# THE MINIMUM DWELLING REVISITED

# THE MINIMUM DWELLING REVISITED

## CIAM'S PRACTICAL UTOPIA (1928–31)

*Aristotle Kallis*

BLOOMSBURY VISUAL ARTS
LONDON • NEW YORK • OXFORD • NEW DELHI • SYDNEY

BLOOMSBURY VISUAL ARTS
Bloomsbury Publishing Plc, 50 Bedford Square, London, WC1B 3DP, UK
Bloomsbury Publishing Inc, 1385 Broadway, New York, NY 10018, USA
Bloomsbury Publishing Ireland, 29 Earlsfort Terrace, Dublin 2, D02 AY28, Ireland

BLOOMSBURY, BLOOMSBURY VISUAL ARTS and the Diana logo are trademarks
of Bloomsbury Publishing Plc

First published in Great Britain 2023
Paperback edition published 2025

Copyright © Aristotle Kallis, 2023

Aristotle Kallis has asserted his right under the Copyright, Designs and
Patents Act, 1988, to be identified as Author of this work.

For legal purposes the Acknowledgements on p. ix constitute an
extension of this copyright page.

Cover design by Eleanor Rose
Cover image: Co-op Zimmer: Interior, 1926. Photograph by Hannes Meyer
© Galerie Berinson, Berlin

All rights reserved. No part of this publication may be: i) reproduced or transmitted
in any form, electronic or mechanical, including photocopying, recording or by means
of any information storage or retrieval system without prior permission in writing from
the publishers; or ii) used or reproduced in any way for the training, development or
operation of artificial intelligence (AI) technologies, including generative AI technologies.
The rights holders expressly reserve this publication from the text and data mining
exception as per Article 4(3) of the Digital Single Market Directive (EU) 2019/790.

Bloomsbury Publishing Plc does not have any control over, or responsibility for,
any third-party websites referred to or in this book. All internet addresses given
in this book were correct at the time of going to press. The author and publisher
regret any inconvenience caused if addresses have changed or sites have
ceased to exist, but can accept no responsibility for any such changes.

A catalogue record for this book is available from the British Library.

Library of Congress Cataloging-in-Publication Data
Names: Kallis, Aristotle A., 1970- author.
Title: The minimum dwelling revisited : CIAM's practical utopia (1928-31) / Aristotle Kallis.
Description: London : Bloomsbury Visual Arts, 2023. | Includes bibliographical
references and index.
Identifiers: LCCN 2023000363 (print) | LCCN 2023000364 (ebook) | ISBN 9781350346185
(hardback) | ISBN 9781350346222 (paperback) | ISBN 9781350346192 (pdf) |
ISBN 9781350346208 (epub) | ISBN 9781350346215
Subjects: LCSH: Apartment houses. | Modern movement (Architecture) | Working class–Housing.
| Housing–Political aspects. | International Congresses for Modern Architecture (2nd : 1929 :
Frankfurt am Main, Germany) | 653 International Congresses for Modern Architecture (3rd :
1930 : Brussels, Belgium) | Existenzminimum
Classification: LCC NA7860 .K28 2023 (print) | LCC NA7860 (ebook) | DDC
728/.314–dc23/eng/20230222
LC record available at https://lccn.loc.gov/2023000363
LC ebook record available at https://lccn.loc.gov/2023000364

| ISBN: | HB: | 978-1-3503-4618-5 |
|---|---|---|
| | PB: | 978-1-3503-4622-2 |
| | ePDF: | 978-1-3503-4619-2 |
| | eBook: | 978-1-3503-4620-8 |

Typeset by Integra Software Services Pvt. Ltd.

For product safety related questions contact productsafety@bloomsbury.com.

To find out more about our authors and books visit www.bloomsbury.com
and sign up for our newsletters.

# CONTENTS

| | |
|---|---|
| List of illustrations | vii |
| Acknowledgements | ix |
| Abbreviations | x |

| | | |
|---|---|---|
| **Introduction** | | 1 |
| | 'Contact zone' and 'practical utopia' | 3 |
| | Structure | 7 |
| **1** | **Genealogies of the Minimum** | 11 |
| | Poverty, 'human needs' and 'minimum' | 11 |
| | Habitation and 'minimum needs' | 14 |
| | Early interventions and reform initiatives | 18 |
| | *Existenzminimum* | 24 |
| | The low-cost housing calculus | 27 |
| **2** | **The 'Small Dwelling' between emergency and aspiration** | 30 |
| | Size and dwelling | 30 |
| | The 'small dwelling' after the First World War | 36 |
| | From the 'small' to the 'smallest' dwelling (*Kleinstwohnung*) | 43 |
| | The pioneering cases of Vienna and Frankfurt | 46 |
| **3** | **International Expert Networks and the housing question in the interwar period** | 59 |
| | The IFHTP encounters the question of mass housing: Vienna, 1926 | 61 |
| | The IFHTP congress in Paris, 1928: The trope of the 'housing for the very poor' | 67 |
| | The IFHTP congress in Rome, 1929: Planning and financing mass urban housing | 71 |
| **4** | **The 'Minimum Dwelling' as Utopia** | 76 |
| | The First World War as rupture: The space of utopia | 76 |
| | Interwar modernism as discourse: Minimum and optimum | 78 |
| | Architecture as revolution | 81 |
| | The private cell, the public sphere and what lies in between | 85 |
| | The Soviet experience: Pursuing the minimum in utopia | 89 |
| | The 'dwelling ration': Social utopia in disguise | 97 |
| | Frictionless living: The studies of Alexander Klein | 101 |

## Contents

| | | |
|---|---|---|
| 5 | **CIAM2: The 'Minimum Dwelling' in focus** | 106 |
| | CIAM and its 'lesser' congresses | 106 |
| | CIAM's first steps and the question of dwelling | 108 |
| | Setting up the first 'working congress' | 112 |
| | The 1929 Frankfurt congress (CIAM2) | 119 |
| | Language matters: The opacity of the *Existenzminimum* | 122 |
| | The aftermath of the Frankfurt congress | 128 |
| | | |
| 6 | **CIAM3: Dwelling as the unlikely hub of modern architecture** | 134 |
| | From CIAM2 to CIAM3: Exploring scales in three-dimensional space | 134 |
| | The elusive theme(s) of CIAM3: The battle of the scales | 136 |
| | The Brussels congress | 148 |
| | The 'minimum dwelling' in CIAM3 | 151 |
| | | |
| 7 | **The CIAM2 and CIAM3 exhibitions** | 157 |
| | The exhibition field in interwar Europe: showcasing the 'minimum' | 159 |
| | The minimum dwelling on show: Exhibiting CIAM2 | 167 |
| | Exhibiting CIAM3 | 179 |

**Conclusions** 190

Notes 196
Bibliography 208
Index 226

# ILLUSTRATIONS

| | | |
|---|---|---|
| 1.1 | Maps 'showing degrees of poverty in London' by Charles Booth | 15 |
| 1.2 | Early examples of 'model housing': the 'model cottages' exhibited at the 1851 Great Exhibition (left) and view of the houses constructed by the *Société Mulhousienne des Cités Ouvrières* in Mulhouse, *c.* 1855 (right) | 19 |
| 1.3 | Robert René Kuczynski's Existenzminimum book and an example of his calculations, comparing the increase in living costs between 1914 and 1920 in Berlin | 25 |
| 2.1 | Aerial image of the Charlottenburg area of Berlin showing typical Mietskaserne (rental barracks), *c.* 1900 | 31 |
| 2.2 | Designs for the improvement of workers' dwellings by the *Verein zur Verbesserung kleiner Wohnungen* | 33 |
| 2.3 | Building of the 'Becque' low-cost typology (Rue Henri Becque, Paris), arch. Jean-Georges Albenque and Eugène Gonnot | 34 |
| 2.4 | Designs for emergency shelters in Breslau, 1920 | 39 |
| 2.5 | Examples of the main types of affordable dwelling prepared for Breslau, *c.* 1924 | 42 |
| 2.6 | Plans for the Dulsberg area of Hamburg, arch. Fritz Schumacher | 45 |
| 2.7 | The extent of the Viennese building programme in the 1920s | 47 |
| 2.8 | Lihotzky's plan for a small kitchen prototype as part of Vienna's housing programme, 1921 | 49 |
| 2.9 | Ernst May's planning vision for the 'New Frankfurt' housing programme | 50 |
| 2.10 | Map and photos of the Siedlungen of 'New Frankfurt' | 53 |
| 2.11 | Jacobus Goettel's plans for the 'cheapest dwelling' | 54 |
| 2.12 | Cover of Franz Schuster's 1927 book on the 'smallest dwelling' (Kleinstwohnung) | 56 |
| 3.1 | Examples of Viennese Höfe constructed by Vienna's municipal authorities in the 1920s | 64 |
| 3.2 | Dwellings for 'undesirable families' in Amsterdam presented at the 1928 IFHTP congress in Paris | 67 |
| 3.3 | Examples of the 'model dwellings' built for Lot XXIV in Garbatella, Rome | 72 |
| 4.1 | Le Corbusier's housing designs for the Weissenhof settlement in Stuttgart | 84 |
| 4.2 | Hannes Meyer's 'Co-op Zimmer: Interior' (1926) | 87 |
| 4.3 | Exhibition of the designs for OSA's 1926 'friendly competition' for a worker's housing prototype | 92 |
| 4.4 | Stroikom typologies A1 and E1/2/3 | 93 |
| 4.5 | Dom-kommuna design by Braschsch and Vladimorov | 94 |

## Illustrations

| | | |
|---|---|---|
| 4.6 | Narkomfin apartments in Moscow, arch. Moisei Ginzburg and Ignatii Milinis (1928–29) | 95 |
| 4.7 | Walter Gropius's ten-storey boarding-house building | 100 |
| 4.8 | Bad Dürrenberg settlement in Leipzig, arch. Alexander Klein | 102 |
| 4.9 | Klein's studies on quality-size-design efficiency for the Kleinwohnung | 104 |
| 7.1 | Werkbund 'model' estates | 161 |
| 7.2 | 'Casa Minima', project by Alessandro Cairoli, G.B. Varisco and Osvaldo Borsani for the Mostra dell'abitazione, V Triennale, Milan 1933. Foto Crimella | 163 |
| 7.3 | Examples of 'model' buildings constructed for the Weissenhof estate in Stuttgart | 164 |
| 7.4 | Interior view of the CIAM2 exhibition in Frankfurt | 169 |
| 7.5 | Examples of Frankfurt dwelling plans exhibited at the CIAM2 exhibition | 171 |
| 7.6 | Dwelling plans from the CIAM2 exhibition | 175 |
| 7.7 | Instances of the CIAM2 travelling exhibition – Zurich (January–February 1930) and Warsaw (March 1930) | 177 |
| 7.8 | Settlement plans featured in the CIAM3 exhibition | 183 |
| 7.9 | Examples of estates featured at the CIAM3 exhibition | 184 |

# ACKNOWLEDGEMENTS

For a project so focused on the study of the international circulation of people, artefacts and ideas, it is ironic that much of the research and writing took place during periods of enforced immobility due to personal and public health reasons. To see it completed, against all these odds, is particularly gratifying on a personal level since at times its very feasibility seemed at stake. Yet it also means that acknowledging the help of all those who supported or engaged with the research is far more meaningful than a standard courtesy. I am deeply grateful for all the support that I received from Keele University – and especially from my colleagues at the School of Humanities. Given all the extraordinary public health restrictions during the lifespan of this project, I am also indebted to all library and archive staff who went out of their way to either facilitate my research visits or provide material in alternative formats during periods of lockdown. The GTA team at the ETH Zurich went out of their way to accommodate my requests and provide helpful guidance during prolonged periods of research at their premises. I am thankful to all of them but I owe a special thanks to Almut Grunewald and Feline Wagner. Further archival research (at the Het Nieuwe Instituut [HNI] in Rotterdam, the Institut für Stadtgeschichte [IfS] and Deutsches Architekturmuseum [DAM] in Frankfurt, the Garden City Heritage Foundation in Letchworth, the archives of the Triennale in Milan) would not be possible without the help, patience and flexibility of the staff curating the collections. During the long periods of enforced isolation that coincided with the preparation of this book I also had the opportunity to reach out (virtually in most cases) to a number of colleagues across the world, with whom I discussed aspects of the research and from whose ideas and advice I benefited enormously. It would be impossible for me to thank them individually here but I would like to make an exception to acknowledge the help of Alessandro Porotto, who was always willing to share ideas and materials with me.

This research was generously funded by a Leverhulme Trust Research Fellowship. Acknowledging only the source of funding, however, would once again not be enough on this occasion. The way that The Leverhulme Trust responded to all the obstacles and accommodated repeated extensions in order to ensure that I made full use of the funds has been humbling. To say that this book and its underpinning research would not have been possible without the Trust's support has a significantly more literal meaning in my case and for this I am deeply grateful.

# ABBREVIATIONS

| | |
|---|---|
| CIAM | Congrès Internationaux d'Architecture Moderne |
| CIRPAC | Comité International pour la Résolution des Problèmes de l'Architecture Contemporaine |
| CPCIH | Comité Permanent des Congrès Internationaux de l'Habitation |
| DAM | Deutsches Architekturmuseum |
| DNF | Das Neue Frankfurt |
| EEST | Archive of Cornelis Van Eesteren, HNI Rotterdam |
| ETH | Eidgenössische Technische Hochschule Zürich |
| GTA | Institut für Geschichte und Theorie der Architektur, ETH Zurich |
| HBM | Habitations à Bon Marché |
| HLM | Habitations à Loyer Modéré |
| HNI | Het Nieuwe Instituut Rotterdam |
| ICP | Istituto Case Popolari |
| IFHTP/IFTP | International Federation for (Housing and) Town Planning |
| IfS | Institut für Stadtgeschichte |
| IGCTPA | International Garden Cities and Town Planning Association |
| IHC | International Housing Congress |
| ILO | International Labour Office |
| IVW | Internationaler Verband für Wohnungswesen |
| OHBM | Office des Habitations à Bon March |
| OSA | Ob'edineniye Sovremennikh Arkhitektorov |
| RFG | Reichsforschungsgesellschaft für Wirtschaftlichkeit im Bau- und Wohnungswesen |
| SA | Sovremmennaia Arkhitektura |
| SH | Schlesisches Heim: Monatsschrift der Schlesischen Heimstätte provinziellen Wohnungsfürsorgegesellschaft |
| SPD | Sozialdemokratische Partei Deutschlands |
| UIV | Union Internationale des Villes |

# INTRODUCTION

The question of how to design and produce affordable, good-quality housing became a central political and social concern in the twentieth century. In 1929, an eclectic international group of avant-garde modernist architects met in Frankfurt to discuss a design programme for this type of housing, seeking new approaches and processes to maximize quality and functionality while making this dwelling widely available and affordable by the mass of the population. The agreed focus of the congress was the product of a multiple awkward elision: literally translated as 'the dwelling for the subsistence minimum' (*Wohnung für das Existenzminimum* in German), it is conventionally referred to in the relevant CIAM literature as 'minimum dwelling'. Neither the original 'Existenzminimum' (in German) nor the 'minimum' (used more opaquely in French) turned out to be easy to define – before, during or even after the congress. The 'subsistence minimum' was a terminology that referenced explicitly the socio-economic profile of the intended residents – the ever-increasing urban population who, by virtue of their own low income and the insufficient supply of affordable accommodation, had been unable to afford good-quality housing in the cities where they lived and worked. The 'minimum', on the other hand, was an even more elusive category, pointing to design austerity as programmatic choice or abstraction in response to scarcity. Conventionally understood in negative terms, as the most basic threshold of tolerability arrived at through extreme reduction and quality sacrifice, by the early twentieth century the term had started acquiring a more positive complexion. A series of further terms were used by the participants, seemingly interchangeably, at the congress to denote reduced size (*Klein-* and *Kleinstwohnung*) and deliberate design minimalism (*habitation minimum* or *Minimalwohnung*). Yet implicit in all these conceptions was the visionary quest for a novel optimal correlation of standard of living (quality), affordability (cost) and mass production (supply).

The Frankfurt congress (CIAM2 in 1929) and the following one in Brussels (CIAM3 in 1930) that tackled this question fell frustratingly short of the organizers' expectations in many respects. Preparation for both events was chaotic, marred by organizational confusion and personal disagreements. The congress proceedings themselves did little to bridge the kaleidoscope of ideological and programmatic positions that divided the participating architects within the ranks of the fledgling CIAM, even on the very meaning of 'the dwelling for the Existenzminimum'. The discussion did not produce an ideal type for the 'minimum dwelling', if ever this were the original intention of the organizers. It even failed to maintain the primary focus on the dwelling itself, with the deliberations switching incongruously between diverse – and ever-larger – architectural scales in the process. If in Frankfurt the dwelling at least dominated much of the congress discussions, this was not the case at the following Brussels congress, where the dedicated housing discussion ended up as little more than an appendix to an event otherwise addressing alternative architectural questions.

In hindsight the two congresses appear either as minor events in the organization's history or at best as important preparatory milestones along a route that led from the group's founding gathering at La Sarraz (1928) to its lionized fourth congress (CIAM4 in 1933). This is after all what key CIAM figures such as its secretary Sigfried Giedion and its later president José Luis Sert claimed retrospectively. Yet CIAM's encounter with the (minimum) dwelling had a fascinating and multi-faceted genealogy. The decision to make mass housing the focus of the group's first working congress(es) did not emerge in an intellectual, political, social or professional vacuum of course. It rather unfolded as yet another episode in a broader and long-standing context of searching for a solution to the problem of providing affordable, hygienic, good-quality and well-designed housing for the masses. This discussion had gathered significant momentum in the course of the late nineteenth and early twentieth centuries but became far more urgent in the wake of the turmoil caused by the First World War. It subsumed diverse layers of pre-existing scientific, sociological, economic and design thinking and then refracted them through a host of contradictory ideological assumptions, national experiences, cultural specificities and professional convictions of those present at the congress. By the time that the CIAM steering group finally agreed that its first working congress would be devoted to the question of housing other international organizations, architectural (such as the International Federation of Housing and Town Planning, IFHTP) or otherwise (e.g. the International Labour Organisation), had already turned their attention to the housing issue in pursuit of innovative solutions that could alleviate the crisis, avert a social explosion and improve living conditions. Meanwhile, a number of state and especially municipal authorities had made impressive, often trailblazing inroads into improving the quality-cost-supply-affordability housing calculus for those with limited means.

In hindsight CIAM's encounter with the 'minimum dwelling' was as short-lived as it was haphazard. Soon after the conclusion of the 1930 Brussels congress CIAM's attention moved quickly to the urban scale, in anticipation of the planned fourth congress to be held in Moscow. Not only did the earlier exclusive focus on housing was subsumed into this broader scale but the very term Existenzminimum – so crucial in determining the identity of CIAM's early history – faded into the background as swiftly and perplexingly as it had come to the forefront of CIAM's first working congress in Frankfurt. The twisted story of its translations and adaptations raises questions as to whether it ever constituted a meaningful shared basis for CIAM's first steps as an international group dedicated to the promotion of the 'new' modernist architecture. Translation woes, however, belied more profound programmatic contestations – what kind of 'minimum' was assumed and for whom, whether such a minimum was determined predominantly by socio-economic factors or extended to a new design idiom or even conception of living, whether it was a problem of managing existing resources more efficiently at times of crisis or it pointed to a quasi-utopian horizon of radical social transformation. CIAM's discourse of 'the dwelling for the Existenzminimum' subsumed and curated – but failed to reconcile – a range of different understandings and personal interests of those present in Frankfurt and Brussels, as evidenced in their congress contributions: Le Corbusier's aesthetic minimalism, his interest in 'light, air, heat' and his fascination with urbanism; Sigfried Giedion's celebration of a new kind of modern 'liberated living'; Walter Gropius's conception of the individual 'dwelling ration' as the atomic level of architectural design and his interest in high(er)-rise building form; Ernst May's correlation of dwelling design with rational settlement planning; Hans Schmidt's concern for the social mission of modern architecture; Helena and Szymon Syrkus's vision of modernist architecture leading the way for revolutionary transformation; or Victor Bourgeois's research on the rational organization of the dwelling in order to meet elevated physiological needs more efficiently.

## 'Contact zone' and 'practical utopia'

Yet CIAM's adventures with the 'minimum dwelling' in 1929–30 left behind a distinctive and significant legacy, not just for the fledgling organization but for the entire international debate on mass housing. The first two working congresses – but also the early CIAM as an inclusive international organization – functioned as a multidimensional and fascinatingly volatile *contact zone*, bringing uniquely together – in cooperation, dialogue, synthesis and crucially friction – a wide range of architects and planners who traversed national borders, ideological fault lines and programmatic polarities. CIAM's discourse on the 'minimum dwelling' owed its novelty less to new radical ideas and more to the decision to promote the organization as a unique and inclusive intellectual-discursive 'contact zone' traversing national, ideological and programmatic fissures while also providing the physical and intellectual space for intense intersections and syntheses. Applied to the field of architectural history, Tom Avermaete described such contact zones as 'intense sites of encounter [including congresses] between different architectural cultures in which ideas, approaches and tools are negotiated, selectively borrowed, partially adapted or rejected' (Avermaete and Nuijsink, 2021, 354). This definition may actually be better applied to other international architectural events of the 1920s (such as the much more widely attended and inclusive International Federation for Housing and Town Planning (IFHTP) congresses) than to CIAM's more restricted and polemical events. However, it is because of the partisan character of CIAM's membership that the organization's congresses functioned as a very different kind of contact zone – a unique meeting site between international avant-garde architectural cultures as an alternative to the canonical spaces of the contemporary architectural establishment. Tension, friction and adaptive synthesis mattered far more than consensus in these contact zones. Albeit tarnished by conflict and lack of agreement about the 'minimum dwelling', CIAM2 and CIAM3 were supremely successful in the broader sense of formalizing and nurturing an alternative avant-garde architectural zone of exchange and productive friction between diverse modernist cultures and architectural conceptions.

There is another reason, however, as to why CIAM's early encounter with the 'minimum dwelling' matters – and this reason has to do with the specific focus on housing. However chaotic, lacking in clear focus and frustratingly inconclusive the deliberations in Frankfurt and Brussels may have been, they did succeed in re-defining the mass affordable and good-quality dwelling as a positive aspiration and a critical hub of multi-scalar transformation of living for all. This happened less by design and certainly even less through any semblance of programmatic blueprint about the form, organization and design of the elusive dwelling per se. Instead the congress proceedings, as well as what preceded and followed them, reproposed the 'minimum dwelling' as something that was positive, universal and transformative even as it referenced economy and austerity or was formed as response to a devastating social crisis. In short CIAM's 'minimum dwelling' thrived in an interstitial space between necessity, emergency and visionary social aspiration, pursuing something that I describe as *practical utopia*.

At first sight, the term 'practical utopia' is paradoxical. In etymological terms utopia constitutes a non-place, inaccessible and essentially unattainable in its entirety or without a total rupture with present conditions. The intrinsic intractability and unreachability of utopia, however, are modulated through the introduction of a practical perspective. As Lewis Mumford argued, mature utopias have a profound reconstructive horizon derived from contextual awareness, in the sense of 'com[ing] to reckon with the world in which they seek realization' (Lewis, 1922, 14). In this sense, the compound term 'practical utopia' indicates both difference from 'impractical dreaming and idle fantasies' and a pragmatic, action-oriented decision to 'plant the seeds of the future in the present' even if the new utopian condition cannot yet be born (Albert and Chomsky, 2017, xiii). Practical utopias tend to be less spectacular and dramatic; but what they sacrifice by compromising with the present they compensate with the liberation from a sense of rigid futural determinism that characterizes grandiose utopias of rupture (Mannheim, 2013, 215–36). In short, practical utopias are transgressive, syncretist and operating in the short term; they privilege a utopian process still in the making with immediate transformative dividends over the mirage of a fully formed ideal futural condition.

For the CIAM members who worked for, and participated in, the 1929 and 1930 congresses, the 'dwelling for the Existenzminimum' came to represent the stepping stone for exploring such a practical utopia for living in the modern world. Designing a housing unit that was optimally efficient in its use of space, resources and facilities, and then deploying it on a mass scale, would deliver on the promise shared among CIAM members that architecture and planning were best placed to (re)shape social behaviour. Re-imagined with the help of modern, constructive planning and social technologies, this optimally minimum/minimal housing unit was intended to shelter, improve quality of life and then re-engineer social relations inside and outside. In short, Existenzminimum was not a bare minimum in size, cost and quality, neither could it be, by definition, a perfectly formed utopian condition. Instead it was debated and pursued as an affordable golden ratio between necessity and utopia for a new society. It was a sweeping yet actionable transformative aspiration that came to exceed the micro frame (individual dwelling) and sanctioned a scalar expansion to the meso (building design, land-subdivision, settlement planning), and eventually the macro frame (urban planning). CIAM's 'minimum dwelling' emerged from the two congresses as neither minimum in the conventional sense of the word nor ironically *a* dwelling per se. The deliberations sanctioned a semantic shift from minimum as bare necessity to a very different, aspirational yet realizable kind of minimum as thoughtful, empowering austerity that promised a radically new conception of living, better for the individual residents and for society as a whole. If the participants disagreed on what this dwelling might be like, what it would feature and how it would be produced, they nevertheless agreed that the 'minimum dwelling' could turn subtraction and austerity into positive values of dwelling design. Their 'minimum' was nothing like the race to the bottom that had characterized earlier approaches to the mass housing question on the basis of a 'zero-sum' size-quality-cost calculus. Instead it sought to determine an abstruse alchemical formula that promised to deliver more (quality, functionality and enjoyment) with less (production and rental costs) and for many more people (something more akin to a conception of good-quality and affordable housing as a universal social right). Largely because of all the disagreements and lack of focus at the two congresses it became clear to most participating CIAM members that any solution to an optimal minimum dwelling would not be found exclusively within the single dwelling but through a much larger modular approach across diverse scales of architectural and planning design that extended from the personal space within the dwelling to the dwelling as a whole, to the building as grouping of dwellings, to the settlement as grouping of buildings, to the city as grouping of settlements, and even to society as a whole.

In 1932, Karel Teige published a detailed book-length work on the affordable dwelling. The book had started its life as a draft summary of the reports on the dwelling situation that individual national chapters had submitted to CIAM's 1930 congress; yet by the time of its publication it had graduated into a gargantuan treatise on global design and policy trends in relation to the question of mass, egalitarian and affordable, modern housing. The title that Teige chose (*Nejmenší byt*, literally 'smallest' apartment) appeared to reference size as a qualitative parameter rather than a purely quantitative benchmark. The book was translated in English as *Minimum Dwelling* seven decades after its publication (Teige, 2002). The translated term is no less opaque than the original 'dwelling for the Existenzminimum' because it retains the tension between a quantitative minimum based on necessity, affordability and tolerability, on the one hand, and a qualitative minimum in a normative and aspirational (in design, social or cultural terms) sense of the word, on the other. Nevertheless, 'minimum dwelling' is broad and opaque in a useful way, drawing attention to the significance of the diverse conceptions of 'minimum' in the discourse of interwar modernism and of the early CIAM in particular.

This is one of the two reasons why I have retained throughout this book the reference to the 'minimum dwelling' as the descriptor of CIAM's early work on housing, even if I consider the term more of a misnomer. The other – and more important – reason has to do with the longer-term significance of CIAM's probe into the meaning of the 'minimum' as an integral part of the broader intellectual framework in which mass housing was debated. Minima – be that of human needs, subsistence income or standard of living – had featured previously in social debates, with housing occupying a mostly peripheral position. Yet CIAM placed dwelling at the very heart of this conversation, as architectural problem but above all as social responsibility. In fact, I argue that CIAM's brief encounter with the elusive Existenzminimum transformed the moral complexion of the entire conversation on the mass low-cost dwelling. The congress proceedings may have done little to bridge the ideological and programmatic positions that divided the participating architects or to shape CIAM's frame of analysis in the longer term. They did, however, embed an enduring 'social' meaning to the problem, as the pursuit of a golden ratio of utopian aspiration and reality grounded on a flexible equilibrium of quality, cost and affordability that could ensure universal deployment in the present tense. While other earlier or contemporary organizations approached the challenge of mass housing as a 'problem' to be mitigated in the margins of architectural practice, CIAM embraced the dwelling for the Existenzminimum as both a challenge and the ultimate noble aspiration of modern architectural practice. CIAM's 'minimum dwelling' was conceived first and foremost as an ethical proposition – a community asset, judged not on the quality of each single unit that it provided but on its capacity for promoting better-quality housing for as many as possible – and ideally for all members of a community. In its wake, the size-reduction rationale of the 'small dwelling' (Kleinwohnung), the design language of 'less is more', as well as the debates on centralization versus peripheral settlement or low-versus-high rise were subsumed into an overarching ethical project of providing good-quality housing to everyone.

This understanding of the 'minimum' as both austere and optimal, aspirational and practicable, utopian and pragmatic, situates CIAM's exploration of the 'minimum dwelling' at the point where three discrete intellectual genealogies of the 'minimum' intersected. The first one was shaped by the need to respond pragmatically and swiftly to short-term emergencies, whether in overall housing conditions and quality standards or in terms of extraordinary shortages of affordable, decent housing due to the pathologies of the modern industrial society and the short-term jolts of the war and the crisis conditions that it generated. The other two shared a radical transformative aspiration but differed in their individual diagnoses of the problem. One was profoundly utopian in the sense that it sought complete rupture with the status quo, positing instead a vision of transformative change that was possible only after the radical reshaping of the existing socio-economic and political order, typically through revolution. The other belonged to the broader radical reformist tradition, underpinned by the conviction that transformative change in the longer term was possible through evolutionary reform from within existing conditions. Of these two, the former saw architecture as the object of revolution while the latter gave architects unprecedented transformational agency as primary subjects of a new society and way of life. While all these genealogies had common roots in the nineteenth-century debates on 'basic human needs' and housing reform, the experience of the First World War and in particular the postwar turmoil dramatically changed their complexion and sharpened their respective propositions. From the turn of the twentieth century onwards, new radical ideas and programmes came to the fore, challenging prior orthodoxies and expanding the scope for transformative agency. Meanwhile the positive embrace of modern canons of rationalization and functionalism; the appreciation of austerity and design simplicity as positive, aspirational blueprints; and the influence of socialist ideas in reproposing dwelling as a universal social asset changed dramatically the contours of the debate on housing reform in the interwar years.

Speaking aphoristically about the programme of twentieth-century architectural modernism, Rem Koolhaas has touched on the 'alchemical' proposition at its heart – 'to transform quantity into quality through abstraction and repetition' (Koolhaas, 1995, 28). I shall return to Koolhaas's quotation (which I have deliberately truncated at this stage) in the Conclusions. It is important, however, to underline how poignant the trope of alchemy is for the history of CIAM's engagement with the 'minimum dwelling' that this book attempts to piece together. Alchemy was a practice of transformation based on separating what is useful and essential from what is not. In doing so, alchemists bestrode the chasm that separated the sacred from the profane. With considerable licence I read into this statement the very essence of the 'minimum dwelling' as a promise to transform crisis and scarcity into a universal, ethically superior optimum, using the dwelling and its components as the catalysts for a profound multi-scalar transformation of collective living in the modern world. In rejecting the long-standing legacies of a zero-sum rationale that had bedevilled the housing question since the nineteenth century, I locate the broader discussion of the 'minimum dwelling' at the dynamic intersection of utopian and highly pragmatic conceptions of architectural agency. The former requires research into the programmatic ideas of a number of architects, paying particular attention to the ways that each understood the problem in ideological and design terms as well as the scope for transformative agency that they had – or thought they ought to have – as professionals. The latter dimension underlines the significance of a historical context of analysis, locating the discourse of the 'minimum dwelling' in broader and longer-term conversations about poverty, habitation, crisis and emergency, urban degradation and the role of the state in guaranteeing social rights. This tension between utopia and necessity, futural aspiration and pragmatic response to the here and now, the single and the universal, programme and realized practice lies at the heart of the book's approach to the 'minimum dwelling' as a practical utopia with universal and ecumenical import.

## Structure

CIAM's 'minimum dwelling' episode occupies without doubt a central place in this book but I approach it as the moment of climactic encounter rather than of genesis. I seek to trace its intellectual, political and programmatic genealogies using a macro-historical perspective that stretches back to the nineteenth century. In analysing CIAM's work on this theme in 1928–30, I recognize its pivotal place in the history of the 'minimum dwelling' that was nevertheless indebted to, indeed was only meaningful and possible because of, a wide range of pre-existing and contemporary intellectual and professional agencies that came together in and around the two congresses of 1929 and 1930 in productive friction. Therefore, this book is essentially about piecing together two 'entangled histories' with multiple fascinating intersections: first, of diverse genealogies of the 'minimum'; and second, of an interplay between utopian, reformist and 'problem'-solving perspectives formulated by a range of professional practitioners in response to the question of mass affordable housing. Although, as it will become evident, CIAM's engagement with the question failed to either settle the discussion or develop a universal formula for the 'minimum dwelling', its distinct legacy ought to be measured less in terms of resolutions or outcomes and more as a dynamic intellectual and discursive process, functioning as a seminal 'contact zone' for the interwar mass housing debate and for the kaleidoscope of ideas and initiatives within the ranks of the then fledgling international modern movement.

The three tropes of 'minimum', 'practical utopia' and 'contact zone' also form the backbone of this book. Chapter 1 traces the origins of the debates about 'minimum' social needs before exploring how they were translated into standards and prompted a range of new initiatives in the domain of housing in the last decades of the nineteenth century. The ways in which the discourse of the 'minimum' oscillated between a moral and a more objective/science-based understanding of housing standards prompted a wide spectrum of reform responses – from surveys to philanthropic housing projects to campaigns for legislative, financial and in the end political reforms. It is in this intellectual context that the first uses of the terminology of what would later feed into the *Existenzminimum* trope appeared, most notably in the form of guaranteeing a minimum income capable of satisfying basic needs and allowing for a modicum of decent living in close relation to contingent economic factors such as inflation and cost of living. The steadily worsening housing conditions for a steadily growing number of urban inhabitants strengthened and added urgency to calls for radical change, whether within the existing system or as the premise of a social revolution. Nevertheless at the turn of the twentieth century the quality-cost-affordability housing calculus remained bound to a zero-sum rationale where the '*minimum*' entailed onerous reductions in some or all qualitative indices.

Chapter 2 deals with the history of a particular understanding of the 'minimum' in housing – size. The history of the small (or, more accurately, reduced-size) dwelling occupied a central place in the intellectual and architectural histories of the 'minimum dwelling'. Initially conceived as an emergency/last-resort solution that was only possible through reductions in cost, size (e.g. the Kleinwohnung typology in early-twentieth-century Germany) and/or quality, it graduated into a more positive and aspirational proposition. Rather than featuring size reduction as a qualitative deficit, this alternative conception of the small dwelling reproposed austerity as an ethical brief that stipulated new conceptions of living, a deeper appreciation of design rationality and in some cases an emancipatory social horizon. As a result, the rationale of the housing calculus started to change, with new variables (such as standardization of construction and new design approaches) introduced into the existing ones (needs-standards, cost-quality, supply-demand, affordability-profitability, etc.) in pursuit of formulas that could stretch or radically alter earlier zero-sum assumptions. The pace of change and innovation accelerated dramatically in the wake of the post-First World War crisis, largely in response to the enormity of the housing crisis and its potentially terrifying social consequences. The dramatic increase in (direct or indirect) public funding and a series of modern construction and design innovations also changed the dynamic of the conventional housing calculus. The result of all these shifts was a range of new multi-scalar perspectives on the 'minimum dwelling' that involved the single housing unit as part of wider distributive, spatial, urban and social arrangements.

Chapter 3 reviews how international architectural networks addressed the question of mass housing in the immediate post-First World War period. Material destruction, political turmoil and socio-economic dislocation as a result of the war combined with fears of a worldwide revolutionary explosion unless effective and timely action to address mass social grievances were to be undertaken. As a result, the question of good-quality yet affordable housing for the masses became a central concern for politicians, municipal authorities, as well as architects and planners – within but also across national borders. The debates hosted by the IFHTP in particular were arguably the most prolific, internationally inclusive and influential, by virtue of the Federation's large membership, plurality of views and willingness to engage with a series of controversial themes at its three 'housing' congresses in 1926–9. The IFHTP operated as the broadest international 'contact zone' for interwar architects in the 1920s. Its three congresses dedicated to issues relating to mass housing (1926, 1928 and 1929) – and in particular its engagement with the question of 'housing for the very poor' – formed milestones in the intellectual genealogy of the 'minimum dwelling', setting the scene for CIAM's subsequent debate on the 'housing for the Existenzminimum'.

In contrast to the focus of Chapter 3 on mass affordable housing as pragmatic response to the postwar emergency, Chapter 4 reviews architectural debates and initiatives motivated by the utopian streak of interwar modernism. These alternative perspectives proposed a new kind of minimum as a design, aesthetic, social and moral optimum. I examine how key figures of the interwar modernist avant-garde like Le Corbusier, Hannes Meyer, Walter Gropius, Nikolay Alexandrovich Milyutin, Moisei Ginzburg, Karel Teige and Alexander Klein put forward new theories about the form, functions, organization and overall role of the modern mass dwelling. The respective propositions of these and other architects involved a radical rethinking of the fundamental premises of habitation: its function of enclosure and marking the boundary between the public from the private; the hierarchy of interim spaces, through which individuals both came into contact and excluded others; the role and spaces of individual freedom and privacy within and well as beyond the dwelling; the flow between individual, group, communal, collective and public spaces in an integrated vision of 'new' living. The metaphor of the individual 'cell' gained traction as the building block of a new modular system linking personal space to private dwelling, building, settlement and finally the city as a whole. Yet I also argue that their quasi-utopian propositions about the dwelling make more sense as discursive actions seeking to propose new or alternative paths and desired outcomes for an as yet undefined optimal future rather than as literal expressions of what 'minimum' and 'optimum' ought to be.

Chapters 5–7 trace the trajectory of the 'minimum dwelling' in CIAM's early history from late 1928 to early 1931. Chapter 5 focuses on the eventful planning for, and conduct of, the 1929 Frankfurt congress (CIAM2). Particular attention is paid to the nine tumultuous months of preparation for the proceedings. Throughout this time the contours of the discussion kept changing as divergent interpretations of what CIAM was and how it should approach the role or direction of the 'new' architecture came to the surface. When the congress did take place in late October 1929, it produced a lot of discussions and significant publicity 'noise' but little in terms of concrete propositions about the optimal shape of the minimum dwelling and was deemed largely a failure by the CIAM leadership at the time.

The preparation for and proceedings of the 1930 Brussels congress (CIAM3) are discussed in Chapter 6. After the inconclusive Frankfurt meeting, this was supposed to become the congress on the 'minimum dwelling'. Yet CIAM3 ended up with a nominal title that kept changing, at least one further key theme, more ideas that were introduced haphazardly and sometimes abandoned in the process and a mind-blowing four exhibition events. The 'minimum dwelling' was tucked into the final day of the official congress programme, overshadowed by other themes and increasingly treated as an embarrassing legacy of the fledgling CIAM's 'child diseases'. In spite of all these problems and deficits, however, the 1930 Brussels congress morphed into the organization's most ambitious, discursively rich, inclusive and pluralistic of its interwar congresses, producing surprisingly rich and productive insights into the problem of the 'minimum dwelling'.

In hindsight CIAM3 represented both the apex and the coda of CIAM's short-lived, fraught and frustratingly inconclusive adventure with housing. Yet in one key respect at least CIAM's two congresses dedicated to mass housing represented a resounding and enduring success: they fulfilled their intended brief as international 'contact zone' for the 'new' architecture. In fact, more than the congress exchanges or resolutions, it was the series of exhibitions and associated publications organized in the margins of the main events that fulfilled the promise of such a productive exchange and became the most consequential legacy of CIAM's first two working congresses. Chapter 7 discusses these outward-facing events linked to CIAM2 and CIAM3 – their curated content but also the planning behind them and their subsequent trajectories. CIAM's exhibitions plugged into a prodigious field of national and international architectural exhibitions that had gathered momentum in the nineteenth and early twentieth centuries. These exhibitions served as places of aggregation of international modernist architectural practice and as canonizing events for the 'new' architecture, in the process absorbing prior sources and examples of innovation in the field of mass housing as part of CIAM's self-constructed genealogy. Their histories too bespeak the exhilarating ambitions and frustrating mishaps that marked the organization's early years and punctuated its ambitious engagement with the Existenzminimum dwelling.

# CHAPTER 1
# GENEALOGIES OF THE MINIMUM

### Poverty, 'human needs' and 'minimum'

Cities have often served as the stirring backdrop to both utopian and dystopian imaginations. The modern industrial city of the nineteenth and early-twentieth century was the window to the densest panoramas of exhilaration and *Angst*. Vignettes of splendour and wretchedness existed side-by-side with an intensity never experienced before (Luckin, 2006). As the optimism about future progress started to wane in the second half of the nineteenth century (Robertson, 2018, 35), the city also stimulated the starkest projections of a bleak future. Here the familiar urban perils of squalor, disease, crime and vice intersected with overcrowding, pollution, exploitation, *machiniste* tedium and the precariousness of wage labour in a bleak everyday struggle for mere survival. The modern industrial metropolis combined scale, intensity and density of experience to the point of an unprecedented sensory overload (Simmel, 1903). It multiplied, amplified and distorted socio-economic, political and cultural polarities, rendering them omnipresent and impossible to escape in rapid, incongruous succession as part of a frenzied everyday rhythm of life.

Poverty, overcrowding, disease and degeneration became objects of a booming enterprise of surveys and data collection sought to quantify and analyse the woes of modern city life (Simmons, 2015, 1–12). They also formed the powerful linchpins of the reformist discourses that gained traction in the course of the nineteenth century. As conditions continued to deteriorate and the subjective perception of these problems fed into intensifying public discourses of crisis and degeneration, the calls for intervention increased, impelling reluctant conservative and liberal public authorities to respond. Not only the framing of the problem but also the field of solutions and strategies of intervention were conditioned by deep-rooted ideological precepts. For conservatives, inequality was rooted in a putative natural order underpinned by traditional precepts of power and authority. For liberals faith in progress was refracted through the dogma of the inviolability of market forces as the optimal arbiter of economic and social relations. For socialists the capitalist system of production was at the heart of the problem of human inequality, thus underlining the necessity for an alternative order produced only through revolutionary rupture. Reformists claimed an intermediate space on this ideological axis, calling for a radical expansion of the field of remedial intervention and more ambitious welfare programmes geared to effecting positive transformations while at the same time obviating a revolutionary escalation. These ideological presuppositions shaped a broader debate on human needs in the nineteenth century that oscillated between 'minimum' and 'optimal' requirements.

Poverty had for long been regarded and scrutinized as a multidimensional problem that touched on anything from socio-economic structures to political decisions to cultural factors to human psychology and morality. The long-standing distinction between the poor 'worthy' of benevolent relief and those viewed as 'undeserving' of any charitable help pointed to a fundamental understanding a poverty as rooted in natural order. It could – indeed more and more people came to accept that it ought to – be alleviated but could not be removed altogether. Poverty could also have a positive meaning when it was borne with dignity or resulted from voluntary renunciation of excess or material possessions altogether (Scott, 2012, 1–15). The intellectual framework for analysing poverty underwent a gradual but significant transformation in the wake of the French Revolution, when the revolutionary notion of equality as a universal social right reoriented public discourse away from providential forces and towards the active construction of a new social order based on citizenship and individual rights (Alfani and Frigeni, 2016, 31–5). Inequality was subjected to a far more rigorous philosophical and practical scrutiny, now approached as a problem with both natural and social dimensions. In contrast to social stasis promoted by traditional models of hierarchy and status/privilege, the modern perspective on poverty was significantly more probing. Fuelled by a strong faith in both human and societal perfectibility, the nineteenth century was marked by growing protest, critique of social foundations, calls for radical change and various attempts to interrogate inequality. This led to a series of attempts to study poverty from a scientific point of view, to analyse its economic and sociological foundations and to measure its effects on the affected individuals and society as a whole (Simmons, 2015, 162).

It was in this rapidly changing context that the question of human needs came to the fore with renewed urgency. Needs, like poverty, had a natural and a social dimension. They included the basic elements both for bodily survival and for the individual's self-fulfilment. While some basic needs could be considered universal and foundational (e.g. the need to subsist and to be sheltered), others were socially constructed and understood in their specific social/cultural/historical context – a condition that made them both diverse and changeable (Pittman and Zeigler, 2007). The nineteenth-century discussion of human needs emerged in a context defined by an acute awareness of both inequality and scarcity. The grossly unequal distribution of resources came to be recognized as a problem through a moral and a pragmatic rationale: it was unjust by virtue of its blatant unevenness to the point that a large proportion of the population could not satiate even 'basic' existential needs; and it was problematic as a model of resource management, especially in times of scarcity when the normal operation of economy and society could no longer guarantee the very survival of those in need. The radical premise of the needs discourse in the nineteenth century was that neither providential nor liberal laissez-faire forces could be trusted to deliver a more equitable distribution of resources that was required in order to fulfil the basic, universal needs of the population. At a time of rapid socio-economic change, however, the meaning and measure of 'basic' needs was also subjected to continuous review and upward redefinition. Campaigners of diverse ideological complexions may have sparred over definitions, diagnoses, indices, priorities and remedial strategies, but they agreed that new forms of intervention were desperately needed to deal with social inequality and avert either degeneration or turmoil (Noonan, 2006).

The resource-centric approach to the satisfaction of human needs in a capitalist wage labour society produced an alternative intellectual and moral framework for understanding poverty. It gradually questioned both providential and liberal orthodoxies about the limits of justifiable intervention in the fight against human inequality. It generated a growth industry of predominantly quantitative research that underpinned and legitimized the increasingly vocal calls for radical reform and active public intervention in order to manage social difference in a more just and equitable fashion. Defining *minimum* universal needs paved the way for new welfarist models of comprehensive insurance and standardized wealth redistribution overseen by rapidly expanding public bureaucracies and professional experts. Inevitably perhaps it also led to a coupling of needs and wages (Simmons, 2015, 33–54). The growing calls for setting wage compensation at a level that guaranteed subsistence and recovery for the working family set the foundations for the campaign in favour of a 'minimum' (or living) wage (Stabile, 2009, 98–102). Whereas laissez-faire liberals predictably rejected direct state involvement to achieve this, others demanded state intervention in order to calculate, force and guarantee the provision of something that resembled a minimum living wage. If the market alone could not guarantee the operation of 'natural' forces of equilibrium, then direct corrective intervention and engineered redistribution were regarded as the only way to restore a modicum of balance. As a result, a veritable science of quantifying human needs and then translating them into minimum wage levels combined with reformist political campaigns to rationalize the economic system and advance the precepts of moral economy.

Using a list of absolute needs as the metric of poverty produced a long and distinguished lineage of scientific research and reformist political campaigns in the past two centuries that transformed the intellectual framework to address poverty and social inequality. Charles Booth's ground-breaking analysis of patterns of poverty in London at the end of the nineteenth century suggested a quantitative poverty threshold range measured in weekly income value (18 to 21 shillings) (Llewellyn-Smith, 1929). At the turn of the twentieth century, Seebohm Rowntree produced another milestone study of poverty, moving the geographic focus to York and the 'poverty line' to a minimum income that was fixed more concretely at 21 shillings (Rowntree, 1901, 87–8). Both Booth and Rowntree resorted to a more or less universal and absolute understanding of minimum human needs for the purpose of setting a workable foundation for analysis of subjective and relative aspects. Booth also introduced a classification distinction between 'very poor' (those with insufficient means to achieve a 'decent independent life') and 'poor' (those with barely sufficient means to attain the same minimum level). In both accounts income and means were used as primary material markers of poverty, but the authors also showed an awareness of complex qualitative factors even when it came to basic minima such as subsistence, accommodation, employment, family composition and expenditure.

However, by the turn of the twentieth century, the needs-based definition of minimum had been found wanting in many respects and had come under sustaining criticism from various poverty campaigners. Assuming that human needs were more or less absolute and stable may have been statistically convenient (it fixed benchmarks against which poverty could be identified in putatively objective terms) but it was unresponsive to changing circumstances and perceptions over time. It was also inflexible in relation to addressing a host of important relative variables. Factors such as context, behaviour, social wealth and contingent events (e.g. a crisis/emergency) had a significant effect on what was – or was perceived as – minimum, if not in kind then definitely in measure and in terms of relative priority. Furthermore, a needs-based minimum showed a bias towards physiological needs (nutrition, shelter) at the expense of the – more subjective and difficult to quantify – psychological and sociological ones. Lastly, translating whatever paradigm of minimum needs into a quantitative threshold was based on the choice of a single measuring unit (e.g. income, consumption) that could only have a partial descriptive – and not normative – value.

In response a growing lineage of survey paradigms inspired by reformist and especially socialist ideas in the nineteenth century attacked the notion of natural, absolute needs for all humans in any given society. They argued that social forces constrained both the understanding of needs themselves and the ability of workers to pursue their satisfaction (Simmons, 2015, 55–78). The intensifying calls for setting a minimum wage soon raised questions about the conditions in which workers earned their income and lived their everyday lives. Between 1839 and 1841 Prussia, Britain and France introduced legislation that standardized minima in terms of child labour. Furthermore, the need to protect humans from disease and the effects of lack of hygiene generated initiatives that called for a qualitative upward redefinition of even those basic, minimum needs. Edwin Chadwick's 1842 report on the sanitary conditions of the working class in Britain directly linked problems with public health, sanitation and housing as key contributing factors to high mortality (Krieger and Birn, 1998). In the wake of deadly epidemics and pandemics in the 1830s surveys questioned the very meaning of an acceptable minimum level of habitation, moving the focus to new concerns such as quality of construction, urban density, overcrowding or sanitary provisions (Harrison, 2017). The effects of epidemic in congested urban areas sprang institutions such as the Paris Health Council to action, generating calls for a building code that stipulated minima of construction and public hygiene standards as basic human needs (Berge, 1992, 116–24). In short, defining minimum needs involved much more than measuring and converting into income units. Quantitative poverty thresholds were useful in quantifying inequality and poverty, but they were inadequate markers of a decent, healthy, independent, secure, dignified and moderately comfortable life.

## Habitation and 'minimum needs'

To dwell means to root oneself to the world by obtaining an intimate delimited space that they could call their own, as a protective shield against the natural elements and a refuge from the unfamiliarity of the surrounding space (Bollnow, 1961; Heidegger,

2006). When Abraham Maslow defined a hierarchical model of basic human needs, he determined a pyramid that started with the most fundamental human (i.e. physiological) needs at the bottom and then moved upwards to safety, belonging, esteem and self-actualization at the top. Maslow's hierarchy indicated a sense of progression from the basic (bottom) to the more complex needs (top). The former were fundamental in the sense of generating the conditions – and releasing the necessary resources – for realizing other needs further up in the pyramid and for pursuing a state of self-actualization (Bay, 1977). Strictly speaking, housing was inserted on the second level (security), being considered a 'deficit' need that arises out of deprivation. Yet so foundational was the need for dwelling that it feeds both upwards and downwards as a factor promoting the attainment of other physiological, psychological and self-actualization needs. Not only does the house provide security but it also promotes and secures the basic physiological needs (food, water, air); it can aid or subvert self-esteem, depending on whether it is used to mark human dignity or promote patterns of social exclusion; and it can advance human self-actualization as expression of personality and as access to other key activities such as employment, education, leisure and culture (Hays, 1995b, 60–86).

Therefore, housing both constituted a fundamental human need and functioned as a receptacle for the pursuit or refinement of a host of other requirements for a secure and dignified life (Lewin, 1913, 13). In the course of the nineteenth century, its meaning had shifted from an elemental association with some form of basic private shelter to an increasingly complex qualitative category that touched on health and hygiene, heat, convenience, as well as an ever-expanding menu of sociological parameters relating to private individual and family life. In his survey of poverty in late-Victorian East London, Booth devoted considerable space to housing conditions, demonstrating how they both marked and contributed to social inequality. Booth used (over)crowding as a primary indicator of poverty – in fact, more accurate than income itself (Booth, 1902, Vol. IX, 1–17). His pioneering spatial mapping of poverty in the British capital demonstrated a strong correlation between income, overcrowding, patterns of employment and social habits (Figure 1.1). His analytical approach showed a far more nuanced understanding

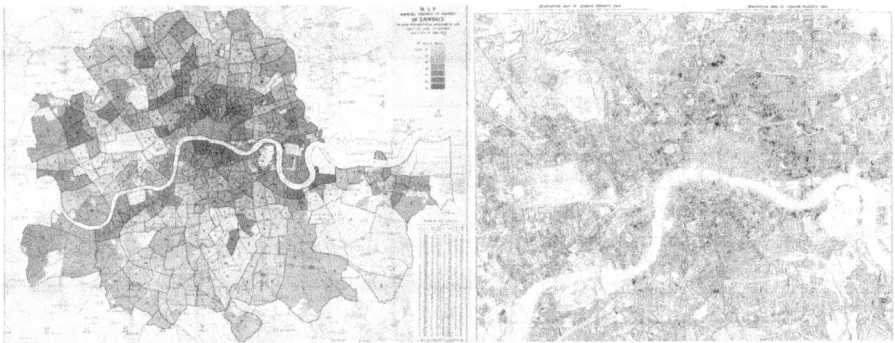

**Figure 1.1** Maps 'showing degrees of poverty in London' by Charles Booth [Source: Wellcome Trust].

of how housing conditions indicated and became conducive to poverty. His survey dedicated a lengthy section of a volume on tenement housing conditions (authored by George Arkell), based on insights gathered from representative visits to particular types of buildings in the area that he researched. The criteria that Arkell used for the classification of the quality of the buildings reflected an awareness of the importance of the basic criteria of light, air, open space and 'sanitary conditions' (a broad category that collapsed qualities such as quality of construction, hygiene, facilities and even room arrangement). His subsequent classification of tenement buildings across a five-step scale from 'very good' to 'very bad' was determined by an elaborate list of sub-indices that related to the four main criteria mentioned above but engaged in a more granular analysis of the elements of each building (windows, staircases, courtyards, etc.). 'Very good' dwellings indicated particular qualities: open access to a space at least as wide as the height of the building itself, direct sunlight even to ground-floor apartments, naturally well-lit staircases and either separate closet and water supply in each tenement (for integrated dwellings) or separate sanitary facilities 'situated conveniently for the tenants, and in a position where it will not attract general attention' (Booth, 1902, Vol. III, 15). By contrast an example of a 'very bad' building in terms of both light and sanitary state is described by Arkell as

> a large plain brick building with six floors, the lowest being half basement. Entering by a gate and ascending a few steps a long passage is reached extending from the front to the back of the building. About half way along this passage is the staircase, and facing it is a window frame from which the sashes have been removed and a sink and water tap placed in the opening. This aperture looks out on a small courtyard. On the staircase is another opening to a second courtyard, long and narrow. These two open spaces light, or are supposed to light, the back tenements their walls have been whitened recently. Close by the sink is the dust-shoot and a closet, and on the stairs is a second closet. This accommodation provides for nearly twenty tenements, one and two-roomed, whose doors open on this passage. The tapper floors are similar, save that the passages are much darker, as they have no light from the street and make a turn at each end to give access to the remoter tenements. The inner walls are dirty, and the plaster has fallen from the roof in patches.
>
> (Booth, 1902, Vol. III, 17)

Beyond ideal types and qualitative classifications, the survey featured vignettes of realistic conditions of life in East London that are often striking. For example, washrooms in older buildings were usually situated either at the basement or on the roof and the unavailability of hot running water meant that tenants had to prepare it in their apartments and then carry it downstairs. A minute single-room apartment was often occupied by a large family (a case of five children was recorded in the survey' sample), had no cupboards or storage space for coal and sanitary wash facilities with numerous other apartments – but it could still cost the equivalent of 15 per cent of the income that Booth had recommended as a poverty threshold. What is also interesting is the implicit assumptions of the authors about what was acceptable or not in terms of hygiene, living space and facilities. Internal water closets that were not fully isolated with floor-to-ceiling walls, dark rooms on the back side of the dwelling, barely lit staircases, shared washrooms, barely functioning drainage and a distinct lack of meaningful personal private 'ration' inside the dwellings were in fact considered tolerable by the authors. Changes in attitudes to what constituted at the time an acceptable minimum of light, sanitation, comfort and appearance could be extrapolated from a comparison between older and more recently constructed tenement blocks. The latter offered distinct advantages in all these areas by featuring more windows, better distributed sanitary facilities and more functional internal fittings or amenities.

The social reformer Octavia Hill contributed to the housing section of Booth's report, focusing on the 'influence of character'. The analysis rested on the premise that density/crowding and human behaviour were more significant causes of distress than any measure of hygiene or comfort in dwelling and any positive effects from education. It included an extensive reflection on the merits of small houses in comparison to large tenement buildings. Hill criticized the latter for multiplying human behavioural defects and for brutalizing otherwise 'gentle' people. In addition, she claimed that the tenement blocks deprived tenants of their individuality and sense of intimate belonging to their dwelling. Meanwhile their visual monotony and lack of character alienated them from their dwelling and community environment (Booth, 1902, Vol. III, 29–36).

Rowntree also understood the central role of housing in the satisfaction of minimum human needs. His survey of York featured a chapter dedicated to housing conditions and to the correlation between overcrowding and social inequality. In comparison to London, York had far fewer tenement buildings, generally larger dwellings in available room terms and notably less overcrowding (defined by Rowntree as a ratio higher than two residents per room). It also had fewer areas that could be classified as 'slums'. However, when he used a different quantitative metric, based on available cubic volume of air per person, Rowntree was forced to lower the minimum to 1.5 persons per average-size room. With regard to 'slum' conditions he admitted that, although these kinds of settlements were less extensive in York than in Victorian-era metropolitan areas such as London or Glasgow, the effects of the vicious circle of insufficient income, overcrowding, poverty and high mortality were very much in evidence. Slum housing was smaller, situated in spatial configurations that prevented sufficient light and air to enter the dwellings (e.g. back-to-back houses, buildings situated in narrow alleyways and small courtyards), with poor supply of running water, unacceptable levels of sanitation, poor construction (measured in terms of quality of external and interior walls and floors, insulation, structural integrity, quality of plumbing), and unsatisfactory standards of hygiene (Rowntree, 1901, 153–8). Finally, the proportion of income going to accommodation in York remained depressingly high, extending in some cases to a quarter of more of wages.

Therefore, housing presented social reformers and state authorities with a degree of complexity that far exceeded the satisfaction of most other basic needs. In many ways modern housing was not just a single need in itself but was key to the satisfaction of other needs, as well as a privileged, intimate space offering unique opportunities to residents for fostering them. While food and clothing were individual needs, housing incorporated diverse scales of social relevance – from the individual to the family and the community; from the inside to the outside space; from the private dwelling to the building, the neighbourhood and the city, and society as a whole. Meanwhile the housing unit was a receptacle of multiple technologies and processes – building, design, heating, domestic economy, social relations, reproduction, relaxation and leisure. All these complexities rendered the task of deducing a universal minimum for housing standards, let alone enforceable regulations across the board and models of good practice, very difficult.

## Early interventions and reform initiatives

With liberal economic orthodoxies firmly in place, for most of the nineteenth century public authorities saw minimum needs at best as a noble aspiration and not a moral responsibility. When it came to housing, they perceived their role as enforcers of elevated general standards, not as proactive agents of housing provision. But even the notion of an absolute needs minimum in relation to dwelling was hard to conceive, let alone enforce. Unlike food (which nineteenth-century natural scientists translated into stable quantities of calories, then nutritional elements), housing had no putatively objective threshold as minimum need beyond that of a mere shelter – a roof over one's head (Bay, 1977). When authorities started to engage with the task of converting minimum needs into concrete housing standards, they encountered only abstract variables that were hard to pin down: ever-shifting benchmarks of air, light and hygiene; expanding conceptions of minimum psychological and sociological needs; technological and cultural changes that transformed the context and content of domestic life, and so on.

Nevertheless, the case for radical improvement of the housing conditions gained traction in the course of the nineteenth century and prompted a growing repertoire of concrete reform action. The traditional philanthropic gesture was no longer deemed effective or sufficient enough to confront a problem that had escalated so rapidly in both scale and quality within the modern industrial urban context. Incidental and parsimonious, acts of charity were deeply embedded in the restrictive moral framework of pauperism and were thus largely devoid of reforming ambition. More alarmingly the mismatch between basic needs and actual conditions of living for workers and the urban poor widened dramatically during the nineteenth century. In the face of this growing chasm important initiatives in the direction of effecting housing reform came initially from a number of either private or collective sources. The history of 'model industrial communities' has provided some of the best examples of improved housing standards in the course of the nineteenth century. As a pathbreaker in early industrialization, Britain offered the earliest and most diverse examples of this trend. Robert Owen's model village in New Lanark, Titus Salt's Saltaire model community in Shipley, Edward Akroyd's housing activities in Copley and Halifax, and the workers' settlements built by the Cadbury and Lever families in Bourneville and Port Sunlight, respectively, were the most renowned experiments in model worker dwellings in the nineteenth century (Frasch and Wyke, 2015). The early British examples soon attracted the attention of continental housing reformers who sought not just to replicate them but to adapt and improve them for the particular conditions of their own countries. In the 1840s, the German social campaigner Victor Aimé Huber travelled extensively in Britain studying workers' conditions of life in the big industrial centres and model housing initiatives. He wrote extensively on the pros and cons of the British experience and devised new schemes for social cooperation before influencing and becoming involved in a not-for-profit building initiative in Berlin (Adam, 2009, 46–50). From the 1850s onwards the German steel magnate Alfred Krupp started turning his industrial facilities in the Ruhr district into a model for an integrated approach to the social welfare of the workforce (Petz, 1990). In France the example of the 'model cottages' exhibited at the 1851 Great Exhibition in London inspired a large-scale experiment in the environs of Mulhouse, where the industrialist Jean Dollfuss established *the Société Mulhousienne des Cités Ouvrières* as the provider of good-quality housing for the workers of his textile factory (Figure 1.2). Only a few years later the iron industrialist Jean-Baptiste André Godin put the ideas of the utopian philosopher Charles Fourier into practice in his plant in Guise, creating model industrial communities on the grounds of his gargantuan *Familistère* – a series of 'social palaces' that provided housing together with a complete set of communal social facilities (Lallement, 2012; Frasch and Wyke, 2015, 182–91). Across the Atlantic in the 1880s, the American engineer and industrialist George Pullman established his own version of an ideal company town south of Chicago (Baxter and Bullen, 2011).

The efforts of nineteenth-century utopian housing reformers did have a significant long-term effect on the framing of the housing question. A deeper awareness of housing

**Figure 1.2** Early examples of 'model housing': the 'model cottages' exhibited at the 1851 Great Exhibition (left) and view of the houses constructed by the *Société Mulhousienne des Cités Ouvrières in Mulhouse*, c. 1855 (right) [Source: *Collection des archives/bibliothèque/Musée Historique de la Ville de Mulhouse*].

as complex human need and a recognition that it involved much more than a mere shelter or a shield against the worst public health hazards would help generate a novel, coherent intellectual framework for apprehending housing as a key driver of social improvement (Gaskell, 1986, 148; Jerram, 2007, 330-1). By challenging the passivity or timidity of public authorities campaigns for housing reform helped establish housing as a critical political and social field where radical reformist or even revolutionary action was possible. They also chalked out and tested in practice alternative scenarios of active, ambitious intervention in minimum standards, social organization and urban planning that would stimulate the imagination of subsequent generations of advocates for radical social change. Nevertheless, whatever the benefits and very often questionable motives, model industrial housing per se was not a viable solution to the growing poverty/housing crisis of the nineteenth century (Gaskell, 1986, 130; Stavrides, 2016, 230). Based on a rejection of the industrial city as the source of physical and moral degeneration (Pick, 1993, 213; Jones, 2014), they were overwhelmingly premised on a flight towards the countryside that was simply not possibly for the vast majority of industrial workers. Their celebration of a romantic view of 'good life' was an ill-suited remedy for what was essentially a problem of urban concentration and crowding. Furthermore, most nineteenth-century model industrial communities were products of a utopian imagination that tended towards heterotopic islands of a new optimum rather than a universal elevated minimum; and were predicated on a tabula rasa – spatial, political, economic, social, cultural – that was hard to create en masse in existing modern cities (Carmony and Elliott, 1980). In this respect the model communities of the nineteenth century were not scaleable outside the contours of a confined, self-sufficient, controlled sanctuary and were therefore unsuitable for tackling the challenge of satisfying the basic needs of the urban workforce and the poor.

Faced with worsening urban problems and social unrest, on the one hand, and growing calls for intervention on the basis of elevated minima for human needs, on the other, government attitudes did begin to shift, very gradually, from the middle of the nineteenth century onwards. A comparison of the 1848 and 1875 Public Health Acts in Britain reveals how within a relatively short period of time both the threshold of tolerability and the scope for state regulation had changed. The 1848 Act put in place a range of measures to protect and promote actively public health. The result was an ambitious step forward in terms of promulgating health standards coupled with a timid approach to housing norms and powers of enforcement. By the time of the 1875 Act the laissez-faire tide had turned decisively. A series of legislative arrangements empowered local authorities – legally and financially – to invest in sanitary infrastructure and implement restrictive public health standards that the Act itself then codified and expressed as a new minimum standard that also affected new housing construction. The next step came in the 1885–1900 period with a series of new acts empowering local authorities, first, to condemn slum-like buildings, then to engage in compulsory land purchases, and finally to become directly involved in the improvement, construction and sale of workers' dwellings, albeit without any form of direct state subsidy (Millins et al., 2006, 15–17). In France the last decades of the nineteenth century witnessed a shift from a reactive public health approach to a new regulatory framework that established the right of public authorities to intervene actively in the housing market. The 1894 Siegfried Act introduced the principle of tax exemption and public subsidy to a number of limited-profit public companies established under the umbrella of the *Société Française des Habitations à Bon Marché* (Shapiro, 1985, 84–110; Power, 1993, 15). The French law was heavily influenced by the 1889 Housing Act in Belgium, which offered wide-ranging fiscal benefits for the private construction of affordable housing for sale. Starting in the 1870s Swedish legislation followed the path of forcing municipalities to devise urban plans as a framework for regulating both public health and housing matters. Although these and other related powers were initially not legally enforceable, the period of 1904–09 witnessed a significant step change in housing policy – first, with the introduction of a public loan system to encourage construction of affordable housing; and second, with the legal codification of powers of intervention with the 1909 Planning Act (Stromberg, 1992, 18–21). The Netherlands introduced a sweeping Housing Act in 1902 that gave unprecedented powers to municipal authorities to survey, regulate and become involved in housing policy and in urban planning as a whole, supported by generous government financial assistance (Stieber, 1998, 15–22). In Germany the federal system delayed the adoption of a centralized housing policy, delegating relevant responsibilities to the individual states. However, from the 1890s onwards, the Bismarckian state insurance funds were allowed to direct funds to private building associations involved in low-cost housing (Rodgers, 1998, 190–2). In addition individual German municipalities had engaged in significant land purchases in and around their area of jurisdiction in an effort to combat speculation with land 're-parcelling' (Wurster, 1934, 97; Ladd, 1990, 186–235). In Italy the lack of a central legislative framework throughout the nineteenth century was partly compensated by the action of individual municipalities. Naples led the way with a comprehensive policy of urban sanitary improvement in the wake of a disastrous cholera epidemic in 1884 that led to extensive demolitions and systematic efforts to improve standards of light, ventilation and public hygiene in the poorer districts of the city (Snowden, 2002, 181–232). At the turn of the century, the then Austro-Hungarian port city of Trieste set up a municipal organization dedicated to the provision of affordable housing explicitly branded as 'minimum dwellings' (*abitazioni minime*; Baf, 1997; ICAM, 1913; Glendinning, 2021, 21). This became the model for the country-wide legislation of 1903 (the so-called Luzzatti law) that enabled building societies to engage in affordable housing provision. The law also paved the way for the creation of a web of Institutes of Social Housing as primary municipal agents for the realization of programmes of housing improvement and construction across the urban centres of the country (Kirk, 2005, 27; D'Amuri, 2013, Ch 3).

All the same, at the turn of the twentieth century even the most interventionist governments continued to shy away from becoming directly involved in housing construction, which was still considered an activity better left to private initiative – albeit within an increasingly regulated framework. Faced with the unwillingness or inadequacy of state intervention both charitable private investors and not-for-profit mutual organizations had became involved in housing earlier in the nineteenth century.

These two models – the first top-down; the other bottom-up – differed in a number of significant ways. Private donors saw their contributions as a form of benevolent investment and expected a healthy (albeit lower than what was the norm in a housing investment at the time) financial reward from the outlay (a system that is typically known as 'five percent philanthropy' (Tarn, 1973)). By contrast self-help companies and a small number of 'pure philanthropy' trusts (like the Peabody or Guinness Trusts in Britain; the *Société Philanthropique de Paris*; the *Verein zur Verbesserung der kleinen Wohnungen* in Berlin) were geared towards the provision of housing to their members without expectation of dividends. On many occasions housing organizations mixed elements of self-help and private investment in order to maximize their capacity for housing output; what made the difference was the relatively lower level of return paid from the investment (typically 2–5 per cent) and the limited control that donors could have on the management of the organization (Dreier, 1997). For example, when the Artisans', Labourers' and General Dwellings Company of London moved from its initial not-for-profit phase to a mixed-investment/impact model in 1874, it set the dividend level at 4.5 per cent (Gould and Lovell, 1895, 222). In Germany the pioneering *Hannover Spar- und Bauverein* operated as a limited-liability company that set the level of dividends at 4 per cent and restricted its housing output to renting (Adam, 2007, 174–5).

Each of these two types of private housing organization played a significant role in redefining the very concept of minimum against government timidity or inaction, promoting higher baseline standards in a larger number of dwellings for the workers and the urban poor. Housing co-operatives were initially limited in numbers and constrained in their housing output capacity for most of the nineteenth century, as dwelling construction costs often exceeded the available capital from their individual members. Nevertheless a series of legislative measures aimed at stimulating the growth of limited dividend/co-operative companies, such as the 1889 German Co-operative Law, provided much-needed legal security desired by private members and gave the co-operative housing movement real long-term impetus that would be properly felt during the twentieth century (Rowe, 1995, 86; Co-op, 2012). By contrast charitable private investment in higher-quality workers' urban and suburban housing (both flats and small dwellings) flourished in the second half of the nineteenth century across a number of countries in Europe and north America. Transnational learning turned Initiatives in one place into blueprints to be reproduced, adapted or rejected elsewhere (Rodgers, 1998, 187). The converted tenements run under a strict disciplinary regime by the organization set up by Octavia Hill in London inspired a series of similar efforts across the continent. The authoritative public research into the social question conducted under the auspices of the Verein für Socialpolitik in Germany emerged as an alternative template for housing policies to the laissez-faire approaches that had shaped the equivalent field in nineteenth-century Britain (Wisselgren, 2017, 46–50). Many American observers were inspired by the British hybrid philanthropic housing provision model but tended to reject its seemingly excessive impact-first approach at the expense of attractive financial returns. When Henry Bowditch set up the Boston Co-operative Building Society in the early 1870s, he deliberately shunned Peabody's 'pure philanthropy' precedent in favour of a profit-first organization that promised a mammoth return of 7 per cent for individual investments (Adam, 2009, 164). While the British and Dutch housing legislation eventually empowered municipalities to become directly involved not only in slum clearance but also in independent housing provision (with Liverpool embarking on this activity as early as 1866) (Holmes, 2006, 79–87; Boughton, 2018, 13–15), France and Germany promoted a system of public financial facilitation and private limited-dividend initiative instead.

The result of all these shifts – in public attitude to housing, professional opinion about minimum needs and law – was that by early twentieth century the overall conditions of accommodation for workers and the urban poor had started to improve. The housing problem, however, refused to go away. In her classic 1934 study of housing conditions Catherine Bauer spoke of a striking irony that marked the nineteenth century: in spite of all the expansive talk about progress, civilization, elevated human needs and social betterment, the modern industrial cities grew uglier, more degrading and less hygienic as time went by (Wurster, 1934, 7–35). Bauer's line of attack was that the activity of the philanthropic organizations resulted in a new kind of sub-standard dwelling replacing slums with a new kind of 'planned slum', as she put it (Wurster, 1934, 81)' that did little to alleviate housing shortage while also degrading further the urban environment. Criticism of the low-cost urban tenements produced by limited-dividend companies and 'pure philanthropy' trusts had remained constant ever since they first appeared on the cityscape of Victorian London. They were censured for their gigantism and lack of design value, resulting in a monotonous, inhuman barrack-like appearance. Nikolaus Pevsner described them as a 'grim parade' with depressing effects (Maltz, 2006, 59; Steadman, 2014, 14). Subsequent critics saw these tenements as one of the main reasons why high-density urban housing was subsequently so intensely disliked as housing typology, in Britain and elsewhere (Interbuild, 6/1959, 29; Tarn, 1973, 44–50). But criticism extended well beyond external appearance, environmental effects and urban segregation (Pooley, 1992). It also touched on the equally monotonous interior design of the dwellings, crushing every sense of individuality and domesticity; on the strict disciplinary power that philanthropic trusts and limited-dividend companies often exercised over their tenants (Cooper, 2005; Maltby and Rutterford, 2016); on their relatively high rents that rendered them unaffordable by the 'very poor';[1] on the ruthlessly selective approach of the proprietors vis-à-vis the kind of tenants that they admitted to the properties;[2] on the barely acceptable standards of living that they afforded to their residents, both inside the dwellings and outside in the surrounding area, in spite of the relative upgrade that they represented in comparison to slums or overcrowded old tenements that they were meant to replace (Wurster, 1934, 22–44; Geddes, 1949, 128); on their inability to address the underlying causes of the low-cost housing shortage, which related to the sky-rocketing price of land, the depression of wages in absolute terms and the absence of subsidy for the rent; and finally, on the relatively small output of this kind of housing provision that was grotesquely insufficient to meet the demand for low-cost housing at a time of mounting urban migration, slum demolition and escalating rents (Gaskell, 1986, 133).

# The Minimum Dwelling

## *Existenzminimum*

The idea that housing, as one of the three most fundamental needs along with food and clothing/heat (Lewin, 1913, 13) and a critical facilitator of higher standards of living (linked to health and hygiene, heat, convenience, as well as an ever-expanding menu of sociological parameters relating to private individual and family life, gender roles, etc.), was a particular facet of the deeper problem of growing social inequality gave rise to new intellectual, political and economic approaches. As 'minimum' needs could now be determined on a more scientific basis, calculated more precisely according to objective quantitative criteria, and associated with a threshold of human dignity that ought to be guaranteed through public intervention, housing became an integral part of the discourse of 'subsistence living'. Legislative interventions in New Zealand (1894), Australia (1900–05) and Great Britain (1909) enshrined minimum wage as part of a corporatist system of wage dispute arbitration (Paterson, 1917; Holcombe, 1910). The development was significant in that it promised a modicum of arbitration in the workings of an otherwise liberal wage economy – but it was not tantamount to the acceptance of some kind of social provision, let alone one premised on human need or taking the moral form of a universal citizenship right (Hyman, 2002). In the years leading up to the First World War the idea of a 'subsistence minimum' was proposed as an alternative – a political commitment to guarantee an elevated tax-exempt income that would enable poor families to subsist.[3] This was part of a discussion that was stimulated by the inability of either the market forces or the timid existing legal instruments to respond to chronic social injustice made worse by cyclical economic crises, inflation and rising prices.

The link between net family earnings and overall quality of life (housing included) pointed to the importance of a decent 'minimum' income as the guarantee of secure subsistence living. This was the conclusion of the German economist Robert René Kuczynski who had conducted forensic work on this theme since the 1910s. In 1921 Kuczynski published a treatise on the 'subsistence minimum' (what he called *Existenzminimum*) that brought together his research findings to that date. Specifying subsistence levels required, first, copious efforts to calculate minimum nutritional needs for survival as an overall calorific value and then breaking them down into different types of food required for a healthy and balanced diet based on earlier scientific research into biological subsistence (Simmons, 2015, 162–8). Housing, light and heating, clothing, education and other expenses were then added to the formula. In reference to housing Kuczynski moved from abstract stipulations to typological proposals – a dwelling with a single room and kitchen – without stipulation of minimum size, quality or amenities (Figure 1.3). This served his primary interest in family income and expenditure in relation to the price index, allowing for easier and more objective comparisons of the cost of a stable Existenzminimum formula before (1914) and after (1920) the war. Yet, while nutritional, clothing and education needs were fixed for each adult male, adult female and child, when it came to housing and heating the assumptions that he used did not take into account fully the effect of variations in family size on the size (and cost)

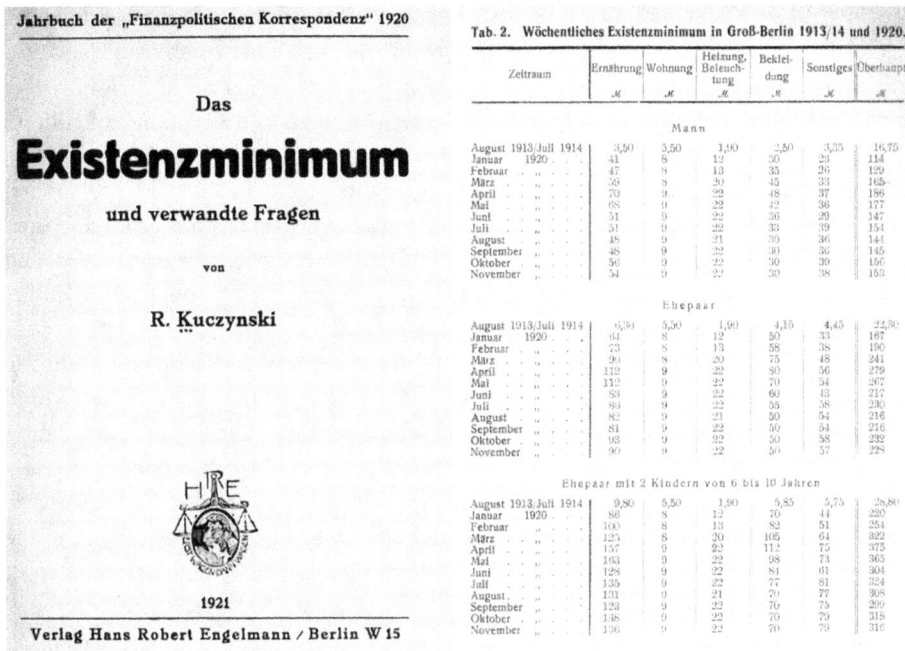

**Figure 1.3** Robert René Kuczynski's Existenzminimum book and an example of his calculations, comparing the increase in living costs between 1914 and 1920 in Berlin (figure columns from left to right: date, food, dwelling, heating, clothing and extra expenses).

of dwelling. He was critical of government-set minimum 'rations' for all basic needs, because he found them either too low or inflexible and irrelevant in actual terms. He noted, for example, that a large number of five-person families lived in smaller and/or crowded dwellings because this is what they could afford at current market prices (Kuczynski, 1921, 15–19). Thus, for reasons of simplicity, his calculations did not delve into qualitative markers of habitation. Instead Kuczynski's primary concern was to show the devastating effect of price rises due to inflation and currency devaluation on the actual cost of the Existenzminimum between and after the First World War, as well as on a shorter-term, month-by-month, basis for then year 1920. His calculations underlined the enormity of the challenge: the weekly expenditure of an average family that was needed to meet absolute existential minima had increased twelve-fold in the short period between the outbreak of the First World War and his census point of 1920, with most of this increase occurring in the period after the end of the war. Kuczynski also used data from his own research in the Berlin area to highlight the severity of the shortage of affordable housing, noting that the rate of wage increases had lagged dramatically behind the rising cost of living, making ever-larger sections of the housing provision unaffordable by the majority of workers. This meant that workers needed to spend an increasingly unaffordable percentage of their wages just to satisfy the most basic definition of Existenzminimum, let alone to fulfil more complex needs associated with quality of life (Kuczynski, 1921). Given how low workers' wages and standards of the Existenzminimum were to begin with, the growing mismatch between income and cost of the individual items in the Existenzminimum reference basket meant that in reality families had to make further compromises, lowering their consumption/expenditure and thus inevitably falling below the subsistence-minimum standard (Holtfrerich, 2011, 38–40; Torp, 2011, 202). The only meaningful solution, as he had consistently argued since 1917, was an extraordinary state intervention to stabilize the economy, then guarantee a subsistence-minimum income calculated in relation to the price index, and finally relieve existing debt commitments for everyone, financed through a one-off tax on property.

Understandably such a discussion acquired fresh urgency and momentum during the First World War years, when unemployment, severe economic disruption and food shortages meant that even existential survival was under threat for a significantly larger number of families. In hindsight it is striking how the predominantly economic framing of subsistence minimum as an income-living costs correlational problem had devoted so little attention to the qualitative aspects of minimum housing as an integral part of the Existenzminimum perspective until well into the 1920s. In 1913 the dissertation work of David Lewin in Heidelberg did contain a brief reference to 'subsistence minimum' housing conditions, with significantly longer discussions dedicated to food and clothing forming the triad of essential minimum needs. Lewin came to the conclusion that 'there is even less evidence of a subsistence level in the housing question than in diet'. He argued that, since housing was a social – rather than a purely biological – need, there could be no absolute and objective minimum measure used for calculation. His brief analysis focused on either physiological or social factors (e.g. quantity and quality of air inside the dwelling; mortality rates per district and type of habitation) without extending the discussion directly to a consideration of size, amenities or design standards. He noted the detrimental effect of overcrowding in urban areas and bemoaned the poor enforcement of even bare minimum standards of housing hygiene and ventilation/illumination. The conclusion that he reached, however, harked back to the same socio-economic fundamentals that Kuczynski used for his own calculations a few years later: gross income inequalities and a growing mismatch between wages and cost of living prevented a significant number of families from rising above the Existenzminimum threshold, forcing them to negotiate unacceptable reductions even in relation to their most basic minimum needs (Lewin, 1913, 51–7). On their part state and municipal authorities did adopt in one form or another the 'subsistence minimum' nomenclature in determining policies of taxation and public welfare but were still reluctant to countenance enforcement of better minimum standards in dwellings without incurring prohibitively higher prices for poorer families. For the majority of Existenzminimum advocates and theorists of that time satisfying the basic need for habitation involved in the first place being able to somehow afford a hygienic shelter. The liberal economic bias of these analyses was conspicuous: there was little interest in subsidized public housing provision, in radical income redistribution policies or in positive enforcement of higher-quality standards of habitation at more affordable prices. Furthermore, nineteenth-century assumptions about class differentiation were easier to leave unquestioned in the more subjective domain of housing than in the scientifically calculated biological needs that allowed for a more universal human perspective. The underlying assumption that poorer families had fewer needs, even 'minimum' ones, meant that the discussion of the Existenzminimum often referenced what Nancy Stieber has described as a 'threshold of tolerability', an extreme reduction of the (Existenz)minimum below which mere survival could not be guaranteed (Stieber, 1998, 83–90).

## The low-cost housing calculus

In spite of significant advances in scientific knowledge, public health regulation, as well as in social awareness and reformist ambition, the reality was that good-quality, low-cost, truly affordable dwellings continued to be in desperate short supply throughout the 'long' European nineteenth century. The mass housing calculus remained desperately distorted by either objective or imposed limits in every domain. The continuing reluctance of state authorities to intervene actively in the facilitation and direct provision of housing – a product of persisting laissez-faire orthodoxies – was a significant impediment to increasing housing output in the far less profitable low-cost segment. The tension between the social imperative of **affordability** and the economic pressures of **profitability** (or at least financial sustainability) for constructors and owners impacted negatively on the system's capacity for supplying cheap and decent houses in sufficient numbers. Even when legislation eventually allowed a number of states to facilitate indirectly low-cost housing (through loans, subsidies, tax exemptions, legal protection, etc.), the result was never enough supply to even approximate rising demand. Not-for-profit initiatives were typically restricted by the limited power of their members to provide enough capital for the expensive business of land purchase and housing construction. At the same time limited-dividend companies were constrained by the levels of their investment and the pressure to deliver financial rewards for their shareholders that would continue to make them attractive destinations for that bizarre hybrid form of nineteenth-century philanthropic capitalism. As a result, the majority of the poorest families continued to live in older, degraded, subdivided, sublet and overcrowded properties in old, new or about-to-become slums because they were still unable to access affordable good-quality housing.

The mismatch between **supply** and **demand** was made worse by yet another paradox. The expanding meaning and rising thresholds of 'basic needs' justified the urgent call for elevated housing standards for all but also inevitably meant increased costs of production and use (Wurster, 1934, 27). Given that public authorities continued to resist any form of active intervention in the housing market beyond modest financial and legal facilitation, most of the new better-quality dwellings ended up being prohibitively expensive for families with low income. In this ruthless market logic a meaningful lowering of cost/rent could be achieved mostly by equivalent economies elsewhere – in dwelling size; in density and plot coverage; in external and interior decoration; in construction quality; in sanitary facilities; in household amenities; and/or in siting – location and distance from the urban core and the places of work (Gaskell, 1986, 147–8). Even otherwise lofty and ambitious slum clearance schemes became a liability: without sufficient replacement of low-cost housing stock in nearby areas poorer residents were forced to relocate further and further away from the core of the industrial city, their places of work and their existing social networks.

In the end the brutal underlying **zero-sum logic** of the housing calculus in the nineteenth century came down to a very basic reality check: in order to promote elevated quality standards and satisfy minimum human needs beyond mere survival at prices that were still affordable by the urban poor and in quantities that could address the growing demand, one or more facets of the system of mass housing production and provision had to change. Advocates of revolutionary transformation were armed with straightforward remedies (communal ownership of land, eliminating the profit variable) based on the prior overturning of the capitalist system itself. Similarly, proponents of a utopian tabula rasa used the premise of abandoning the modern city altogether as the only way to unlock radical possibilities to improve living standards for the population. Neither of these pathways was meaningful to those advocating a reformist and gradualist approach. For them the primary challenge was to get the maximum quality, affordability and supply dividends by convincing or forcing public authorities to take a significantly more active role in the regulation, financing and production of housing for the masses. Their fight was primarily one against entrenched convictions and practices that in their eyes stifled the process of radical social improvement within the broad contours of a modern industrial capitalist society. Change in this direction was slow and tentative until the turn of the twentieth century. When the pace eventually quickened, especially in the wake of the First World War, the entire mass housing calculus was transformed, its conventional zero-sum logic challenged and rejected in favour of aspirational alternatives.

In spite of their obvious differences, these revolutionary, utopian and reformist projects shared a conviction that the housing market did operate on a ruthless zero-sum logic and thus there was little or no space for magical solutions without substantial prior change in either the entire system or in some of its components. Gradualist reform had yet no meaningful recourse to its own version of a revolution – no shortcut to indulge and no conceivable alchemy to turn to. There were only two further variables that, in theory, could upset the zero-sum logic of this operation and would in effect revolutionize the meaning of the 'minimum' in the dwelling – but they both remained largely untapped until the First World War. The first concerned the actual **costs** of producing standards-compliant affordable housing. These were derived more or less directly from land, labour, equipment, material and amenity prices. So long as these parameters remained either accepted unquestionably or outside the realm of intervention, there was no further device that could change the zero-sum principle of this activity or generate further margin for significant economies. Modern technological and management advances, however, were about to disrupt this equation, paving the way for a series of transformative modalities in the form of rationalization, standardization, prefabrication and modular construction. Principles of rationality, function and efficiency were already evident in other fields of production throughout the nineteenth century – in factory building and management, in industrial infrastructure, even in the very techniques of building higher and safe buildings faster. Yet the realm of housing, viewed as a primary expression of human individuality, remained largely impervious to these innovations until the turn of the twentieth century. The second untapped variable concerned **design** and aesthetic values associated with dwelling. Elevated minimum standards of housing design (both exterior and internal) and comfort had been abstracted from traditional ideals of nineteenth-century 'bourgeois' living because this was deemed at the time the only conceivable conduit of social improvement for the poor. It was not only 'model' dwellings that reflected and reproduced filtered-down versions of aristocratic and middle-class ideals of life (Gaskell, 1986, 145); any 'minimum', whether of human needs or standards of domestic life, was arrived at by deducting from the bourgeois desires, aspirations and their domestic menagerie all the way down to a perceived threshold of tolerably 'good enough'. A radical break with the past that extended to the positive adoption of a functional, indeed minimalist approach to interior and exterior design based on science and technology would eventually disrupt and transform the zero-sum dynamics of the low-cost housing calculus (Gartman, 2009, 10–23). It would also enable the rethinking of other variables such as preferred optimal size and configuration, amenities and equipment, as ingredients of a new kind of 'minimum' that promised to be not only – and not primarily – more economical but crucially better because of it.

Neither of these two variables was seriously considered as a field of experimentation and innovation in the field of mass housing by professional experts and gradualist reformers until the turn of the twentieth century. When they did enter the reformist imagination, as a result of both professional fascination with the modern sublime and urgency to respond to the post-First World War housing crisis, they turned the conventional housing calculus upside down and rendered a very different understanding of 'minimum dwelling' possible.

# CHAPTER 2
# THE 'SMALL DWELLING' BETWEEN EMERGENCY AND ASPIRATION

### Size and dwelling

The dwelling may be an intimate, personal space – a 'state of mind' (Young, 2011, 290) associated with the idea of a 'home' – and it invariably has a cultural and social context that distinguishes it from place to place and from time to time. Yet in its most elemental form it is 'a room with a horizontal floor and ceiling, vertical walls and certain dimensions' created by humans for their daily life (Doxiadis, 1972, 2–10). As a deliberate enclosure for protection and reproduction the dwelling defines and is defined by space. Size and volume, therefore, are its most fundamental parameters.

It is no coincidence that the room has been considered as 'the smallest unit created by man, which serves all basic purposes' (Doxiadis, 1972, 1). In its most elemental form the dwelling can be a single room; in fact, this is how the history of permanent habitation begins, or an interconnected network of rooms with differentiated functions. It is possible to conceive of the room-dwelling scheme in two ways: as a single enclosure with internal subdivisions or as a modular system of semi-closed units forming together a self-contained habitation. Either way, however, the dwelling demarcates an enclosed intimate space where a human or family seek to satisfy their needs. The room itself is a kind of irreducible minimum – the smallest unit, the atomic scale of more complex and extensive habitation formats. Size defines it spatially and volumetrically but is also determined by the functions that it encloses and permits or otherwise their fulfilment. Until the twentieth century, size was closely linked to quality of life and status. A larger dwelling was typically reflective of higher social Standing, income and quality of life. Moreover, larger size allowed for more (and better) amenities to be enclosed within the dwelling, thereby promoting (in theory at least) better living standards. The model of the bourgeois abode remained the cultural benchmark of good living and therefore served as the starting point for deriving – through a series of reductions – the more economical dwelling for the working classes and the urban poor.

Other factors beyond geometric size refracted the cost of the dwelling. Density was one of them. Dwellings in single-family houses or low-rise buildings increased the price while multi-storey residential blocks allowed for a more intensive (therefore economical) use of land, particularly in cities where space came at a premium due to high demand. Land coverage was another, with higher-density development that encroached on open public space bringing the cost down. The quality of construction and amenities also played an important role in determining the cost and price of the dwelling. Finally, location mattered enormously. The closer the dwelling was to highly valued assets (city centre, 'good' neighbourhoods, places of employment, etc.) the more expensive the land and the higher the housing unit's cost relative to other units of similar size and specification. Cost reflected not only objective factors but also prevailing subjective social and cultural attitudes.

Therefore, size was a core component of the conventional housing calculus but not a self-referential focus thereof. The main challenge facing reformers at the turn of the twentieth century was not the size of the dwelling per se but size in relation to other factors, some of which concerned the dwelling (e.g. available space per resident, health and hygiene) while others related to the block (e.g. density, distribution, land coverage, privacy) and siting (e.g. surroundings, distance from work). Each dwelling had a spatial context that refracted its key size metrics. This is why the Berlin *Mietskaserne* (the notorious 'rental barracks' used extensively after the introduction of the 1862 Hobrecht plan) (Figure 2.1) became synonymous with urban housing degradation: regardless of the size of individual apartments (generally small due to the interest of the owners to extract the highest possible rental income) they suffered from overcrowding, poor sanitation, insufficient ventilation and light, and poor construction/amenities (Berndt, 2004; Rousset, 2020). The combination of speculative building practices and subletting (in itself a collateral effect of poverty and high rental prices, as well as of inadequate dwelling stock) resulted in overcrowding within the dwelling in addition to the high

\*__Figure 2.1__ Aerial image of the Charlottenburg area of Berlin showing typical Mietskaserne (rental barracks), *c.* 1900 [Source: Getty].

density of land plots in poorer neighbourhoods (Jerram, 2007, 156–70). Therefore, the earlier 'open small dwelling' offered the worst of all worlds: small size, poor amenities, crowding, lack of privacy, unhygienic living and still relatively high cost and poor value for money (Fehl, 1988, 98–9; Lenger, 2012, 107). If it represented a minimum, it was the kind of a lowest common denominator that in fact depressed even the most fundamental human needs purely for reasons of profit (for the constructors) and cost (for the tenants).

Attitudes to smallness in dwelling started to change gradually from the last quarter of the nineteenth century. Rather than basing the size-reduction formula solely on the requirements of profitability or of cost reduction, more thought and energy went into maximizing affordability and basing the design of the dwelling on the intended inhabitants' real needs and uses. While most older housing stock consisted in large apartments of three, four or more rooms with a sizeable surface area, the needs of the buyers and renters were moving in the opposite direction, namely towards more compact dwellings featuring a significantly smaller number of rooms (Jerram, 2007, 156–70). Furthermore, there was a cultural shift away from the 'open' dwelling (one shared by more residents than those belonging to a single nuclear family, typically including relatives but also private renters (Lenger, 2012, 107)) and towards solutions that promoted 'closed' family occupancy (Fehl, 1988). Size remained a trade-off but the ensuing size reduction was increasingly presented by its advocates as a lesser evil, unlocking proportional gains in quality, affordability and enhanced scale of deployment. In France the new official term *Habitations à Bon Marché* (literally 'good value', HBM) gained currency from the 1890s (Dumont, 1991, 7–30), later to be complemented with the even more literal *Habitations à Loyer Modéré* (lower-rent/affordable dwellings, HLM), subsuming size reduction to the pursuit of a better quality-cost ratio. In Italy the adjectives 'popular', 'economic', 'fast' and in some cases even 'minimum' were used instead (Rutar, 2006). Even in Germany, where the terminology of the 'small dwelling' (Kleinwohnung) remained in use, a number of reform initiatives such as the Berlin-based Organisation for the *Verein zur Verbesserung kleiner Wohnungen* (Improvement of Small Dwellings) that appeared in the last two decades of the nineteenth century saw the 'small dwelling' typology as part of a reform solution to the problem of living conditions among the urban workers rather than as a stop-gap measure to address a housing crisis (Bullock, 1988, 177; Fehl, 1988, 118–22) [Figure 2.2]. Whether as apartment in a reformed urban block or as single-family house (detached or in row) in the suburban periphery, the small-dwelling typology involved 'closed' dwelling units of between one and three sleeping/living rooms excluding kitchen space to be used by a single-family unit. Over time the room number specification also acquired an overall surface numerical expression, indicating a dwelling on no more than 75 m$^2$, the actual figure depending on the number of people in the family household (Hagen and Ostergren, 2020, 162). In the context of this new logic size reduction responded to the need for cost-efficiency while also attending to minima of comfort and decency.

At the same time the focus of low-cost dwelling design also began to shift to the bigger scale of block reform, as a further strategy of maximizing cost dividends while also effecting overall improvements in the residents' quality of living. A stream of new

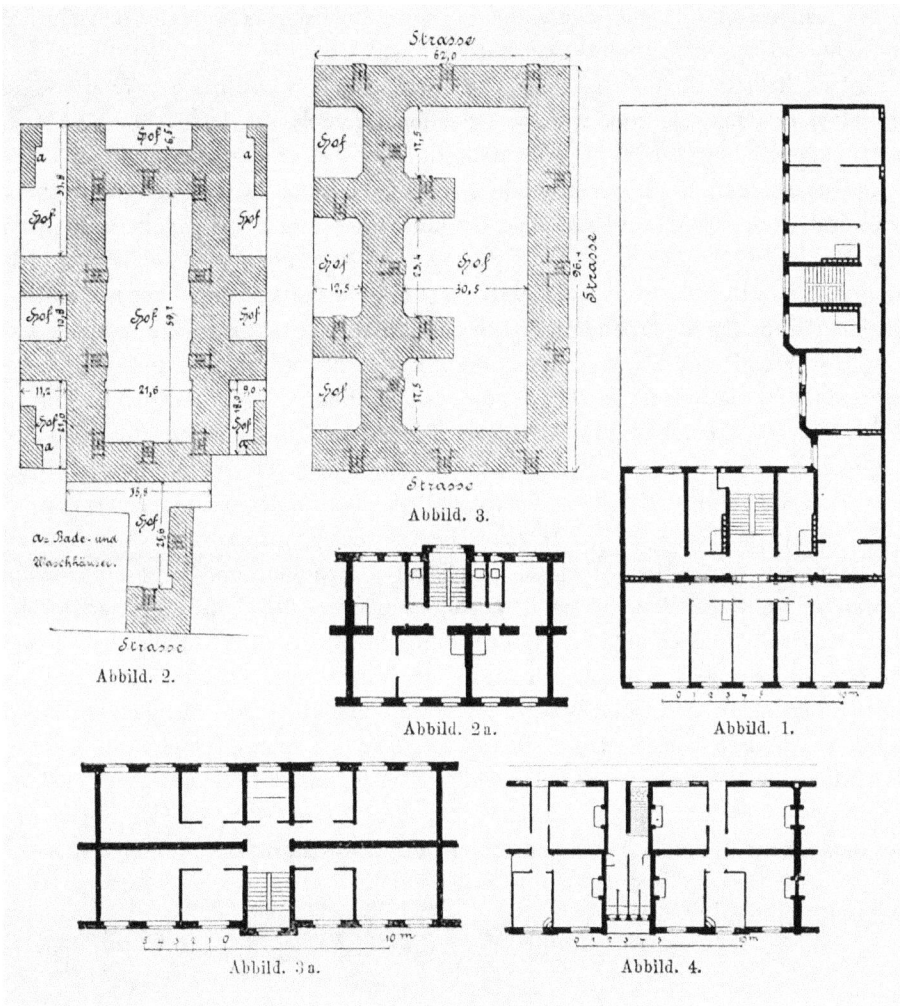

**Figure 2.2** Designs for the improvement of workers' dwellings by the *Verein zur Verbesserung kleiner Wohnungen* [Source: *Deutsche Bauzeitung* 25 (1891): 181–2].

ideas around the turn of the twentieth century about how purposefully designed small dwellings could deliver a higher standard of living for the masses at a more affordable cost when combined with plans for a reformed urban block. At two special conference and exhibition dedicated to the improvement of urban apartments that took place in Berlin in 1891 and 1892 the most innovative solutions focused on the distribution of small dwellings in such a reformed urban block (Bosch Abarca, 2017, 103–4). The shift of focus from the individual dwelling to the block and to the broader use of land in the urban setting was a pragmatic choice since the scope of design innovation regarding the individual dwelling was still very limited at the time. Even so, however, new ideas about how to combine an efficiently designed perimeter block with ample open space for recreation and sufficient illumination opened up new opportunities for rejigging the conventional logic of the housing calculus (Sonne, 2005).

In the light of all these developments designing and constructing reduced-size dwellings gradually acquired a more aspirational complexion, paving the way for a more extensive engagement of public authorities, cooperative organizations and other social stakeholders to the construction of affordable small dwellings of good-quality specification in pleasant urban settings. In France important legislative interventions in the 1890s and 1900s (Siegfried Law in 1894; Strauss Law in 1906; Ribot Law of 1908; and Bonnevay Law in 1912) promised to inject urgency to the task of addressing the housing problem in the rapidly expanding French cities. A special 1905 competition organized by the Rothschild Foundation for a 'model' housing complex in Paris generated strong interest (127 submissions overall) but produced a solution that was far from scalable in either design or financial terms (Ford, 2018). More specific focus on the actual design of the economical dwelling was evident in the two dwelling typologies that emerged from the 1912 competition organized by the city of Paris[1]: the 'Emile Zola' and 'Henri Becque' typologies (named after the streets where the first such apartment blocks were erected following the competition). The first type featured separate rooms for sleep, cooking and eating and featured private sanitary facilities that constituted the benchmark for the standard Habitations à Bon Marché (HBM); while the second was a 'rudimentary' version of the first type that compressed all living functions into a family hall and comprised of a further sleeping room divided by partition typically amounting to *c*. 30 m² and intended for those rehoused from the demolished slum settlements (*taudis*) (Dumont, 1991, 115). A mixture of paternalism and social prejudice vis-à-vis the urban poor underpinned the specification of the 'Becque' type (Figure 2.3) since its severely reduced character was justified on the grounds that the inhabitants of slums had different 'minimum' needs

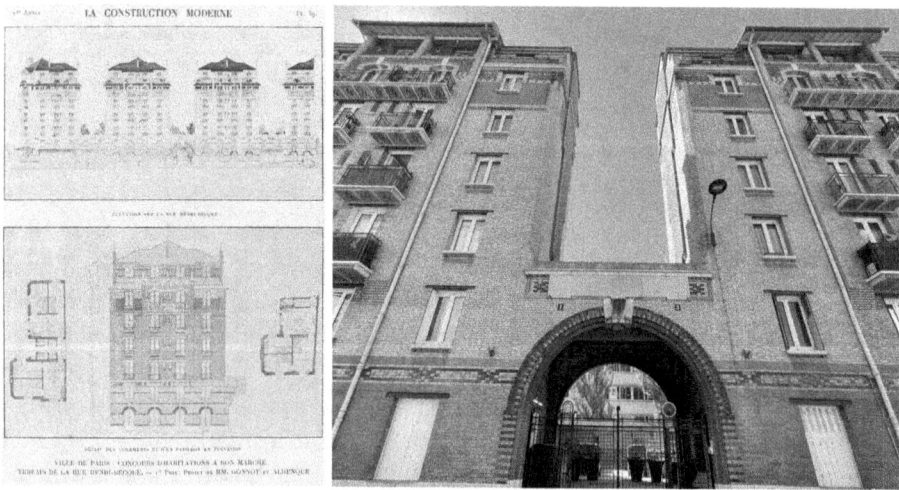

**Figure 2.3** Building of the 'Becque' low-cost typology (Rue Henri Becque, Paris), arch. Jean-Georges Albenque and Eugène Gonnot [Source: [left] *Zentralblatt der Bauverwaltung* 55 (1913): 359; [right] Author's photo.

and only deserved a transitional lodging to prepare them for the elevated quality of the standard HBM (Fijalkow, 2006, 13). By contrast, the higher specification of the Zola type, which was by far the most common form of HBM housing produced in France before the First World War, underlined the shift of attitudes in relation to dwelling quality for the masses. Attention to interior and exterior design, convenient location within the urban core, thoughtful distribution to accentuate ventilation and illumination and an explicit stipulation in the architectural brief to avoid the semblance of 'barracks' contributed to a more aspirational framework for municipal housing (Dumont, 1991, 151–21; Rudolph, 2015, 59–64).

In Germany new associations dedicated to the research and promotion of the small dwelling appeared in most major cities, such as Frankfurt, Dresden, Munich and Hamburg. A series of new regulatory instruments put in place since 1873 culminated in the 1902 Law for Promotion of the Construction of Small Dwellings, which introduced a number of qualitative standards of size and functionality for the typology: a tiered system of min-max dimensions for different dwellings configurations (30–35 m$^2$ for single-room, 35–48 m$^2$ for two rooms; up to 60 m$^2$ for three rooms), maximum allowable number of dwellings per corridor and number of building floors, inclusion of facilities such as kitchen, toilet and storage facilities (Kähler, 1985, 52–3). In addition, the renewed interest in the small dwelling became part of a broader cultural reaction to historicist ostentation and material excess that had marked models of middle-class domesticity in the nineteenth century (Ekici, 2018, 565–73). In this context, austerity, simplicity and objectivity (*Sachlichkeit*) did not simply derive from a sense of dire emergency and a rationale of deficit. Instead they became linked to purposeful simplification of design and decorative taste in order to enhance the functionality of the dwelling (Forty, 2000, 249–55; Mallgrave, 2009, 207–11). Prominent figures of the reform movement made notable contributions to the housing reform debate in support of the design and moral principles of the Kleinwohnung, such as the Berlin-based jurist Paul Felix Aschrott who was active in the ranks of the *Verein für Socialpolitik*, VfS (Association for Social Policy) and participant in the Association for the Improvement of Small Dwellings (Albrecht, 1891; Fehl, 1988, 112–16). Architects too became increasingly more interested in design innovation on the scale of the small individual dwelling. Among them was the building director of Hamburg (1909–33) Fritz Schumacher (Schumacher, 1919); the architectural theorist Friedrich Ostendorf and Heinrich Tessenow, who – along with Hermann Muthesius, Richard Riemerschmid and other key figures of the German Werkbund – designed Hellerau, the first garden town in Germany in 1908–11 (Tessenow, 1916; Arnold, 1993; Schwartz, 1996, 107; Adler, 2004; Harris, 2012). In his writings, Tessenow eloquently highlighted the importance of the small/economical dwelling for the vast majority of the world's population and called for a radically new framework for conceiving it as an autonomous and not derivative design challenge. Not only did he claim that bigness was no better than smallness but he continued with the even bolder assertion that 'through smallness we improve on bigness' (Kindt, 1982, 41).

Singing the praise of design efficiency and standardization marked the beginning of a radical departure from the crude zero-sum logic of the nineteenth-century housing calculus. Yet it also turned out to be polarizing, mapping onto increasingly acrimonious debates about standardization of construction and building typologies versus aesthetic individualism or aesthetic nationalism (Anderson, 2003). In Germany there were many critics of this novel vision of simplified and austere architectural canon. The fault lines actually ran deeper, dividing even the proponents of architectural simplification that informed the entire debate on the small dwelling at the beginning of the twentieth century. As the architectural critic Karl Scheffler noted on the eve of the war, two different paths to architectural austerity had already started to collide, the one using history and tradition as the guiding principle for abstraction and the other deploying radically new and universal architectural forms (Scheffler, 1913, 73–6). The debate came to a head at the first Werkbund exhibition organized in Cologne in 1914, where Muthesius's 'theses' in favour of standardization and industrial efficiency came under sustained criticism from the point of view of artistic freedom and individuality (Conrads, 1971, 21; Campbell, 2015, 57–82). Meanwhile the standard equation of better living with a flight or at the very least distance from the metropolis persisted as a strong orthodoxy in architectural design. Even reconceptualized and integrated in a reformed urban block, the small urban apartment continued to be widely regarded as a serially suboptimal solution (reduced size, economical construction and high-density urban site combined to a de facto lower quality of living) at a time of breakneck urbanization. Even as the focus on smallness was acquiring a more positive moral complexion and the value – practical and social – of urban living for the workers was being reappreciated (Sonne, 2005, 59; Eisenschmidt, 2019, 20–75), it proved hard to shake off the negative aura of metropolitan life associated with the reduced-size and -quality apartments of the Berlin Mietskaserne or the Viennese Bassena apartments (consisting of one room and kitchen with basin) (Jäger-Klein, 2005, 170)).

When Schumacher published his treatise on the Kleinwohnung in 1916, he assumed a sombre tone that framed the question of mass living in a rapidly expanding metropolis as a social 'problem' that called for radical remedial action in the very short term. By circumventing the crude dichotomies of the past (city versus countryside, individualism versus mass production, bigness versus smallness), he called for pragmatic solutions capable of delivering tangible and scalable improvements (Schumacher, 1932, 52–6; Schubert, 2021, 2–4). Social responsibility and design aspiration mixed with a crushing sense of *Angst* in the face of an escalating social emergency. Through the pages of his detailed study of the typology of the Kleinwohnung Schumacher suggested that the best strategy was a proactive, reform-minded pragmatism whereby size reduction and urban siting could be part of the solution to the housing question rather than spurned as part of the problem thereof.

### The 'small dwelling' after the First World War

By the time that Schumacher compiled the preface to the second edition of the same book on the small dwelling in 1919 the magnitude of the challenge had exploded in the wake of the First World War. The conflict that broke out in 1914 turned out to be one of those epoch-defining seismic events with a legacy of unprecedented disruption for many years after it had ended (Roberts, 2006, 166–8). In the particular domain of housing the First World War catalysed a wide range of profound changes that turned almost every aspect of the housing calculus upside down. The period up to the outbreak of the conflict had experienced cyclical sequences of housing over- and under-production by the private market that had already aggravated the conditions of overcrowding and affordability (Jerram, 2011, 321–37). There was frequent talk of a severe 'housing crisis' in the decades leading up to the Great War, courtesy of a housing market still dominated by the whims of the private sector with limited public intervention to compensate for either intensifying demographic pressures or the boom-and-bust cycles of private housing construction. Yet, as building activity virtually ground to a halt during the years of the conflict, the housing shortage soon reached unprecedented proportions (Bauer, 2020, 119–23). Material destruction and large refugee movements only made an already grave situation desperate. Predictably it took years even after the end of the war for the private market to recover, let alone effectively meet the escalating and urgent demand (Silverman, 1970, 117; Sieder, 1985, 37–8). Against previous laissez-faire orthodoxies and cultural biases, public authorities (state and municipal) did finally step in far more actively in order to alleviate the housing crisis with both funds and facilitating construction initiatives. However, the financial side of the operation remained fraught with difficulty until well into the 1920s: rampant inflation and extreme currency fluctuations sent costs to dizzying heights and restricted the public sector's margins of financial manoeuvre. Once again, the housing calculus hit the wall of financial scarcity against the backdrop of enormous supply-demand backlogs and escalating construction costs.

The scale and urgency of the problem in the immediate post-First World War years far exceeded anything previously experienced and thus required radically new solutions. The most pressing task involved providing some form of housing to all those who had found themselves unable to access an abode at the end of the war as a result of hardship, migration or material destruction. Requisitioning systematically unused property, both residential and otherwise, offered a short-term solution in Vienna and the Soviet Union during the difficult postwar years (Willimott, 2017, 442). Yet this was little more than a stop-gap palliative measure. The even bigger challenge was how to resume housing construction and scale up the capacity for affordable housing with immediate effect at a time of extreme dislocation and volatility. This was the test that confronted Ernst May when he took up his first major architectural job as technical director of the Silesian Rural Settlement Authority (*Schlesische Heimstätte*) in February 1919. May arrived in Breslau (today Wrocław in Poland) at the age of thirty-three, following apprentices with Raymond Unwin in London and some freelance work in Frankfurt that was interrupted during the war. The role that he was asked to perform in Breslau was formidable, again due to a combination of chronic problems with housing and new extraordinary challenges that had to do with the city itself. Breslau occupied a geographically marginal position in the history of the unified German state, located in the eastern province of Silesia. This marginality was only enhanced in the wake of the territorial losses imposed on the defeated German empire in 1919. A city with historically high density, Breslau saw its population increase dramatically in the years leading to the First World War, as part of a wider picture of acute urbanization that affected Germany and other European countries at the time. Yet the chronic housing shortage was further exacerbated by the migration flows of ethnic Germans that followed the postwar territorial losses in the east and the eventual partition of Silesia (the easternmost part of which was awarded to the new Polish state), with Breslau receiving a large share of the displaced population due to its location close to the new border with Poland (Ascher Barnstone, 2016, 23–4; Karch, 2018, 96–147). In response to the extraordinary challenges facing the city in the immediate aftermath of the First World War the municipal administration decided on a new programme of radial housing expansion in order to absorb population growth as quickly as possible while lowering density in the old metropolitan core and elevating overall standards of living (Kähler, 1985, 339–40).

In the first instance May had used the notion of 'emergency shelter' (*Notheim*) – a special category of affordable and swiftly produced housing geared to refugees and special groups of workers most seriously affected (Henderson, 2002, 191; Urbanik, 2014) – to imbue a number of his cost-cutting design choices (reduction in room and apartment size, in some typologies stretching down to 26–34 m$^2$; standardization of construction elements, processes and equipment, etc.) with an aura of existential social imperative (Figure 2.4). Very soon, however, he also embarked on a far more ambitious programme of rapid expansion of satellite settlements (*Siedlungen*) in the outskirts of the city with the kind of productivity and attention to detail that became the trademark of his later Frankfurt portfolio. The decline in individuality and the monotony of the Siedlungen, he argued, was a reasonable prize to pay for serving the overriding social goal of swift access to decent housing for as many as possible in the extraordinary circumstances of post-First World War Germany.[2] The streamlining of housing typologies and building norms opened a workable path to the standardization of material procurement for building construction. He responded pragmatically to the severe postwar housing shortage and scarcity of municipal resources with a typological compromise: the basic unit for Breslau's new urban policy would be the typical Kleinwohnung.[3] May justified this choice by invoking both necessity and emergency – the enormous scale of the housing shortage versus failure of the open market to provide solutions and scarcity of public resources to compensate; but he also aligned this choice with the vision of peripheral, lower-density settlement development as a strategy for maximizing quality dividends for the residents. His main target of criticism remained the ghost of the Mietskaserne that in his opinion offered a kind of false economy, sacrificing living standards for cost-efficiency. A consistently harsh critic of high(er)-rise urban residential development on grounds of typology and siting, he immediately dismissed suggestions that this form of high-density construction, which he found alien to German building traditions and suitable only for downtown commercial accommodation, could provide a viable solution to the slow pace of recovery in the postwar housing market.[4] He therefore claimed that the combination of Kleinwohnung type and peripheral Siedlung planning/siting offered the best compromise of quality, cost-efficiency and speed of response to the housing emergency, displaying a balance of short-term pragmatism

# The 'Small Dwelling'

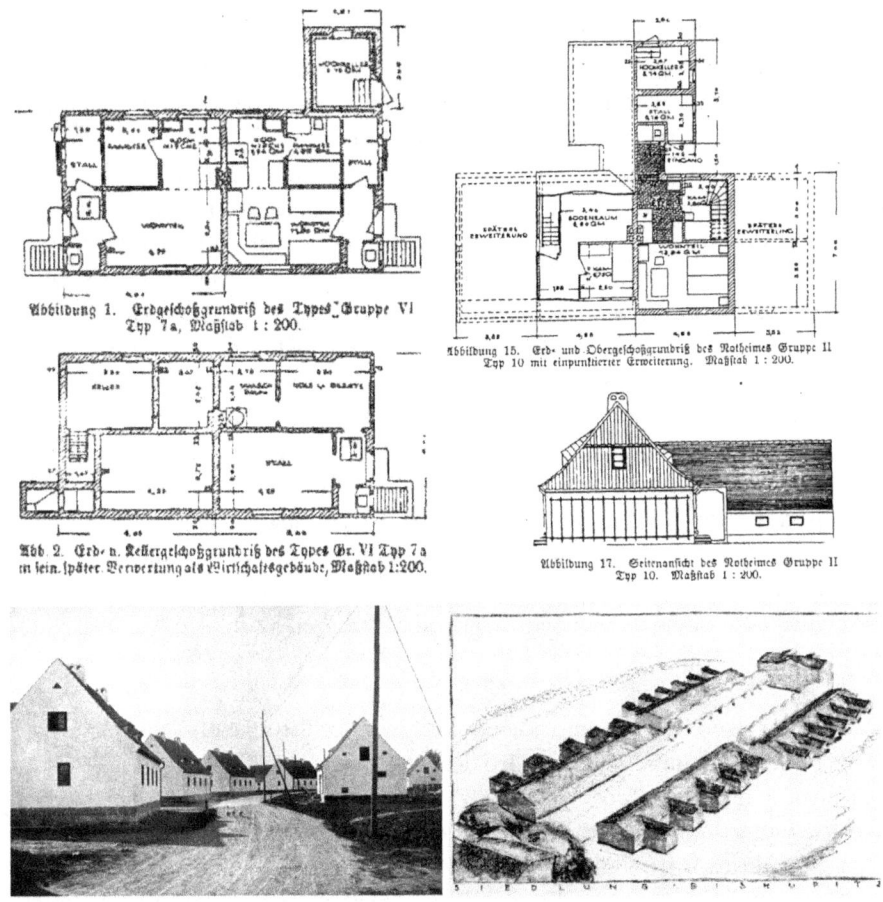

**Figure 2.4** Designs for emergency shelters in Breslau, 1920 [Source: *SH*, 1/2 (1920): 1–10].

and longer-term commitment to social improvement that became the trademark of his architectural career in the 1920s.

In 1919–20 May was still thinking of the small dwelling as a hybrid, extended and more economical form of the 'small (family) house' two-storey (plus basement) building with pitched roof and ground-floor access to a small private garden. Translated into *Kleinhaus*, this dwelling typology had already been hailed as a positive housing innovation by German architects and a preferable alternative to the small dwelling in a high-density urban block (Stübben, 1907; Muthesius, 1918). But May also made the design process more efficient by proposing two standard dwelling types in size configurations (differing in the number of bedrooms) and multiple combinations of detached and semi-detached building groups. Each unit featured a living room with connected, well-ventilated small kitchen (*Wohnkuche*).[5] In a series of articles published by the journal *Schlesisches Heim* (SH) that he directed between 1920 and his departure for Frankfurt in 1925 he defended his fondness of precise typological standardization on the basis of necessity but he also presented it as a positive choice that promoted design rationality and functionality. In his view, the 'essential basic forms' of housing had remained largely intact over time and did not need be extrapolated right from the start in every single new housing project. Norms were both efficient and a guarantee of good, context-sensitive practice. This was true of every individual component of the dwelling design, from determining the most effective and rational usage of available floor space to the shaping of roofs; the design of furniture; and the provision of equipment, utilities and storage facilities. May treated a delicate path between genuflection to regional tradition and praise for modern design and construction principles. He opted for a more traditional exterior design that invoked memories of the local rural village and its vernacular forms; but he also defended his decision to keep decoration to a minimum on grounds of both economy and authenticity (Henderson, 2002). When he defended standardization and industrial methods of construction, he presented this more as a pragmatic and necessary than a preferable, let alone dogmatic, solution.[6] Yet, even as he invoked necessity and social interest as primary guiding principles of his work, he did sketch a 'more or less distant' all-encompassing optimal future solution, for which he considered his Silesian work as a practical map that had resolved dead ends and highlighted clear paths forward. He described his method as imbued with determined and aspirational realism:

> [w]e have taken the facts into account here and, for the sake of a policy of what can be achieved, initially disregarded demands that we have in mind as later goals in favor of the directly possible. It is no longer necessary to explain in detail today that a perfecting of the small house floor plan to the last consequence is only conceivable if we previously brought together the living conditions of thousands, which are the same, the type. The type cannot be designed and cannot be ordered; it develops.[7]

Size reduction remained of course a key consideration, not only because the mere typology of the Kleinwohnung/Kleinhaus was predicated on the reduction of overall floor space but also due to the severely limited resources available for housing construction in the midst of the postwar crisis. In 1921 May published an article in the SH journal with the eloquent title 'How far can the surface area of the small house be reduced'. The article provided a framework for a series of individual studies and attempted innovation in every aspect of the design of the 'small dwelling'. Without entering into a discussion of changing family structures and social norms, he advocated a typical standard of a three-bedroom home (one for the parents and two for the children, separated along gender lines), a 'living room' (*Wohnraum*) with adequate kitchen facilities (*c.* 20 m² in total), internal bathroom and small private garden. In his design typologies for the Silesian 'emergency shelters', he calculated that a dwelling unit could promote good 'minimum' standards of life in a dwelling of *c.* 40 m², with provisions for future expansion of the surface area to 70 m² by the residents when more favourable economic conditions permitted it.⁸ By 1924 he would feel confident enough to formulate an all-embracing architectural and planning vision that linked the individual components of the dwelling to large-scale settlement planning and then to the political project of forging a new modern society. All aspects of his research and practice in all architectural scales (floor plans, construction management, innovation in materials and building methods, furniture, decorative elements, garden design, satellite settlement planning) combined with a series of sociological insights about gender and domestic economy, mobility, private and public life in a modern society to produce a programme that was notably closer to his later work in Frankfurt in 1925–30.

The culmination of May's approach in Breslau was a toolkit of standard small-size dwelling 'types' that represented the distillation of all insights gathered from experimenting with different configurations, techniques, materials and design assumptions in the preceding four years. Eleven 'basic types' with four further variations, ranging in size from 40 to 144 m² but typically in the 50–70 m² range, offered a tried-and-tested menu of configurations to suit diverse living arrangements and family sizes (Figure 2.5).⁹ In addition, May also developed a special typology for a two-floor 'middle-class house' (*Mittelstandhaus*) of significantly larger proportions (125 m²) but with standardized wood construction, built-in furniture and a flat roof. This prototype mediated the new elevated 'minimum' standards for low-cost housing and the 'optimal' dwelling arrangement that he had in mind as the desired destination for the 'more or less distant' future. In contrast to his work on the reform of the Kleinwohnung and the emergency shelters, which was predicated on sheer necessity and forced reduction, May's middle-class dwelling prototype was proposed on a platform that coalesced 'minimum' and simplicity as a positive choice. The symbolic message was unmistakable: rather than being regarded as a sub-optimal solution to housing emergencies, standardization of construction represented the way forward for the entire housing sector (Henderson, 2002, 208). Pre-fabrication too was considered desirable, as speed and efficiency of construction were important whether in times of acute emergency or not. Overall size mattered less than the internal organization of the dwelling along functional lines that reflected modern life. Vernacular elements could be reconciled with a decidedly modern functional design and aesthetic philosophy that transcended bitterly fought fault lines like the shape of the roof (Pommer, 1983). May borrowed language and arguments from his work in the field of low-cost/emergency housing in order to justify his design choices for the middle-class house: there would be the most 'rational management' of household tasks for an era 'without the help of domestic workers'; a well-designed, functionally separated and adequately ventilated 'living kitchen' was appropriate even for middle-class households; and the 'simple and practical' decoration underlined the 'clear definition of the forms as they arose from the respective purpose' without the use of any 'unnecessary ornamental elements'.¹⁰ All in all this prototype proposed a radical reversal of the calculus that led from the good-quality 'minimum' to the 'optimal' dwelling: rather than approaching the former as a savage reduction of the latter, it was the 'optimal' dwelling that now emerged as an adapted and expanded version of the new functional 'minimum' type.

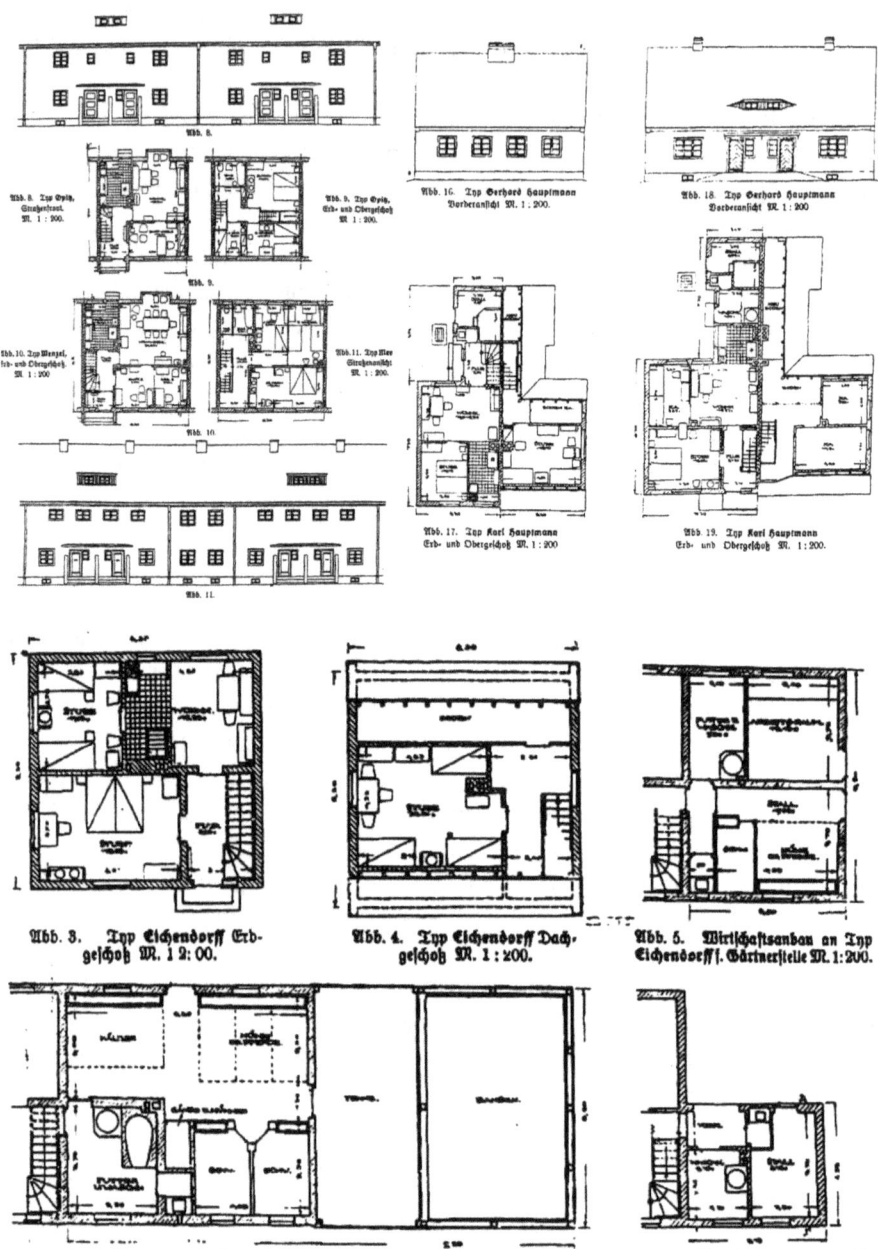

**Figure 2.5** Examples of the main types of affordable dwelling prepared for Breslau, c. 1924 [Source: *SH*, 5/3 (1924): 71–6 and 5/4 (1924): 99–117].

The alchemy worked. By the end of 1919 Breslau had gone from a virtual collapse of housing construction to an impressive record of 367 new peripheral settlements offering a spectacularly improved quality-cost-affordability proposition.[11] Since May's portfolio was not confined to the city of Breslau but covered the entirety of German-controlled Silesia, his work delivered significant improvements in both housing supply and elevated dwelling quality across the entire region. Housing construction per annum increased from *c.* 1500 units to more than 3700 between 1919 and 1923; the rate of increase in metropolitan areas was even more impressive, rising by more than five times during the same period.[12]

## From the 'small' to the 'smallest' dwelling (*Kleinstwohnung*)

The emergency situation that confronted May in Breslau was far from unique in post-First World War Germany. In Hamburg those in need of new homes rose from 6,000 in 1919 to 37,000 only 4 years later and nearly doubled once again in the following decade (Kähler, 1985, 79–81). It soon became clear that the private sector – predictably in hibernation during the war years – could not provide the much-needed solution, not least because the dire financial situation and political uncertainty made housing an unattractive investment. A newly elected social-democratic (SD) municipal administration embarked on a radical programme of expanding the supply of good-quality and affordable dwellings to cover the escalating demand with noble intentions and enthusiasm but severely constrained resources. Schumacher, who kept his job of city architect, soon realized that even his technically elaborated Kleinwohnung could not provide anywhere-near enough dwellings to meet demand in the first postwar years. Working in Hamburg and Cologne (1919–22), he directed his attention to planning for future urban expansion in peripheral zones, taking advantage of the increasing involvement of the municipal authorities in the housing sector and the ability to purchase new lands for future suburban development (Milan, 2019; Schubert, 2021).

Similar challenges confronted municipal authorities and architects in many other parts of Germany. The situation remained challenging until well into the early 1920s due to a combination of high inflation and dearth of government funding, leaving limited margins for large-scale construction projects involving affordable housing. Nevertheless, it was becoming increasingly evident that the political and cultural framework was changing in ways that would generate a new kind of momentum for urban social housing. A growing consensus on the need for increased public involvement in housing provision produced institutional, financial and political instruments for significant municipal intervention in the domain of housing, particularly in those municipal authorities where the SPD had gained power post-1918 (Lieberman, 1998, 28–44). On a national level, the new Weimar Constitution of February 1919 included a formal pledge 'to ensure that every German has a healthy home and that all German families, especially those with many children, have a place of residence and business that meets their needs'

(Article 155). The same article provided public authorities with significant powers of land expropriation 'to satisfy housing needs, to promote settlement and land reclamation and to improve agriculture'. The 'healthy home' formulation may have been vague and largely devoid of explicit normative content; but it did provide one of the very first instances of legally codifying access to decent housing as a universal citizenship right.

The last but arguably most important in practical terms component that transformed the housing calculus was the decision to channel significant public financial resources to the goal of constructing affordable and decent housing in sufficient numbers and speed. Financial stabilization from 1923 onwards was accompanied by the eventual introduction of a special rental tax (*Hauszinssteuer* or *Gehaudeentschuldungssteuer*) in 1924, levied on 'unjust' wealth earned by homeowners during the years of hyperinflation as a result of the sharp decline in actual mortgage debt (Von Saldern, 2009, 208). The tax promised to generate an unprecedented level of public funding for a significant expansion of public housing provision in the second half of the 1920s. The introduction of the Hauszinssteuer ushered in a period of unprecedented expansion in housing construction by public and cooperative societies in order to compensate for the chronic quality problems of the German housing stock and the collapse of provision in the years during and after the First World War (Silverman, 1970, 115–16). The effects of this policy change were immediate as they were transformational in the medium term, before the 1929 global financial crisis brought the experiment to a shattering standstill.[13]

The government's decision to allocate a significant portion of the tax proceeds to housing construction and the willingness of municipal authorities to prioritize the construction of affordable dwellings had a transformational effect on the entire social housing sector and marked a dramatic shift of public consensus regarding the role of public authorities in the provision of housing. The housing situation, however, remained challenging. Even during the 'good' years of the Weimar Republic (1924–29), it proved difficult to just keep up with housing demand. In Hamburg the municipality took advantage of increasing funding from the central budget to create building companies in partnership with trade unions and expand its role in the city's building programme; yet the rise in the output of affordable dwellings was merely catching up with the prewar average pace of new construction (Silverman, 1970, 125–6; Kähler, 1985, 111). Reducing the size of the individual dwelling could only go that far – down to *c*. 48 $m^2$ for the smallest (1–1.5 room) apartment typology to be precise. Increasing the density of the new peripheral settlements by opting for higher-rise developments also had a limit in Hamburg – typically four and on occasion five storeys – that was both a practical and a programmatic choice, as was the overwhelming preference for the perimeter-block building typologies.

The search for a new framework that could align developments in all domains (funding, land use, rationalization of construction, building typologies and housing design) continued in pursuit of the elusive formula that could supercharge construction of affordable housing on a sufficiently larger scale. In 1927 Schumacher oversaw a special ideas competition for reduced-size dwellings destined for the extension of the Dulsberg settlement in the north of the city (Becker and Knott, 1992, 180; Popp, 2018)

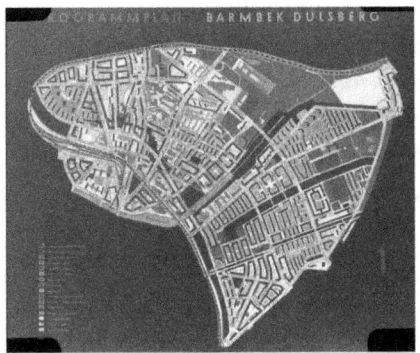

**Figure 2.6** Plans for the Dulsberg area of Hamburg, arch. Fritz Schumacher [Source: *Staatsarchiv Hamburg* and *Fritz Schumacher Gesellschaft*, respectively].

(Figure 2.6). The area had already served as a showcase of different scenarios of small-dwelling construction, based on a radical 'reassignment' (*Umlegung*) of the existing land that became possible after the decision to redraw the boundaries of the original city plan in favour of adopting a version of the row typology (*Zeilenbau*); but the final extension of the settlement was reserved for what Schumacher described as 'the cheapest form of housing, the smallest apartment (*Kleinstwohnung*) … [achieved] through rationalization in the use and development of the land, as well as in the economy of the building operation' (Schumacher, 1932, 54, 59). Here some of the winning designs took size even further down to 40–44 m$^2$, primarily by compressing the dimensions of the main room down to 12 m$^2$ (Kähler, 1985, 124; Schubert, 2021, 10).

Schumacher described the Dulsberg experiment as nothing short of a 'miracle' – the result of an intellectual process of thinking out of the box to challenge embedded orthodoxies about domesticity, planning, and design. It was premised on thoughtful minima and achieved through a series of studied economies from the 'reassignment' of the land to the design of the building to the arrangement of the individual dwelling to the construction methods and materials, which nevertheless resulted in commendably high standards of living for the residents. This description of the superlative Kleinstwohnung verged on alchemy – maximizing quality and affordability gains by cannily and thoughtfully using modern design and construction practices to reduce the use of space resources and increase densities. Still, even with the benefit of continuity of tenure and increased state funding, Schumacher's Hamburg programme fell short of either the affordability or the scale tests. By 1930 the city had been forced to set up a special commission to investigate ways to reduce costs further, especially in the face of spiralling construction costs that translated into higher/unaffordable rental and purchase prices (Kähler, 1985, 95). The conclusion of the investigation appeared to suggest that, in order to bring costs down again, a wholesale reduction in *all* qualitative indices of the Kleinstwohnung (not only size but construction, fittings and density) would be necessary. By that time the 'fat years' of the Republic were definitely over and the cumulative effect of reduced funds and escalating interest payment for all the loans that had oiled the housing construction machine in the 1920s brought the ambitious housing projects, in Hamburg as well as elsewhere in Germany and beyond, to an infelicitous end (Peters, 1933). Scaling up the deployment of various Klein(st)wohnung solutions tested in the previous years to approximate the growing demand at sustainably affordable prices had proven to be the most intractable of all challenges.

## The pioneering cases of Vienna and Frankfurt

Was there another way to deal with the compound tests of quality, affordability and scale? By the time that the various public housing programmes in Weimar Germany received the critical funding boost from the central budget, a radical scheme of mass affordable housing construction had been well underway in the city of Vienna (Blau, 1999). This municipal initiative had begun far more modestly in 1919 as an emergency response to the extraordinary housing pressures caused by the First World War and the collapse of the Austro-Hungarian empire that followed it; but by 1923 it had entered its heroic phase of large-scale urban 'people's housing palaces' (*Volkswohnungspalast*) that would last until the late 1920s (Hautmann and Hautmann, 1980, 76). The approach that the architects of the so-called 'Red Vienna' took was predicated on a series of actual trade-offs: higher urban density through large perimeter blocks, simplification of aesthetic design, strict standardization of construction and dwelling typologies, and of course size economies in an effort to bring costs down while promoting significantly higher standards of hygiene and comfort for the dwellers in comparison to the older urban tenement blocks. The typical Viennese Kleinwohnung was small in size – typically either 38 m$^2$ or 48 m$^2$ in the first phase of construction (1923–26), with the minimum dimensions sometimes reduced to 32 m$^2$. It was also rather basic in its amenities (small if functionally redesigned kitchen, no built-in furniture, minute toilet) and distributed across multi-floor apartment blocks organized around an internal courtyard. The lack of other amenities, private such as bathing and laundry, was compensated by a parallel programme of generous investment in good-quality collective services located within the residential ensembles. The housing complexes also provided a wide range of social services (nursery and playrooms, larger kitchen facilities, library, recreation facilities, etc.) as part of a programme of shifting many of the traditional domestic functions from the private to the communal domain.

Yet the key significance of the Viennese programme did not lay in typological or construction innovation. Instead it related to the authorities' ambition to scale up the operation in order to benefit as many people in need as possible. Here cost economies were used to extend the programme's supply and genuine affordability for the user – and it was this combination of focus that set the Viennese building programme apart, especially during the first half of the 1920s when nothing else of comparative ambition and scale existed across the continent. Much that the concept of affordable good-quality

## The 'Small Dwelling'

'minimum' housing as a universal social right had gained currency across post-First World War Europe, aided by the renewed popularity of 'municipal socialism' projects (Medina and Monclús, 2018, 23–9; Gruber, 1991, 45–72), the Viennese municipality embarked on its most ambitious concrete realization. Emergency in the case of post-1918 Vienna meant not only unprecedented demand for affordable and decent housing but also a deeper social and economic crisis caused by the war and the political vacuum in the former Austro-Hungarian lands that followed it (Kohlrausch, 2019, 42–8). Taken together, these two challenges called for the most extreme kind of intervention: immediate and dauntingly large-scale, providing relief and averting a social and humanitarian catastrophe (Harris, 1999, 287–9) but without either guaranteed state funds or a political structure to support it. Yet it somehow happened (Jahn, 2014). The city authorities stepped into the vacuum with an innovative financial plan based on the direct progressive taxation of private property to fund the most ambitious in scope and social vision plan for affordable housing construction across the city (Figure 2.7). At the height of its building programme the city hosted the 1926 congress of the International Federation of Housing and Town Planning (IFHTP) and presented to the one-thousand delegates not only ideas

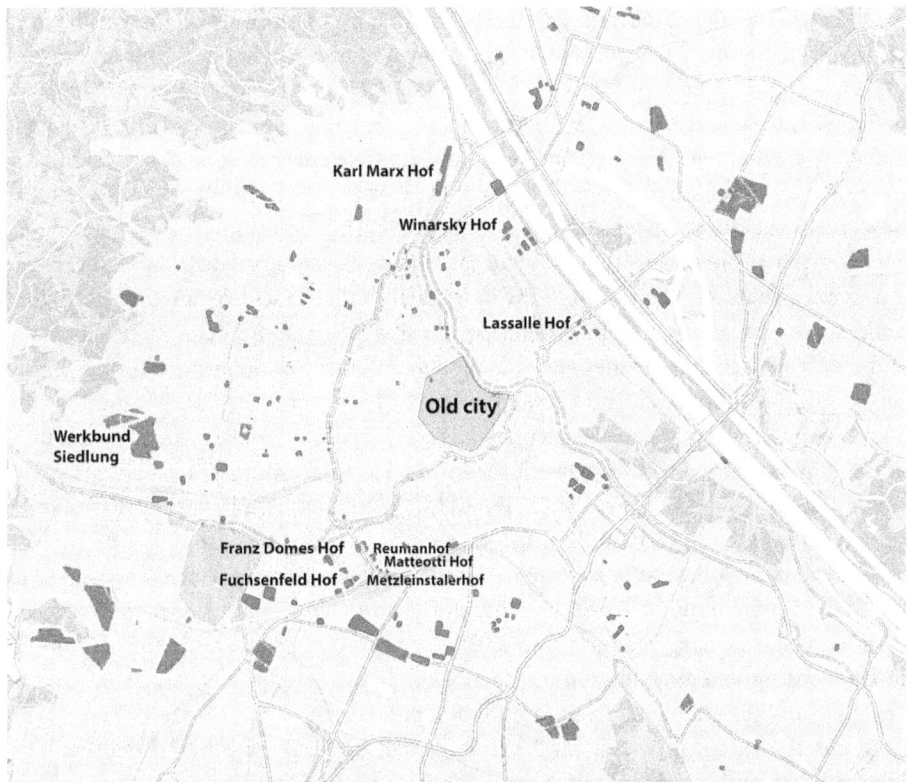

**Figure 2.7** The extent of the Viennese building programme in the 1920s.

but a formidable register of 25,000 already realized dwellings as well as an even more ambitious programme for the near future already underway (see Chapter 3). By the time that economic crisis and the rise of (Austro)fascism had brought it to an end in the early 1930s the total tally was nearly 60,000 housing units (Gruber, 1991, 46–9).

In post-First World War Vienna extreme emergency supercharged ambition and innovation. Size reduction and increased density remained key facets of the municipal programme but they now served a different order of priorities: not producing the most compact or innovatively designed or hygienic or pleasant or ground-breaking dwelling; not bringing costs down to an absolute minimum in order to save money; not making further savings by moving further and further away from the urban core; but instead masterminding a thoughtful compromise at the service of the more ambitious goal of producing more good-quality dwellings tantalizingly close to the metropolitan centre at breakneck speed that could be sustained over the medium term, and then making them available at a price that was truly affordable even by those with severely reduced income. The criticisms raised against the Viennese building programme ranged from quality to contemporary standard accusations of 'socialism' coming from the right to subsequent disdain for alleged concessions to architectural/design/aesthetic conservatism (especially in comparison to the contemporary Siedlung alternative settlements (Davidovici, 2017; Blau, 234)) to political naiveté (Porotto, 2019, 853–4). Yet novelty was never in short supply in the housing programme of 'Red Vienna' – and it came in both minima and maxima. The reduced-size Viennese kitchen (*Spülküche*) of 4 $m^2$ and eventually 3 $m^2$ designed by the young Margarete Lihotzky in the early 1920s, 'built on scientific principles based on the new working methods of rational housekeeping ... [and chosen] not only to save space and money, but most of all to save time', served as eloquent evidence of how severe scarcity could lead to design and sociological innovation (Blau, 1999, 182–5; Elsaesser, 2006; Hochhaeusl, 2013) (Figure 2.8). In terms of spatial distribution of spaces across a whole range of scales from the individual room to the dwelling to the building and to the city as a whole the Viennese housing programme excelled in efficiency and clarity – again not for the sake of a 'model' statement or publicity stunt but in the service of maximum scale and speed (Porotto, 2016; Porotto, 2017a). In addition, the Viennese housing programme entertained its own version of social alchemy by turning 'minimum' housing into a framework for mass education towards a radically new way of life (Sieder, 1985, 36; Stavrides, 2016, 109–16). Neither as trailblazing in design as some of its contemporary modernist estates in other parts of Europe nor as socially revolutionary as some of the collectivised housing projects implemented or planned in the Soviet Union in the late 1920s (see Chapter 4), the Viennese housing project excelled as an all-encompassing modular framework that reproposed the optimum 'minimum dwelling' as the one that allowed in practice the highest number of people in need to benefit from the better living conditions that it offered.

It was the extent to which the Viennese small-dwelling housing programme was underpinned and defined by powerful ideological and sociological transformative aspirations that set it apart from other contemporary projects regarding a redefinition of the 'minimum dwelling and rendered it an influential prototype for similar initiatives

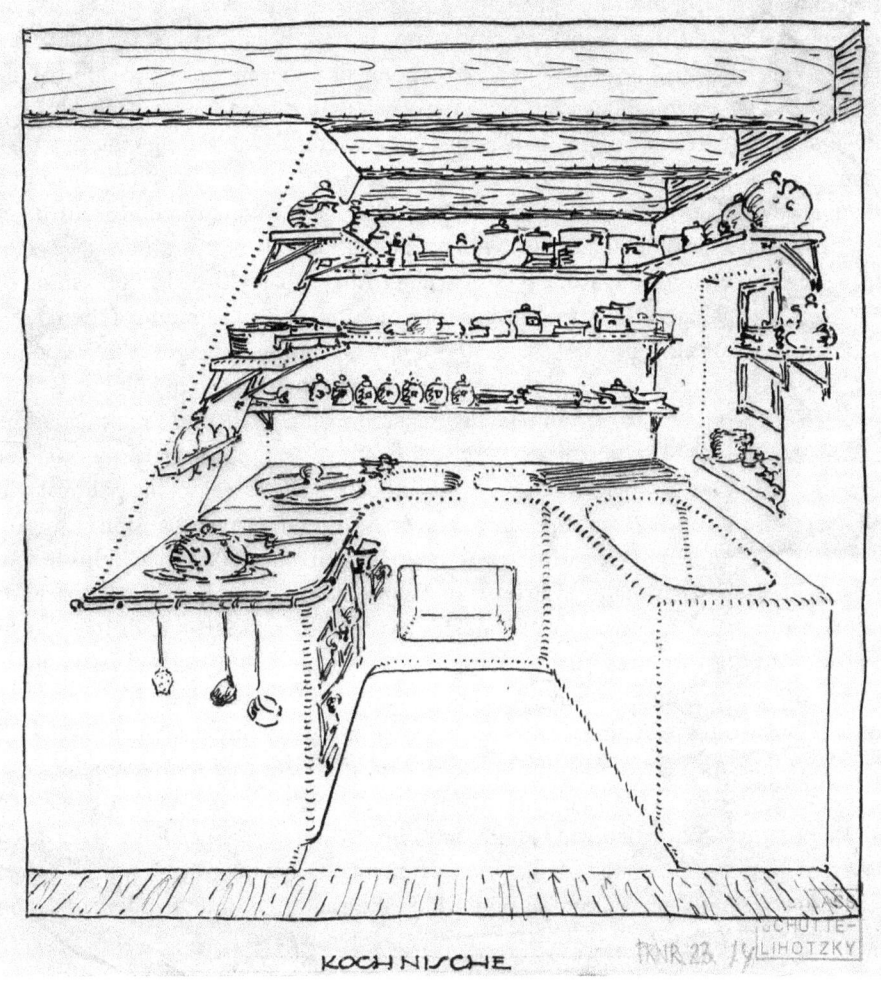

**Figure 2.8** Lihotzky's plan for a small kitchen prototype as part of Vienna's housing programme, 1921 [Source: *Universität für angewandte Kunst Wien, Kunstsammlung und Archiv, Nachlass Margarete Schütte-Lihotzky/Luzie Lahtinen-Stransky*, Inv. Nr. 23/4].

elsewhere'. By the time that he left Breslau to take up a new role as city architect (*Stadtbaurat*) of Frankfurt (1925) Ernst May had witnessed enough of the spectacular achievements in affordability and scale that would become the hallmarks of the entire history of housing in 'Red Vienna' for the rest of the 1920s. May subscribed to the idea of housing as a universal social asset that ought to be extended as widely as possible across the weaker sections of society. But his strong programmatic preference for peripheral settlements instead of urban high-density apartment blocks put him at odds with the preference of the Viennese housing programme for the gigantic urban Hof. The Frankfurt peripheral settlements constructed during May's tenure (1925–30) constituted the basis for one of the most impressive in scale and quality, forward-looking in design and programmatically sophisticated public housing projects of the interwar period. While his 'New Frankfurt' (*Neue Frankfurt*) programme has not been regarded as trailblazing in its design (Heynen, 1999, 65), domestic economy or underpinning conception of life (Lane, 1986, 294–6), its unique value lay in the coherent unity and complementarity of its individual construction, design and planning components. It was through the extensive deployment of the row house typology (*Zeilenbau*) and the 'satellite' (*Trabanten*) planning principles that May was able to connect organically object, room, dwelling, settlement and the universal goal of large-scale deployment of affordable housing as a social right for the masses (Henderson, 2013, 400–1) (Figure 2.9). This multi-scalar conception of emancipatory, egalitarian and universal 'smallness', rooted in a celebration of thoughtful simplicity and a strong sense of social responsibility, alchemised emergency into a quasi-utopian design and planning opportunity for his architectural vision in Frankfurt.

May had the good fortune to make his transition from Breslau to Frankfurt at the peak of this favourable political and financial parabola in the history of the Weimar Republic. This was a moment when the local authority had the vision, the political will and the funds to launch a transformational programme of housing expansion (Clingan, 2000; Lane, 2006, 261–8). The crushing pressure of emergency that shaped his tenure at the Schlesische Heimstätte in Breslau had subsided to a degree to allow space for a more aspirational approach to the housing brief. The Frankfurt authorities sought someone with the vision and proven expertise to carry out an integrated programme of 'housing construction, urban extension, and settlement planning' that was very much aligned with the Weimar consciousness of housing as a universal social service.[14] May's personal pitch focused on his impressive record of realized projects in Silesia at a time when so much of building activity across Germany had declined or come to a halt.[15] Frankfurt's mayor Ludwig Landmann, who had set in place a highly centralized system of municipal administration, was instrumental in granting the new Stadtbaurat a brief that combined power, central support, funding and significant freedom of action

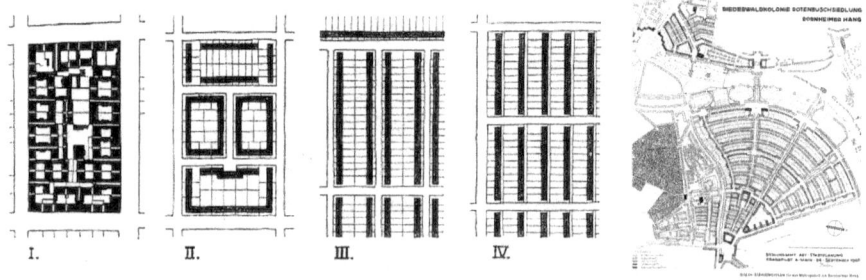

**Figure 2.9** Ernst May's planning vision for the 'New Frankfurt' housing programme. Left: the historical dissolution of the traditional block in favour of 'row-housing' (Zeilenbau) [DNF 4/2–3 (1930): 24]. Right: Riedervald, example of peripheral settlement (Siedlung) [DNF 2/8 (1928): 25].

in matters of design, management and execution of the housing and urban planning initiatives (Kähler, 1985, 221–6).

During his hugely productive Frankfurt tenure, May operated equally as an architectural designer and as a highly gifted urban operations manager. He approached the two tasks of the project as complementary tasks geared to a unified campaign (Heynen, 1999, 155) but, while he maintained tight control over the latter, he relied heavily on co-opting the expertise of others in the former. The collaborative ethos that had marked his earlier work in Breslau continued and expanded in Frankfurt. He relied on the vision of other architects such as Mart Stam, Adolf Meyer and Eugen Kaufmann, who took command of particular housing projects and contributed design ideas to the overall municipal building programmes. He was instrumental in bringing pioneers of modern functional modular design to Frankfurt, such as the designer Margarete Lihotzky with whom he had stayed in contact since his days in Breslau (Elsaesser, 2006, 35–6; Hochhaeusl, 2013; Schütte-Lihotzky, 2019, 105). He was internationally minded, travelling extensively to observe other planning initiatives and taking active part in the proceedings of organizations such as the International Federation of (Housing and) Town Planning (IFTP/IFHTP), which was presided by his former mentor Raymond Unwin. When he became a pivotal founding member of CIAM in 1928, he mediated the divide between the more traditionally minded IFHTP and the new, more avant-garde architectural group. The mediation was both organizational (he attended IFHTP's 1926 and 1928 congresses at the same time that he played a key role in organizing CIAM's first working congress in Frankfurt) and programmatic (his housing and planning views remained rooted in a low-density and decentralized approach to urban expansion, displaying an enduring alignment with a lot of earlier garden-city ideas that were an anathema to many of his avant-garde CIAM colleagues) (Wagner, 2016, 114–17). As member of CIAM's steering group he also played an important role arbitrating in the programmatic and personality clashes with the Werkbund (of which he remained a member since 1918) that threatened to destroy CIAM in the late 1920s (Kallis, 2020, 6–12).

May brought to Frankfurt an already highly elaborate understanding of a 'minimum' modern dwelling programme, forged in the extraordinary challenges that he had faced during his Breslau stint (Schwartz, 1996, 216; Oberlander and Newbrun, 2011, 64). He stuck with the small-dwelling (Kleinwohnung) typology that he had worked with in Breslau rather than attempting to reinvent the typological wheel, as, for example, Le Corbusier had sought to do with his housing experiments in the early 1920s (the 1915 Maison *Dom-Ino* or the 1922 *Maison Citrohan* (Curtis, 1996, 109–10; Moos, 2009, 84–8)) or Ludwig Hilberseimer and Hannes Meyer had attempted with their radical 'cell' designs (Hays, 1995, 173; Ottillinger, 2009, 38; see also Chapter 4). The new public housing programme that he devised in 1925 involved a series of innovative refinements of the familiar reduced-size dwelling but refracted his earlier design ideas through the modern prisms of industrial production, typification and modular functional design. May promised that the Neue Frankfurt programme would resolve the postwar housing shortage within ten years of sustained, centralized building activity. Individual dwelling units would have to be designed on the basis of the most rigorous functional economy, with an overall surface area 'no more spacious than necessary'. This would require the rational redesign of kitchen facilities, the concentration of washing activities in a single room and the socialization of other traditional household activities such as laundry. The extent and scope of communal facilities increased over the years of May's Frankfurt tenure, combining new ideals of living (e.g. day care centres, theatres, youth centres, radio rooms) with necessary cost economies (Henderson, 2010, 327). Here the thoughtful integration of necessity and positive aspiration encompasses the totality of May's planning vision from the design of private family spaces to neighbourhood configurations and his entire Trabanten philosophy of decentralized settlement (Porotto, 2016, 91–101). Standardization of components and building methods and mechanization of construction would contribute to the dual goals of economical building and rapid construction en masse while at the same time propagating good-quality rational design. When it came to the external design of the dwelling units May emphatically rejected 'any reference to past stylistic eras' and the 'excessive individualism' of bourgeois design practices. Anticipating criticisms that standardization of design, construction and individual components would promote dull uniformity and lack of individualism, he underlined how Frankfurt's new building programme involved a collaboration of different architects who were allowed to handle the entire design of the settlement buildings with a high degree of design freedom and individual creativity even as they fulfilled the directives of a general plan and followed a set of clear design guidelines (Figure 2.10).[16]

In spite of the wide range of breakthroughs in design and construction that the Frankfurt housing programme absorbed, size reduction per se continued to matter to May as a strategy for facilitating large-scale deployment of affordable housing. The municipal magazine that he curated featured a series of contributions on this theme, posing the question in its most basic cost-quality form. In the 1928 issue the Berlin architect Jacobus Göttel reframed the conundrum as one geared first and foremost to affordability ('the cheapest dwelling'). His design prototype (Figure 2.11) examined the possibility of further reducing his earlier assumption of the 'minimum' size of a typical family dwelling from 48 $m^2$ to 38 $m^2$) in an otherwise still low-density building arrangement that promised to bring rental price down to an acceptable level of 25 per cent of the benchmark wage of a factory worker.[17] A year later Wilhelm Hagen, chief of the municipal health office, published an analysis based on biological and sociological observations that suggested a revised framework for the 'smallest dwelling' (Kleinstwohnung). True to the fundamental premises of May's overall programme, Hagen did not depart from the orthodoxy of Trabanten settlements. The typologies he suggested featured private garden space and often balconies, adhering to the low-density orthodoxy and rejecting the temptation to sanction high-rise residential alternatives purely on the grounds of cost-efficiency. Nevertheless, further reductions of size could still be advocated on the basis of streamlining domestic functions and eliminating outdated traditional living practices. He came up

The 'Small Dwelling'

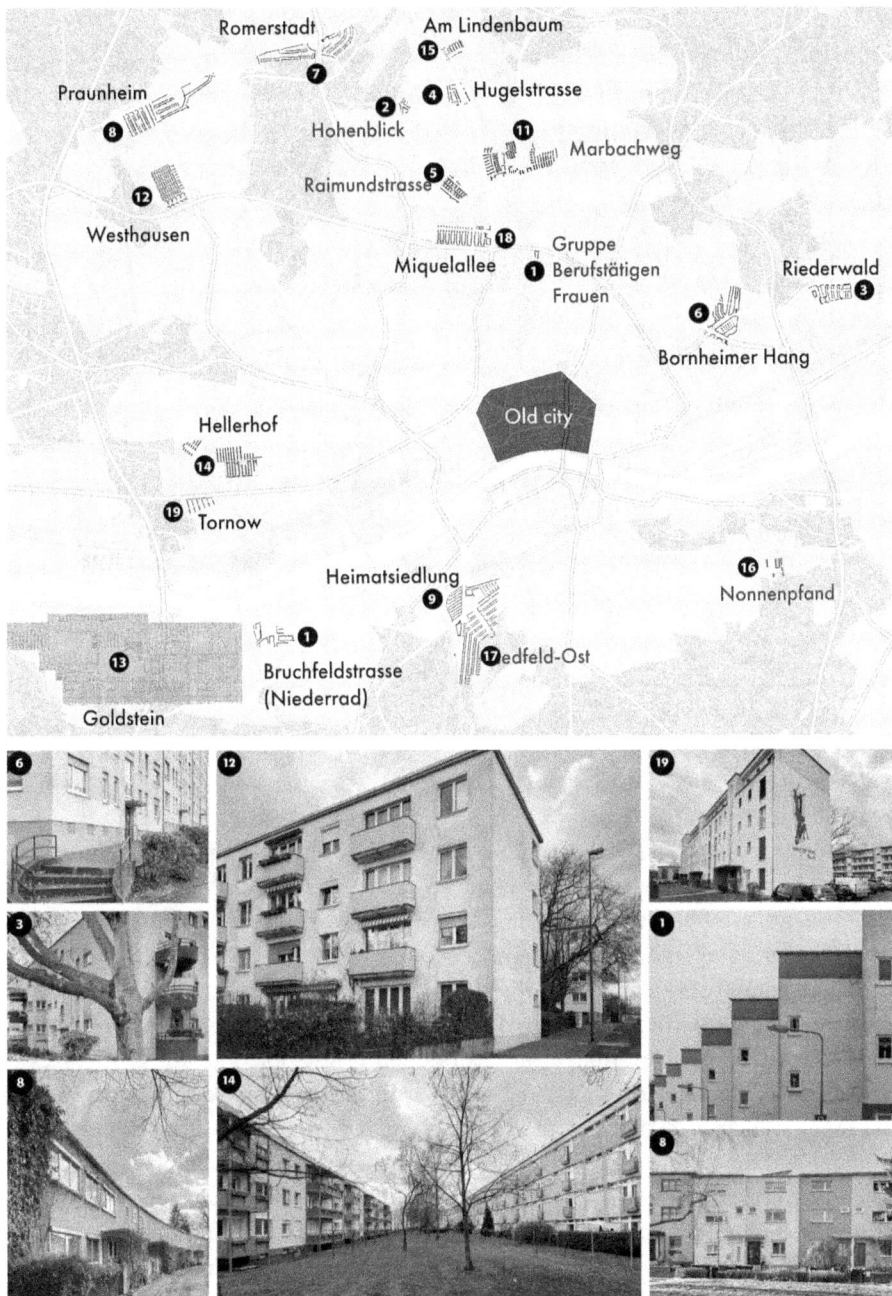

**Figure 2.10** Map and photos of the Siedlungen of 'New Frankfurt'.

## The Minimum Dwelling

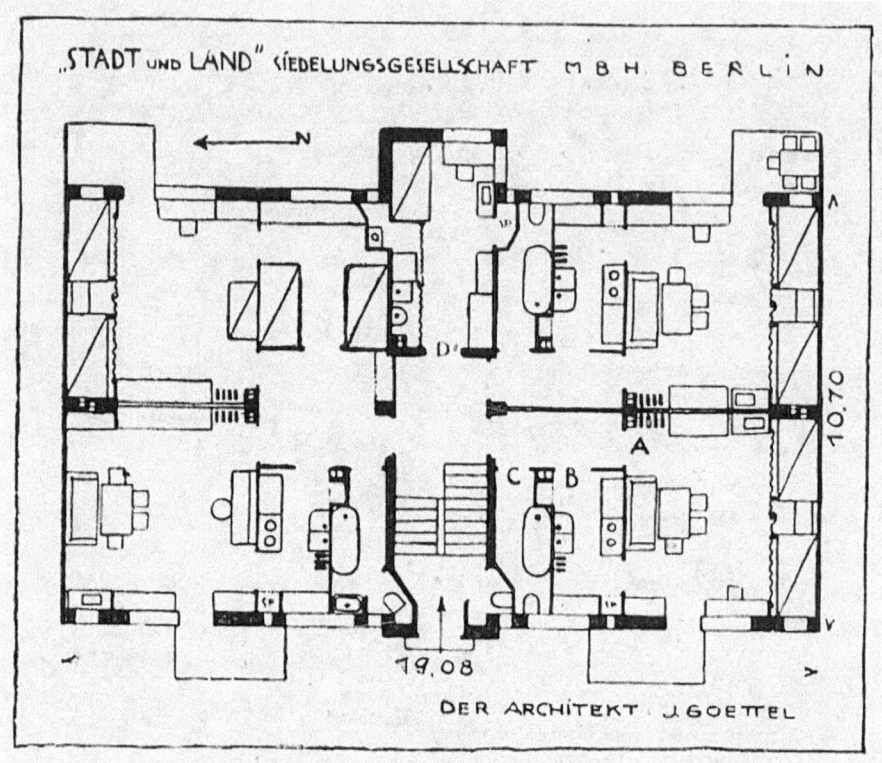

**Figure 2.11** Jacobus Goettel's plans for the 'cheapest dwelling' [Source: *DNF* 2/2 (1928): 111].

with a formula of a *c.* 50 m² apartment for a four-person family, with small but functional kitchen space (a relatively easy undertaking given the advances of the 'Frankfurt kitchen' design in terms of space and design efficiency), a ruthlessly functional living room, washroom with shower and bedrooms that allowed children to be separated by gender.[18]

Yet the Frankfurt version of the Kleinstwohnung was more than a superlative 'small dwelling' in its conventional reductive form. Instead it was proposed as a novel dwelling paradigm made possible through the intersection of multiple modern genealogies of 'minimum' habitation. Here functional spatial arrangement, typological standardization and rational interior design met the studied simplicity of a new 'Taylorized' domestic economy and the austere aesthetics of the new Sachlichkeit. There were echoes of Vienna in the Frankfurt programme that involved key figures of the modern movement who worked in both cities during the 1920s. Apart from Lihotzky, Anton Brenner, a young graduate of the Arts School in Vienna who had worked on a number of municipal projects, also came to Frankfurt in 1926. Another young Viennese architect Franz, Schuster followed a similar trajectory. Schuster, who had worked under Heinrich Tessenow's guidance in the pioneering Hellerau settlement project in Dresden before, had returned to Vienna to play a leading role in 'Red Vienna', working alongside Adolf

Loos and Otto Neurath (Panerai et al., 2004, 151) before departing for Frankfurt in 1925. The three of them worked together on a number of projects in Frankfurt under the auspices of the municipal 'standardization' department. While in Frankfurt Schuster also turned his attention to the typology of the Kleinstwohnung, producing ideas and plans that suggested a reversal of the process through which the interwar reduced-size dwellings had been typically arrived at (Figure 2.12). Rather than starting with size reduction as a cost-saving goal and then trying to fit as many traditional functions and components as possible in the new configuration, he subjected the composition of the apartment to a rigorous test of austere functionality, eliminating 'useless burdens' of the past and reducing forms to their purest, most efficient expression (Henderson, 2013, 188). Crucially he also approached the apartment as a modular ensemble of spaces, configurations and design components, with thoughtfully redesigned furniture playing a critical role in unlocking new possibilities for both space reduction and elevated quality of life (Schuster, 1927; Schuster, 1929). Such a holistic conception of the apartment as the sum of fixed and movable, construction and organization modules mapped onto May's overall multi-scalar plan for his 'New Frankfurt' as the organic aggregate of innovations from the micro (component) to the macro (Siedlung and city as a whole) scale.[19]

The increasing interest in the 'smallest' and 'cheapest' dwelling reflected an optimistic belief in the power of rationality, austerity and standardization to deliver, with 'minimum' means, genuinely optimal living standards for all through a radically new conception of modern living. The complexity of the housing calculus, however, meant that the kind of work that May was pursuing in Frankfurt in relation to the Klein-/Kleinst-wohnung was often chasing a moving target. This is because the whole formula depended also on broader contextual factors such as wages and inflation beyond the control of architects or municipal authorities. By the time that Schuster refined his 'smallest dwelling', the social legitimacy of the entire Neue Frankfurt housing experiment had come under renewed scrutiny. The otherwise impressive housing record of May's team in Frankfurt appeared to have failed the litmus test of universal affordability – by no means a problem unique to Frankfurt as Schumacher had also found out in Hamburg towards the late 1930s (Schubert, 2021, 10). Even the cheapest new Klein(st)wohnung units in decentralized settlements were appreciably costlier to produce and then rent out than what the minimum wages of Frankfurt workers could justify. May's small-size apartments were simply not affordable enough for their intended social function. The question of quality-needs-cost balance was restated with renewed urgency in the pages of the municipal magazine *Das Neue Frankfurt* in 1928–29. The response of May's team to this new challenge was flexible and pragmatic. They set the absolute size minimum for the overall dwelling surface area at 38–40 $m^2$. This was the zero point of the Frankfurt Kleinstwohnung in terms of size, as it had been for the early Viennese housing programme. Any further gains, May argued, could only come from rational internal organization of functions and equipment.[20] Inevitably quality would suffer on a per-dwelling basis but this translated into significant gains in terms of the broader social goal of expanded affordability and scale of production. In one of his last major estates, Westhausen, smaller dwelling sizes were combined with significantly

**Figure 2.12** Cover of Franz Schuster's 1927 book on the 'smallest dwelling' (Kleinstwohnung).

higher-density/-rise building forms in order to increase the affordability of the produced dwelling units (Porotto, 2019a, 851). No matter how programmatically wedded he was to the low-density settlement and thoughtful size reduction up to an absolute minimum that guaranteed a good level of comfort, his primary concern remained affordability and mass provision. He was thus ready to compromise on building height and density if such concessions advanced the goal of decent housing as universal social right.

\*\*\*\*\*

The typological differences between the Viennese and Frankfurt housing experiences in the 1920s are of course hard to ignore. By virtue of their contrasting approaches to density, building organization (*Hof/Siedlung*), siting (urban/peripheral), spatial arrangement (block/row) and genuflection to the modernist minimum aesthetics, the two cities occupied very different places along the spectrum of views that sharply divided architectural opinion in the interwar years (Porotto, 2019a). In addition, they were underpinned by different sociological assumptions about the balance between individual, collective and public life, as well as by divergent assumptions as to how the transitions between them ought to be negotiated (Porotto, 2016, 91–6). If anything, the Viennese experiments exhibited a higher degree of programmatic flexibility in order to accommodate the municipality's social mission of providing decent housing for the largest possible number of citizens (Hochhaeusl, 2013). By contrast, May's New Frankfurt scheme was grounded more firmly on a number of 'hard' programmatic assumptions (decentralization, low density, access to privatized garden, etc.) that, even when revisited in the late 1920s in the light of the limited affordability of apartment types for those with lower incomes, were not seriously questioned by the design team.

Nevertheless, the Vienna and Frankfurt affordable housing programmes that took shape in the course of the 1920s encapsulated all that had changed so dramatically in the intellectual grounding of the 'minimum' affordable dwelling for the masses in the first decades of the twentieth century and started to take concrete shape in the years after the First World War. The extraordinary set of challenges generated by the 1914–18 conflict and by the tumultuous transition to a new postwar normality in the 1920s meant that the prior framing of the housing question in terms of emergency remained dominant in postwar debates across Europe. Size too remained a key signifier of the 'minimum', and it is not a coincidence that the first instances of radical innovation derived from revisiting the conventional typologies of the small/reduced-size dwelling. What did change, if only gradually, was the discursive complexion of the 'minimum dwelling' in its diverse variations ('reduced-size', 'good value', 'lower rent', 'economical', etc.), shifting from a purely literal/reductive and more-or-less pejorative to a moral imperative and eventually normative and increasingly aspirational frame. Using the perspective of human needs and underlining the importance of providing a dignified/hygienic shelter to all those in need, this kind of dwelling was now actively advocated as an efficient, thoughtfully designed container of better living and as a scaleable proposition that bespoke a social ambition to improve living conditions for society as a whole. As important was the parallel shift towards active public intervention and the associated recognition that, since housing was a wider social asset, satisfying the human needs of decent habitation had paramount significance for society as a whole. The discourse of social emergency provided the impetus not only for a substantial increase in the supply of these minimum affordable dwellings in the first decades of the twentieth century but also for a range of innovations in typological and spatial design, production methods, as well as political action that in the end subverted the zero-sum logic of the housing calculus. Given the universal nature of the challenge, it also brought together political and professional groups willing to share experiences and good practice, to learn from one another, and

## The Minimum Dwelling

explore common strategies for addressing the housing question. The 1920s provided the momentum and the organizational space for all these agencies to come together in established and new 'contact zones'. Whether out of sheer anxiety to solve a 'problem' or driven by aspirational frames of radical reform and utopian transformation, these networks supercharged and universalized the discourse of the 'minimum dwelling', imbuing it with a (more) positive social tenor along the way.

# CHAPTER 3
# INTERNATIONAL EXPERT NETWORKS AND THE HOUSING QUESTION IN THE INTERWAR PERIOD

As a field that involved not only design and construction but also a wide range of broader issues – from public health to social inequality to urban planning and governance to social and political stability – the housing question invited both interdisciplinary expertise and international exchange. It also plugged into a rapidly expanding international communication sphere, marked by publications, congresses and exhibitions. The International Housing Congress (IHC) was one of the earliest examples of this international dimension, starting its life as an event parallel to the 1889 Paris world fair but gathering momentum in the years leading up to the First World War (Horne, 2002, 231; Biles, 2010, 45–50). At the turn of the twentieth century, the international garden-city movement provided an alternative model of organization, starting from a national association in Britain but capitalizing on the successful diffusion of its programme across the continent and the evolving trans-national network of personal and organizational contacts to form the International Garden Cities and Town Planning Association (IGCTPA) in 1913 (Geertse, 2016). Inter-municipal co-operation too gathered momentum at the turn of the twentieth century, initially through informal communication among reform-minded local agents but gradually developing its own national and international networks of trade unions, co-operatives and tenants associations (Rodgers, 1998; Saunier, 2004; Saunier, 2008). The year 1913 also saw the formation of the International Union of Local Authorities (*Union Internationale des Villes*, UIV), an organization that oversaw a number of conferences and publications across Europe, both before and after the First World War (Gaspari, 1997; Payre and Saunier, 2000; Dogliani, 2002). Since each of these - and other similar - networks had its own priorities, agenda, and mode of operation, there was as much antagonism and friction as genuine collaboration between them (Geertse, 2012, Ch 1); yet together they contributed to the formation of an active inter- and trans-national dialogue on housing in the early twentieth century (Rodogno et al., 2015).

The turmoil caused by the First World War accelerated dramatically this already unfolding cross-border networking momentum. Architects were among the first to embrace the new challenges and, when they did so, they demonstrated a keen willingness to ground their claim that their expertise was best placed to provide optimal solutions to the crisis (Kohlrausch, 2019, 64). Already-established organizations such as the IGCTPA and the UIV resumed and expanded their activities – the former eventually deciding in the mid-1920s to add 'housing' to its title (renamed International Federation for

Housing and Town Planning, IFHTP, in 1926) and remit. In addition, a wider range of organizations such as the International Cooperative Alliance and the newly formed International Labour Office (ILO) engaged more extensively with the housing question. New organizations too, such as the International Federation for Housing (*Internationaler Verband für Wohnungswesen*, IVW) – a more radical group that splintered from the expanded IFHTP – were formed to account for ideological and programmatic disagreements regarding the housing question (Geertse, 2015, 3).

The urgency of post-First World War reconstruction of the war-ravaged areas, particularly in Belgium and France, stimulated further national and international discussions about the best future form of housing and town planning. It is no coincidence that many figures who became associated with the campaign for modern, affordable and high-quality dwellings for the masses in the 1920s had been heavily involved in the various reconstruction efforts after the First World War. In Britain Raymond Unwin, a key figure in the garden-city movement and the IFHTP, worked closely with the British government during the First World War, contributed to the drafting of the 1918 Tudor Walters report on housing and shaped the influential 1919 Housing and Town Planning Act that placed affordable council housing at the heart of the reconstruction effort (Bayliss 2001: 169-74, 68-78). In continental Europe politicians (like Louis Loucheur and Henri Sellier in France (ie France; ) and Emile Vinck in Belgium) and younger architects (like Raphael Verwilghen, who headed the Belgian Office for the Devastated Regions; Jean-Jules Eggericx, who became head of the Architectural Office of the same organization; and Victor Bourgeois in Belgium; Ernst May and Hans Scharoun in Germany) promoted ambitious agendas of housing reform in their respective countries, using reconstruction as a silver lining in the otherwise dismal legacy of the Great War. There were cases where architects experimented with new forms and techniques, such as in the Belgian garden city of La Roue (1920–21) where Eggericx and other designers tested various affordable housing hypotheses; in Bourgeois's cubic *Cité Moderne* (1922–25), or in a number of settlements designed by teams involving Louis van der Swaelmen, like Le Logis-Floréal (1922–24, with Eggericx's involvement) and Kapelleveld (1922–26) (Smets, 1977, 140–3; Van Loo, Anne, 1996; Lambrichs, 2000; Kafkoula, 2013, 178–80). Furthermore, the pressing need to address the multiple postwar crises coalesced with broader, far more ambitious demands for radical change.

In these circumstances housing became both a primary practical priority, as part of satisfying the basic human need for shelter now under threat, and a symbolic terrain for rehearsing all sorts of competing visions of social, political and cultural transformation. On their part architects and planners seized the opportunity to inject deeper transformative meaning to their professional discourse and practice, becoming not simply builders of new abodes or engineers of new towns but aspiring alchemists of whole new worlds. While the immediate postwar political momentum for radical housing reform subsequently petered out or was tempered by harsh economic realities, it helped solidify a cross-border communication frame that invested all sorts of specific national challenges relating to housing, poverty, social inequality or quality of life with an international significance and relevance. This trend suited architects, planners and municipal experts as it allowed them to develop shared diagnostic languages and prescriptions whose applicability, they claimed, transcended national boundaries and whose anticipated optimal effects were universal. The result was that the post-First World War conversation on housing became a symbolic proxy field where not only diverse architectural programmes but also political, cultural and social visions competed for normative status and universal sanction.

## The IFHTP encounters the question of mass housing: Vienna, 1926

Given the international popularity of the garden-city model for the reconstruction of the devastated territories in the continent, the IGCTPA/IFHTP occupied a central role in the immediate post-First World War discussions about planning and housing. Unlike the UIV the Federation had sustained its operation during the war and stepped quickly into the reconstruction debates by organizing the 1915 congress for the reconstruction of Belgium and arranging for a number of Belgian exiled architects to study the British experience in garden-city construction. It also resumed its normal activities soon after the armistice, holding its first postwar congress in Brussels (September 1919) and maintaining a regular – annual or biennial – pattern of meetings throughout the 1920s (Geertse, 2012, 70–95; Allan, 2013, 40–8, 614–15). As an organization that had strategically opted for the propagation of a more narrow programmatic agenda based on the British garden-city schemes as opposed to a broader town planning agenda, the IGCTPA dedicated its five first postwar congresses (1919–22) to debating strategies for the international promotion and diffusion of this particular planning model. As its membership grew significantly over this period, however, and in the light of the slow postwar recovery of both the UIV and the IHC, the IGCTPA eventually expanded its scope of interests, starting with the debates about regional planning at the 1923 Göteborg and the 1924 Amsterdam congresses (Buder, 1990, 146–7).

By that time the reinvigorated organization was ready to move on from its earlier focus on reconstruction along garden-city lines and to take the leap into the broader discursive sphere of urban planning that was previously the primary domain of the UIV and the IHC. The ambitious extension of focus was also communicated through name changes, as a result of which the 'garden city' component was initially demoted (1924) and then dropped altogether (1926) from the title. The Federation's goal, as formulated at the beginning of the Amsterdam congress,[1] was the widest possible representation and exchange of views on town planning and housing, a task that also depended on expanded country membership (Riboldazzi, 2009, 49–62). The Federation also actively sought closer links with other international organizations such as the League of Nations and particularly the ILO. The latter connection was important due to the ILO's de facto focus on matters of quality of life for working populations. Both the 1924 UIV and the IGCTPA congresses were held in Amsterdam in short succession and representatives of the two organizations discussed plans for closer co-operation. At the conclusion of the IGCTPA congress an ILO resolution was read and discussed, calling for 'healthy dwellings at low rentals in garden cities or urban communities under proper conditions of health and comfort' (IFHTP 1924, 10–11, 85). This same pursuit had also formed a central component of the workings of the Permanent Committee of the International Housing Congresses (*Comité Permanent des Congrès Internationaux de l'Habitation*, CPCIH), whose members had failed to revive the organization in the post-First World War years and eventually decided to join the IFHTP in 1928 as a section with special expertise in housing matters (Saunier, 2007; Pont, 2014). At the same time that this CPCIH-IFHTP alliance was being forged, particular groups within the ILO were pushing hard in the direction of expanding the organization's competence in matters of public housing, producing an impressive range of statistical studies on postwar housing conditions in Europe (e.g. ILO's 1924, *European Housing Problems since the War*) and ambitious plans to extend comparative research activities in the near future (Saunier, 2010, 199–200).

Therefore, the significant membership and organizational expansion of the IGCTPA/IFHTP in the course of the 1920s gave it significant clout but came at the cost of increasing ideological and programmatic heterogeneity that inevitably generated frictions and divisions. Compared to the relatively modest in size early postwar meetings (Göteborg was attended by *c.* 300 delegates) the number of attendees grew to *c.* 500 in Amsterdam, reached 1000 in Vienna and comfortably exceeded this number in Paris in 1928 (Allan, 2013, 615; Riboldazzi, 2013b, 164). The absorption of the CPCIH in 1926–28 ought to have strengthened the IFHTP's credentials as the primary forum for the housing debate in the 1920s; instead it generated acrimony and resulted in a damaging split in 1929, when a group of members protested at what they perceived as the IFHTP's efforts to crush the relative autonomy of the housing section and left the organisation to form the IVW (Wagner, 2016, 97–144). Ideological fissures (particularly the different approaches of socialists and liberals), cultural mistrust (a perceived schism between Britain and the continental countries in terms of administrative practices and social traditions) and personality clashes were inevitably multiplied in the wake of the IFHTP's organizational and membership expansion, transforming in the process the Federation's congresses into far more diverse and often combative events. The tone of the conversation at the Amsterdam congress was overwhelmingly amicable and driven by a concerted attempt to promote synthesis of views or even consensus; yet this was to change dramatically at the Vienna congress of 1926, when the combination of a far more diverse membership and a significantly broader perspective on both town planning and housing created conditions for a more confrontational congress.

That Vienna was the host city in 1926 was very significant. German and Austrian members had been initially prevented from re-joining the organization after the First World War. They had been allowed to come back to the fold in late 1922 but the fact that they were chosen to host the regular congress was a significant sign of normalization. Just like their re-admittance had an immediate effect in shifting the Federation's discursive agenda towards regional planning, the choice of Vienna – a city whose administration (*Gemeinde*) was already engaged in an extraordinary in scale and ambition programme of affordable housing construction by the mid-1920s (see Chapter 2) – highlighted how the IFHTP was determined to take its new housing brief very seriously (Geertse, 2016,

740). The congress tackled two questions that had become central to the architectural conversation in the 1920s, particularly in the continent where the task of postwar reconstruction and the pressure to respond to the housing shortage were more pressing. The first was land tenure and its significance in terms of both affordable housing provision and regional planning. This discussion drew attention to the problem of speculation that drove housing prices upwards and highlighted the limits that legislation placed on public authorities in terms of acquiring land through expropriation that lay within the boundaries of the urban or regional plans. Ernst Hein, Vienna's chief engineer, explained the benefits of the city's dual approach to the problem – a combination of acquiring peripheral areas and expropriating urban lands that together stimulated housing construction en masse and drove rental or sale prices down. There was general consensus among the speakers that existing laws placed significant restrictions both to the acquisition and rational use of land for housing and public facilities, even if considerable progress had been made in a number of countries since the turn of the twentieth century to that effect. But Hein suggested that the optimal future solution to the problem lay in empowering public authorities to control land both within and in the periphery of the urban areas.[2]

The second headline topic of the 1926 Vienna congress concerned the study of benefits and drawbacks involved in the construction of single-family cottages and apartment buildings. The proceedings delivered a rich and animated discussion on this topic, but they also underlined how difficult the process of achieving programmatic consensus in an organization with a much more larger and diverse membership had become. Vienna, as the city engineer Franz Musil noted in his address to the congress, had pioneered an ambitious programme of social housing that challenged many of the prewar orthodoxies – namely that urban expansion needed to be planned in a decentralized way, that low density was the sine qua non of better-quality housing, that good-quality dwelling ought to be a fully privatized unit of housing and that the dwelling size could not be reduced without an equivalent decline in the quality of life that it offered. Unsurprisingly Musil sang the praises of the city's building programme – approximately 32,000 new urban dwellings of considerably higher quality built between 1922 and 1927.[3] He did pay the necessary tribute to the benefits of the family cottage sited in a low-density peripheral residential area surrounded by ample green space and with good transport links to the urban centre; but he also stated that this approach alone was not enough to either address the overriding problem of housing shortage or improve fast enough the conditions of living in older urban tenements (Jahn, 2014; Maderthaner, 2017). Faced with a sub-optimal choice between quality of the individual dwelling unit and increasing supply, Vienna had opted for a strategy that prioritized the latter without either sacrificing or over-specifying the former.

The bold Viennese approach to mass housing was essentially based on the Kleinwohnung form (literally small apartment dwelling),[4] a housing typology known for marking a departure either from the single-family home or from the *Kleinhaus* (small detached house up to two storeys containing up to two apartments) (Schuster, 1927, 1–2; Lorbek, 2018) (see also Chapter 2). The 'small dwelling' type used in Vienna typically involved a reduced-size apartment of 38–48 m$^2$, in a medium- or large-size residential block, with the parallel provision of communal facilities for the

## The Minimum Dwelling

block residents. Already used in small numbers across the city before the First World War to speed up the pace of construction, the Kleinwohnung typology had also been used in Germany prior to the war and had over time gained popularity among the constituency of housing reformers for its promise of efficiency rather than any of its individual design merits (Jerram, 2007, 157–77; see also Chapter 2). However, the Kleinwohnung typology promoted by the Viennese municipal administration from 1922–23 onwards was far more aspirational and socially minded than the prewar experiments in Austria and other countries of continental Europe. Apartments were arranged in large courtyard blocks (*Höfe*) and organized in small numbers around staircase access through an entrance from the courtyard interior (Porotto, 2017a; Porotto, 2017b, 5–10; Porotto, 2019b) (Figure 3.1). They featured rationalized kitchen spaces (typically in the form of the Viennese 'kitchen niche', originally developed

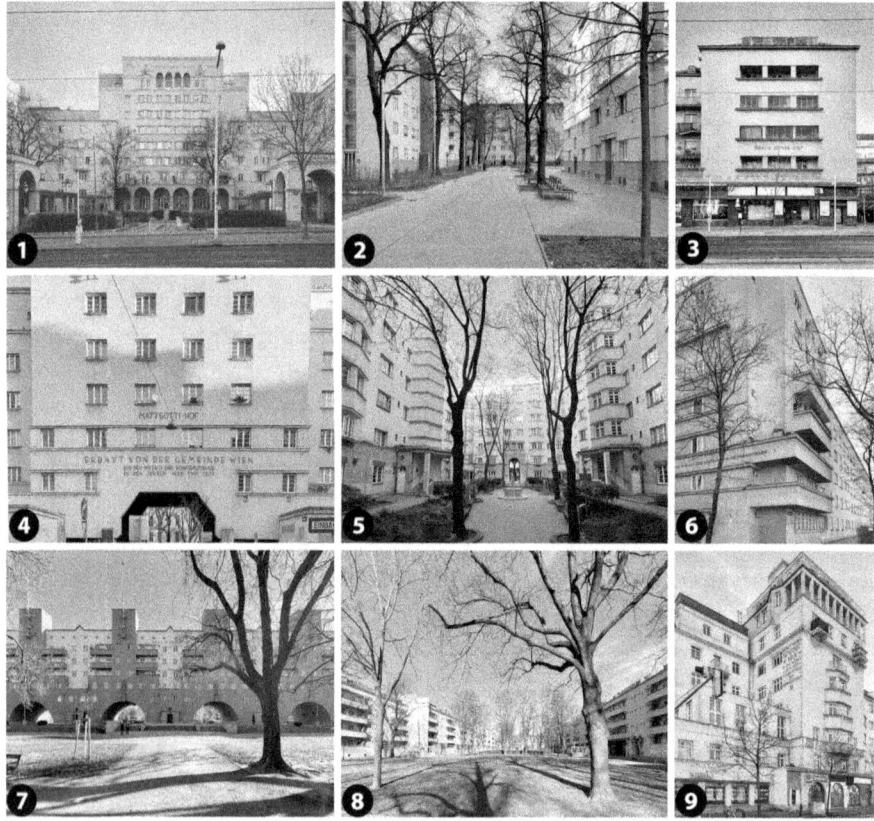

**Figure 3.1** Examples of Viennese Höfe constructed by Vienna's municipal authorities in the 1920s. (1) Fuschenfeld Hof; (2) Metzleinstaler Hof; (3) Franz Domes Hof; (4–5) Reumann Hof; (6) Werkbund estate; (7–8) Karl Marx Hof; (9) Matteotti Hof; (10) Winarsky Hof; (11–12) Lasalle Hof [Source: IFHTP, 1926].

by Margarete Lihotzky for the earlier emergency settlement units constructed in the early 1920s and then adapted and refined for use in the municipal apartment blocks (Hochhaeusl, 2013)), private toilet facilities, living and sleeping spaces to suit families of different sizes. The reduction of space inside the dwelling – and the associated loss of certain facilities, such as shower or bath – might have been dictated by the ruthless logic of financial austerity but was infused with moral significance as part of the municipality's efforts to use the available funds to extend the benefits of hygienic living to as many residents in need as possible. In addition, the provision of an extensive network of communal facilities within the blocks themselves (not only washing but also kindergartens, libraries, social and leisure spaces (Schmid, 2019, 136–48)) marked a relative shift from the strictly private dwelling enclosure to the hybrid semi-private/semi-public spaces of the Höfe, which emerged from its spatially transitional status into a primary component of residential life.

The Viennese municipal building programme was peerless at the time of the 1926 IFHTP congress in terms of both scale and quantity–quality ratio. The congress itself offered the city a unique opportunity to showcase its achievements and stake a strong claim that it represented a tried-and-tested model for modern social housing whose rationale and execution could inform the broader international debate. During their stay, delegates were treated to a series of site tours as well as to two exhibitions – one dedicated to the two themes of the congress and the other focused exclusively on Vienna and presenting its urban development from ancient times to the work of the Gemeinde in the 1920s.[5] In presenting various aspects of the municipal housing programme, Vienna's representatives mixed positive and defensive arguments to explain the preference for the large residential blocks in the urban core. The typological solution was presented as a practical compromise that delivered an optimal ratio of quality, scale/speed and cost. In placing the construction of Kleinwohnungen (or Volkswohnungen – people's apartments – as Musil and others had described them in more positive, socially aspirational terms in the municipal literature[6]) within a context of emergency and practical compromise, the Viennese representatives did not openly depart from the Federation's revered position that single-family cottages represented the optimal solution to both housing and (as part of decentralized settlements) town planning in the future. Instead they compared them to the existing conditions of living for most people of low incomes inside the city and the emergency situation generated by the postwar housing shortage. The message was, rather than waiting for improved conditions that may have permitted a more extensive construction programme based on single-family dwellings in peripheral settlements, the Gemeinde had to act in conditions of hardship that were far from uncommon in large parts of the continent after the First World War. Furthermore, public ownership of land – an area in which Vienna had invested considerable resources, resulting in the city owning a quarter of the urban lands[7] – had enabled the authorities to embark quickly on social housing construction in and around the city, using not only apartment blocks but also *c.* 3,500 cottages, without relying on the private sector. Lastly, they invoked other practical benefits of their centralizing approach, noting, for example, that extending the city through a large number of peripheral settlements instead would have required significant expenditure for the provision of adequate transport links to the city centre.[8] All in all, the official Viennese representatives recast the municipal programme as a compromise – but an optimal one if the measure of success shifted from the quality of each individual dwelling to the social consequences of a large-scale building programme for the community.

Inevitably each of these two features of the Viennese housing programme – dwelling in urban blocks and public provision – generated controversy at the congress. The discussion that followed the individual presentations was surprisingly animated by the usually consensual standards of the IFHTP. British delegates in particular, including Charles Purdom, one of the founder of Letchworth and Welwyn garden cities, criticized the host city for its aggressive promotion of public construction at the expense of private initiative.[9] The British architect Mark Elgood underlined the ongoing consensus within the Federation for the single-family cottage dwelling with private garden and suggested tenements of only a small number of floors in exceptional circumstances or as a transitional measure until financial and legal conditions permitted a more extensive application of the decentralized approach.[10] Different perceptions on both matters, however, also divided delegates from other countries, particularly in relation to public ownership of land. Criticism of the Viennese housing model came from all possible directions and was linked to a wide range of programmatic disagreements – for amounting to 'complete socialisation' of land, for subjecting building to political considerations, for imposing uniformity and crushing every sense of individualism, for depriving its tenants from the all-important contact with nature and for putting financial considerations ahead of quality of living for its tenants. Among the critical voices were proponents of the peripheral settlement movement in Germany, such as the social democratic president of the Anhalt parliament in Dessau Heinrich Pëus, who dismissed the use of the Kleinwohnung typology by the Gemeinde Viennese as at best a lesser-evil 'transitional' measure that had to be abandoned when conditions of financial and social stability returned; and Berlin's chief city planner Martin Wagner (also affiliated to the SPD), who urged for a less centralized approach to public building that allowed the residents themselves to 'have a share in building activities' through municipal building societies and co-operative organizations.[11] The IFHTP's president Raymond Unwin oscillated between covert criticism (criticizing centralization of housing in urban centres and the lack of individuality in apartments as befitting a society of 'automats … and Robots'[12]) and emphasis on the IFHTP's role in hosting the widest possible international exchange of views on contemporary problems. The general congress of praise for the Viennese housing experiment could not conceal the rapidly growing tensions between radical social housing reformers and the traditional core membership of the organization, a tension that would bedevil the Federation in the following three years and result in the 1929 split (Riboldazzi, 2009, 79–91).

## The IFHTP congress in Paris, 1928: The trope of the 'housing for the very poor'

Two years later, the members of the IFHTP met again in Paris. The agenda of the proceedings in 1928 was even more ambitious in coverage and multidisciplinary, with five different themes, and an attendance that was significantly larger than in Vienna (Riboldazzi, 2013b). The congress programme included sessions on three topics – 'housing for the very poor', building costs and 'mass and density of buildings' – that were bound to deepen ideological and programmatic fault lines within the expanded Federation. 'Housing for the very poor' represented the IFHTP's attempt to expand into a social agenda for housing that targeted the needs of the working population, including those with very low incomes. Adopting a neologism for a concept of housing based on income was bound to cause definitional confusion among the delegates. Some restricted the term to those who, albeit in employment, did not earn enough to benefit from existing programmes of affordable and subsidized housing construction, whether as owners or tenants. Others took a broader approach that included all forms of poverty, including homelessness, living in slums (a theme that gained traction in the IFHTP conversation and graduated into being one of the core themes of the 1931 congress in Berlin) or even those deemed 'undesirable' by Arie Keppler, Amsterdam's housing director (Figure 3.2),

Logements pour familles indésirables. Amsterdam.

**Figure 3.2** Dwellings for 'undesirable families' in Amsterdam presented at the 1928 IFHTP congress in Paris [Source: *IFHTP* 1928, I, 42].

or 'parasitic' by the Spanish delegate Federico Lopez Valencia.[13] In many ways the formulation of the theme lent itself to an old-fashioned perception of this social category as necessitating special treatment in terms of housing that diverged from quality norms otherwise applicable to the rest of the population.[14] The definitional confusion around the notion of the 'very poor' brought to the surface ideological divisions among delegates who considered the provision of housing for this group as an extraordinary form of benefit and those who approached it as a matter of ethical imperative towards society on a par with education and public health (the last point was made passionately by the Belgian senator Emile Vinck).[15] Other divisions concerned the extent and duration of public assistance beyond the normal instruments of financial facilitation (e.g. loans and favourable tax treatment) aimed at bringing rental prices down to a level that would be affordable by most, if not all, citizens. The views of Lawson Purdy, New York's Charity Organisation Society, that the problem of affordable housing could be solved through natural market forces alone were criticized by the majority of European delegates who were willing to countenance some form of public intervention.[16]

However, the most interesting facet of the congress discussion on the 'housing for the very poor' concerned the link between 'minimum' human needs and housing quality standards. Unwin dismissed the idea that a 'cheap house' had to be equated with a 'less good' one; instead the differentiating factor had to be space, amenities and level of comfort, not standards or basic facilities.[17] Some delegates appeared willing to accept that different 'minimum' standards would also have to be defined for the special category of the 'very poor'. Giuseppe Gorla, vice-president of Milan's Institute of Social Housing (*Istituto Case Popolari,* ICP), epitomized the traditional paternalistic and disciplinary view of housing for the poor by describing his organization's experiments with special forms of accommodation made available as emergency shelter and enforced 'schooling' for the 'very poor' families. Gorla acknowledged that this kind of dwelling ought to satisfy the residents' basic needs – but these needs, in his opinion, differed from those of the rest of the population and thus justified a kind of accommodation that offered significantly lower quality and amenities. He argued that social housing was a right that ought to be extended only to those who had proved that they were responsible citizens and tenants willing to fight their way out of poverty. Thus, the provision of temporary accommodation for the 'very poor' in Milan also served the purpose of monitoring their behaviour and redirecting only the 'worthy' tenants into the standard housing system of the ICP.[18] Gorla and the other members of the Italian delegation spoke of the Italian state's experiments with a new type of hotel-like accommodation for this special social category that was inspired by the boarding house or hostel typologies (Villani, 2012, 147–8; Bertani, 2014; Kallis, 2017, 271–5).

The views expressed by the Italian delegates (also supported by various Dutch and British representatives) were singled out for criticism by one of the congress's chief rapporteurs, Henri Sellier, head of the Paris departmental office of affordable housing and mayor of the garden city of Suresnes. In his view the concept of the 'very poor' had only a relative meaning due to both different standards of living in each country and different views as to whether it ought to be limited to workers or stretched further to include everyone living in poverty. He objected strongly to the practice of segregating the poor from the rest of society. Furthermore, he supported the view that dwellings made available to this social category ought to at the very least satisfy a series of universally accepted 'minimum' standards of living and never fall below them even in times of crisis. He mapped the spectrum of views expressed at the congress, with Vienna occupying one end (rents universally low to be affordable by everyone) and the United States on the other (no special public provision for the very poor).[19] Even if the majority view at the congress was that some form of public intervention was required, the question of whether it ought to promote housing for the 'very poor' as part of a universal social right framework or as a conditional and/or temporary allowance stood in the way of any form of meaningful consensus in Paris. To make matters worse, delegates who otherwise agreed on the need for some degree of public intervention diverged in terms of what form and strategy was best – lowering housing standards to a bare minimum of tolerability to ensure sufficient provision in the short term; facilitating construction through public financial instruments (loans, tax); subsidizing construction and/or rental costs to render the dwellings affordable; or bringing costs down through the use of modern construction techniques and building materials.

The conversation on the housing for the 'very poor' intersected with another session dedicated to building costs. The session's chief rapporteur Robert Schmidt, director of the planning board for the Ruhr district, had argued that technological innovation alone – central purchase of building materials, pre-fabrication or standardization of plans and components – could reduce building costs by up to half and thus pave the way for making an elevated standard of dwelling affordable by substantially more people with lower income.[20] It was clear in the session plenaries that innovations in this field were expected to go a long way towards bringing costs down and thus compensate to an extent for the rapid postwar increase in the price index. Delegates discussed the merits and limits of a series of experimental techniques (steel frames, substitute materials such as cork or slag cement for the walls, standardized fittings) as either alternatives or supplements to public subsidy. However, at one point in the plenary discussion, Schmidt also referred to another promising variable – rational design and use of space – and pointed to the relevant research carried out by the Ukraine-born architect Alexander Klein. Klein had conducted a series of scientific studies of domestic space usage and internal circulation for Germany's Research Society for Economic Efficiency in Building and Housing (*Reichsforschungsgesellschaft für Wirtschaftlichkeit im Bau- und Wohnungswesen*, RFG). His findings were exhibited at the Paris IFHTP exhibition as examples of best practice in terms of how to maximize dwelling quality through the most efficient organization and use of 'minimum' space across a variety of family-size scenarios (Savorra, 2015, 68–72).

Klein's work remains hard to categorize. While his designs were conceived as practical norms for mass-produced, low(er)-cost and affordable housing in Germany and his methodology was rigorously empirical, they also derived from his vision for 'frictionless living' that had all the characteristics of a 'practical utopia'. His dwelling prototypes belonged to a select register of works that featured both in the IFHTP and CIAM panorama of exhibitions (Bevilacqua, 2011; Korbi and Migotto, 2019). For all these reasons, I discuss Klein's dwelling designs later on in this study (see Chapter 4). For the 1928 exhibition, however, featuring Klein's work was important because it aligned with the specific historical context of the Paris congress. The event took place only days before the parliamentary debate on the proposal of the French labour minister Louis Loucheur for an ambitious new housing law. Loucheur himself held a special place in the congress's official opening, in recognition of his enduring efforts since the end of the First World War to promote legislation in favour of mass affordable dwelling construction in France. He welcomed the delegates and, together with senator Paul Strauss, emphasized the significance of this coincidence of the congress with the crucial parliamentary vote (IFHTP 1928, I, 20–6). The Loucheur law was indeed approved in mid-July 1928, making at last significant amounts of public funding available (in the form of low-interest loans) to facilitate the construction of affordable good-quality dwellings on a scale unprecedented for France – 200,000 new homes were anticipated within five year from the introduction of the law (Gustiaux, 2015). The French programme favoured low-density solutions in garden-city developments and was geared towards home ownership over time, reflecting Loucheur's belief that root-and-branch housing reform was the best strategy to prevent revolution and maintain social harmony (Benton, 1984, 55). It was also comprehensive in its coverage, in theory extending from the IFHTP's category of the 'very poor' to the bulk of the working classes and, through additional measures introduced in 1930 as part of the Bonnevay law, to the professional middle classes as well. Dwelling plans differentiated between social status, offering progressively more space, better functional separation and upgraded amenities with every step up the social pyramid. The earlier 'Becque' and 'Zola' prototypes (see Chapter 2) formed the basis for the two main typologies of Habitations à Bon Marché (HBM) – the 'minimum' (*rudimentaire*) and the 'ordinary', respectively), to which two further categories of higher specification were added in the course of the 1920s and 1930s (the 'improved' HBM and the 'reduced rent' dwelling) (APUR, 2017).

Besides celebrating the new French housing initiative, the Paris congress also served as a forum for bringing into contact relevant experiences in public housing from a wide range of countries across political divides at a moment where optimism about public housing was at its peak before the dramatic retrenchment caused by the global financial crisis of 1929. The presence of a small but active group of delegates from the Soviet Union in Paris marked a period of closer, though short-lived, relations between Soviet co-operative housing institutions and the IFHTP. The IFHTP leadership used a carefully calibrated language to refer to the key Soviet plans for collective housing and made light of the fundamental programmatic difference between the mixed private-public experience in Western Europe and the exclusively public housing provision in the Soviet Union.[21] At the same time a sizeable delegation from (Fascist) Italy also took active part in the congress proceedings. Consisting of some of the highest-ranking experts working for the Milanese and Roman branches of the public ICP and headed by the organization's president Alberto Calza Bini, the size and quality of the Italian representation in Paris illustrated a concerted effort on part of the Italian architectural establishment to put Italy on the international map of good practice and innovation in housing and urban planning (Riboldazzi, 2013; Kallis, 2020a, 607–8). Again, the IFHTP leadership steered clear of the political minefield, brandishing instead its inclusive ethos and openness to a diverse range of strictly professional perspectives.

## The IFHTP congress in Rome, 1929: Planning and financing mass urban housing

Fourteen months after the closing of the proceedings in Paris the IFHTP's next congress kicked off in Rome (12 September 1929), in suitable pageantry at the imposing municipal administration building on the Capitoline Hill, with a separate national exhibition dedicated to housing and regulatory plans for a series of Italian cities hosted in the city's primary exhibition venue.[22] For the Italian organizers, this was a unique opportunity to exhibit Rome and Italy to the world as a fount of both peerless heritage and modern innovation. At the official opening of the congress proceedings Calza Bini spoke briefly about the 'regenerative fervour' with which the Fascist regime had tackled the big questions of urban housing and planning. This is why, he explained, the organizers had arranged for a series of parallel exhibitions showcasing the best examples of public housing constructed or planned by the regional branches of the ICP and other state organizations; and for a series of organized visits to particular housing projects (Kallis, 2020a, 611–14), including 'a small, modern quarter [in the garden town of Garbatella in the southern periphery of Rome] that was constructed in four months … product of the harmonious collaboration between builders, architects, and workers' (Figure 3.3).[23] Once again Unwin sidestepped the strong ideological investment by the Italian organizers and decided instead to focus in celebratory terms on the extension of views represented in the ranks of the Federation that the 1929 congress represented. In his opening address he made clear that 'we appreciate each other's differences … [and] do not seek to copy Rome'; the greatest contribution of the IFHTP's international congresses, he claimed, lay in 'arous[ing] in all nations equally appreciation of what has been done in others'.[24]

The 1929 congress agenda combined the IFHTP's core interests in urban planning with the Italian organizers' primary concern for modern interventions in historic urban areas. Two sessions (replanning old and historic towns to meet modern conditions; and methods of planning for the expansion of large towns, with special reference to old and historic towns) were dedicated to this broader theme (Glendinning, 2013, 208). One further theme (financing working- and middle-class housing) continued the 1928 conversation on housing for the 'very poor' and on building costs. The fifth topic, however, marked a significant departure for the IFHTP. Titled 'planning apartment housing schemes in large towns', it represented the most significant shift away from the Federation's garden-city programmatic origins and a growing willingness to consider, however conditionally, higher-density and -rise metropolitan housing as one of the pragmatic solutions to the housing emergency. The differences of opinion on this matter that had generated a lot of animated discussion three years earlier in Vienna were also evident in the diverse national experiences and attitudes outlined by the various national reports in Rome. The IFHTP's

## The Minimum Dwelling

**Figure 3.3** Examples of the 'model dwellings' built for Lot XXIV in Garbatella, Rome [Source: (Top-right) reprinted with the kind permission of the *Archivio Innocenzo Costantini, Biblioteca Comunale F Cini, Comune di Osimo*, Italy; (Top-left), (Bottom-left & Bottom-right) Author's photo].

programmatic position that optimal habitation could only be provided by single-family houses in low-density decentralized new settlements was not questioned. However, now a stronger sense of realism appeared to prevail, leading most delegates to accept that a combination of financial pressures and practical challenges meant that urban apartment dwellings had to be recognized as part of the solution. Debates about building height and density monopolized the plenary discussion, with an unusually broad spectrum of views expressed and attitudes divided not just along national but also individual municipal lines. Given that the entire discussion was framed in a language of necessity dictated by practical limits (lack of funds, high land values, ongoing demand for urban dwellings, need to rehouse former residents of 'slums'), the question was essentially one of defining the absolute minimum of quality in high(er)-rise apartment construction that enabled economical construction en masse. For the overwhelming majority of delegates, this meant determining the highest 'tolerable' number of floors for the residential blocks – and less so the minimum size of the individual apartment dwellings.

The session's rapporteur Frank Minshull Elgood reminded the congress of the Federation's assumed position that height should be restricted to three floors – but he also acknowledged that this represented a desired 'optimum' that was not always feasible.[25] Implicitly this statement opened the way for more elastic attitudes to building height, if not necessarily to density per se, as Elgood also underlined the importance of the proportion of open space in high-rise urban settlements. The director of the Rotterdam Housing Department M J I de Jong van Ellemeet raised the 'threshold of tolerability' in relation to building height to four storeys.[26] The Danish delegate F C Boldsen and the chief architect of Dresden Paul Wolf spoke of new approaches to the design of the multi-storey residential block with communal facilities that allowed scaling up to nine floors without theoretically significant compromises in quality of life.[27] George Risler, president of the French *Union Nationale des Federations d'Organismes d'Habitations à Bon Marché*, offered a similar perspective and defended building types up to five floors.[28] Those delegates who advocated going higher than the Federation's previously assumed three-storey maximum prefaced their suggestions with the obligatory caveat that this represented a 'lesser evil' approach, meaningful only as a relative improvement vis-a-vis the slum-like conditions in which large portions of the urban poor continued to live. Five or even six storeys emerged as a new limit that was still practical when supported by new technological and construction innovations to keep overall costs per unit down while still regarded as representing a tolerable sacrifice in overall quality of life for the residents. Milan's municipal engineer Cesare Albertini argued against the use of such apartments for large families. Arie Keppler, Amsterdam's housing director, advised against rehousing former slum residents in high-rise apartment blocks. Ernst May, Frankfurt's chief architect, cautioned against increasing the number of floors too much, even when elevators allowed it and savings could be significant, because such a form of living could degenerate into a new kind of slum environment.[29] Lawrence Veiller, director of the US National Housing Association, underlined that technical and security advancement had made possible the construction of residential blocks for those less well-off up to ten or even fifteen floors but added that he viewed this development with considerable alarm, both from a quality point of view and as a safety risk.[30]

It was the two members of the Liverpool delegation that made the most sensational contribution to the session on apartment buildings. Hugo Rutherford defended his city's choice to erect urban blocks of up to six storeys by pointing to their financial and practical benefits, claiming that through this solution it was possible to rehouse twelve times more people in the city and close to their places of work than if the single cottage typology had been used. These, he claimed, had been well-received by the new tenants and the benefit of reduced commuting times and city traffic outweighed any comparative shortfalls in privacy and quality of living environment. Lawrence Keay went even further: with thoughtful use of large-site planning in peripheral urban areas, full deployment of elevators, and increased use of communal facilities for recreation or even cooking, blocks of up to ten floors would allow a larger number of workers to live in good-quality apartments close to their places of work and personal associations.[31] Keay had no problem emerging as the provocative outlier at the Rome congress, urging the Federation to abandon its earlier assumption of a three-storey maximum. In this respect, he came close to a form of positive support for high-rise apartment construction that had first been aired by a Soviet delegate at the 1928 Paris congress.[32] The discussion at Rome was inconclusive and no amended consensus view emerged from the proceedings. Nevertheless, the fact that an organization that was the organizational child of Ebenezer Howard, the nous of the garden-city initiative, and was so heavily invested into the international promotion of the garden-city agenda seemed increasingly willing to give exposure to a discussion on horizontal urban housing development was significant. The topic came up in different forms in subsequent IFHTP congresses (most prominently in the 1937 Paris congress but also as part of the Federation's growing interest in rehousing residents of urban slums that was one of the key themes of the 1931 Berlin and 1935 London meetings). While the Federation's declared programmatic position remained unchanged throughout this period, if anything these conversations underlined a growing margin between optimum and acceptable minimum.

*****

Ernst May, Victor Bourgeois and Raphael Verwilghen from Belgium; Hendrik Berlage and Cornelis van Eesteren from the Netherlands; Hans Bernoulli from Switzerland; and Alvar Aalto from Finland were names that appeared on the attendance register of both IFHTP congresses during the 1920s and CIAM meetings from 1928 onwards (Geertse, 2012, 165–76; Riboldazzi, 2013b, 161). Of those May (who attended the 1928 and 1929 congresses as part of the Frankfurt municipal delegation) and Verwilghen were most actively involved in both, as well as in a number of other parallel expert 'contact zones' in the 1920s and 1930s, such as the UIV and IVW. This said, most avant-garde modernists who subsequently became involved in CIAM never appeared either in the ranks or at the congress registers of the IFHTP. The persistence of the garden-city idea as the Federation's programmatic orthodoxy, coupled with an enduring commitment to urban decentralization and low-rise construction, was a polarizing proposition for the majority of the younger architects who saw themselves as the vanguard of the 'new' architecture in the 1920s. At the same time the IFHTP's mainstream design orientation and ideological neutrality could never appeal to those modern architects who approached housing as an engine of revolutionary radical political, social and cultural transformation. More importantly, however, the IFHTP was the de facto forum for professionals who were already embedded in municipal organizations and public building programmes geared to problem-solving rather than aspirational design thinking or radical transformation. It is thus not surprising that already established architects like May and Verwilghen, who had been originally attracted to the premise of Howard's and later Unwin's vision and remained passionate advocates of peripheral settlements as part of their professional practice, felt far more at home in the professional milieu of the IFHTP than passionate advocates of urban centralization and high(er)-rise apartment-based construction like Le Corbusier or Walter Gropius. CIAM, on the other hand, recruited the bulk of its active members from alternative professional networks and communication spheres, striving from the start to differentiate itself from the established international expert networks of the time. Its bid for international inclusiveness was tempered by its strict programmatic adherence to the canons of the 'new' architecture that excluded or dissuaded a large number of architectural practitioners.

Nevertheless, CIAM's itinerary from the sweeping declarations of the founding meeting at La Sarraz in 1928 to the 'minimum dwelling' agenda that dominated its first two working congresses in 1929–30 cannot be uncoupled from the evolution of the housing and planning debates in the international domain of interwar architecture. Connections went beyond personality overlaps or institutional linkages[33]; they concerned shared or intersecting intellectual genealogies and discursive practices even as they often diverged in programmatic terms. The obvious matter of chronology is part of the explanation: CIAM was a relative late-comer in this competitive and increasingly active international expert field. By comparison the IFHTP's involvement in the post-First World War reconstruction debates confronted its members with the harsh realities of emergency and forced them to negotiate the assumed 'optimum' of the garden-city typology against the urgent need for an ameliorative, scaleable and affordable 'minimum' in mass housing conditions. However, it was the IFHTP's uninterrupted institutional presence and activity, its sweeping international character and its unique at the time ability to confer expert legitimacy upon views on planning expressed in its congresses and publications that ensured the organization's dominant role in the international architectural scene during the interwar years (Buder, 1990, 142–4). It was against this backdrop that the IFHTP decided to expand its focus to matters of town and regional planning, affordable housing, building and land costs, 'housing for the very poor', slum clearance, urban density and high-rise residential construction. In retrospect the Federation's three 'housing' congresses in 1926–29 mapped a series of new issues and exposed – often unwittingly – new points of programmatic conflict, many of which would be revisited and recast by CIAM members in Frankfurt and Brussels. It is no coincidence that at the 1930 CIAM congress in Brussels (see Chapter 6) three of the four themes (rational land subdivision, high- or low-rise, and minimum dwelling) echoed the core topics of the Federation's earlier housing-related congresses in 1926–29. In this respect the IFHTP and CIAM histories intersected and interpenetrated more productively than is often assumed.

# CHAPTER 4
# THE 'MINIMUM DWELLING' AS UTOPIA

## The First World War as rupture: The space of utopia

The First World War began with a domino effect of old-style chauvinistic bravado and ended up as a trademark cataclysmic 'black swan' event in global history. The young Walter Gropius was not alone in coming to the immediate conclusion that 'the old stuff was out' (MacCarthy, 2019, 102). The sense of violent rupture generated by the war and then by the unprecedented postwar crises catalysed a desire for radical new ways of thinking and a 'new beginning' that promised to liberate the modern human from the shackles of the past (Griffin, 2007, 1–14). Despair with, and aversion to, the world that had produced the conflict and now seemed convulsing, exhausted and broken, amidst the devastation and trauma of four years of unparalleled brutality, also whipped up a new sense of exhilarating opportunity. Gropius captured the sensation of seismic transition in 1919:

> Today, the artist lives in a time of disintegration devoid of dogma. He is mentally alone. The old forms are broken, the frozen world is loosened up, the old spirit has been knocked over and in the midst of being cast into new form. We waver and we do not yet recognise the new order.
>
> (Gropius, 1995)

The premise of a radical new beginning, of a vast creative slate blissfully purged from the accretions of an exhausted 'old' world invited all sorts of maverick creative forces to break open and convey visions of a 'new' world into the tangible future (Lane, 2013, 51–76; Barnstone, 2017, 1–4). In announcing the death of the old these artistic currents posited the exhilarating possibility – or even imminent expectation – of a veritable cosmogony, even if or perhaps because, as Gropius confessed, the precise contours of this new world were still opaque. Architecture, however, possessed a cosmogonic impulse in a more literal sense of the word. The 'new building' mantra of interwar modernist architecture bridged the metaphorical and the practical, the utopian and the realizable. It premised a new world that was as much an anthropological, ethical, cultural and social category as it was an architectonic, physical, spatial and experiential one (Barnstone, 2017, 1–4). The Berlin-based architect Bruno Taut tried to cancel the distinction between utopia and lived practice by declaring in 1920 that he no longer wished to draw utopias in principle but "absolutely *tangible* utopias that stand with both feet on the ground" (Pruden, 2018, 13; emphasis added). The new architecture that he and other avant-garde architects envisioned in the post-First World War years was both new building and new living – not just reconstruction amidst the detritus of the war but a momentous leap into something authentically novel, creative, morally superior and better.

There was another momentous event that deepened the sense of an end-time (*Endzeit*). The Bolshevik revolution in Russia sent shockwaves that travelled fast and far, feeding both intoxicating hope and extreme *Angst* in different political and social groups on a global scale. That so many in the ranks of the modernist architectural avant-gardes aligned themselves one way or another with the revolutionary left is hardly surprising in this respect. The consolidation of Bolshevik rule, precarious though it was for quite a few years after the 1917 revolution, was seen as the irrefutable proof that the Marxist teleological scheme of history was reaching its climax, an end-time that could render the most total of utopias tangible, actionable, practicable. Yet the upheaval in Russia fed dreams of radical rupture even amongst circles opposed to revolutionary Marxism, from the moderate left all the way to the ultra-nationalist right (Berghaus, 2000). The Bolshevik victory served as a poignant reminder that the experience of the war and the shockwaves caused by the 1917 revolution had rendered a 'return to normality' if not undesirable then practically impossible (Antliff, 2007).

Amidst the psychological disorientation, material devastation, economic dislocation and escalating shortage of dwellings for citizens and refugees alike (Gatrell and Zhvanko, 2019), the housing question emerged from the debris of the First World War with even more acute significance and social relevance. A blend of transformative aspiration and a grave sense of social responsibility in the face of crisis and emergency led many architects and critics in the interwar years to embrace the subject of housing as one of the most urgent and noble goals of the movement of the 'new' architecture. Its pioneers staked their claim that they were best placed to translate the longing for a new world into space and form (Blake, 1960, 176). When it came to housing, modernist architects claimed to have worked out a formula that promised to deliver better with less – and all that for many more beneficiaries. In this chapter, I explore the utopian intellectual strand in the history of the modernist 'minimum' dwelling. I make extensive use of the trope of 'alchemy' in order to capture the disruptive intent of design innovation as formal, spatial-functional and sociological re-invention of habitation. I trace the intellectual processes through which the modernist dwelling absorbed, developed, condensed and unified a series of discrete novel ideas that ranged from individual components to the dwelling unit as an integrated 'minimum' functional system to its scaling as building, community, city and way of life. This process involved a radical rethinking of the fundamental premises of habitation across diverse scales and functions: its role as an individual and collective 'cell'; its enclosing and sheltering function, separating the public from the private; the hierarchy and distribution of uses across interim spaces, through which individuals both came into contact and excluded others; the role and spaces of individual freedom and privacy within and beyond the dwelling; the flow between individual, group, communal, collective and public spaces in an integrated vision of 'new' living. I argue that the architects' utopian propositions about the dwelling make more sense as discursive actions seeking to propose the shape of radical transformation for an as yet undefined optimal future rather than as literal expressions of what 'minimum' and 'optimum' ought to be. In spite of their significant programmatic and ideological differences, these path-breaking architects collectively opened up the debate on the 'minimum' dwelling to the possibility that minimalism and austerity could become the foundation for a universal 'optimum' for individual and collective life; and illustrated how dwelling – disassembled, reimagined, recomposed and inserted into bigger spatial and sociological frames – could be transformed into the engine room of the 'new' world.

## Interwar modernism as discourse: Minimum and optimum

Associating anything 'minimum' with the utopian sphere is counter-intuitive. Minimum indicates the smallest, the most basic quantity of something, below the level of which it ceases to serve its intended purpose or have its expected effects. It makes sense as a defensive guarantee and a threshold rather than an ambition in itself, let alone a utopian alternative. But what if this 'minimum' is not merely a reluctant concession but indicates the *right* measure of something[1] where too much or too little can be detrimental (Kuchenbuch, 2016, 149–50)? Such a meaning opens up a path for transformative aspiration that links the austerity of the 'minimum' with the aspirational state of the 'optimum'. The minimum-as-right cannot be deemed a utopia in the sense of a perfect teleological condition but it can be elevated to the status of a critical agent that unlocks new pathways towards it. It functions like the anticipatory consciousness that Ernest Bloch associated with the longing for the 'new', the dramatic pull away from an insufficient, seemingly dying present towards a *not-yet* determined utopian future. It is the possibility, the intuition of a utopia rather than a defined vision and conscious destination that guides this utopian impulse, as a process and not an outcome (Bloch, 1995; Levitas, 1990 and 2010; Thompson, 2012).

To appreciate the transformative ambition that underpinned the discourse and praxis of modernist architects in the interwar years it is important to appreciate modernism's encounter, indeed collision with history. Modernism came of age at the time when the contradictory forces of revolutionary rupture, crisis and transformative aspiration were in maximum swing. Crisis and opportunity, crisis *as* opportunity for a 'new' sense of time and call for judgement (Koselleck and Richter, 2006), defined the landscape in which the modernists of the 1920s encountered the extraordinary challenges of the post-First World War conditions. The potential of the 'new' radiated ever more brightly and alluringly through the cracks opened up or rather deepened by the conflict and its unsettling aftermath. In the circumstances of crisis, dislocation, disorientation and uncertain flux modernist architects stepped in with a mighty toolkit: the promise of progress and liberation; the intellectual vision of the 'new' world; and the technical and design wherewithal to construct it (Larsen, 2001, esp. 1–12). They claimed that they were uniquely capable of moving from despair or shapeless anticipation to the active construction of the 'new'. In an extraordinary article titled 'New Epoch + New Art' and published on the first issue of Frankfurt's municipal magazine in 1926, the art historian,

## The 'Minimum Dwelling' as Utopia

member of Ernst May's *Neue Frankfurt* team, and co-editor of the journal Fritz Wichert captured the intoxicating anticipation of the 'new':

> We believe that the world is in the midst of a tremendous change, a change in style and personality that humanity has never or rarely experienced in the course of its thousands of years of earthly life. We live through a great moment in the history of the world in the change of the soul, of the house, of the household goods, of the speaking, sounding and visual arts. A feeling is already growing towards the certainty that a new humanity will seize the inhabitants of the globe and will one day replace the old torn state of mind.

The plus sign in the title was significant. The world was on the cusp of something radically new, whose shape was still to be decided. History, art and architecture were the key ingredients of a mighty chain reaction that would alchemise 'a new humankind'.[2] Like their counterparts in the fledgling Soviet Union modernist architects elsewhere perceived their role as that of the primary subjects of a dual historical transition – away from decadence and towards the utopian premise of the 'new' (Kermode, 2000, 100). Yet Soviet architects in the 1920s benefited from a significantly more potent and clear narrative for both the start and the end of the transition, with a cogent villain (capitalist society and 'bourgeois' way of life), a clear path forward (destruction of the capitalist economic and social system) and a potent teleology of a perfect society as destination. By contrast in the West, modernist avant-gardes lacked either the equivalent of the complete break with the past or the teleological horizon of future utopian transformation. Instead they had to concoct their own utopian projects in bizarre circumstances of both rupture from and partial continuity with the present-past that they had revolted against. The result was a far more asymmetrical transition: while the past appeared to them exhausted, the 'new' future remained ambiguous, fuzzy, contested and uncertain. The Western discourse of a 'new' architecture could posit a past to which it had decisively turned its back but no seismic break, no post-revolutionary tabula rasa, nothing like a total storyline of starting anew and no clarity of a single destination or path ahead.

Could all that amount to an alternative kind of 'revolution', an antidote to the destructive frenzy unleashed by the Bolshevik revolution and its bloody aftermath, an alternative future of radical transformation through technical and design innovation alone, in which architecture retained its agency without losing its autonomy as aesthetic endeavour (McLeod, 1983, 144)? Le Corbusier certainly thought so, but his 'revolution' was essentially ameliorative, open-ended and malleable by the architect's creative impulse (Jeanneret, 1987, 8). Ludwig Mies van der Rohe eulogized industrialization and technical innovation as the panacea for all social and economic ills (Mies van der Rohe, 1971). The Berlin architect Martin Wagner foresaw a system of construction and management that could transform the dynamics of the housing calculus by reducing costs by 40 or even 50 per cent (Wagner, 1925). Gropius came to a similar enthusiastic conclusion about the promises of modern technological innovation in construction.[3] Theirs was a simulated, controlled revolutionary explosion, a paroxysm of Fordist utopian optimism where the *deus* was the *machina*. Some retained a primary commitment to the goal of a 'real' social revolution, the only route capable of eliminating the persistent structures of the present-past and thus removing the obstacles to radical change that stood in the way of the 'new' world. Others pursued an optimistic radical social reformism that promised egalitarian access to a set of minimum benefits-as-universal rights and opened up a new horizon of profound socio-economic transformation accessible to all members of society.

Architects debated all these challenges and propositions both within national or ideological silos and across them, united in a shared uncompromising rejection of past forms, a common faith in the transformative power of new industrial techniques and a conviction that the 'new' architecture was at the very least a pivotal agent of transformation if not the single universal elixir. Through national and international fora, through a profusion of written texts, through exhibitions and landmark model experiments, they engaged in a productive but often de-centred and frustratingly polyvalent conversation about the toolkit and the longer-term direction of the change they wished to pursue. In this sense, interwar modernism in the west operated more like a discourse of cultural revolt than a self-assured revolution. Sarah Goldhagen suggested understanding modernism in such discursive terms rather than as a movement defined by more or less coherent aesthetic and design canons (Goldhagen, 2005). She argued that

> modernist buildings, projects, urban plans – including their stylistic positions – as well as manifestos, exhibitions, and other contributions, have been proposals or hypothetical propositions offered up, either actually or hypothetically, to an identifiable community of recipients (architects, urbanists, critics, curators, historians, and theorists) with the intent of testing that proposal's merit and validity.
> (Goldhagen, 2005, 159)

Such an approach shifts the fulcrum of the history of modernism from the architectural products to the rationale that led to their proposition and the language through which they were expressed and justified as 'optima'. Goldhagen underlined the importance of the architect's 'socio-ethical intentions for the forms he designed: what the practitioner believed his forms would signify to the society and the people for whom he designed' (Goldhagen, 2005, 155). As a polyphonous trans-national and trans-ideological conversation also bearing the imprint of architecture's own intrinsic tensions between art and commercial activity with permanent effects, individual expression and social relevance, it was bound to be polysemic and fraught with contention. Yet its intellectual pluralism and dialogical pathos reflected its dynamic historicity, its sweeping scale of modernist architecture's social ambition and the productive tensions of its 'not-yet' utopian horizon (Daniel and Moylan, 1997; Buchanan and Irr, 2006, 249). The diversity, indeed disparity, of the outcomes belied the coherence of the questions that they were seeking to answer and the language that communicated their alignment with a more or less defined set of prognoses, oppositions and objectives (Goldhagen, 2005, 159–61).

Goldhagen invoked the analogy of a professional conference to highlight the discursive character of modernism; and this is an analogy that runs through this book.

## The 'Minimum Dwelling' as Utopia

Ideas, conference papers, articles, treatises, as well as 'paper' plans, 'model' experiments and realized architectural projects were the all-important individual discursive statements of a 'new' architecture, not-yet crystallized, in search of its 'new' identity and transformative purpose. Journals, galleries, meetings, informal or formal visits, congresses and exhibitions became the primary loci of this conversation. In this way they also functioned as 'contact zones' (Pratt, 1991; Falser, 2015, 221; Hernández and Nuijsink, 2020), physical and/or ideational, bringing together – in dialogue, synthesis and conflict – diverse personal interpretations and propositions that vied for universal validity. The different voices and the contradictions of what they proposed as 'optimum' often overshadowed their convergence on the challenges they sought to address: how to square utopia with reality, ambition with necessity; how to balance technology, construction, functional design and art; how the 'new' ought to best mediate radical change and continuity with aspects of tradition; how to satisfy most human needs for more people while working with limited means; how best to respond to the need for social transformation. The theme of the 'minimum-optimum' that is the focus of this book was only a subset of this much broader conversation. It was a pivotal one to begin with, however, and grew in significance in the course of the 1920s, as the sweeping transformative ambitions of the architects participating in the conversation grappled with competing political loyalties and programmatic priorities in the face of the challenging circumstances of the post-First World War world.

### Architecture as revolution

No other figure in the annals of early modernism has attracted so much attention and notoriety as the Swiss-born architect Le Corbusier (Charles-Édouard Jeanneret). His influence on the debates about the 'minimum dwelling' within the ranks of CIAM will be reviewed in more detail later (see Chapters 5–7). It is interesting, however, to note that, before developing his sweeping theories about the urban scale that largely defined CIAM's legacy from the 1930s onwards, Le Corbusier engaged with the single dwelling as elemental unit of transformative architectural agency across all scales. In his 1923 treatise *Towards a New Architecture*, arguably the most influential and widely commented treatise of the 'new' architecture, he put forward a conception of architectural agency that straddled design and construction, rationality and emotion, the part and the whole, setting a new and hugely influential benchmark of how complex ideas about architecture could be communicated in an affective, intellectually expansive and visually sumptuous format (Curtis, 1986, 28–37). His modular approach to architectural design was evident in the ways in which he developed a number of elemental units (the typologies of the *Maison Citrohan* and *Dom-Ino* cubes; the use of pilotis to lift the building and keep the ground free; the vertical integration of patio space; the free, flexible facade; the interior open, equally flexible plan) that supplied the units for a number of different scenarios of horizontal and vertical scaling. These formed the basis of pretty much every project that he undertook, with varying degrees of success, throughout the 1920s – from individual buildings (Cook

House; Villa Stein and Savoie; the two houses that he designed at the Weissenhof estate in Stuttgart) to whole settlements like Pessac; from low-cost to bespoke, luxury housing; from dwelling shells to stacked villas (*immeubles-villas* (Schnoor and Kromrei, 2013)). As Le Corbusier explained in the buildup to the 1925 Exhibition of Decorative Arts in Paris, his architectural programme encompassed 'every detail of household furnishing, the street as well as the house, and a wider world still beyond' (Curtis, 1986, 46).

Le Corbusier proceeded with what can be described as a unique translation of minimalism from the aesthetic idiom to its disaggregation into elemental components ruled by precise rational and utilitarian design logic (Blake, 1960, 14–19). It is in this context that Pier Vittorio Aureli has reappraised the Maison Dom-Ino (1914), a project developed with post-First World War reconstruction in mind and one that Le Corbusier himself described as 'the pure and total design of a whole building system' (Corbusier and Jeanneret, 1946, 22). For Aureli, this was above all an elemental form and structure of enclosure produced through a series of extreme reductions in design and construction processes, followed by their rendering into residential plan. The tabula rasa of the empty (floor-less) prototype not only served the intentions of adaptability (by the planner and the resident) and scaleability but also emphasized how design minimalism was intricately linked to the deliberate emptying of the domestic space from the social and cultural accretions of the past. Its blank canvas was a generic, rationally derived shell ready to be filled by the instances of the 'new' world that he, like other modernists, so passionately evangelized (Gregh, 1979; Aureli, 2014). The perspective drawing of the empty two-storey concrete rectangular prism with which the Maison Dom-Ino has been most closely associated underlines Le Corbusier's approach to minimalism as a design method and its product as a prototype mould, not a finished architectural artefact and even less so a strict architectural and design canon (Picon, 2014; Eisenman, 2014, 142).

Minimalism went a step further in Le Corbusier's designs for the Maison Citrohan, dating back to 1919–20 and presented in prototypical model form at the 1922 exhibition of the *Salon d'Automne* in Paris. Unlike Dom-Ino, the Maison Citrohan was presented as a formed habitation: although still conceived as a simple concrete cube, its interior was structured into more familiar functional subdivisions (the double-height living room, the bedrooms on the second floor and the guest rooms on the top floor). In addition, the model emphasized a number of other characteristics, such as the pilotis (in the 1922 version), the roof patio and the enlarged horizontal windows that Le Corbusier would soon formulate into his five points of architecture (Moos, 2009, 79–80). Absolute purity of forms, precise standardization of components and extreme design efficiency that referenced the modern industrial logic of car production combined with projections of optimal biological, sociological and psychological functions of habitation. But it was the way in which Le Corbusier justified his design that disclosed more accurately his idiosyncratic understanding of 'minimum':

> Until now, a dwelling has been made out of an inconsistent grouping of many large rooms; in the rooms there was always too much space and always not enough space. Today, fortunately, we no longer have enough money to carry on with

these uses and as we do not want to consider the problem in its true light (living machine – *machine à habiter*) we cannot build in cities and a disastrous crisis ensues. ... Since the price of the building has increased fourfold, it is necessary to reduce by half the outdated pretensions of architecture and at least by half the [size of the] cube of the houses. From now on, the problem is in the hands of the technical expert: we need to call upon the breakthroughs of industry and change our mindset completely. And the beauty? There is always [beauty] where there is the intention and the means to achieve proportion .... One should not be ashamed of living in a house without a pointed roof, with smooth walls like metal sheets and windows like those of factories. But what we can be proud of is having a house as serviceable as a typewriter.

(Corbusier, 1924, 200–1; emphasis added)

Here were the familiar categories of the time-old housing calculus – but turned upside-down. Size reduction mutated into a positive and intentional strategy of rupture with the past and liberation from the cultural and social conventions that had stifled innovation. The real deficit, according to Le Corbusier, was not size reduction but its opposite – the progressive enlargement of the dwelling according to the logic of bourgeois notions of domesticity, as marker of social status, that had resulted in a chaotic accumulation of spaces, rooms and objects that cluttered space and disrupted domestic life. Thus, designing for the absolute 'minimum' in volume, plan, construction process and fittings only made sense if the starting point was the empty, austere shell. Improved affordability was a necessity, a motivation for design innovation and a desirable outcome of this radical design process but far from its sole or primary driver. Instead minimalism served as a positive choice geared towards the promotion of a completely new conception of habitation and living.

Le Corbusier's influence on the history of the 'minimum dwelling', not to mention in terms of shaping CIAM's programmatic agenda, remains as complex and divisive nowadays as it was in the 1920s and 1930s. He was as consistent and passionate a proponent of the 'new' architecture's alchemical potential as few within the ranks of the modernist movement. A particular section in his Towards a New Architecture treatise suggestively titled 'Architecture or Revolution' and his subsequent incongruous political misalliances during the 1920s and 1930s (Fishmann, 1982, 182–7; McLeod, 1983; Antliff, 2001; Jarcy, 2015; Perelman, 2015) have supported an interpretation of his propagation of a 'new' architecture as an ideologically charged counter-revolutionary strategy (Brott, 2013; Brott, 2016; Brott, 2017; Brott, 2017). Nevertheless, the Le Corbusian vision assumed far more primary architectural agency in the production of the revolutionary 'new' world than most of his CIAM fellow travellers were willing to countenance. His belief in the transformative power of mechanization, radical design innovation and rigorously rational reappraisal of the entire context of living (including habitation but as unit of a much wider system of urban planning) placed him on the utopian edges of the spectrum of programmatic views expressed in the ranks of CIAM in the 1920s. His suggestion that design and process – arguably the two least probed variables of the housing calculus until the interwar years [see Chapter 1] – could alchemise that elusive utopian condition of 'more with less for all' reflected an unconditional conviction that architecture could become more revolutionary than any political or social revolution (Jameson, 1985, 71).

A further standard objection raised against Le Corbusier's (as well as Mies', Gropius's and other modernist pioneers') approach to 'minimum' was that it promoted a 'minimalist' design of objects, forms and entire houses that was otherwise geared to individualism and luxury – less strictly rational than a mere excuse to turn an engineered semblance of simplicity into conspicuous consumption (Schuldenfrei, 2018, 182–3). Undoubtedly, his experiments with reducing objects and building forms to a 'minimum' very often resulted in designs, models and sketches that appeared to shun affordability. His reworking of the Citrohan prototype for the Weissenhof housing exhibition in Stuttgart (Figure 4.1) morphed into the most grotesquely expensive dwelling in an estate that was already far costlier than what even an average family could afford at the time (Jackson, 2016, 25). Contemporary criticisms noted that the fittings inside most dwellings resembled traditional artistic artefacts than machine-produced mass consumer products, more akin to the tastes of the 'middle class than to the precepts of functionalism'.[4] Even his prototype designs for the supposedly affordable *Maison Loucheur* in France skirted the ceiling of stipulated cost (Benton, 1984, 58). Le Corbusier defended the real-life character

**Figure 4.1** Le Corbusier's housing designs for the Weissenhof settlement in Stuttgart [Source: Author's photo].

of his two houses in the estate by pointing to their suitability for 'many normal families'. Every habitation, he argued, was assembled from the same pool of elemental design elements just like all words are composed from the same alphabet, regardless of its size, configuration or interior design.[5] As a result his two Weissenhof dwellings bespoke the same understanding of human habitation needs based on a flexible minimum that was at the same time proposed as the basis for an optimum conception of domestic life. He thus turned the process of deriving mass affordable housing solutions upside down using the Maison Citrohan prototype as an optimum 'model' that suggested a wide range of other results – smaller or larger, more or less costly but essentially derived from the same type and logic of habitation (Corbusier and Jeanneret, 1946, 150).

## The private cell, the public sphere and what lies in between

In his various designs for different housing prototypes and projects Le Corbusier used the metaphor of the 'cell' (*cellule*) as the smallest possible enclosure for optimum habitation, by which he meant the satisfaction of elevated 'basic' needs – both physiological, such as light and air – and psychological – such as isolation and relaxation (Moos, 2009, 143). His cell was the realization of the minimum of habitation in space and volume. It included the provision for basic functions mapped onto the internal space but it was a complete, self-referential minimum system of design and construction as an emptied three-dimensional container. The experience of the medieval monastic cell unit that he encountered during one of his early trips to Italy exerted a lasting fascination on him that surfaced in his textual descriptions of many projects that he built in the interwar years (Leatherbarrow, 2017, 95). These cells underpinned his design philosophy and descriptive language in relation to a series of subsequent projects, from the houses of his *Plan Voisin* to the student accommodation of the Pavillon Suisse (1930–32) and the dwelling units of the *Cité de Refuge* Salvation Army hostel (1932–33) in Paris and his postwar *Unité d'Habitation* in Marseilles (Rendell, 2017, 81–96). His project for the Fruges quarter in Pessac (1924–26) provides a snapshot of how a basic (5 m × 5 m) prefabricated 'cell' as empty unit mass could then be externally modified, proportionately scaled up (or down if needed) or stacked in a number of different configurations (Lévy, 1988; Hsu and Shih, 2006).

The trope of the dwelling as an elemental and intentionally minimal 'cell' was familiar to, and cherished by, many of Le Corbusier's avant-garde contemporaries. Ludwig Hilberseimer used the term to indicate the basic unit of design (the individual room) that served as the primary module of architectural scaling and unified programmatically the entire urban scale (Hilberseimer, 1927, 182; Tafuri, 1969; McEwan, 2018, 92). Marcel Breuer based his designs for minimum apartments exhibited at the Parisian *Salon des Artistes Décorateurs Français* in 1930 on the 'dwelling cell' (*Wohnzelle*) as the basis of a new conception of urban habitation based on the typology of the hotel or the boarding house.[6] Hans Schmidt considered the 'room cell' (*Raumzelle*) as a minimum, standardized and industrially (re-)produced, shell for dwelling design, offering unique advantages in terms of functional innovation and affordability (Huber, 1993, 24). The idea of a clearly defined living cell, strictly individual and private, as the minimum of residential enclosure was also invoked by Soviet architects in the 1920s such as Nikolay Milyutin, Ivan Nikolayev and Moisei Ginzburg (Buchli, 1998; Buchli, 1999, 65; Shvidkovskiĭ, 2007, 359), as well as by radical avant-garde modernists with strong ideological affinity with the Soviet revolutionary experiment such as Hannes Meyer and Karel Teige (Aureli, 2017, 28–30). Moreover, Walter Gropius based his elaborate sociological analysis of minimum habitation on the importance of an individual 'dwelling ration' (*Ration Wohnung*) (Gropius, 1930, 26–7). This was also a primary concern in Ernst May's attempts to re-imagine the conventional reduced-size dwelling (Kleinwohnung) typology as a minimum-optimum of affordable modern habitation for his Frankfurt residential projects in the 1920s (Mumford, 2000, 31).

Yet the emergence of the figurative lingua franca of the 'cell' belied the very different programmatic positions of the architects who invoked it in the 1920s. For Le Corbusier the 'cell' was the product of a technical and biological conception of the 'minimum'. His gospel of external isolation and internal lighting and respiration led him to a sophisticated technological approach to the problem of minimum habitation but his quest for universally applicable processes and standards shaded the sociological parameters of the discussion out of the picture. The users of his dwellings were only impressionistically factored in the discussion, without much of a social background or cultural legacies and with limited reflection on the realities of social inequality that posed the problem of the good-quality/low-cost mass habitation in the first place (Uhlig et al., 1994, 58–62). This supra-ideological dimension largely explains the fact that his ideas and designs attracted the attention of as ideologically diverse audiences as the Soviet constructivists (Cohen, 1992) and the Italian rationalists, the latter perceiving their role as serving the interests of the Fascist revolutionary project (Rifkind, 2012; Brott, 2013; Billiani and Pennacchietti, 2019, 73–87). However, this was not the way in which many of his avant-garde modernist peers in the 1920s understood and addressed the problem of the minimum dwelling. For them the quest for a new 'minimum' was not primarily a technical or design conundrum, even if both these variables were recognized as having critical significance in the process. In spite of their ideological and programmatic differences Gropius, Schmidt, May or Mart Stam within CIAM, as well as Soviet architects in the 1920s, approached the question of the 'minimum dwelling' as an integral part of modern architecture's social moment. Their 'revolution' lay in proposing the new 'minimum' in habitation as part, however critical, of a loop of social, political and anthropological transformations in-the-making, in which the dwelling both captured radical shifts already happening and foreshadowed, anticipated or expedited the processes of radical societal transformation.

It is in this context that Hannes Meyer published the provocative image of his so-called 'Co-op Room' (*Co-op Zimmer*) in 1926 (Figure 4.2). The staged photograph of a sparse single room with a low bed frame, one open and another folded chair, a table with a gramophone, a shelf on the wall and a caption reading 'The Dwelling' was used by Meyer as illustration for his article titled 'The New World' (*Die Neue Welt*).[7] The text referenced architecture only tangentially. It read like a panegyric on the constructivist

**Figure 4.2** Hannes Meyer's 'Co-op Zimmer: Interior' (1926). Vintage print, 16.1 × 16.3 cm [Source: *Galerie Berinson*, Berlin].

spirit of the 1920s ('Today every phase of our culture of expression is predominantly constructive'); a Futurist celebration of speed ('we live faster and therefore longer. We have a keener sense of speed than ever before, and speed records are a direct gain for all'); a call to dissolve all sorts of traditional boundaries – of space, states, forms of art, areas of productive activity, 'high' art and everyday material life; an evocative depiction of a new, liberated, mobile human ('the semi-nomad of our modern productive system has the benefit of freedom of movement') living in a rapidly dissolving old world on the exhilarating cusp of new forms, new processes, new modes of expression and new spaces ('yesterday is dead'); and an elegy to mechanization, standardization and industrial efficiency as the absolute matrix for the 'new world' that the article referenced in its title. For Meyer the role of the architect and the artist was to ride the constructive wave, turn their backs on the past, purge their minds from the 'knowledge of the past [that] is a burden weighing upon us', and become the engineers and producers of the 'new world … with the means of today' (Djalali, 2015).

The contents of Meyer's Co-op Room illustrated a modicum of 'basic' physiological (protection, sleep, heat, rest) and psychological (the gramophone) needs. If what was shown, however, was the author's figurative and polemical image of a future single minimum cell for the modern ascetic 'nomad', what of the other 'needs' that were either absent or only elliptically referenced on the photograph? Here Meyer's own background as an architect who made his name through a series of innovative projects for the Freidorf co-operative settlement in Basel in 1919–21 (Hays, 1995, 85–7), where he lived until 1926, provides important clues. His mottos 'co-operation rules the world' and 'the community rules the individual' embedded his image of the minimum Co-op Room into a broader shift away from traditional economic processes and social norms towards a 'new' world of collective living as a positive aspiration. Freidorf was conceived by Meyer as a practical model of a co-operative garden suburb of about 620 inhabitants, living in low-rise row houses designed in close collaboration with the architect and organized around a central square and play zone. Communal facilities for schooling and day care, guest facilities and various meeting and activity premises were housed in a large central co-operative building (*Genossenschaftshaus*) constructed in 1922–4. At the time Freidorf was portrayed as a model intentional community reflecting the benefits of co-operation as the threshold to a more collective form of living.[8] It was there that Meyer experimented with the technical side of building standardization alongside his social concern for a co-operative version of the conventional garden-city paradigm (Panerai et al., 2004, 108). But while his commitment to standardization and Taylorization grew in his subsequent architectural work, the co-operative dimension was absorbed into a revolutionary socialist outlook that marked his later design practice at the Bauhaus (1927–30) and eventually in the Soviet Union (1930–6) (Dearstyne, 1986, 206–19; Bosma, 2014; Djalali, 2015; Poerschke, 2014, 104–15; Tomita et al., 2014). Freidorf represented a more modest negotiation of individual, community and public spheres, seeking to strengthen the role of the intentional (co-operative) community while preserving the traditional role of the family unit in the private domestic domain. It remained an island of exception that could only have a limited effect on the world beyond the triangular plot of the settlement. Gradually Meyer became convinced that design abstraction, technical innovation and the embrace of industrialization could not by themselves produce a new architecture capable of serving the 'needs of the people' (*Volksbedarf*):

> [this realisation] forced me to give up the errors of my former liberal and reform-minded interpretation of social conditions. It was a step-by-step process, as I had been particularly exposed to such interpretations through my professional connections with neutral co-operative movements and with independent trade-unionism. ... Some of us 'progressive architects' ... strove to 'give form to the functions of society through its buildings'. ... By this attitude we architects brought the social factor to the fore as the chief determinant of architecture and called this architecture 'functional', although actually it was at the service of a social apparatus that is more and more evidently falling apart. No wonder that this attempt to reform bourgeois architecture ran aground ...[9]

The conclusion that he reached was that the family unit, traditionally seen as the 'building block of bourgeois society', was rapidly losing its economic and social significance. Thus, the role of the 'new' architecture was to move beyond the token 'reformism' of the bourgeois collective forms (the philanthropic compounds; the commercially run boarding houses and hostels; the centralized heating systems, kitchens and modicum of social services in many functional residential blocks or settlements). The 'collective dwelling of the future' would reflect and accelerate these processes along the road that led to the constitution of a new society. The illustrated cell was the new absolute minimum space of habitation rediscovered amidst the wreckage of the earlier sacrosanct bourgeois notion of domestic privacy. It also signified the emergent, entirely re-engineered 'new world' where conventional notions of privacy had became intentionally eviscerated in favour of socialized forms of life and familial domesticity had been superseded by collective organization. Outside of the cell the modern person would cease to be a private or semi-private one and enter the public sphere without intricate staged transitions or overwrought spatial negotiations. The new socialized world had to be organized on the basis of how a series of diverse groups and individuals united by the physical proximity of their habitation and by varying social ties straddled, tempered and re-negotiated the public–private dichotomy (Chermayeff and Alexander, 1963). Rather than being limited, incidental or transitional, the sphere of collective life graduated into the fulcrum of the new social organization, in the process subsuming and transforming functions and spaces traditionally embedded in bourgeois domesticity.

## The Soviet experience: Pursuing the minimum in utopia

If Meyer's view of an architecture serving and accelerating a new, egalitarian and collectivized socialist society was a minority proposition in the West during the 1920s, it referenced a conversation that was already in full swing in the Soviet Union at the time. A number of architects and urban theorists proposed a wide spectrum of design solutions that, while addressing the mounting housing emergency and the lack of funds, sought to give concrete form to the utopia of a collectively organized society. The goal itself, the desired social destination of the revolution, was not at stake. Instead their main conundrum was how this ideal new society could be best achieved, how the change could be fast-tracked and what agency architecture had in this process. Initial ideas for addressing the housing question sought to adapt tried-and-tested models of either de-centralization through garden cities and peripheral settlements or high-density/-rise urban concentration (Movilla Vega, 2020, 1–2). These measures, however, were treated as little more than stop-gap palliatives until more radical interventions were forthcoming (Buchi 1998: 160–1). With the Five-Year Plan (1928–32) providing the political momentum for change, the Soviet Constructivist avant-garde led the chorus of voices that called for an immediate leap into utopian self-realization.

A series of projects and competitions in the mid- and late 1920s scoped out a range of solutions provided that these could be linked one way or another to the ideological orthodoxies of Marxism-Leninism, the priorities of the Stalinist policies and the Soviet revolutionary discourse. Unsurprisingly collectivized life gained a totemic status in this discussion (Willimott, 2017, 440). The question was posed as such: should the collectivized society be immediately assumed to be the sole guiding principle of residential architecture that would catalyse a total revolution in the primary realm of everyday life or should the process of change be managed over years, decades even, to proceed in tandem with social education and cultural transformation (Andrusz, 1984, 114–15)? The two tendencies fought an ideological and intellectual battle over the ownership of the revolutionary project, soliciting competitions that were called to re-imagine a 'new life' and a 'new Soviet person'. In his 1929 *Socialist Cities* treatise, Leonid Sabsovich proposed a fully-fledged collectivized domestic sphere that denied any space (literally as well as figuratively) to the traditional family unit and granted only a modicum of privacy to the individual (Cooke, 2005, 32). The future of the new socialist city, he argued, was there and then – and anything from the provision and consumption of food to the raising of children would be fully socialized and organized efficiently in large complexes that addressed all the needs of the worker's everyday life. As for private space, Sabsovich suggested that a minimal enclosed 'cell' of just 4–5 m² and equipped with only a modicum of functional, space-saving furniture be made available to each worker for strictly individual use. This cell(ular) imagined space – anonymous, fiercely egalitarian and minimum ad extremis – appeared as an even more reduced and expunged version of Meyer's interior. In both cases the radical reduction of space, amenities and 'art' that it entailed was a projection of a new conception of minimalism that was transformative rather than reactive, utopian even as it responded to pressing economic and political contingencies. For Sabsovich the cell represented the smallest autonomous space of the revolution; a test tube in the vast and complex experimental apparatus developed in order to reform everyday life that also included new containers dedicated to work, food, hygiene, education, recreation, exercise, socialization and so on – all intended to catalyse a new revolutionary consciousness. As such it was conceivable in, and because of, the new, vast, multi-functional and de-centred organism of collective life (DeHaan, 2013, 43–7).

It is far from coincidental that the debate on the optimal form of habitation was a subset of a broader, increasingly acrimonious conversation about the merits and pitfalls of urbanization. The city of the past, it was argued, was steeped in capitalist patterns of exploitation that the Soviet state aimed to obliterate. Similarly, the private dwelling belonged to the superseded bourgeois epoch that would be overwritten by the 'new life' (*novyi byt*) engineered by the revolution. As for the family, the conventional unit of dwelling residents, it was now deemed to reproduce traditional forms of oppression that the revolution sought to supplant with the emergence of the liberated 'new Soviet person'. When the head of the Organisation of Contemporary Architects *Organizatsiya Sovremmennaia Arkhitektura*, OSA Moisei Ginzburg met with Le Corbusier in Moscow in 1928, he pointed out to him that, unlike the 'new architecture' in Western countries, architects in the Soviet Union had the advantage of the revolutionary reality in their favour. This allowed them, he argued, to proceed more daringly and build completely new forms of habitation, settlement and social organization (Cooke, 2005, 30–1). The optimal solution was to be found in novel spatial constellations of everyday life that arranged and connected all these pieces into organic, functional, as well as ideologically orthodox super-containers. It was in this context of radical disaggregation and re-aggregation of everyday life into a new collective organism that the new housing type of the *domkommuna* emerged in the Soviet Union in the second half of the 1920s. When, in 1926, OSA's journal Contemporary Architecture (*Sovremmennaia Arkhitektura*, SA) announced an ideas-'friendly' competition for a worker's housing prototype (Figure 4.3), the phrase 'organic condition' was deliberately used in the accompanying brief to describe the nature and scale of the project in mind. Every component of the project was to be studied individually and then assembled into an integrated revolutionary ensemble. Submissions were expected to advance innovative solutions that could promote and accelerate the sweeping goals of the reform of Soviet everyday life. The backdrop of the competition, however, was dire: the cumulative results of the collapse of housing construction during the sequence of savage wars combined with a massive population influx into the cities after the end of the Civil War and the new Soviet state's severe shortage of financial resources to produce an unprecedented housing crisis. Thus the 1926 competition tempered its utopian subtext with an overarching rationale of practical necessity and austerity. The challenge was to come up with solutions to re-design single-family dwellings that cost no more than a family room in a communal apartment and functioned better as a transitional arrangement to the future utopia of the novyi byt. The eight architects' responses[10] featured a series of communal facilities and spaces, proposed in the spirit of purging the legacies of bourgeois life and responding to the need for economies that would allow the expansion of a programme of good-quality housing for the masses. They also approached the brief from the 'transitional' perspective, in most instances incorporating private cooking facilities in the proposed dwelling typologies. They diverged, however, in terms of the best strategy to manage the pace and process of transformation, as well as the optimal scale of the dwelling solutions and building configurations of the private-collective ensemble (Crawford, 2014; Movilla Vega, 2020, 2–5).

The 1926 competition convinced the newly established Building Committee of the Russian Republic (*Stroitel'nyi komitet*, Stroikom) to establish a new commission tasked with extrapolating standardized dwelling typologies, with OSA playing a key role in the process. The result was a series of dwelling types (from single 'cell' to a multi-room apartment) tested against six basic distribution and 'stacking' schemes (A-F) forming residential blocks that assumed diverse scenarios of collective living (Movilla Vega, 2020, 7). The study used rigorous scientific methods and benchmarks (e.g. volumetric efficiency) to test various design, distributional, and grouping hypotheses and to allow useful comparisons on the basis of plans and tabulated data. As befitting the 'transitional' character of the projects for which they were designed, the dwelling types were flexible and adaptable. They covered the widest range of living scenarios – from single-person 'cells' (in some cases as small as 6–8 m$^2$) to multi-room 'family' apartments; from 'sleeping cabins' with shared amenities to fully equipped, self-contained dwelling units; and from a fully collectivized residential block to a more conventionally private family living arrangement. More than the size of each dwelling, it was the kitchen – whether it was included or not; and, if provided, its dimensions, placement within the dwelling, and level of amenities

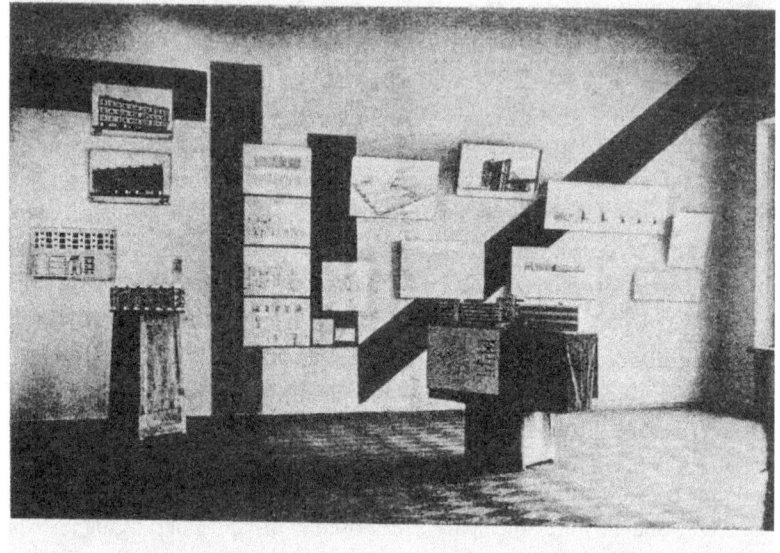

**Figure 4.3** Exhibition of the designs for OSA's 1926 'friendly competition' for a worker's housing prototype [Source: *Sovremennaja Arhitektura (SA)* 1927/4–5: 129].

## The 'Minimum Dwelling' as Utopia

that it offered (autonomous space or niche or the minimal kitchen cabinet) – that emerged as one of the key differentiators across dwelling and block typologies.

The entire Stroikom typology was based on a strict modular analogy: using volumetric efficiency as benchmark, each dwelling unit was disassembled and recomposed from individual 'cellular' components and then scaled up in horizontal and vertical aggregations to building organisms. In its diverse typological articulations across the A-F matrix, the metaphor of the 'cell' was the single most significant innovation of the Stroikom research (Figure 4.4). The radical proposition of the one-room cellular variants (A-1/C-1/F-1) lay in recognizing the individual cell as the smallest, irreducible building block of a new vision of optimal collectivized living. Sleep, intermittent relaxation, personal reflection and a minimum space for keeping personal belongings were imported into the cell, while the rest of the physiological, sociological and psychological needs would be satisfied through an optimal combination of collective and shared facilities within an efficient radius from the cell itself.

Individual cells based on the Type-E prototypes were the most potent catalysts for *byt* reform. In one project for an experimental dom-kommuna by Stroikom architects Mikhail Barshch and Vladimir Vladimirov, adult accommodation (Figure 4.5) was to be provided in variants of the Type-E spatial scheme, with a complex hierarchy of shared-access spaces organized within and across the different buildings of the complex. Designed for a population of 1680 people, the project envisaged a separation according to age (adults in one block; children distributed into two buildings, one for school-age

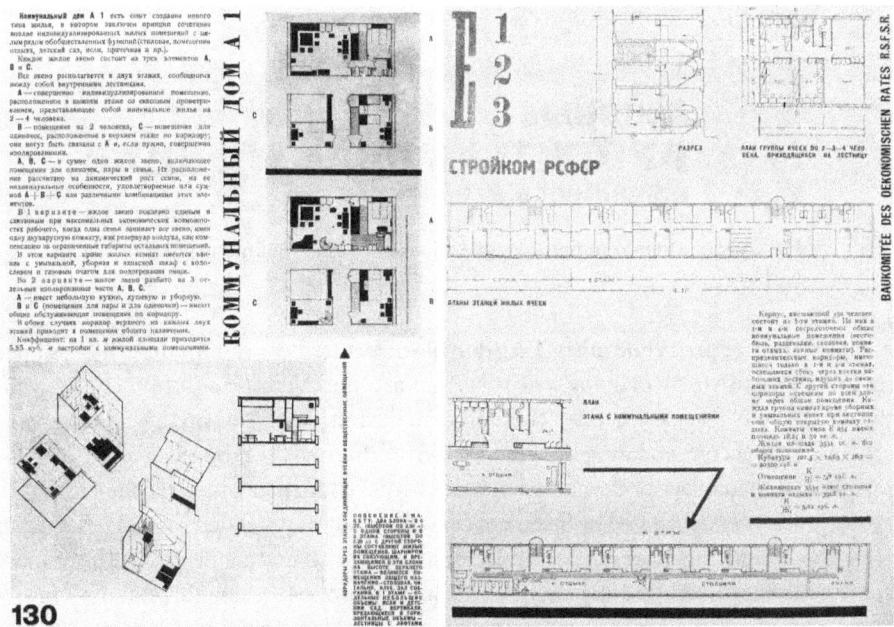

**Figure 4.4** Stroikom typologies A1 and E1/2/3 [Source: *SA* 1929/1: 19 & *SA* 1927/4–5: 130].

**Figure 4.5** Dom-kommuna design by Braschsch and Vladimorov [Source: SA 1929/2: 41–3].

and the other for pre-school age). The adult block featured E-1 minimum 'cells' designed for individual use (6 m² of living space plus sanitary unit (Vujosevic, 2013, 741–2)), while the other two blocks destined for children used dormitories based on the Type-F spatial scheme, each accommodating between 28 and 30 children. But the balance between the private and the collective domains was stretched even further in one of the residential group prototypes developed by Stroikom (E-1-2-3), a block intended for 450 inhabitants. Here the Type-E units were specifically designed for shared adult use, with the floor space of the unit adjusted accordingly (17 m² for two, 24 m² for three and 30 m² for four). Such an adaptation of a 'cell' originally designed for individual use as the basis for a minimal shared arrangement deprived the enclosure of its modicum of privacy even in relation to rest, relaxation or personal hygiene. This arrangement represented the closest that the Stroikom experiments came to a fully-fledged collectivized and communal residential space, where not only the family but the very notion of minimum privacy had been obliterated, with their associated functions re-distributed in structures of shared and collective living (Movilla Vega, 2015, 257–8). In contrast to Sabsovich's minimum 'sleeping cabin', the communal version of the Type-E unit (E-1-2-3) intentionally disembowelled the last vestiges of privacy. This had two significant implications: first, it allowed the extreme physical shrinking of private space – not only in its familial variant but also in terms of the personal 'ration' – and reduced habitation to an anonymous space with little or intentionally no affective qualities; and second, it went hand-in-hand with the most radical re-distribution of basic needs to an actively communal/collective domain, which replaced the traditional familial habitation as the non-public hub of life, and diffused their satisfaction from the concentrated dwelling space to a number of inter-related spaces. If anything, the needs that were recognized as minimum, basic, important or even desirable became in theory extended; it was dwelling as a private or semi-private space that was dissociated from most – and in some cases nearly all – of them.

The most emblematic of OSA's dom-kommuna, the Narkomfin that Ginzburg designed together with Ignatii Milinis and the engineer Sergei Prokhorov (Figure 4.6), straddled the categories of a prototype, a model and an experiment precisely because it negotiated the tension between pragmatism and utopia, process and outcome, 'transitional' present and 'optimal' future. Divided into functional blocks (one for living, another for communal facilities, a third one for centralized mechanical services and a fourth one for the raising of the children), it featured a combination of private, semi-private and variable communal spaces, each with its precise transitional logic, subsumed into the overarching logic of the organic ensemble (Buchli, 1998; Buchli, 2017). Dwellings were of four main types, differentiated by size, intended use and facilities. The F-type was

**Figure 4.6** Narkomfin apartments in Moscow, arch. Moisei Ginzburg and Ignatii Milinis (1928–29) [Source: Robert Byron's photographs].

the smallest (36 m²) and assumed extensive use of collective facilities by the users. The other two – the fully-fledged privatized family K-type and the 2F (volumetrically double F cells for larger families but with the addition of privatized utilities) – provided some form of kitchen space and extended up to 90 m². All these units had private bathrooms and separated bedrooms, with the main living room differentiated by function (eating, work, relaxation). Dormitory-style minimal cells, by contrast, were single-room units without kitchen facilities but easy access to separate communal spaces; only one of these types featured a private bathroom (Rendell, 2017, 33–49). All dwelling types gravitated towards a minimum: spatial arrangements were strictly determined by the most efficient satisfaction of physiological and psychological needs (e.g. east-west orientation, thoughtful use of colour), amenities were economical (e.g. use of foldable and multi-purpose furniture) and size was kept under strictly functional control. Yet the minimalism of Narkomfin's dwelling units was tempered by the collective provisions in the other blocks and served as a physical mini-rehearsal of the desired optimum of fully-fledged collective living.

One of the penthouse apartments of Narkomfin's residential block was reserved for the economist Nikolay Alexandrovich Milyutin. Milyutin rose to the important position of Commissar of Finance of the Soviet Union in 1924–29. In this capacity he was one of the prominent and authoritative figures in the debates about urbanization, housing construction and the new Soviet *byt* in the 1920s and 1930s. He was a strong believer in the benefits of socialized living but belonged to those who argued for a slower, more pragmatic and less ideological transitional approach (Kopp, 1970, 185; Andrusz, 1984, 115). It was Milyutin who had commissioned the construction of Narkomfin in the first place and his wish for such a bespoke apartment unit sacrificed the rooftop solarium featured in Ginzburg's original plan. Milyutin had written extensively about dwelling cells and new concepts of habitation, culminating in his book *Sotsgodor: The Problem of Building Socialist Cities*. He devoted a significant portion of his analysis to the 'living cell', a strictly personal space (in contrast to most of the 'cells' in the Stroikom-OSA dom-kommunas that indicated dwelling units) with which he associated a specific minimum set of individual needs such as sleep, retreat, personal hygiene, reading and safe-keeping of personal items. In its minimum conception this cell would occupy a surface area of just 8.4 m² and barely 22 m³ in volume, although it could be extended when economic and other practical considerations permitted it. A strong and consistent proponent of the *novyi byt*, Milyutin defended his hostility to the traditional institution of the family as a significant obstacle to the promotion of collective living according to the ideological precepts of communism. The personal cell existed, in his view, as the only defensible space of minimum individual privacy, beyond which there was no other diaphragm or intermediation between the Soviet person and the collective-public domain (Milyutin, 1975).

On their part OSA architects defended the ideological validity of their dom-kommuna projects by presenting them as 'social condensers'. The term paid direct tribute to the modern technological advances of electricity and machine. Just like electronic condensers channelled the current and multiplied its power, their social translations would shape and intensify the transition to the desired destination of a radically new communist society (Clark, 1995, 231; Cooke, 1995, 112–13). As Ginzburg stressed,

> this task of life-construction, the task of creating social condensers for our epoch, receives its completion only by being crystallised in particular material forms, vestured in flesh and blood; and by embodying a new set of architectural features impacting on human psychology and sensually perceived by it. The task of life-construction, having started with the organisation of forms for the new life, of new *byt* and labour processes, concludes with the materialisation and figuration of architectural objects – spatial containers for these forms of new life.[11]

Distillation into physical, organized, integrated form and amplification of the momentum for individual as well as societal transformation: here was the succinct expression of the social condenser's concatenation of minima and maxima. The resulting forms posited a new role for the revolutionary architect as a formidable social alchemist, with the power to transform humble materials (the minima) into new potent forms with exponential effects (maxima) and then to convert them into a social panacea (absolute and unconditional optimum, ergo utopia).

## The 'dwelling ration': Social utopia in disguise

In 1928 Karel Teige argued that real 'freedom consists in leaving the home'. He became convinced that post-revolutionary architectural innovations in the Soviet Union paved the way for an impending utopia of dwelling 'without incarcerating walls' in a fully collectivized modern socialist society. Just like the foundation of family life, the very idea of privacy inside the dwelling now had to be questioned as yet another outdated legacy of the bourgeois world (Häußermann and Siebel, 2021). The 'cell' analogy was interesting in this respect because it offered the possibility of an – minimal and functionally residual – individual (semi-)private space within this new collective universe without the intermediate stage of a conventional group-private family abode (Chermayeff and Alexander, 1963, 121; Nerdinger, 2013). In his view the Soviet housing experiments in the 1920s mapped the entire spectrum of transformative possibilities all the way to the total obliteration of the private and family domains in pursuit of full-scale collective living – especially in the early, fully socialized Soviet 'communal apartments' (*Kommunalka*) and the youth communes (Schlögel, 1998; Pott, 2009; Messana, 2011; Evans, 2014).

Teige was critical of fellow modernist architects in Europe because he believed that they had sought to revolutionize the dwelling without first challenging its traditional association with the private enclosure of the family unit or its menagerie of bourgeois domesticity.[12] And yet the Western architects mentioned by Teige in his critique had already grappled in their work with the notion of the individual private cell-like space in relation to public-private domain of habitation. At the 1929 CIAM2 congress in Frankfurt key figures of the group such as Sigfried Giedion, Gropius and Schmidt reflected on the future optimal role of the private dwelling in relation to both the public-private and the private-family-public axes. In this context the terminology of the 'dwelling ration' (*Ration Wohnung*) was used to designate a minimum of personal space within the dwelling. This ration encapsulated the idea of a modicum of privacy and individual self-fulfilment as a spatial and organizational expression of an egalitarian and inalienable right for all those living together and the surest guarantee that the dwelling arrangements were capable of satisfying their real biological, sociological and psychological needs of the individual as well as the family unit. Like a 'cell' but more conceptual and flexible than physical and associated more positively with personal needs, the 'dwelling ration' was integrated into a hierarchy of domestic spaces that sought to reconcile the private functions of the dwelling enclosure with an increasing, again affirmative emphasis on communal life. Peter Sloterdijk highlighted the sociological differences between Soviet modernism's focus on the collective sphere and western modernism's focus on privacy in the dwelling but also their critical equivalence:

> Just as Soviet modernism was condensed into the myth of the communal apartment, which was to be the press that would mint a New Man fit for the collective, so too does Western modernism gather itself under the myth of the [private] apartment, where the liberated individual, who has been made flexible by flows of capital, devotes himself to the cultivation of his relationship to himself.
> (Sloterdijk and Fabricius, 2007, 89–90)

In his preface to the published proceedings of CIAM's 1929 Frankfurt congress (see Chapter 5), Giedion used the 'ration' trope twice. On the one hand, his motto 'every person must be allocated their own dwelling ration' (Giedion, 1930, 8) used the same cell-like trope to describe it as a space inside the dwelling enclosure, twice removed from the non-private sphere (the outside public as well as the other members of the household). On the other hand, he described the congress goal as determining the 'smallest ration for dwelling' (*Mindestration Wohnung*) that guaranteed the satisfaction of biological and sociological human needs while being affordable and scalable as a mass resource. In spite of their semantic differences the two 'rations' shared a perception of the minimum as a positive and aspiration consideration – the former as a space of retreat and freedom for the individual, the latter as an enclosure that marked the boundary of the public sphere. In either of these two instances, and in contrast to the Soviet dom-kommuna typologies, domestic privacy was posited as an asset – its function emancipatory and constitutive of the person's autonomy, liberation and self-fulfilment, its status constitutive of the optimal dwelling itself. What had changed with the trope of the dwelling ration, however, was the rationale of the private-public threshold: conventionally used to demarcate the intimate domestic space from the outside world, it now ran through it and generated a novel assemblage of transitional spaces between the individual, the family and the public sphere (Sloterdijk and Fabricius, 2007, 92).

The individual dwelling ration did not need to be (and in fact was not typically envisioned as) a separate space physically demarcated and inaccessible to others; it could be carved from existing spaces of the dwelling in which the individual lived as a member of an intentional dwelling community. When Gropius or Schmidt invoked it as the only valid measure of the modern habitation, they meant that even the most affordable dwelling destined for those with the most restricted financial means ought to be determined by a minimum amount of space necessary for the comfortable satisfaction of every dweller's fundamental individual and collective needs (Gropius, 1930; Flierl, 1965). It represented the most elemental minimum of habitation, whose precise spatial value could not be fixed for all use cases (as we shall see, it was typically assumed to be 12–14 m$^2$ but in some cases it could be stretched into single figures). This is because the ration was determined by both measurable physiological standards (ventilation, illumination, insulation, mobility, hygiene) and sociological considerations (equality, independence, emancipation, leisure, enjoyment, self-fulfilment). Thus, it represented both quantity (space, air, light, heat, etc.) and quality (function, comfort, retreat, personal reproduction) in its most efficient and productive correlation. Whatever the actual numerical value ascribed to it, the figure could also form the guide for calculating the optimal minimum size for the dwelling depending on its residents: the numerical value assigned to the ration multiplied by the number of residents within the dwelling unit gave a rough guide for the optimal-minimum space.

Gropius's conception of the dwelling ration evolved continuously throughout the 1920s. He experimented with and adapted the sociological, technical and typological principles of his dwelling design philosophy. The fullest and most sophisticated presentation of his ideas came on the occasion of his contribution to the twentieth annual exhibition of the *Société des Artistes Décorateurs* held in Paris in 1930. Gropius, who curated the 'German Section' of the exhibition together with his former Bauhaus collaborators Marcel Breuer and László Moholy-Nagy, used the exhibition format to represent a quasi-utopian image of modern habitation derived from the methodical clustering of radically revised interior components – spaces and rooms, functions and uses, objects and subjective feel (MacCarthy, 2019, 229–30). There Gropius posited the 'dwelling ration' as a physically separate space for each member of the household. He also re-imagined the dwelling's living spaces as intermediate semi-communal areas for the semi-private family unit – a further positive nuancing of the transition from individual to family to public spaces. As he explained, these interim spaces – neither private for each individual nor public because they excluded those not belonging to the family – bespoke a radically new idea of living based on 'non-committal' forms of contact and co-presence.

Gropius's 1930 exhibit illustrated how the typology of the boarding house could be used to provide optimal 'dwelling rations' to each individual as well as harmonious spaces where residents could come together in various scenarios and degrees of intimacy when they desired so. Thus, there were installations of integrated living-sleeping rooms for individual men and women subtly joined with living and functional areas where they could congregate with other residents of the complex, reduced-size apartments for families without children, and a number of spectacular communal areas (bar, dancing room, study room, library, etc.) where larger groups of people could come together. The rooms could be experienced as self-referential spaces and, where appropriate, as

**Figure 4.7** Walter Gropius's ten-storey boarding-house building (exterior and interior common room) exhibited at the Werkbund 1930 exhibition in Paris [Source: *Die Form* 5/11–12 (1930): 283–5].

components of more complex spatial configurations that approximated a revised idea of the family dwelling enclosure. What brought all these rooms together, however, was Gropius's building 'container': a ten-storey urban apartment block that represented a normative shift to communal living (Overy, 2004) (Figure 4.7). The high-rise apartment block presented in Paris was Gropius's version of the 'social condenser' – a clustering of optimized spaces and functions that expressed in physical form and accelerated social change through a novel arrangement of individual, family and communal spaces (Miller, 2017).

Gropius's programmatic embrace of the 'dwelling ration', however, served a further significant goal. The choice of the word 'ration' bespoke a synergy of rationality, austerity and allowance. Beyond reflecting Gropius's optimism for the ability of the industrial methods of construction and design to enhance the efficiency of the construction process (Seelow, 2018), it also promoted an understanding of the modern dwelling as a positive social asset and a minimum right for every person, regardless of income, gender or age. This social dimension was indicated by the special meaning of 'ration' as limited but inalienable allowance, essential for the satisfaction of elevated personal needs. The title of an article that he authored for the Werkbund journal *Die Form* in 1926 revealed his order of priorities – 'how to construct cheaper, better, more beautiful dwellings'. Reduction in cost while maintaining high standards became the key that unlocked the social utopia of universal housing. His understanding of the dwelling as a technology of methodically putting together spatial and functional modular components into integrated ensembles intersected with his belief that only through public intervention and co-operative involvement could the new dwelling fulfil its social mission.[13] By eliminating excess and rationalizing design in order to improve dividends relating to quality of life the 'dwelling ration' was the proverbial golden ratio of individual freedom and social harmony disguised as a humble threshold of comfortable, dignified subsistence extended to all.

In this crucial respect Gropius strayed decisively into a utopian territory of his own. His faith in the power of new industrialized techniques, new materials used in innovative constructions methods and new design precepts based on the precision of a machine-like assemble practice confronted the harsh limits of the conventional housing calculus with the embrace of more, not less industrial rationalization of the design and building processes (Fehl, 1990; Seelow, 2018). He, not unlike Le Corbusier, was heavily invested in the promise of industrial production and standardization as the primary agents of profound social and cultural transformation. From his early ideas about a pre-fabricated 'Living Machine' (*Wohnmaschine*) (Saldern, 1991) to his experiments with steel houses in Dessau, he pursued an idiosyncratic fusion of technocracy, rigorous standardization and social responsibility. He sought a unique third way between the self-referential design machinism of Le Corbusier and the socio-economic analysis of revolutionary socialist architects who approached the housing crisis as entrenched in the normal operation of the modern capitalist system. In a more socially minded variation of the Le Corbusian rhetorical dilemma 'revolution and/or architecture' Gropius refracted Fordism through the prism of radical social reformism to achieve the 'ideal' affordable minimum dwelling for all (Seelow, 2018, 7).

## Frictionless living: The studies of Alexander Klein

Their significant differences notwithstanding, the housing designs of the Soviet constructivists and the premise of the dwelling ration used by Western avant-garde modernists shared two convictions – first, that the dwelling ought to do more than satisfy the biological and psychological needs of its residents, extending into sociological standards of optimal living; and second, that these sociological parameters had changed dramatically and could no longer be based on earlier assumptions about bourgeois domesticity. If the Soviet avant-garde modernists of the 1920s premised their utopian dwelling on the professed panacea of revolutionary rupture that would destroy once and for all the old world and open up the space for a wholly new way of living, the dwelling ration was based on an alchemical formula whereby rational design, standardization and technological efficiency would be capable of maximizing the biological and sociological dividends of the modern minimum dwelling. Either way the new dwelling would have to be reflective of, and conducive to, new optima of habitation and new minima benchmarks. There was a third way, however, that did not presuppose a revision of the sociological framework of modern habitation but instead sought to extract dividends by rethinking the design of the dwelling according to the profile, observed habits and mapped practices of its users. The case of the Ukraine-born architect Alexander Klein illustrated this different path to determining a minimum that was at the same time verging on the optimal without straying into sociological biases. Klein had already established himself in Germany as one of the leading theoretical experts on the subject of small-size dwelling. His rigorous empirical science-based studies on movement, use of space, room arrangement and spatial practices within the dwelling had drawn attention to the importance of rational, user-centred design in the configuration of the mass dwelling. His typologies had been widely accepted as a canon by Germany's leading institute in housing research (*Reichsforschungsgesellschaft für Wirtschaftlichkeit im Bau- und Wohnungswesen*, RfG) and his scrupulous empirical studies (a combination of site analysis, surveys and innovative graphical representation of the findings) were widely considered as the most accurate and objective research framework for determining minima in size, amenities and spatial organization of the economical mass dwelling. This reputation earned him a place of honour at the 1928 IFHTP exhibition in Paris (see Chapter 3). It is thus not a coincidence that, even without executing a large number of housing projects himself (Lueder, 2017, 82–5), Klein exerted significant influence on a number of 'experimental' housing settlements in Germany in the period between the mid-1920s and the advent of National Socialism, from the Sommerfeld and Fischtalgrund estates in Berlin (the former largely based on his RfG floor plans; the latter also featuring small model family dwellings designed by him[14]) to the settlement of Bad Dürrenberg in Leipzig that he designed by himself in 1927–28 (Kress, 2011, 163–77) (Figure 4.8).

In many ways Klein was the ultimate design alchemist. He believed that with the help of science and scrupulous observation rational spatial design was capable of transforming the modest dwelling into an optimal container of human life, satisfying more human needs (not just biological but social and indeed psychological) better than most existing – and far more expensive and generous in space terms – dwellings of the same size. By studying human circulation within the dwelling and by organizing spaces efficiently on the basis of their intended functions he was able to derive min-max

**Figure 4.8** Bad Dürrenberg settlement in Leipzig, arch. Alexander Klein [Source: *Bundasarchiv* 102-09733].

configurations of space and internal organization that multiplied biological and mental satisfaction for the dwellers. In his view it was not the size of the dwelling that determined its qualitative elements but space in relation to arrangement of its components (rooms, passages, furniture), the interfaces between them and the circulatory practices that they encouraged or prevented (Lueder, 2017, 88). As his studies demonstrated, the same dwelling size or even the same ratio of space to number of residents could result in a wide range of living experiences that could enhance or diminish the quality of life that they offered. In fact, Klein paid particular attention to space as an intimate perception, studying design strategies for enhancing the subjective experience of spaciousness at eye level and the effect of free areas within the dwelling (Lueder, 2017, 89, 99; Korbi and Migotto, 2019, 302–6). His research showed that size reduction alone – without adjustments in its internal configuration and the updating of its usage profiles – resulted in a negative alchemy of disproportionate quality deficits in relation to any cost benefits, creating awkward narrow passages, cluttering, functional shortfalls, significant penalties in terms of ventilation and lighting, as well as an overall negative effect in terms of psychological satisfaction.[15] At the same time, however, he was equally scathing in his critique of avant-garde modernist dwelling solutions that, in his opinion, showed scant regard for and understanding of either housing spatial design or the residents' practices. This brought him into direct confrontation with some key protagonists of the modern movement in the second half of the 1920s, who appeared to him as determined to subject functional common sense to design or ideological dogma.[16] Instead Klein deployed his rigorous data-driven methodology to demonstrate how his own ten key dwelling prototypes (covering a range of sizes, number of residents, configuration and distribution of rooms (Figure 4.9)) could cost less than existing alternatives while still delivering significantly higher quality dividends.[17] His typological propositions avoided questioning existing sociological assumptions about the dwelling, such as the changing shape of the modern family, the merits or otherwise of collective living, as well as the shifts in gender roles or in functions of particular rooms (Korbi and Migotto, 2019, 306).

Klein came to the conclusion that the best balance between economy and quality could be achieved in a dwelling space of between 45 m$^2$ and 70 m$^2$ for a range of one- to three-room abodes. The yardstick for his calculations was the novel concept of 'frictionless (*reibungslos*) living'. In his view friction deformed the domestic space by confusing the room functions and impeding mobility flows within and across the different dwelling spaces (Hill, 2003, 14; Celedon, 2013). The minimization or even complete elimination of friction within the dwelling presupposed a meticulous study of a range of other elements such as the placement and function of doors and windows, the range and positioning of furnishings and the connections between the rooms.[18] In this sense Klein not only reimagined the reduced-size apartment but also imbued it with transformative potential through a novel min-max formula capable of delivering optimal quality of life to its residents.[19] Size per se, distribution across buildings, site planning or construction innovation interested him less than the organization of the dwelling itself as modular ensemble of rooms. His Bad Dürrenberg garden settlement served as his greatest practical realization of his vision of 'frictionless' living: initially conceived as

# The Minimum Dwelling

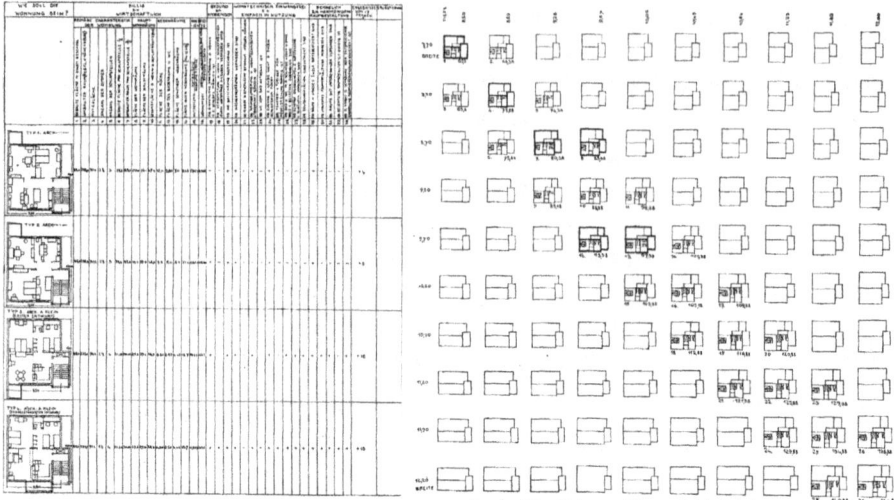

**Figure 4.9** Klein's studies on quality-size-design efficiency for the Kleinwohnung [Source: *Zentralblatt der Bauverwaltung* 48/34 (1928): 54, 7–8].

a partnership with Gropius that in the end he executed by himself, the project offered Klein the opportunity to implement his studies in a real-life setting, offering a wide range of *c.* 1000 dwelling scenarios (41 m² for two-room variations, 54 m² for three and 68 m² for four) in both higher-density blocks and row-housing developments (Kress, 2011, 172–4). Yet once again his focus was on the avoidance of friction within the individual dwelling (Koch, 2016, 4), otherwise relying heavily on Gropius's original work on the spatial organization of the settlement and its residential containers.

****

Unlike in Klein's methodology where it invoked loss, the trope of 'friction' has been used in a positive and productive sense in this chapter. This is because the term can also indicate the creative chemistry produced through international contact, active engagement and vigorous exchange of different programmatic views. If we approach all these divergent propositions as discursive rather than normative statements, invested with sweeping aspiration to redefine the entire context and intellectual apparatus of the discussion on the minimum in habitation, then their friction was generative of radical possibilities that turned the conventional housing calculus on its head and questioned almost every previous assumption about the process of producing affordable dwellings of good quality. In different ways they all resorted to some kind of 'cell' metaphor as the building block of 'new' living, within and beyond the residential space. This 'cell' or 'room' or 'cabin' or 'ration' united and divided them. Whether invoked as a dwelling category or denoting some kind of discrete space within a complex network of other interlinked spatial components that formed part of a much broader programmatic conception of living, defining and designing the 'cell' was at the very heart of their diverse quasi-utopian propositions. Starting from this 'cell' and moving across ever-larger architectural scales, they converged on the dwelling as the hub of a profound future social transformation of living that stretched from the individual space to the family and the community as a whole. What this transformation would be, what kind of optimum it would reflect and how it would be realized remained part of the exciting discursive field that gave interwar modernism its fascinating energy, ambition and diversity. Inevitably, however, they all challenged and revised the framework in which habitation as a whole, and the 'minimum dwelling' as a subset thereof, ought to be discussed – not as a problem to be solved in and by itself but as the radically re-designed and re-dimensioned hub of a much wider transformation of living from the individual space to the family, and the community as a whole. Thriving in the post-First World War sense of an interregnum, this discussion strayed into the fascinating terra incognita of a not-yet crystallised vision for a better future world.

# CHAPTER 5
# CIAM2: THE 'MINIMUM DWELLING' IN FOCUS

### CIAM and its 'lesser' congresses

The historiography of the 'modern movement' and of CIAM in particular has come a long way from the earlier attempts to hallow CIAM4 and the 'Athens Charter' as foundational moments in the history of twentieth-century modernism or conversely as the source of all that is wrong in the modern cityscapes of the twentieth century (Sadler, 2004, 34–7). Ex post facto the trajectory from the founding La Sarraz *'réunion'* (assembly) to the Frankfurt congress (CIAM2, 1929) to the meeting in Brussels (CIAM3, 1930) and eventually to the – repeatedly postponed – fourth congress (CIAM4) lent itself to a narrative of orderly programmatic progression from the single dwelling to the building, the block, the neighbourhood/settlement and the city as a whole. Sigfried Giedion, CIAM's general secretary, articulated such a schema on numerous occasions in the early 1930s, and he restated it in the preface to José Luis Sert's publication *Can Our Cities Survive* in 1944:

> CIAM began by investigating the smallest unit, the low-cost dwelling. It then proceeded to survey the neighbourhood unit found in urban settlements, and finally widened its scope to include an analysis of present-day cities, with suggestions as to what the approach should be in the attempt to solve the problems of human communities in our day.
>
> (Sert, 1942, x–xi)

In essence, what key CIAM figures and earlier histories of the 'modern movement' sought to articulate afterwards with the mythology constructed around CIAM4 was a partisan genealogy of CIAM4's Athens Charter as a revolution foretold at the first meeting of La Sarraz and forged purposefully at the two intervening congresses (1929, 1930) (Panerai et al., 2004, 110). This narrative depicted CIAM4 as both climax of an alleged evolutionary continuum from the first to the fourth congresses; and a portentous turning point that set a new radical path for the history of modern architecture. The tension between these two assumptions about the role of CIAM4 is hard to reconcile: while the former points to linear continuity, orderly progression and unity of purpose, the latter exaggerates the status of the fourth congress as a qualitative, paradigmatic 'critical juncture' that generated both ruptures with the past and novel powerful path dependencies for the future of modernist urban planning norms. Both schemes, however, reduced the volatile chemistry between competing visions and forces within the organization to a sequence of supposedly major junctures (CIAM1/CIAM4) and minor, incremental moments (CIAM2/CIAM3).

These earlier orthodoxies about the role of CIAM in the history of interwar modernist architecture and its path from inception to the stardom have long been revisited and deconstructed (Gold, 1998; Ciucci, 1999, 572; Gold, 2007, 58–77). In lieu of alleged continuity of strategic intent and clarity of vision alternative genealogies have come to the fore that were notably less direct and continuous, less orderly and uniform, more plural and contested than originally suggested. Furthermore, there is now an important – and rapidly growing – body of research specifically on CIAM2 that has reappraised the organization's productive discussion of the 'minimum dwelling' in spite, rather than because, of the congress outcomes. Attention has been drawn to the rich typological experimentation with the trope of the 'minimum dwelling' that predated CIAM's interest in the theme and informed the discussions at its two housing-focused congresses. It is clear that CIAM's engagement with the 'minimum dwelling' did not unfold in an intellectual vacuum. Recognizing the significance of housing for modern architecture at the meeting of La Sarraz reflected broader international debates, political discourses and relevant professional practices already well underway in many parts of Europe. Furthermore, the intention of CIAM's founding members to establish an organization that functioned as a productive inter-/trans-national forum and canonical body for the fledgling modern movement made perfect sense when viewed as a distinct part of a wider – and again already formed – international communication sphere in the domains of architecture and urban planning. Even if CIAM was very different from the IFHTP or the UIV either in programmatic or in organizational terms, they all thrived in a drastically expanded transnational field of circulations, exchanges and dialogue. Mass affordable housing was already firmly on this discursive agenda. It mapped onto a broad, highly diverse spectrum of relevant pre-existing socio-political and architectural perspectives on affordable housing by self-proclaimed modernists within and outside CIAM as well as by other architects of very different programmatic persuasions going all the way back to the nineteenth century (see Chapters 1–2). All this, and the crossovers in membership between these and other fora throughout the 1920s, meant that CIAM's interest in the 'minimum' dwelling was not and cannot be read as a self-referential path.

This said, CIAM's engagement with the theme of the 'minimum dwelling' across diverse architectural frames and scales at the Frankfurt and Brussels congresses was distinctive, pioneering in ambition and profoundly consequential. The choice of the 'minimum dwelling' as a theme mattered enormously for the fledgling CIAM as a vehicle for fostering productive cooperation within its ranks and for registering its distinct programmatic voice on the burgeoning international architectural field. It also served as a strategy for integrating the heterogeneous trends of the 'new' architecture into a universal programmatic canon capable of addressing the totemic 'housing question'. The congress proceedings and insights produced at CIAM2 and CIAM3 provided a wealth of fertile intellectual insights that refracted the contemporary architectural discourse of the mass affordable dwelling. Even more than the congresses themselves, however, it was the dynamics of exchange, confrontation and synthesis forming in the interstices of the congresses in 1928–30 that proved to be the most productive facet of CIAM's early work.

## The Minimum Dwelling

By the time that the Brussels congress wrapped up its proceedings and thus completed the cycle of the 'minimum dwelling' debate that had started in the months after the La Sarraz gathering, CIAM had redefined the intellectual scope and parameters, if not the actual typology, of the 'minimum' dwelling. In this respect the conflicts, frustrating near-misses and indeed dead ends that marked the two congresses were at least as important as their featured keynotes, joint summaries and resolutions.

## CIAM's first steps and the question of dwelling

CIAM began its life on the whim of a small circle of avant-garde personalities from the field of architecture and culture. In the absence of a shared programmatic manifesto, not to mention a clear organizational structure and ethos, the early CIAM relied more heavily on enlisting the active support of key figures of the modern movement from the widest possible sample of European countries. The early, more ambitious plans for a high-profile founding congress had to be scaled down to the far more modest and informal 'assemble'.[1] The La Sarraz meeting ended up being little more than an exploratory gathering of a loose coalition of the willing – a select but inherently unrepresentative group of architects from a relatively small number of countries united in their opposition to the architectural establishment (the controversial outcome of the competition for the new headquarters of the League of Nations in Geneva supplied the cause celebre and a suitable rallying cry) and in their advocacy for a 'new' architecture, who nevertheless remained divided by different programmatic priorities and ideological beliefs.[2] Invitations also had to perform a balancing act between different generations and nations. While the majority of the attendees were young and at an early point in their careers, there was also a number of invitees who had impressive portfolios of executed designs (e.g. Hendrik Berlage in Amsterdam; Ernst May in Breslau and Frankfurt; Victor Bourgeois in Brussels), held important institutional positions (e.g. Hannes Meyer as director of the Bauhaus in 1928–30; Hugo Häring as a founding member of the German *Ring* collective) or had risen to celebrity status among national or international circles of the 'new' architecture (e.g. Le Corbusier). In addition, exclusions and absences were as important as attendances. Important figures like Adolf Loos, Erich Mendelsohn or Auguste Perret were approached but refused to accept the invitation. Walter Gropius and Mies van der Rohe did not attend either, although as members of the Ring their voices were nominally present in institutional guise. Cornelis Van Eesteren and Jacobus Oud were repeatedly invited but neither could turn up, much to Siegfried Giedion's frustration who strongly desired a balanced Dutch representation that mediated between the 'old' Berlage and the radical Mart Stam.[3] El Lissitzky and Moisei Ginzburg planned to attend but were denied entry into Switzerland, marking the beginning of a fraught relationship between CIAM and Soviet architecture. While Italy and Spain were represented by young architects (Juan de Zavala/Fernando García Mercadal and Alberto Sartoris, respectively), there was only rudimentary attendance from Eastern Europe (Szymon Syrkus from Poland) and no representation from the Scandinavian countries,

Czechoslovakia (Karel Teige was invited but could not attend), Britain or the United States (Mumford, 2000, 16–18; Seelow, 2016, 10–14).

With no organizational structure or formal membership to rely on, CIAM's secretary Giedion stepped in to provide both much-needed logistical support and strategic direction. His critical role ahead, and in the aftermath, of the La Sarraz assembly remained undiminished in subsequent years. His Zurich base became the de facto directional hub of CIAM. Giedion engaged in an extraordinarily prolific and sustained activity, sending constantly invitations and reminders, cajoling invitees into involvement, expanding the international reach of CIAM's network, mediating between personal differences, programmatic dichotomies and national sensitivities. He remained largely agnostic about CIAM's political profile and ideological direction, choosing instead to promote the organization as an inclusive international movement with as wide membership and representation of architectural views as possible. The early CIAM bore the unmistakeable imprints of his all-embracing vision and untiring planning work, as he agonized about the viability of the incipient venture and cared deeply for its ability to become a truly representative, canonizing fulcrum of the 'new' architecture. Ahead of the La Sarraz gathering, he shared his immediate priorities with Van Eesteren: he wished to 'involve as many [personalities] as possible but I also need to check who we can work with in the future'.[4] Striking the right balance between the widest possible and most representative international membership, on the one hand, and productive cooperation, on the other, was a delicate task, especially since the fledgling CIAM needed every bit of the propaganda capital that its most prominent members could offer, in spite of their strong convictions and personality quirks; but he remained optimistic about the prospects of the venture in this respect.[5] He was forced to navigate difficult characters (the 'egoistic' Le Corbusier; the unpredictable Stam), complex cultural dichotomies (the tensions between 'French' and 'German' conceptions of the 'new' architecture), as well as profound programmatic and ideological polarities (the co-existence of socialist members with delegates from Fascist Italy; the divisive discussion about capitalism and the 'social' role of the modern architect).[6]

Arguably more important than who was included in the membership list was the level of the members' involvement in the running of CIAM and active participation in its meetings. Giedion bemoaned the absence of both Gropius and Van Eesteren from La Sarraz. The strong presence of younger members with professed socialist views (Stam, Hans Schmidt and Paul Artaria, Meyer) at the founding assembly of 1928 meant that the ensuing declarations 'veered to the left'.[7] Le Corbusier turned out to be the least reliable key personality: against his initial misgivings, he became actively involved in the preparation of the La Sarraz meeting, drafting a series of programmatic statements that were heavily revised in the process; subsequently he oscillated between decisive formative contributions and long periods of absence, silence and inactivity that unsettled Giedion. Both the more established figures and the young members joined the CIAM fray with already strong ideological and programmatic convictions that proved impossible to reconcile in the process. Adherents to the garden-town principles (May, Bourgeois) clashed with supporters of urban centralization and high-rise construction (Gropius,

Le Corbusier). For some participants the 'collective' nature of the new organization of society was treated as a cornerstone of modern architecture's transformative capital; in fact, Schmidt had proposed this topic for the La Sarraz meeting.[8] This was, however, a position either not fully shared by those who were willing to countenance a degree of collective operation or rejected altogether by others. A similar programmatic variation related to the question of standardization, with proponents of full mechanization and pre-fabrication of the entire dwelling pitted against those who were willing to embrace it only for simplifying the production of components and fittings (Ciucci, 1999, 559–63). Urbanism held a quasi-mythical status in the architectural visions of some key members (most notably Le Corbusier), while other participants considered the term either too abstract or too under-developed to be of use, positing instead the importance of dealing with smaller and more familiar scales first before engaging with broader picture of urban design. Meanwhile supporters of the relative autonomy of architectural work never saw eye-to-eye with those who believed that the 'new' architecture depended first and foremost on functionalism, technical innovation, standardization, mechanization and in the end the suppression of aesthetic individualism for the benefit of social equality. Socialist-minded members could not condone the prospect of aligning their work with either industry or any state authority that would inevitably put them at odds with their deeply felt social conception of architecture and vehement critique of the operation of the capitalist system (Hays, 1999). Both sides could profess their belief in the 'revolutionary' promise of the 'new architecture' but their respective 'revolutions' collapsed very different, in the end essentially unreconcilable, socio-political visions (see Chapter 4). These and numerous other differences could not be reconciled or set aside, no matter how hard Giedion worked in the background to smooth out creases and mend chasms. Contingent factors such as how many representatives of the different trends were active in the organizational dialogue and indeed present in CIAM's planning meetings in subsequent months and years made a big difference in influencing the short-term direction and priorities of the organization.

Finding the most apposite architectural scale as a starting point for CIAM's deliberations was thus of paramount significance for the efforts to integrate – if not fully reconcile – diverse perspectives into a working framework for collaboration and partly compensate for all other differences, programmatic and ideological alike. The La Sarraz declaration – product of intense, sometimes acrimonious negotiation behind the scenes and synthesis of opposing views that nevertheless fell short of a coherent programmatic manifesto – eulogized the need for a new overarching programme of architecture, based on rational design principles, a wholehearted embrace of new technological advances and an emphasis on the 'social' role of modern architecture. Yet the declaration that was published at the end of the gathering resembled much more a wishful mapping of issues than a well-defined and practical roadmap for future action (Conrads, 1971, 12–21). The differences reflected in the two versions (French and German) of the document highlighted two main challenges: first, the difference in architectural terminology between the two languages, partly related to the objective difficulties in translating particular concepts like urbanism but also pointing to culturally grounded discursive variations that affected the ways in which architects from different countries referred to common issues[9]; second, and more importantly, the existence of profound ideological chasms, rooted more in personal belief than in divergent national or lexical practices, that set key participants at La Sarraz at odds in relation to key programmatic questions (Gold, 2013, 59–60; Long, 2016). There was, however, an even deeper chasm that was laid bare at La Sarraz and affected the ways in which different CIAM members viewed the method and long-term goals of the organization: While Le Corbusier arrived at the Swiss chateau armed with sweeping aspirational statements about the 'revolutionary' role of the 'new' architecture as something akin to a panacea for all modern ills, others ascribed to architecture a more modest ambit – one whose main task was to engage in factual and scientific analysis of the existing conditions first before arriving at practical solutions for transforming the design and function of individual components from the single object to the dwelling to the city as a whole. The official text of the meeting's was a marvel in diplomatic balance and judicious synthesis of divergent views but this was only achieved by evading contentious topics and editing out divisive language to the point that the text of the final Declarations ended up as two largely separate French and German versions unrepresentative of the breadth of opinion expressed at La Sarraz. Gropius criticized the declaration document as too abstract and 'dilettantish', lacking the practical and factually grounded foundation that the new organization needed in order to ensure that future congresses would be more productive.[10] 'Urbanism' did occupy a cardinal place in the final text, privileging the larger frame of the city as the most valuable unit of programmatic deliberation and action for the organization; but the order of significance of its individual components was left wide open, reflecting tensions and disagreements among the highly disparate group that assembled at La Sarraz (Moos, 2009, 269). Dwelling was identified as one of the three primary functions of urbanism but without any hint of its future centrality for the organization's early congresses (Jones, 1999, 106–9; Stoppioni, 2007; Champy, 2009, 97–119; Gold, 2013, 57–60). Meanwhile the need for a rational development/division of land (the nominal title of CIAM3 – see Chapter 6) emerged as a key component of the third thesis in the declaration, as was the idea that large-scale functional zoning (one of the main tenets of the 'Athens Charter') had to be recognized as the fundamental guiding principle of the new urbanism that CIAM evangelized (Gold, 1998, 229–31).

What followed the conclusion of the proceedings at La Sarraz confirmed the uncertain and fragile results of CIAM1. The founding assembly ended up being an international 'propaganda' affair, albeit again less so than initially hoped for, but achieved little in terms of generating firm organizational structures or routines that could set the venture on a concrete path to its first working congress. The declarations of the meeting fell short of any coherent or actionable programmatic agenda capable of generating path dependencies. The discussions at the chateau had also done little to iron out prior disagreements among the disparate group of participants and even less so to formulate a clear strategy about the next steps. A few encouraging developments (e.g. the constitution of a French group in the autumn, in spite of initial fears that internal personal and programmatic divisions would obstruct the process) could not compensate for growing signs of an uneasy relationship with the Ring[11] – a complex problem that would escalate, fester and disrupt the early CIAM's operation for years to come, all the more alarmingly given how important and sizeable the German representation was (Jones, 1999, 99–109; Somer, 2007, 31; Stoppioni, 2007). The only tangible organizational advance was an agreement to set up an executive group (*Comité International pour la Résolution des Problèmes de l'Architecture Contemporaine*, CIRPAC) to oversee the preparation of the future congresses, provide strategic leadership to the group and coordinate the publicity efforts that were so important for elevating CIAM's profile in the international architectural dialogue (Mumford, 2000, 26).[12] Predictably the onus for keeping whatever momentum alive and planning for the next congress fell on Giedion, whose trademark strategy was to use his prolific epistolary activity to keep members informed, involve them in the next tentative steps and coax promises of either involvement or future attendance from an expanding web of contacts.[13] Yet whatever momentum had been generated by CIAM1 did not translate into a concrete roadmap for the next steps of the organization. There were a breakthrough relating to the location of the next congress, with Frankfurt emerging as a strong candidate by December, following Bourgeois's suggestion at La Sarraz.[14] The choice of preferred venue, however, did not imply in any way a clear sense of thematic focus for this make-or-break congress; in fact, Giedion still thought that the most suitable topic for the next meeting would be to tackle the critiques of the 'new' architecture and the discourse of the 'pseudo-modern'.[15]

## Setting up the first 'working congress'

The chequered path that led from the La Sarraz gathering to the Frankfurt congress featured two important organizational milestones: the first preparatory meeting that took place in Basel in early February; and the meeting of the congress keynote speakers in Karlsruhe in late September 1929. Of the two, the first turned out to be the most consequential, both for giving shape to the congress and for influencing the medium-term direction of the entire CIAM venture. The congress itself, originally scheduled to take place in late September, had to be postponed by a month and eventually took place on 24–26 October. From an organizational point of view, it was an improvised, chaotic and very often frustrating affair, with Giedion – and to an extent the CIAM president Karl Moser – in Zurich and May with his colleague Stam in Frankfurt bearing most of the planning burden. Organizing a first major international event was a challenging task to begin with; but CIAM's multiple idiosyncrasies as a loose coalition of strong personalities keen on unconventional improvisation without the support of fixed institutional structures added to the steep learning curve.

The CIRPAC Basel preparatory meeting (2 February 1929) was well-attended. Apart from Moser, who chaired the proceedings as president, Giedion, May and Stam, it featured Le Corbusier, Bourgeois, Marcel Breuer (Hungary), Schmidt (Switzerland), Häring (Germany), Josef Frank (Austria), Sartoris (Italy), José Manuel Aizpurua and

Luís Vallejo (Spain) and Syrkus (Poland). The minutes of the meeting illustrate how the participants had arrived in Basel with strong views but no clear sense of the precise focus of the first working congress. Only the Swiss group came to the meeting with a coherent proposal for the theme of the forthcoming congress. The proposed scheme was largely based on Giedion's earlier suggestion for an analysis of the obstacles to the 'new' architecture (Somer, 2007, 25), organized under seven sub-headings: land ownership, political and administrative decision-making, current building legislation, construction and design stakeholders, administrative process, consumer demand and architectural education. The Swiss proposal also featured a skeleton agenda, with each of the seven areas of focus introduced by a rapporteur and taking up half a day, with the final section of the congress devoted to a presentation of Frankfurt's programme of housing construction as a case study of how the 'new' architecture has addressed all these challenges.[16] There was no specific mention of housing as a thematic focus in the Swiss proposal, however. Schmidt, himself part of the Swiss group, criticized it for being too broad and lacking in clear focus. He arrived at the meeting with a fully-fledged alternative scheme for a three-day housing-themed congress, with the first day devoted to the perspective of the user, the second day focusing on the relation between the existing regulatory framework for construction in each country and the technical requirements of good-quality construction, and the third day tackling questions of financing and reform of land ownership. In contrast to the original Swiss proposal, Schmidt's scheme provided the first nudge towards a single congress focus on the dwelling scale, but it was more refracted through his personal belief in the social dimension of the 'new' architecture (Huber, 1993, 26–8, 34–9).

May cautioned against overspecifying the congress's agenda at such an early stage in the planning cycle or introducing too many sub-topics to the programme, proposing instead a broader umbrella term (*Wohnungsbau*, housing construction). Le Corbusier, on the other hand, was instrumental in introducing the first of the two key ideas that eventually shaped the theme of CIAM2 – the question of determining the 'minimum' in dwelling design (he used the French term *habitation minimum*). What exactly he had in mind when he summoned this terminology cannot be safely inferred from the meeting's minutes – and it was precisely this linguistic and semantic ambiguity in CIAM's discourse on the 'minimum dwelling' that would generate its fair share of misapprehensions and tensions in the process. That the Swiss architect considered any discussion of the 'minimum' as only a subset, however important, of a much broader discussion about the programme of the 'new' architecture and urbanism is highlighted by how little he said to elucidate it (admittedly in the face of an apparent agreement by the other participants) and by how quickly he moved on to other suggestions at the Basel meeting. He was particularly interested, he said, in including a detailed discussion of 'new' techniques in housing construction, as well as a consideration of the financial and land implications vis-a-vis existing restrictive and outdated legislation that stifled innovation. But he was also keen on expanding the frame of reference to other issues, be that of land reform, of circulation within the dwelling, of its biological requirements (air, light, sound, heat) and of matters of 'domestic economy'. These and other more technical suggestions by

Le Corbusier were greeted with suspicion by those – Häring, Breuer, Schmidt – who advocated a stronger alignment of the organization's discourse with an agenda of 'social' responsibility. Breuer spoke in favour of engaging such a social dimension of the housing question and of strengthening references to it in the official title of the congress. He was outspoken in his defence of the modern architect's social mission and accused the other participants of being too cautious and 'dull' in their handling of the proposed dwelling theme. On his part Le Corbusier countenanced a number of suggestions for expanding the scope of the congress theme but resisted proposals that favoured a politicized discussion on the broader 'social' dimension of the dwelling, arguing instead for a rigorously technical and scientific approach as befitted the professional ethos of architects. Yet, in hindsight, his seemingly off-the-cuff reference to the 'question of the minimum' produced a genuine turning point in CIAM's early discourse.

Another point of disagreement at the Basel meeting concerned the methodological approach to be adopted at the Frankfurt congress. The animated discussion pitted once again Breuer against Le Corbusier but also involved May and Häring. As the topic of the dwelling started to take hold, both Häring and May cautioned against the danger of duplicating the work of other organizations that had already established their credentials in related matters on the international architectural scene. May pointed out that the topics of land reform, dwelling size and financing had already been discussed at the 1928 Paris congress of the International Federation for Housing and Town Planning (IFHTP) (see Chapter 3), which he had personally attended and whose conclusions he rated highly. Häring, warned against the prospect of a self-absorbed congress that ignored the significant prior work on affordable housing by the members of the Frankfurt-based International Federation for Housing (*Internationale Verband für Wohnungswesen*, IVW) – in essence a breakaway faction of the IFHTP with a particularly strong interest in mass housing.[17] The ensuing discussion may have seemingly concerned the remit of the forthcoming Frankfurt congress but in fact touched on the question of CIAM's raison d'être as an incipient venture fighting for its own niche in an ready crowded field of relevant international bodies. Le Corbusier argued that the theme itself did not matter as much as the scientific precision of the method and the clarity of the congress outcomes. Breuer, however, understood the entire CIAM operation as an ideologically progressive, highly partisan initiative, explicitly aligned with the socially transformative dimension of the 'new' architecture that could only realize its full potential with the formulation of a 'manifesto' based on a single agreed ideological position. This suggestion alarmed both May and Häring who for different reasons believed that CIAM ought to function as an inclusive forum enabling the broadest representation and exchange of different views without committing to a manifesto-like set of principles. Months later, when the preparation for CIAM2 was well underway, Gropius raised similar concerns about the distinctiveness of CIAM's approach vis-a-vis the IVW, the IFHTP or even the German government's RFG. His preference for a focused and rigorously scientific approach based on biological and technical aspects of architecture,[18] as an alternative to what he criticized as either aesthetic or political propaganda,[19] came with a warning against the prospect of turning CIAM into a dilettantish talking shop. For him, as well as his colleague Schmidt, the fledgling organization desperately needed clarity of programmatic direction and joint alignment to a single position.[20] He was appreciative of the work carried out by existing organizations on the questions of housing and urban planning but believed that CIAM ought to ground its distinctiveness on firm programmatic and propagandistic ground by fully adopting the partisan perspective of the 'new' architecture.[21]

As the discussion on the congress theme in Basel ran the risk of degenerating into a damaging ideological and personal confrontation, the conciliatory interventions of Schmidt, Häring and finally May jointly introduced the second component that was to prove critical in terms of defining the actual focus of CIAM2 – *Klein-* or *Kleinstwohnung*, namely small or smallest dwelling. The attempt to find a balance between the social-political and the technical-scientific dimension without over-committing CIAM to one or the other was evident in all three suggested congress titles: Schmidt proposed the scheme 'socially just Kleinwohnung', Häring put forward the motto 'Kleinstwohnung and [its] social requirements' while May suggested an even more inclusive formulation that combined the 'right to the Kleinstwohnung' with a focus on 'modern technique' and '[concrete] realisation'. But it was the shift from housing in general to the small(est)-size dwelling that was by far the most consequential development. Even as at that point Moser intervened to move the discussion to other organizational matters, asking for the exchange of views on the precise theme of CIAM2 to resume at a later point, the lexical shift to a size-determined housing focus proved a significant turning point that – together with the seeming acceptance of the Lecorbusian 'minimum' – generated a critical path dependence, aligning the Frankfurt congress with the question of dwelling size, construction efficiency and social affordability.

A one-day preparatory meeting for CIAM's first working congress proved to be too little to resolve the multitude of thematic, programmatic and organizational issues facing the organization. Moser's early promise to return to the consideration of the precise theme at the end of the meeting was quickly forgotten. Instead the remainder of the discussion revolved around urgent matters of preparation for the congress, an associated exhibition that would function as the all-important propaganda showcase of CIAM's international credentials, the formation of national groups of delegates and financial-operational matters. It was agreed that each day of the Frankfurt congress would feature a thematic keynote speaker, followed by discussion sessions on each sub-theme. In an effort to ground CIAM's distinctive approach to the dwelling question on solid scientific and factual principles, the CIRPAC chose the methodology of questionnaires, prepared and circulated ahead of the congress by the keynote speakers and completed with data from each national group represented at the congress.[22] There was a clear understanding that the quality of the questionnaires themselves and of the information supplied by the delegate groups would make or break the work of the congress.[23] Since the precise list of the day themes had yet to be fixed (and this was a task that took months to finalize, as will become evident, causing confusion and delays that plagued the entire CIAM2 operation), who was to be responsible for each questionnaire and on what precise theme data would be solicited remained unresolved for months.

The official report on the first preparatory meeting that was issued shortly afterwards in both French and German versions provides an honest and telling reflection of the largely inconclusive discussions in Basel. Mirroring the discursive linguistic bifurcation of the La Sarraz assembly, the official theme of CIAM2 was described very differently in each version – 'social claims and technical realisation of the minimum dwelling' (*habitation minimum*) in French; and 'the small-size dwelling (Kleinwohnung) and its social and technical solutions from the perspective of the new architecture' in German.[24] The official report issued at the conclusion of the Basel meeting featured a draft programme with a day-by-day breakdown of speakers and activities; yet the topic of the first congress day was marked as 'not yet fixed'. The published draft programme as a whole bore scant resemblance to the eventual conduct of CIAM2: the date was eventually moved by a month, the duration was reduced from four to three days and the daily subthemes and list of speakers continued to change for months to come. Even if the dwelling appeared as the sole focus point in the interim congress title, the proposed third day of the congress was to be dedicated to a discussion of the 'urgent reform of the urban land question for the benefit of public health' – a reference to what eventually became the official title of CIAM3 in 1930 and evidence of an ongoing lack of consensus within the organization as to the preferred architectural scale for CIAM's future proceedings in Frankfurt and beyond. Even the impressionistic rendition of the congress title did not appear to have stopped further suggestions for ancillary topics to be included in the final programme. Syrkus went away from the Basel meeting with the impression that both land reform and domestic economy would be eventually included as sub-themes for the third congress day.[25]

Within a month from the Basel meeting, however, key figures became concerned that the proposed ambit for CIAM2 was too vague and overambitious to form the basis for a productive working congress. When Giedion attempted to co-opt the then chief architect of Berlin Martin Wagner into the congress, he received a terse negative response: Wagner not only objected to what he perceived as elitist, undemocratic operation of the organization but also rejected the draft programme as too incoherent and thus unlikely to make any meaningful contribution to the cause of the 'new' architecture.[26] Wagner's rebuff prompted a rethink within CIAM and resulted in a swift decision to abandon the topic of land reform altogether.[27] Day-specific topics also came under review, eventually leading to the decision to use the second day as a mere opportunity to elaborate the topics of the keynotes from the opening sessions.[28] By June 1929 Giedion had become worried that the agenda was excessively focused on technical aspects and tried to reintroduce the question of financing into the programme – a suggestion that was nevertheless quickly dismissed by May as counter-productive.[29] The position of Gropius was the most bewildering: even as he was pressing for a reduction of the original list of subtopics, he was also making repeated attempts to introduce the theme of building form (*Wohnform*) into the CIAM2 programme[30] and appeared supportive of the conflation of the dwelling and the land reform themes for the Frankfurt congress.[31] Such a tendency to initially include a profusion of ideas for congress topics and then decide to move them to subsequent events became a standard long-term practice in the history of interwar

CIAM that explains the actual sequence of congress themes from Frankfurt to Brussels and then to Athens far more accurately than any preconceived orderly scale transition from the dwelling to urbanism that Giedion claimed afterwards.

The only other official preparatory meeting for the Frankfurt congress took place nearly eight months later – and within only a few weeks from the opening of the congress itself.[32] By that time the congress had taken a very different direction and overall shape, more out of improvisation and trial-and-error than intentional planning. Giedion insisted that a meeting of the keynote speakers ahead of the congress was critical as it provided the last opportunity to iron out organizational/procedural problems and improve the quality of the congress proceedings.[33] The meeting, held in Karlsruhe on 29 September 1929, was attended by Giedion and all prospective speakers – Bourgeois, Schmidt, Gropius (the first CIAM meeting that he was officially involved in) and Pierre Jeanneret who was nominated to stand in for Le Corbusier and would deliver the jointly authored keynote at the congress in his cousin's absence. The meeting was productive[34] and a final congress programme was issued shortly afterwards: the first day would feature the talks by Gropius (sociological foundations of the minimum dwelling) and Bourgeois (the programme of the minimum dwelling), followed by the keynotes by Schmidt (critique and improvement of the regulations on the minimum dwelling) and Jeanneret (the Karlsruhe protocol quoted a similar title to the one by Schmidt but the final title was set to change again in the lead-up to the Frankfurt congress).

The reasonably optimistic mood following both the Basel and the later Karlsruhe preparatory meetings belied the chaos and constant frustrations that marked the intervening period. If investing so much in the questionnaires appeared a sensible solution on paper, in practice the formula adopted in Basel could only work through coordination and adherence to strict deadlines. The responsibility for drafting each of the two questionnaires was delegated to different – and very busy, as it turned out – members (Bourgeois, Gropius, Le Corbusier), with early March initially considered the absolute deadline for the circulation of the two exemplars to the national groups.[35] With no questionnaires in sight in early April, however, Giedion used anything from extreme deference to stern warnings about an impending disaster in Frankfurt to coax those responsible for drafting the texts into action.[36] The knock-on effect of this initial delay was very significant because the questionnaires themselves were dispatched too late to the national groups,[37] with most responses arriving too late to be processed ahead of the Frankfurt congress. In the end Gropius worked together with Schmidt and Artaria to deliver the first questionnaire in early July;[38] it took Bourgeois, however, until early September to finally release his own survey form.[39] The two questionnaires were sophisticated and forensic. The first – and by far the most exhaustive and far-reaching one – covered anything from economic considerations (wages, cost of living and rent levels) to sociological (nature and size of the household), biological (air, sound, light) and technical (housing typologies, internal configuration, etc.) parameters of the 'minimum dwelling'. By comparison the second questionnaire was a more focused and technical document, gathering data on existing building regulations in each country but also asking very specific questions about a wide range of 'minima' – size and height of the dwelling, size of individual rooms and spaces, size of openings, building-plot ratio, external walls, etc.[40] When they were finally circulated, no one questioned their quality. Asking, however, national groups to respond to two lengthy and demanding documents with high-quality data, and then tabulating and comparing all the information in order to make insights useful for the congress keynote speakers, required far more time than was available after all the initial delays.

The questionnaire debacle was the main reason behind the eventual postponement of the congress from September to October. Stam, who together with his colleagues of the *Oktobergruppe* (Franz Schuster, Josef Gartner and Adolf Meyer who died in the midst of the preparations for CIAM2) had assumed a critical role on the Frankfurt side of the planning operation, was the stronger supporter of postponement. In early June he launched a scathing critique of the entire planning operation, complaining about missed deadlines and miscommunication between Zurich and Frankfurt.[41] Schmidt soon echoed similar misgivings, aware that the four-month delay in the circulation of the first questionnaire had already exhausted the time needed for data collection and analysis ahead of the original September date.[42] At some point in early summer even Giedion came round to the view that a postponement – until December or even the spring of 1930 – would be a good idea.[43] The much shorter one-month deferment that May negotiated did provide just enough breathing space to put preparations for a 1929 congress back on track[44] but it proved too little too late. By the time that the entire CIAM planning operation had gathered momentum in the late summer and late autumn, everything had fallen behind – not only the questionnaires but also the responses, the plans for the exhibition (see Chapter 7) and even the official invitations and hospitality arrangements in Frankfurt.[45]

The organizational mayhem was exacerbated by the fraught situation in many national groups. Given the size and importance of the German group within CIAM, the increasingly fractious relationship with Häring personally and with the Ring at organizational level alarmed the CIRPAC and became a source of major frustration throughout 1929 without achieving any lasting resolution.[46] The situation with the French group was almost as problematic, owing to intensifying personal and ideological differences among its members, with Le Corbusier sinking into apathy and complete silence during the late-spring and summer months of 1928.[47] The erratic behaviour of the Swiss star architect became a source of exasperation even for the usually diplomatic and deferential Giedion, who implored him, to remain engaged with the CIAM venture and provide much-needed leadership.[48] Efforts to build up a national CIAM group in Czechoslovakia fell flat over the summer, when the Czech representative Jaromír Krejcar informed the Zurich secretariat that there was insufficient interest in the venture among his colleagues.[49] Another last-minute appeal to Teige to help with the formation of the group, provide data for the congress questionnaires and come to Frankfurt on CIAM expenses fell flat (Misa, 2008, 89).[50] The final tally of seventeen countries represented at the Frankfurt congress was a disappointment for Moser and Giedion, who had worked hard since La Sarraz to extend the organization's international reach. The eventual lack of any representation from the Soviet Union in particular, notwithstanding repeated approaches to Ginzburg and Lissitzky,[51] was particularly frustrating, especially given the growing significance of Soviet urbanism for the 'new' architecture (Cohen, 1992; Mumford, 2019; Wolfe, 2011, Ch 4). Giedion did not fare much better with his personal approaches and invitations. In addition to Wagner's brusque refusal to become involved, another key German figure, Bruno Taut, dismissed the entire CIAM operation as 'dilettantish' and refused to take any part in the proceedings.[52] In spite of his renowned expertise in the field of social housing, Henri Sellier, the mayor of the French garden-town of Suresnes and director of the Office of Affordable Housing (*Office des Habitations à Bon Marché*, OHBM) of the Paris region, was approached too late to be able to attend.[53]

## The 1929 Frankfurt congress (CIAM2)

That the congress and the associated exhibition did take place in the end felt like a small triumph of the commitment and resilience shown by both the Zurich secretariat and the Frankfurt organizing hub during the chaotic few months ahead of the new opening date of 24 October. The final programme looked impressive in its thematic coverage and line-up of distinguished speakers. This was the first full opportunity for CIAM members to engage in serious discussion about their individual ideas and practice, to exchange views about their respective national experiences and to explore new avenues for international professional collaboration in order to advance the cause of the 'new' architecture. The actual congress was preceded by a social evening at the botanical gardens on the evening of 23 October. The following morning the two short opening talks by May (as host) and Giedion (as secretary) marked the official opening of CIAM2 and set the scene for two full days of keynotes and discussion.[54] The proceedings on 24 and 25 October were conducted behind closed doors, as per Gropius's suggestion, to allow for more elaborate technical discussion and create an environment conducive to a candid exchange of views.[55] Two keynotes – the one by Gropius on the first day and the other by Schmidt on the second day – were meant to offer a critical discussion of the comparative data from the two congress questionnaires. The other two main speakers (Bourgeois and Jeanneret) shared the same broad topic ('minimum dwelling'). All keynote presentations stimulated discussion during the afternoon segment of each of the first two days, even as they revealed disagreements about the scope, purpose and intended future of the organization.

Ahead of the keynote presentations, Giedion and May delivered short – though no less programmatic – addresses to the delegates. Giedion introduced the Frankfurt congress as a milestone in CIAM's organizational development towards a genuinely transnational collaborative venture in support of the cause of the 'new' architecture. Presenting the small La Sarraz 'assembly' as a decisive step towards the success of the CIAM initiative and the expansion of its international membership,[56] Giedion hailed CIAM2 as a proper 'working congress' with a deliberately small group of recognized experts in the field of housing which, albeit far from homogeneous in programmatic terms, involved only professionals who shared a profound belief in the transformative potential of modernist architecture and excluded those whose 'attitude and work is linked to a bygone era'. Giedion presented the focus of the Frankfurt congress on the 'minimum dwelling' as the direct product of programmatic consensus achieved at the Basel preparatory meeting of February 1929; a grotesque, if understandable for publicity reasons, misrepresentation of the chaotic and turbulent nine months that intervened between the Basel meeting and the congress itself. In justifying the focus on the 'minimum dwelling' for CIAM's first working congress, Giedion spoke of an enormous social problem whose roots lay in the early industrial society but which was allowed to fester and was now affecting millions of working families across the world. He then stressed that CIAM's goal in Frankfurt was not to simply examine and compare the current situation regarding the shortage of good-quality, affordable dwellings across those countries represented at the congress proceedings but to produce an authoritative analysis of the causes of, and solutions to, the problem (Giedion, 1930).

May's opening statement was similarly short, offering a succinct programmatic statement of his – and Frankfurt's – approach to social housing. For him the dwelling was the vital 'cell' of modern architecture as well as the elemental unit of a modern modular urban planning at diverse, complementary scales. He located the problem of the 'minimum dwelling' at the intersection of four critical but competing priorities – quality, size, affordability and supply. He rejected the zero-sum logic of the nineteenth-century housing calculus that had justified onerous reductions in quality and size in order to keep costs down and meet emergency demand, arguing instead that a decent, pleasant and affordable dwelling for all was not only morally desirable but also possible. He observed that in the post-First World War years new housing stock had offered significantly better quality but tended to cost more – the result of steep increases in the cost of materials and in the overall price index, thus becoming either unaffordable by lower-income families or too expensive to produce in sufficient numbers. Modern construction techniques and standardization had already delivered significant reductions in the cost of the dwelling unit but they could not solve the affordability problem by themselves. The same could be said about the rational design and functional organization of domestic spaces, on the basis of new insights about the biological, sociological and psychological requirements of modern habitation. As a result of improvements in these two key areas, size had lost much of its earlier associations with dwelling quality. For this reason, May appeared willing to countenance a further push in the direction of size reduction (the fundamental principle of the conventional Kleinwohnung) in order to extract further dividends in terms of quality, affordability and supply for as many as possible. Funding, however, remained at the heart of the affordability conundrum: without generous and proactive public involvement in the entire housing cycle (land availability, planning, construction and financing) the 'minimum dwelling' could never become a universal social right. May did not expect that the congress would be able to specify the exact typological and technical requirements of such a dwelling but he hoped that the CIAM debate would direct the focus of dwelling design to the full satisfaction of minimum biological, sociological and mental requirements of the residents (Giedion, 1930, 10–16; Steinmann, 1979, 40–2).

## CIAM2: The 'Minimum Dwelling' in Focus

The keynote talks differed in terms of both focus and understanding of the 'minimum dwelling' congress theme. Gropius engaged with the sociological foundations of the minimum dwelling, analysing the enormous changes that modern life had already affected on individual, family and public life. He outlined how the family had gradually lost its universal status as a modern dwelling community and how traditional gender roles had been eroded. The cumulative result of the reduction in the average size of the households, the growing number of people living alone and the changing assumptions about the gendering of domestic spaces necessitated a radical reassessment of dwelling design. Gropius also struck at the heart of the conventional association of dwelling size with either quality of life or social status. When it came to specifying the 'minimum', he emphatically rejected basing the design and the costing of the dwelling on the basis of the minimum income of the working population (the basis used by economic theories of the Existenzminimum – see Chapter 1); instead he proposed a qualitative biological definition of the elevated minimum that both modern techniques and public funding ought to make truly affordable and available to everyone.

The two keynotes by Bourgeois and Le Corbusier-Jeanneret covered similar conceptual territory but in significantly different ways. Bourgeois spoke with meticulous detail about the biological requirements and technical standards of the 'minimum dwelling'. True to the intention of the organizers to focus not only on analysis and comparison of the present situation but also on optimal alternatives for the future, Bourgeois made a series of practical design recommendations for individual rooms (small kitchen but well-equipped with modern amenities; separate living/eating room for the family; small shower room for washing; side room for children); for healthy air and light circulation (speaking in detail about the window as a critical instrument thereof); for the optimal size for the 'dwelling ration' (20 $m^2$ for one person, 35 $m^2$ for two people and 10 $m^2$ added for every extra person); for modes of efficient insulation and centralized heating; and for what he called 'household education' (optimal use of furniture, rationalization of the household process).[57] In his in absentia address Le Corbusier defined the 'minimum dwelling' in only tangential terms, choosing instead to talk at length about the recent Loucheur law in France and his own ideas about a 'fully industrialised' affordable dwelling design that was fast, efficient and relatively cheap, matching the simplicity of the modern automobile production line. He then moved to a rambling discussion of his broader programmatic positions about dwelling design, talking about the standard frame, the use of iron and reinforced concrete, the free facade and open plan, the pilotis and the importance of functional and standardized furniture. His motto of 'air, sound, light' as the most sound biological basis for design and construction decisions concerning the 'minimum dwelling' underpinned his call for a 'hermetic house', impervious to humidity and dust. He praised novel construction principles and methods that underlined the urgent need for standardization, industrialization and 'scientific truth'. In Le Corbusier's view the 'new' architecture alone could furnish the ultimate solution to the problem of the minimum dwelling through novel functional design and fully industrialized construction principles (Giedion, 1930, 28).

Schmidt dealt with the issue of planning and building regulations on both national and local levels. His talk echoed one of the principles of the La Sarraz declaration concerning the detrimental effect on antiquated laws on housing construction. For him the entire system of housing production had rendered the goal of high-quality and affordable dwellings for all working population impossible. This was because state and local supervisory authorities, owners of land and buildings, constructors and residents existed in almost complete isolation from each other. No matter how restrictive and out-of-sync the existing building regulations actually were, Schmidt argued that there was little point in changing the legislative framework without also effecting radical changes in the entire productive process. The only alternative would be to develop a new, flexible system of building rules that could fully protect the residents from speculation while allowing maximum freedom to the architect to design each dwelling in close partnership with the user (Giedion, 1930, 43–6).

Across the four keynotes there were unmistakeable indications of the speakers' desire to inscribe dwelling into a wider scale of architectural intervention that extended outwards and upwards from the dwelling 'cell'. Cautioning against a fragmentary approach that favoured displacement of the new housing groupings away from the existing city, May urged his colleagues to 'integrate the sum of these living cells into the town plan' and to pay particular attention to the interstitial spaces and the provision of adequate services for the new communities (Bourgeois et al., 1931, 10–16). In their addresses Gropius and Le Corbusier converged on two key programmatic observations: first, that individual life was gradually giving way to – arguably superior – collective forms of urban living; and second, that a combination of sociological, technical and economic factors called for a reassessment of the earlier ideal of a single-family decentralized house, with Gropius advocating higher-rise building forms and Le Corbusier defending the benefits of urban concentration. Bourgeois and Gropius spoke in favour of basing the re-design of the modern dwelling on sociological foundations that took on board the profound transformation of the structures of modern family life (Smets, 1977, 148). But it was predictably Le Corbusier who effortlessly switched the reference scale inwards and outwards from the dwelling frame, talking about the rise of the age of the machine, then changing perspective to talk about the problems of circulation of cars on an urban scale, before marshalling the aesthetic arsenal of functionalism against the legacies of decorative architecture and historicism (Huber, 1993, 8–10, 26–7; Barr, 2011).

### Language matters: The opacity of the *Existenzminimum*

There was a semantic elephant in the Frankfurt congress hall, however. May's address referred almost exclusively to the 'dwelling for the Existenzminimum' (*Wöhnung für das Existenzminimum*), a term that also featured in the official title of his talk. With the exception of Giedion's occasional reference to the Existenzminimum – either as an income-related concept or in relation to the official title of the congress exhibition, the other keynote speakers showed scant or no interest in using the term. This was only partly attributable to the linguistic bifurcation of the early CIAM's discourse into French and German versions. While the German term 'Existenzminimum' was very hard to render in other languages and thus almost entirely unusable in the French-language keynote talks of Bourgeois and Jeanneret-Le Corbusier, Schmidt's talk, albeit delivered in German, still did not make a single reference to it (Korbi and Migotto, 2019, 300–2). The term had begun to creep into the German-language CIRPAC communications and guidelines during the late summer and early autumn of 1929, first in relation to the title of the exhibition and later in the description of the official congress theme itself.[58] However, it was never used in a systematic and consistent way by CIAM members, often replaced by or used interchangeably with other German-language terms and was mostly associated with the conventional typology of the Kleinwohnung. There was no mention of the Existenzminimum in either of the two questionnaires distributed ahead of CIAM2. Meanwhile the French version of the official CIAM2 documents neither adopted the term nor made any effort to translate it in more literally. Even in the final version of the CIAM2 programme, the German term 'dwelling for the Existenzminimum' was translated in French as 'habitation minimum' (minimum dwelling).

Considering how the terminology of the Existenzminimum has come to define the proceedings of the Frankfurt congress and the early CIAM's discourse on housing, it is surprising how little the term itself appears on either official or private documents ahead of CIAM2. May had showed no interest in incorporating the Existenzminimum in his architectural writings until well into the autumn of 1929, even if he, like other socially committed architects working in the Weimar Republic and other European countries at the time, was familiar with the contours of the economic debate on subsistence minima and the social dimension of basic human needs. Equally surprising was Giedion's shunning of the terminology in official CIAM documents and personal correspondence. The CIAM secretary had made reference to dwelling design for the 'Existenzminimum' in his 1929 *Liberated Living* booklet (Giedion, 2019) and was clearly conversant with the nuances of the term as he had referred to 'housing for people who merely subsisted' (*Leute mit der Existenzminimum*) in an article that appeared in Frankfurt's municipal architectural journal in June 1929.[59] Yet, although at the time of the Basel preparatory meeting in February he was putting the final touches to his publication, he – like everyone else – snubbed the term during the discussion on the congress theme and hardly ever used it in official CIAM documents until July. Even after the term had started appearing in official press reports, organizational guidelines and draft programmes afterwards, Giedion preferred to reserve it mostly for the exhibition rather than the description of the congress theme itself.

There were two main problems with the nomenclature of the Existenzminimum for the CIAM2 congress. The first was a practical one: although the term came to occupy a pivotal place in the proceedings, the exhibition and the subsequent publication, it was neither properly defined in its novel architectural context for the purposes of the congress discussion nor consciously adopted by keynote speakers as CIAM's programmatic lingua franca. It could be argued that Giedion was deliberately resorting to more familiar terminology or more descriptive alternative terms when he compiled outward-facing documents. For example, the final version of the CIAM2 programme began with the phrase 'the problem of building dwellings at affordable rents for the least privileged class of the population' before deploying casually the opaque official terminology of the Existenzminimum as synonym.[60] Nevertheless, the lack of clarity regarding the congress theme that had bedevilled the Basel preparatory meeting was never properly addressed in the ensuing months. If in the end the Existenzminimum terminology somehow prevailed in the official nomenclature of CIAM2, it was neither due to active and conscious collective choice nor reflective of a programmatic consensus among CIAM members.

The second problem related to profound cultural and programmatic dichotomies among the members of the early CIAM. As mentioned earlier, it was Le Corbusier who at the February 1929 preparatory meeting had suggested a congress focus on the question of 'minimum'. In contrast to the precise term 'Existenzminimum' that was unwieldy in other languages, the abstract language of the 'minimum' provided a tentative conceptual common ground among the participants of the Basel meeting. And yet it is revealing that all German-speaking CIAM members instantly linked the discussion of 'minimum' with the typology of the conventional Kleinwohnung. That the minimum equated with smallness in this particular context made perfect sense to the German, Swiss and Austrian architectural traditions, where the term 'small-size dwelling' had been familiar and popular since the nineteenth century (see Chapter 2). By contrast, the French term 'habitation minimum' had a more muddled meaning: although size was always implicit in any discussion on the affordable dwelling in France (be that the earlier HBM or the 'reduced-rent' houses of the 1928 Loucheur law), the French 'minimum' was contextually flexible enough to accommodate anything from lower cost or quality sacrifices to functional design abstraction (Dumont, 1991, 156; Kühl, 2001, 123; Matysek-Imielińska, 2020, 42). The semantic difference between the French and the German renditions of the congress theme was never resolved through the adoption of a corresponding terminology, even after the conclusion of the congress. Giedion appeared to treat Kleinwohnung and Existenzminimum as interchangeable terms in the context of the CIAM2 proceedings in the German language. Given, however, his role as secretary and de facto nous of the planning operation for the Frankfurt congress, he was also obliged to communicate with other CIAM members in both German and French. It is therefore interesting that he could refer to the congress theme as 'Kleinwohnung' when he corresponded with May[61] while using the term 'habitation minimum' as the congress and questionnaire title in his guidelines to the French-speaking Bourgeois or in his invitation to Sellier.[62]

The lack of a clearly defined and consistently used congress terminology resulted in a grey linguistic zone where different terms and translations, as well as a series of variants and hybrid neologisms, vied for attention and sanction at the congress without a clear winner. Schmidt preferred the term 'Minimalwohnung' for the questionnaire that he prepared for the congress.[63] He and Gropius used the same term in their keynote addresses in Frankfurt, again without providing any definitional cue as to the term's specific meaning or relevance for the official congress title. The term was also adopted by other members of the Swiss group at CIAM2.[64] 'Minimal' was of course not an exact synonym of 'minimum', but it did go some way towards bridging the lexical gap between the German terminology (Kleinwohnung/Existenzminimum) and the 'minimum dwelling' used in the French texts. But it was another size-related variation that added to the babel of terms at CIAM2 – Kleinstwohnung or literally 'smallest dwelling'. On one level the difference between Klein- and Kleinst-wohnung appeared as a simple problem of degree, the latter being the absolute zero of the former in terms of overall size reduction. Yet in his theoretical treatment of the 'smallest dwelling' (Frankfurt-based at the time) Franz Schuster (see Figure 2.12) had associated it with the absolute qualitative inversion of the conventional 'bourgeois' large-size dwelling and a call to re-think the small dwelling from scratch. Schuster presented this as a necessity caused by scarcity of resources and the uncritical reproduction of outdated ideas about architecture and domesticity – but a necessity that was morally vindicated on the grounds of pursuing a full solution to the housing question that afflicted millions of people across the world (Schuster, 1927, 1–2). Thus, the Kleinwohnung was no mere superlative Kleinwohnung, no mere product of yet another savage reduction in size without questioning the entire framework in which dwelling was understood and approached as a design question; instead it was a radically new dwelling typology with its distinct intellectual complexion and methodological blueprint. The slippage from one to the other had not troubled the participants of the Basel preparatory meeting, when, within minutes from each other, Schmidt's proposal for a congress title based on the 'Kleinwohnung' was countered by alternative ideas from Häring and May that adopted the 'Kleinstwohnung' variant. Nevertheless, the two terms continued to be used in a seemingly interchangeable manner by Giedion and Moser in subsequent months, as synonyms for the Existenzminimum and its own variations.[65] The official programme of the Frankfurt congress[66] used both terms as perfect equivalents alongside the official terminology of the Existenzminimum and all its paraphrases. To confuse matters even further, the 'habitation minimum' terminology used by Bourgeois was rendered in English as 'minimum dwelling' – bringing it into line with the translation of Schmidt's and Gropius's 'Minimalwohnung' in the congress publication that appeared in 1930; but the very same term was translated as 'Kleinwohnung' in the German-language summary of Bourgeois's keynote that was provided by Schmidt at the congress.[67]

The babel of terms, paraphrases and translations at CIAM2 did not stop with the keynotes but extended into the discussion that followed each talk. Individual participants stuck more or less to their pet terms but did not seem troubled by other concepts being used as synonyms or equivalents. The only term that was conspicuously absent was 'Existenzminimum', even after two days of proceedings in theory dedicated to this very theme. This said, the post-keynote discussion sessions were more productive in terms of determining the actual meaning of the congress discussion and extrapolating some points of tenuous consensus. May argued that the very notion of a 'minimum' for subsistence ought to be calculated in relation to absolute (and more ambitious) biological and sociological requirements. At a congress where keynotes dealt in forensic detail with either biological parameters of the dwelling – such as ventilation and illumination – or sociological ones – for example, family composition, gender roles, patterns of work and leisure – the suggestion to use absolute units as benchmarks for the 'minimum dwelling' was a significant step in the direction of giving a more concrete shape to the congress discussion. No matter how prominent the terminology of the Kleinwohnung was among German-speaking participants at CIAM2, it was increasingly clear that determining the 'minimum dwelling' had moved beyond conventional efforts to merely reduce surface space in order to cut down construction costs. As Frank noted, the real challenge was to find ways to produce dwellings that met elevated requirements efficiently, in sufficient numbers to meet social demand and at a cost that – without sacrificing quality – could render this new kind of dwelling affordable to all working population.[68] As a result, dwelling size and cost were no longer seen as absolute benchmarks of the 'minimum' dwelling.

Aside from deploying different nomenclature, each keynote speaker also privileged different scales of architectural analysis. Bourgeois's talk was the closest to the dwelling scale in title and content alike. Le Corbusier's keynote roamed a vast territory from the interior design of the dwelling to the building form and the entire frame of urbanism. Schmidt's contribution on building regulations blended the dwelling and the urban scales, in hindsight foreshadowing the momentum towards urbanism that marked CIAM's trajectory from the La Sarraz assembly to CIAM4 and beyond (Kallis, 2020). By comparison Gropius covered his own distinctive ground at the congress, presenting the 'minimum' as a potential basis for 'optimum' dwelling design with sociological parameters considered as important as biological ones in determining typological, distributional and urban planning decisions. Even if the discussion at CIAM2 lacked a clear definitional and conceptual scaffold, it offered opportunities for the participants to articulate in more detail their views on what made the 'minimum' dwelling different from its reduced-size or -quality predecessors and on what set CIAM's approach apart from other contemporary architectural organizations. The diversity of the keynotes provided more than enough inspiration and controversy to animate the subsequent discussion. In response to Bourgeois's elaborate presentation of the biological and typological dimensions of the minimum dwelling during the second day of the congress, the discussion moved to a detailed exchange of views about the size, function and arrangement of individual rooms as part of a strategy to reconceptualize and redesign the modern dwelling. May, Gropius and Aalto drew attention to the elevated significance of the kitchen as the true 'laboratory' of the modern house – a small separate room that nevertheless held the key to the rethinking of the entire spectrum of daily functions of domestic economy and to the integration of the room components of the dwelling into a thoughtfully connected whole in spatial and psychological terms.[69] This discussion also echoed what Gropius had claimed in his keynote on the previous day about the rapidly changing sociological parameters of modern habitation, especially the relationship between individual, family, community and the state, resulting in the relegation of 'the importance of the family unit in the [modern] sociological picture'. Gropius argued that the smaller size of the average family, as well as the increase in the number of divorces, childless couples and people living alone presented architects with a new challenge to rethink the functions of the modern house in the context of a more collective organization of life.

But it was another section in Gropius's keynote that generated the most lively discussion at CIAM2. The Bauhaus founder used part of his talk to evince a strong preference for a form of semi-collective living based on the housing type of the multi-storey apartment block as a superior alternative to individual family houses. His conception of architectural space in this respect was already strongly three-dimensional, arguing in favour of grouping of dwellings in both vertical and horizontal scales. Throughout the 1920s he and other architects like Peter Behrens, Ludwig Hilberseimer, Hannes Meyer and van Eesteren had embraced the opportunities offered by a three-dimensional approach to architectural design, showing how high-rise construction could create fruitful tensions in the cityscape and articulate a strong image of urban modernity (Hays, 1995; Eesteren, 1997, 23; Hake, 2008, 124–33; McEwan, 2018). At CIAM2 Gropius defended vertical development not only on grounds of efficiency of construction and cost-effectiveness (thereby helping bridge the gap between cost of production and the average family income) but more importantly due to its alleged sociological and cultural benefits.

That Gropius ended up including a sizeable chunk of his keynote on the topic of high-versus-low-rise construction in an address otherwise dedicated to the minimum dwelling was far less arbitrary than it would seem. His efforts to include the topic of building form in the CIAM2 programme [see above] had been thwarted only by Giedion's and May's decision to slim down the congress agenda for practical reasons during the summer of 1929. This is why Gropius's excursus into the question of high-rise construction surprised and divided the delegates in Frankfurt. Stam and to an extent Schmidt objected to the discussion as a matter of principle, arguing that it involved a very different scale of architectural resolution to the one adopted for CIAM2 (the single dwelling). Members of the Frankfurt delegation (May, Hans Kampffmeyer and Hagen), together with Häring, took issue both with the programmatic position expressed by Gropius and with his decision to insert it in his keynote against congress thematic guidelines. Using arguments that had for long been restated by supporters of the garden city (Kampffmeyer was also involved in the IFHTP), they questioned the universal suitability of the tower block in modern urban housing design, especially for families with children. In spite of some support from delegates (e.g. André Lurçat called for more floors to be added to the building form of the Frankfurt 'minimum dwelling'), Gropius bowed to pressure and reluctantly agreed to retract this section of his talk.[70]

At the end of the Frankfurt congress efforts to extract a set of agreed design, construction and typological guidelines for the 'minimum dwelling' failed. The existence of profound ideological and programmatic disagreements among CIAM members combined with lack of usable data from the questionnaires to prevent in the end the publication of any congress resolutions. It is evident from the organizational paper trail that Schmidt in particular had worked consistently over the summer and autumn to put in place an efficient structure for soliciting data (questionnaires), collating the responses (summary template) and producing some kind of overarching resolutions from the congress. The Swiss architect had also drafted a template form for summarizing the findings of the second day of the Frankfurt proceedings that was only partly completed in the wake of the discussions, reflecting both lack of consensus and of usable data.[71] The summary template predictably skirted the more controversial discussion points at CIAM2 (e.g. minimum size of rooms, height of building/number of floors, aesthetic guidelines, the question of public ownership of land); yet it also attempted to establish the foundations of a collective programme for the minimum dwelling that rested on an aspirational set of biological, sociological and technical new minima. Schmidt had also prepared a draft version of what could have become the official 'theses' of CIAM2.[72] The 'minimum dwelling' was presented as both an emergency practical response to the crisis and a sociological necessity in view of the rapidly changing contemporary patterns of life. Schmidt's draft text recognized that some universally applicable minimum standards (about overall size and dimensions of individual rooms, internal configuration, equipment, insulation, heating, illumination, etc.) would be highly desirable due to 'the proceeding equalisation of living demands and needs through modern economy and production'. In an attempt to find a compromise formulation that would be acceptable to delegates with markedly divergent ideological and programmatic positions, the draft noted that the provision of mass housing could not be left entirely to market forces; it thus required at the very least the active involvement of public authorities in planning, construction and funding. The draft text was also critical of 'illusory' ideas that the good-quality dwelling could be made affordable to all simply through modern production and construction techniques. The real programmatic contribution of Schmidt's text, however, lay in its attempt to demolish two of the most common misconceptions surrounding the discourse of the minimum dwelling: first, that the minimum dwelling related to minimum size, overall surface area and/or size of individual rooms; and second, that the same 'minimum' could only exist as a meaningful social construct in direct relation to minimum family income (Brysch, 2019, 326). The alternative conception of the 'minimum dwelling' that the draft document sketched was a hybrid one – partly born out of socio-economic necessity and partly embraced positively for its sociocultural benefits – that ought to reflect an objective 'standard' based on human needs and a social right to decent, affordable housing for all (Huber, 1993, 26–7).

## The aftermath of the Frankfurt congress

In contrast to what had transpired in reaction to Gropius's lecture on the first day of CIAM2, the discussion that took place on the afternoon of 25 October, second day of the Frankfurt congress and final session of the closed-door proceedings, was less contentious and more focused. Schmidt's scrupulously researched and detailed talk, in conjunction with the technical insights from Bourgeois's keynote on the previous day, provided a framework for debating the 'minimum' on a more concrete and productive basis. Late into the discussion, Stam called for the determination of the congress's guidelines regarding the minimum technical and other requirements of the modern dwelling. At that point May intervened to remind the delegates that the organizational problems of the previous months had deprived CIAM2 of its most valuable resource – usable data from all its member countries that would have allowed meaningful comparison and evidence-based synthesis of findings. He also asked participants not to comment individually to the press about the congress proceedings and positions, leaving the outward-facing communication entirely to the Frankfurt office. The tone of May's interjection was sobering: the congress, he argued, was not ready to publicize its positions because its practical outcomes had been negligible at that stage.[73] This was the first clear indication that CIAM2 would refrain from issuing official resolutions on the theme of the minimum dwelling; and that the topic of the minimum dwelling would be carried over one way or another to the next congress, scheduled to take place in Brussels a year later.

May was predictably far more outspoken in his private correspondence with Giedion. His post-congress evaluation letter to Giedion was uncharacteristically long and candid by May's measured standards. He was unequivocal in his verdict that CIAM2 had not been a success, something that he attributed to organizational mistakes and misjudgements. Some of these May considered inevitable for a fledgling organization, although he expected that CIAM would have learnt a lot of lessons from the trials of the La Sarraz assembly more than a year earlier. Other misadventures, however, were entirely avoidable in his opinion, including the ponderous questionnaire system, the delays and the lack of consistency in the data provided in the responses of the national groups. He proposed for the future that all responses from the national groups be submitted at least four weeks ahead of the start of the congress for all the data to be tabulated and analysed rigorously. Still May reserved the most pointed critique for his own CIAM colleagues and congress participants who had approached the theme of the dwelling for the Existenzminimum as a 'problem of worldview' (*Weltanschauungsprobleme*) rather than as a practical architectural challenge. Only if architects had spent first a period of time in an actual worker's dwelling in order to understand the needs of its residents, he claimed, could their contribution to the debate of the minimum dwelling become useful and productive in practical terms. Until that happened and a sense of practical realism prevailed, nothing of real value could ever come out of the CIAM congresses, he warned.[74] A week later an ever more scathing attack on the Frankfurt congress came from Josef Frank, who informed Giedion that he resigned from his role as representative of the Austrian group and wished no further contacts with CIAM. Frank, unlike May, pointed the finger directly to the keynote speakers – Gropius and Schmidt in particular – accusing them of being superficial, dilettantish and not deserving a place in an otherwise serious professional congress. But the problem for Frank lay even deeper: it concerned key CIAM personalities, how they 'talked past each other' and ignored anything that did not fit their ideological or programmatic agenda. Frank concluded his resignation letter by deriding the key findings of the discussion in Frankfurt and by expressing the view that, with the same approach, the same personalities and their 'intrigues', and the same loosely defined topic carried over from Frankfurt to Brussels, there was hardly anything else he could contribute to the congress or CIAM as a whole.[75]

Frank's resignation was by far the most spectacular immediate fallout from the Frankfurt congress. More alarmingly, however, it also mapped out the deep ideological and programmatic fissures that ran through CIAM membership and that the Frankfurt congress had failed to reconcile: the extent of the architect's 'social' role; the tension between biological, sociological and technical priorities in dwelling design; the question of architecture as art or technique; the urbanization-decentralization debate. In his own assessment of CIAM2 Giedion bemoaned the chaotic planning ahead of the congress that had resulted in an essential bifurcation between keynotes and discussion without either a clear conceptual agenda or an effective organizational structure to amalgamate the two components.[76] Giedion was also aware of the deeper programmatic fissure when he confided to Gropius that the following congress could only succeed if it balanced more effectively the practical details with the bigger picture and the factual with the inspirational. This entailed continuing to work with members of very different convictions and even difficult personalities at almost any cost – but with a stronger operational structure.[77] With Le Corbusier absent – literally and metaphorically – from the forefront of CIAM and with the Ring architects increasingly divided over future participation, there was no margin for further high-profile fallouts.

In publicity terms the Frankfurt congress turned out to be hugely successful. Press reports and specialist presentations appeared soon afterwards on a number of outlets, reaching a much wider expert and public audience than either the congress or its Frankfurt-based events could ever garner. Both the Zurich secretariat and the Frankfurt congress hub worked hard, if not always in unison, to maximize the publicity momentum and the popularity of the exhibition (Barr, 2011, 34–5). The predictably mixed press reviews greeted CIAM2 as an important, if flawed and essentially incomplete, milestone for the 'new' architecture. The overwhelming majority of the reports commended the choice of congress theme and the novelty of the methodological approach followed at Frankfurt. The more focused discussion on building regulations that took place on the second day was generally recognized as the more valuable part of the congress proceedings[78] and there was near-universal praise for the CIAM2 exhibition.[79] Yet, beyond summarizing the key points from the keynotes and offering impressionistic comments on the proceedings, press and specialist reports that appeared in the wake of CIAM2 could not offer any specific insights into any breakthrough or progress that was achieved in Frankfurt.

Still, even if the Frankfurt congress itself was regarded by the CIAM organizers as a failure due to its chaotic planning, unfocused proceedings, ill temper and lack of resolutions, it was a productive one in the longer term. The programmatic impasse destroyed any hopes that the question of the minimum dwelling could be approached as a predominantly typological problem in need of universally applicable scientific standards. Such a conclusion was frustrating for the participants but turned out to be a blessing in disguise. In spite of the continuing lexical and/or semantic conflation of 'minimum' with small(ness) – particularly in the German-language context – size retreated further into the background of the programmatic discussion on the modern affordable dwelling. Similarly, it became clear that neither technical shortcuts nor design alchemies alone could provide a sustainably affordable and scaleable solution to the contemporary housing problem without fundamental changes in the broader administrative, socio-economic and/or legal context. The failure of CIAM2 to determine an alternative conception of the minimum dwelling – beyond the dissociation of the minimum from income and its closer alignment with scientific biological standards – may have appeared as an anti-climax to CIAM's steering group at the time but it did open up a broader discursive space for alternative understandings of the problem, if not exactly manifesto-like declarations, practical solutions or blueprints for immediate action. The willingness of the congress speakers to expand the scale of the discussion beyond the individual dwelling (be that urbanism, building form, land policy or political will) unwittingly produced the most consequential programmatic advance through a process of elimination: the minimum dwelling could not exist as a single, standalone technical or typological blueprint unless biological, sociological and technical standards aligned with the 'social' goals of making it affordable and accessible to all members of society, regardless of their income. Writing in Frankfurt's municipal journal shortly after the conclusion of CIAM2, May offered his own vision for an all-embracing programme capable of delivering the Existenzminimum dwelling for all. While avoiding rigid programmatic or ideological statements, he produced a formula that was not based on a single panacea but underlined the need for placing the discussion of the single dwelling into a composite frame with multiple interconnected parameters: modular composition that subsumed all scales from the individual domestic object to the room to the dwelling to the site and the settlement; rationalization and standardization of all components and processes of housing construction; attention to the biological and sociological standards; root-and-branch revision of land policies and building regulations; overhaul of the system of financing and the operation of local administration; embrace of modern technical methods and construction systems.[80] Others like Schmidt and later Teige came to similar conclusions while sponsoring very different ideological assumptions and optimal prescriptions for the future: the minimum dwelling ought to be one that was better – even optimal – to live in, because and not in spite of its planned austerity, offering a more enjoyable and liberating life for each and every of its residents, constructed efficiently to meet social demand and then made available at a cost that rendered it accessible to a significantly larger section – some would argue, even the entire – working population (Aymonino, 1971, 81–2).

And what of the Existenzminimum, a concept with demonstrably very few roots in the architectural discourse of the 1920s that CIAM attempted to bring to the frontline of the discussion about mass affordable housing? In early 1929 Giedion published a short, ebullient in tone and sumptuously illustrated manifesto-like book with the title *Liberated Living* (*Befreites Wohnen*). The publication project took shape and was completed in a real hurry (Mumford, 2000, 31–4) during the short period between the founding meeting of CIAM at La Sarraz (June 1928) and the group's first congress in Frankfurt (CIAM2, October 1929). It was intended as a propaganda statement for two recent trends that had converged: first, an unprecedented belief in the total transformative agency of modern architecture; and second, a recognition that housing design could become the laboratory of a new human and society as expansive horizon of modern architecture (Giedion, 2019, 6). Giedion dedicated a key portion of his book to the theme of 'dwelling for the Existenzminimum'. This, he claimed, was 'the most important task of contemporary architecture'. Giedion defined the problem as 'building dwellings for people with the most limited means'; but it was clear that he also held a normative conception of the dwelling – living liberated from the weight of permanence, of unaffordable rents, of domestic labour, of oppressive interiors and of unhygienic conditions of living. The dwelling that Giedion had in mind was the vehicle for 'a new form of life' for all:

> The minimum subsistence dwelling must offer more comfort than the typical bourgeois housing today at a lower price. That is, it must be better organised and must possess a higher LIVING VALUE.
> 
> (Giedion, 2019, 11–12; all emphasis in the original)

As intriguing, however, was Giedion's consistent terminology and signification of the Existenzminimum dwelling as a quality-cost-scale problem that the 'new' architecture could finally solve. The term, which would soon become the historic tag line of CIAM's Frankfurt congress, was still shrouded in ambiguity, devoid of a clear intellectual lineage in architecture up to that point; and Giedion offered little further conceptual clarity beyond equating it to an abstract minimum level of basic human needs, typically defined in statistical terms against prices and wages, and to the social group consisting of people with very low income that placed them close to, or even below, this minimum. The subsequent deliberations ahead of and during the Frankfurt congress did not resolve its ambiguity. 'Existenzminimum' has been taken for granted as the seminal description of the CIAM2 proceedings, enjoying wide adoption in the relevant international literature; but it has also served as a pejorative notation in many critiques of twentieth-century functionalist architecture as a whole, both in interwar and post-1945 years (e.g. De Carlo, 1970; Architecture Today, 2001, 5; Marzot, 2002, 67–8).

As bewildering as the term's hasty adoption in the CIAM nomenclature in 1929–30, however, was its swift demise. In the same article that appeared in the Frankfurt municipal magazine in November 1929, May used the term sparingly and came to a sobering conclusion in the wake of the Frankfurt congress:

> It should not be an exaggeration if we write that today we are at the beginning of this work and that it will probably take years before international cooperation between the civilised countries succeeds in finding a solution to the problem of housing for a living wage. … We are experiencing the morning of an era that sees the noble task of building in satisfying the living needs of the broad masses. It is therefore no coincidence that the International Congress for New Building (CIAM) chose this topic [dwelling for the Existenzminimum] for its first major conference, and it is again not surprising that, despite careful preparation of the conference, it has not achieved any results yet.

It seems that even May all but abandoned the term as a programmatic blueprint after CIAM2. The majority of future occurrences of the 'Existenzminimum' related to the international exhibition and the homonymous book-length publication of the conference proceedings (see Chapter 7). Nevertheless, though short-lived and soon to be eclipsed, CIAM's brief discourse of the Existenzminimum transformed the moral complexion of the entire conversation on the mass low-cost dwelling. It may have done little to bridge the ideological and programmatic positions that divided the participating architects or shape CIAM's frame of analysis in the longer term (the shift to the larger urban scale was already in place by 1930–31). It did, however, embed an enduring 'social' meaning to the problem, as the pursuit of a golden ratio of utopian aspiration and realism grounded on a flexible equilibrium of quality, cost and affordability that could ensure universal deployment in the shortest possible term. Unlike the IFHTP, which approached the challenge as a 'problem' to be mitigated in the margins of core architectural practice, for CIAM the problem of the dwelling for the Existenzminimum was both a challenge and the ultimate aspiration. The frame was universal and egalitarian: CIAM's 'minimum dwelling' was conceived first and foremost as an ethical proposition – a community asset, judged not on the quality of each single unit that it provided but on its capacity for promoting better-quality housing for as many as possible – and ideally for all members of a community. In its wake the size-reduction rationale of the Kleinwohnung, the design language of 'less is more', as well as the debates on centralization versus peripheral settlement or low-versus-high rise were proposed as complementary, flexible and debatable variables subsumed into an overriding ethical project of providing good-quality housing to everyone.

# CHAPTER 6
## CIAM3: DWELLING AS THE UNLIKELY HUB OF MODERN ARCHITECTURE

**From CIAM2 to CIAM3: Exploring scales in three-dimensional space**

If CIAM's 1929 Frankfurt congress had a theme of sorts and a more defined programmatic focus to begin with, the Brussels congress that followed it in 1930 has proved much harder to pin down in programmatic terms. Starting its life as a mere follow-up to the unfinished business from Frankfurt on the 'minimum' dwelling, it ended up hosting an incongruous patchwork of ideas, themes and architectural scales. The balancing act of fitting the dwelling alongside building height, land subdivision (what became the official theme of the congress in the process) and urbanism (an intention that gathered momentum ahead of the congress but was then toned down for practical reasons) in the CIAM3 agenda proved arguably too hard for the organizers of, and participants in, Brussels. As a result, CIAM3 lacked focus, coherence and anything vaguely resembling resolutions about any of its themes. Rather than an organic sequel to CIAM2, the Brussels congress ended up resembling more an unintended prolegomenon to CIAM4. Nevertheless, the planning for and conduct of the Brussels congress functioned as a steep learning curve for CIAM. More out of contingency than design it closed down programmatic pathways and opened up new ones, effecting in the process significant changes in organizational dynamics and recalibrating longer-term strategies through both negative and positive feedback. In the process CIAM3 did arguably far more to signify and elaborate the organization's distinctive take on the 'minimum dwelling' and on the 'new' architecture as a whole than CIAM2.

CIAM3, the organization's second working congress, took place in Brussels in late November 1930, a mere thirteen months after the conclusion of the Frankfurt event. In hindsight it may appear as the ultimate transitional occasion in the history of the early CIAM, occupying an awkward spot between the panegyrical founding of the organization in 1928 and the legendary fourth congress en route from Marseille to Athens in 1933. Its count of shortcomings and mishaps was high: dysfunctional organization, lack of thematic focus and coherent scale of analysis, absence of congress resolutions, ideological chasms and personal frictions, headline absences and departures, and so on. Lessons from the preparation and conduct of the Frankfurt congress weighed on the minds of the organizers – but, because of CIAM's loose modus operandi and Giedion's conscious efforts to avoid confrontation, old defects and new problems beset the

Brussels congress from the first stages of its organization. Some of the most disruptive developments could not be anticipated – for example, the sudden resignation of Karl Moser from CIAM's presidency; or the equally unanticipated departure of key CIRPAC figures for the Soviet Union (May, Stam, Schmidt) who were in fact heavily involved in the CIAM3 preparations. The lack, however, of a clear programmatic vision for the Brussels congress and the very different perspectives of key CIAM members about the direction of the organization meant that once again the preparation cycle was marred by confusion, delays, lack of coherent thinking and high-profile – if mostly privately expressed – personal grudges.

CIAM3 was supposed to become *the* congress on the 'minimum dwelling', following from the frank admission that the Frankfurt congress had not delivered a forensic analysis and authoritative guidelines on the topic. In theory the early agreement to carry over the topic from CIAM2 to the 1930 Brussels congress[1] had offered the organizers a much clearer focus and sense of direction. This meant that now the CIRPAC did not have to spend too much time determining the congress theme as it had to do at the same point in the CIAM2 planning cycle. However the advantage was squandered in the months leading up to the congress, with an unprecedented profusion of further topic ideas that kept battling for the soul of the congress and the movement until the last moment. Unlike CIAM2, where the organizers decided at a sensible point in time to limit the discussion topics and thin down the agenda while investing heavily in the single exhibition event, CIAM3 ended up with a nominal title that kept changing, at least one further key theme, more ideas that were introduced haphazardly and sometimes abandoned in the process, and four concurrent exhibition events. The 'minimum dwelling' ended up being tucked into the final day of the official congress programme, overshadowed by other themes and increasingly treated as an embarrassing legacy of CIAM's 'child diseases'. It was also quite possibly rescued from obscurity by the ongoing success of the CIAM2 exhibition spin-offs (see Chapter 7) and by the unexpected stir caused by the summary keynote on the topic delivered by the Czech delegate Karel Teige.

Given that the eventually official title of CIAM3 (*Rationelle Bebauungsweise*, rational land subdivision) was only tangentially linked to the original intention to engage in more detail with the unfinished business from Frankfurt on the topic of the (Existenz-) minimum housing, it would be reasonable to approach the Brussels congress as little more than a footnote in CIAM's brief encounter with the minimum dwelling. Instead I argue that the 1930 Brussels congress was the organization's most ambitious, discursively rich, inclusive and pluralistic of its interwar congresses. Far more than its Frankfurt predecessor, it ended up being the signature housing congress of the early CIAM, delivering surprisingly rich and productive insights into the problem of the 'minimum dwelling'. It also marked the climax and at the same time the end of an era in CIAM's early history – an era linked as much to particular personalities as to their particular programmatic vision for the 'new' architecture.

# The Minimum Dwelling

## The elusive theme(s) of CIAM3: The battle of the scales

The decision reached at the end of the Frankfurt congress to carry over the discussion of the minimum dwelling to the next event provided much-needed focus and direction to the CIRPAC planning efforts that had been sorely lacking during the preparation of the Frankfurt congress.[2] The swift acceptance of Victor Bourgeois's offer to host the 1930 congress in Brussels was also a welcome development that was communicated immediately to CIAM members and key contacts targeted for future participation.[3] The initially depressed mood within the ranks of the organization after the conclusion of the Frankfurt proceedings gradually gave way to a more optimistic outlook for the future. In the remaining months of 1929 Giedion and May prioritized work on the two most important public-facing legacies from CIAM2 – the exhibition that was about to embark on a successful international outing; and the eagerly anticipated congress publication. This, however, as well as ongoing problems with the structure of the German and French national groups,[4] also meant that the organization of the Brussels congress took a back seat until late in the winter of 1930.

The preparation cycle for CIAM3 began in earnest with the meeting held at Le Corbusier's atelier in Paris on 3 February 1930. This was the first of three such planning meetings, with the second taking place also in Paris in May and the third one hosted in Frankfurt in the following September. The choice of Paris as location for the meeting was a welcome indication of Le Corbusier's renewed engagement with CIAM after a hiatus of more than half a year and his absence from the Frankfurt congress. It was also useful for the CIAM leadership in its efforts to rebalance – if mainly on the symbolic level – the German and French influence on the organization. As it turned out, the first Paris meeting was poorly attended, with Gropius and May failing to turn up and with the more temperamental Stam representing the German side at the discussion.[5] The meeting was also overshadowed by the sudden announcement of Moser's resignation from the presidency of CIAM only days earlier.[6] Giedion had sought to postpone the crucial preparatory meeting that would determine the theme of the Brussels congress, fearing that without the presence of two of his most dependable interlocutors at that stage the discussion about fixing the congress theme could become unduly influenced by the agendas of those present.[7] In the end, however, the urgent need to set in motion the preparations for CIAM3 as quickly as possible in order to avoid a repetition of the planning chaos that had beset the previous year's congress prevailed in the minds of the CIRPAC delegates.

The February Paris meeting was chaired by Bourgeois as official host of the 1930 congress. Yet it was the presence and contribution of Le Corbusier that proved once again pivotal. This was not the Le Corbusier of the 1929 Basel meeting where he had called for practical and focused proceedings anchored on the dwelling scale and had done more than anyone to define CIAM's particular angle on the topic by introducing into the CIRPAC discussion the language of the 'minimum' (see Chapter 5). Instead this time the Swiss architect launched into an impassioned and sweeping defence of adopting architectural scales wider than the dwelling. Although at the beginning of the discussion he appeared hostile to the idea of introducing a discussion on urbanism at CIAM3 before having resolved the fundamentals of the discussion on housing, he then turned the problem upside down by suggesting that the question of the 'minimum dwelling' could not be effectively addressed without revisiting a host of broader issues – from the sociological uses of the modern dwelling to the planning laws to the existence of communal services to the design of neighbourhoods and communities, and so on. The key point, according to Le Corbusier, was to use the Brussels congress to transition the discussion from the minimum habitation as individual 'cell' (the single dwelling) to its modular iterations as building, quarter and in the end city as a whole. Although he cautioned against debating urbanism in broad and abstract terms, he ended up defending its critical place at the 1930 congress by identifying its all-important intersection with the housing question – the 'subdivision/parcelling of land' (Kallis, 2020, 11–12). This was the only way, he argued, that a discussion of urbanism could add real value to the CIAM proceedings without sacrificing the clear and practical focus of the congress.[8]

The official press report that was issued at the end of the lengthy February 1930 preparatory meeting restated the earlier position that the theme of the 'minimum dwelling' would continue to be the main focus of the Brussels congress. It added, however, that the discussion would also be expanded and elaborated to include the question of 'rational land development'.[9] The French and the German versions of the February press report reproduced the bifurcated language of CIAM2 regarding the 'minimum dwelling' (*habitation minimum* in French; *Wohnung für das Existenzminimum* in German) but resorted to similar terminology to render the newly introduced focus on land development for CIAM3 (*parcellement du sol/Bodenparzellierung*, respectively). The relatively understated discursive shift from dwelling to land was suggestive of a more consequential furtive scale leap towards urbanism as the default CIAM frame (Gold, 1998, 231). Yet the change of plan sanctioned by the CIRPAC delegates, who had arrived at the Paris preparatory meeting well aware of the earlier decision to reserve the topic of urbanism for the organization's fourth congress, was less surprising than it might have appeared at first. The programmatic link between land development and social housing had been recently explored at the recent IFHTP congresses in Vienna (1926) and Paris (1928) (see Chapter 3), with more and more architects realizing that the path to a socially progressive housing policy passed through a radical overhaul of land ownership and subdivision practices (Domhardt, 2012, 178–9). The question of land reform (*Bodenreform*) had surfaced as a strong candidate for becoming the key topic of the third day of CIAM2 during the spring and summer of 1929, supported in particular by Gropius and by the Swiss group.[10] That it was eventually dropped from the Frankfurt congress had to do with attempts to shorten the event and simplify the agenda – but it was assumed that land reform itself would become an important part of CIAM's future conceptual transition to the wider scales of architectural analysis.

Furthermore, Gropius revived his original attempt to include a discussion of optimal building form and height that had caused so much acrimony when it was mentioned – contra programme – in Frankfurt. This time his proposal enjoyed Giedion's enthusiastic endorsement. The CIAM secretary had been following the discussion on high-rise residential architecture at the 1929 IFHTP congress in Rome and, like Gropius, was keen on incorporating this dimension to the CIAM discussion on the minimum dwelling. Ahead of the Paris preparatory meeting, Giedion and Gropius exchanged a series of personal letters discussing the best way to mastermind the incorporation of building height into the CIAM3 discussion. Gropius was evidently smarting at having been rebuffed in Frankfurt, pointing the finger at Stam but also blaming May's 'clumsiness' for the embarrassing debacle.[11] Giedion had already been in contact with the two English architects (Rutherford and Keay) who had raised the topic of high-rise residential building form at the IFHTP congress, with a view to inviting them to give presentations at the forthcoming Brussels congress (Somer, 2007, 39–40).[12] Gropius's absence from the February CIRPAC meeting, however, meant that the topic had to be proposed by Giedion himself, in what can only be described as an awkward and largely unsuccessful attempt to get it accepted into the official CIAM3 programme.[13]

There were two further proposals concerning the theme of the Brussels congress that attempted to square the circle of continuing the discussion on the 'minimum dwelling' while also cogently addressing a broader set of issues. The first came from the Belgian member Raphael Verwilghen, who was also heavily involved in the 1930 congress preparations. Verwilghen's scheme had been submitted to the CIRPAC ahead of the February meeting and was quoted extensively during the discussion at Le Corbusier's atelier. Based on his extensive experience from designing housing schemes in Belgium, Verwilghen's scheme suggested a gradual shift of CIAM's analysis towards a significantly larger urban scale. The proposed shift, however, followed a thoughtful modular approach to negotiating and integrating different scales of architectural analysis, leading incrementally and organically from the individual minimum dwelling to urban planning through the 'grouping of minimum dwellings' into novel building forms and neighbourhood/settlement plans (Grulois, 2011). Verwilghen also outlined a three-stage structure for the forthcoming congress with the first two relating directly to the 'minimum dwelling' and featuring a comparison between historical and contemporary examples; and the third stage exploring a workable method for moving from the individual home to the urban scale by examining different groupings of dwellings in surface area, volume and height.[14]

It was this last point – the extension beyond the individual building plot and towards the settlement and the entire city scales – that proved inevitably contentious. Verwilghen's proposed framework for CIAM3 could not be accepted in its entirety because it veered too far in the direction of large-scale settlement design (even with his suggestion that the discussion of settlements be limited to those with an overall size of up to twelve hectares). For those, like Stam and Bourgeois, who had arrived at the Paris preparatory meeting eager to defend the centrality of the dwelling scale against overextension towards urbanism, Verwilghen's scheme was a step too far in that direction. And yet, in hindsight, so much that featured in this early proposal subsequently shaped the congress and exhibition preparation. It was Verwilghen's suggestion for a 'congress-promenade into the exhibition' that was ground-breaking, because it essentially provided a cogent methodology for partly disaggregating the two key CIAM3 components and their respective modes of discourse (congress-verbal versus exhibition-visual). He argued that any link between the minimum dwelling and urbanism might not have been appropriate for a congress keynote at that stage but it could inject a new kind of programmatic dynamism to the graphical presentation of plans in the various exhibition activities planned for CIAM3. This suggested a change of approach to the relative balance between the congress and the exhibition: while in Frankfurt the exhibition was in theory designed to reinforce the themes of the congress proceedings, what Verwilghen proposed for Brussels was an exhibition that was both significantly autonomous from the congress keynotes and a further 'promenade' into the anticipated theme of the following congress.

The second fully formed proposal about CIAM3 that was discussed at the February preparatory meeting came from the Danish group and was significant in a different way. While not departing from the earlier decision to maintain the 'minimum dwelling' as the core theme of CIAM3, the Danish scheme suggested an interesting division of methodologies: on the one hand, the 'minimum dwelling' as a fact of international modern architectural practice through the best examples that had already been realized under existing conditions and regulations; on the other hand, a reflection on the 'minimum dwelling' as it ought to be, with its novel normative conceptions of living, opportunities for better quality of life for the masses and a consideration of what steps could bring this alternative future within the reach of modern architects.[15] This fundamental distinction cut across all sorts of ideological and programmatic fissures, not only within the ranks of CIAM but also across the entire professional communities of modern architects and urban planners. It was essentially pointing to the existence of two different approaches to the housing question and two different associated languages with which to articulate diagnoses and solutions – a present-focused, pragmatic, practical, reform-oriented one versus a future-oriented, utopian, disruptive, indeed revolutionary alternative.

Although sensibly formulated and enjoying Giedion's support, the Danish proposal touched raw nerves at the Paris February meeting, provoking a somewhat tart exchange between Stam and Le Corbusier. The two prominent CIAM figures were divided by significant professional, programmatic and ideological differences, even if they were both drawn to the transformational promise of the 'new' architecture. The Swiss-born architect's unique approach to external form, his hyper-advocacy of *machinisme* and his at best erratic political stance had already turned him into a bête noire in the eyes of committed socialist architects such as Meyer, Schmidt and Stam (Bernardi, 1995, 101). At the February 1930 Paris meeting Stam appeared to favour a more factual, evidence-based and pragmatic focus for the forthcoming Brussels congress, reminding the participants that CIAM2 had been criticized precisely for its perceived lack of practical focus and tendency to digress into wild projections of diverse utopian imagination. Le Corbusier did not disagree with the essence of the separation proposed by the Danish group but reacted to Stam's crude realism-utopia juxtaposition; for him it was the utopia of today that was bound to become good practice in the near future. The two architects also disagreed on whether the CIAM3 exhibition ought to show only realized housing exemplars or include a portion of planned or 'paper' projects. The exchange remained generally courteous in tone and the discussion appears to have moved on quickly to other, more pressing organizational matters for the impending Brussels congress.[16] It did reveal, however, a growing divergence of perceptions among key CIAM participants about the very raison d'être and future strategic priorities of the organization (Somer, 2007, 34–7).

The February meeting ended on a positive, if inconclusive, note. In spite of important absences and the often awkward personal chemistry among the attendees, it achieved a significant conceptual shift from the 'minimum dwelling' to the nomenclature of 'land subdivision', even if it left the details of the associated scale transition largely undetermined. It also produced a series of important decisions about the management of the questionnaire system (in theory two sets would be sent out to national groups shortly after the meeting, one produced by Schmidt and the other by Le Corbusier); and the organization of the CIAM3 exhibition itself. Clearer guidelines for the national groups were issued and early deadlines were set in order to avoid a repetition of the problems that had beleaguered the Frankfurt congress.[17] In the weeks that followed the meeting, however, the attention of the organizers in Zurich, Brussels and Frankfurt was diverted by a series of crises regarding national groups (most notably, once again, the German *Ring*) and the publication from CIAM2 that nearly caused a rift between Gropius and May and threatened to destroy the last remaining chances of a constructive German representation in the organization after the bitter fallout with Häring (see Chapter 5). In addition Le Corbusier continued to be an unreliable interlocutor, delaying the preparation of his questionnaire on technical innovations in dwelling design.[18]

By the time that the second preparatory meeting took place in mid-May, again in Le Corbusier's atelier in Paris, it seemed that little progress had been made towards giving a more definite shape to the Brussels congress, in spite of the impressive preparatory work carried out by the members of the Swiss group (Schmidt and Rudolf Steiger in particular) to that effect. Technically this was not one but two meetings separated by three days. The first of these meetings on 17 May was disrupted by the absence of the main congress organizer, Bourgeois. This otherwise minor inconvenience forced those present (Le Corbusier, Moser, Giedion, Steiger and Gropius) to hold off the discussion of the bulk of organizational matters for the follow-up meeting, scheduled to take place on 20 May. Instead, on Moser's proposal, discussion moved to the questionnaires and the exhibition. The result was a bizarre exchange of views on wider programmatic and methodological questions, prompted by a fully formed proposal from the Swiss group but then largely monopolized by Le Corbusier. In Schmidt's absence Steiger presented an overview of the Swiss scheme to the attendees, based on a detailed comparison between three major Swiss cities – Zurich, Basel, Geneva – that united different scales (city-block-building-dwelling), time dimensions (historical development and contemporary conditions) and methodologies (overview of existing situation plus proposals for optimal future arrangements).[19] The Swiss scheme was fascinating because, quite like Verwilghen's proposal at the February meeting, it sought to integrate more organically the congress discussion and the exhibition activity. It also sketched, however elliptically, an analytical approach that fused rich historical data and up-to-date social evidence with urban morphology. In essence it set up a framework for analysis and a visual scheme for presenting evidence that promised to feed productively into, and amplify the outputs of, each other. Given the already agreed plan to dedicate the fourth CIAM congress exclusively to urbanism, the Swiss proposal also provided a thoughtful roadmap to extend methodically the discussion from the minimum dwelling to the city without losing sight of the individual significance of the different architectural scales and their interconnections.

Le Corbusier responded to Steiger's presentation with characteristic enthusiasm and loquaciousness. He was once again on ebullient form, traversing architectural scales with rhetorical flair and oscillating between rigorous scientific realism and sweeping utopianism. He arrived at the meeting with yet another scheme to extend the planned discussion on the minimum dwelling and land subdivision towards his favourite theme of urbanization. In many respects this was a rerun of his disagreement with Stam at the February meeting over utopia and pragmatic realism – but revisited more expansively from the viewpoint of a new doctrine of urbanism. Le Corbusier's fundamental proposition was that there could be no aspirational discussion on the 'minimum dwelling' unless modern technical innovations were deployed to their maximum effect in the context of a radically reformed building legislation and land policy. He also observed that, however sophisticated and effective the methods and norms of modern architecture may have been, they could not be realized under the existing regulatory regime. Therefore, he argued, a radically new urban doctrine was desperately needed in order to open the way for the revolutionary changes envisioned by the 'new' architecture. Reverting to utopian tropes, Le Corbusier claimed that new construction and site-management techniques already constituted a 'revolution' – but one that was nevertheless stifled by 'ancient' building regulations and modes of municipal decision-making. Given that Schmidt had already engaged with this precise topic at CIAM2 and Giedion had pressed for dedicating part of the congress work to the theme of obstacles in the way of the 'new' architecture, Le Corbusier used his positive assessment of the Swiss scheme to align the critique of the present conditions with the formulation of a radical new doctrine of urbanism that would supposedly set CIAM apart from other contemporary organizations.

In the course of appraising the Swiss scheme and promoting the programmatic link between architecture, urbanism and social development, Le Corbusier used one of his serial digressions to link land subdivision to density. Summoning his already published plans for the *Ville Contemporaine* and the *Plan Voisin* for Paris (Passanti, 1987) and reflecting his hardening critique of suburbanization and urban decentralization, he called for a rational 'urbanisation of the city centres in height and space', with new typologies of high-rise housing stacks designed in close collaboration between architects and a wide range of experts from the economic, technical, sociological and health professional fields. The absence of May – one of the most fervent and persistent proponents of the lower-rise/-density *Trabanten* principle at the time (Kähler, 1985, 20–44) – from the meeting made this attack on peripheral development easier to interject. In addition, however, it provided the perfect opportunity for Gropius to put once again on the table his own proposal for aligning minimum dwelling and land management with building height and the opportunities offered by high-rise residential development. Gropius defended the programmatic significance of high-rise construction in the context of the discussion on the affordable good-quality housing by linking Le Corbusier's vision of centralization with Schmidt's research on building regulations. His was a short intervention, hampered by the fact that the meeting lacked consistent translation and was generally monopolized by Le Corbusier's long and rambling monologues in French. Giedion, who had earlier helped with the translation of Steiger's presentation, stepped in once again to render a summary of Gropius's proposal in French. But the discussion was inconclusive beyond charting a possible path for the conceptual passage from dwelling to land development to urbanism.

Following Gropius's brief intervention, the discussion was swiftly overshadowed by another Lecorbusian soliloquy – the first of two passionate tributes to Soviet urbanism at the Paris preparatory meetings. Invoking the contemporary experiments in the Soviet Union as a guiding principle for CIAM's future work fed easily into the growing consensus within the organization on the shift to the urban scale and the plans to hold the fourth congress in Moscow. It was of very limited use, however, in terms of settling the topic for the forthcoming CIAM3. Moser tried on numerous occasions to refocus the discussion on clarifying the precise conceptual focus of the Brussels congress but to no avail. The first May meeting ended with broad agreement on Schmidt's proposal, notwithstanding reservations expressed by some attendees about its logistical feasibility for CIAM3 given the relatively short time remaining; and with an even more vague discussion on a further proposal by Le Corbusier premised on a separate questionnaire linking the 'minimum dwelling' with the three topics of ventilation, sound-proofing and illumination. In light of the apparent lack of clear agreement regarding the precise topic for the Brussels congress at the end of the 17 May meeting, it is therefore surprising that Moser opened the proceedings of the second gathering three days later by declaring this subject already settled and moving the discussion to other organizational matters.[20] This time the presence of Bourgeois provided more of a practical focus for the discussion in comparison to the earlier meeting, allowing a series of decisions to be taken about the dates of the congress (originally 2–4 October), the extent of the exhibition material (Bourgeois insisted on a maximum limit of twenty urban case studies due to complexity of the process of gathering and standardizing the material from so many different sources), and a strict deadline for both the production of the visual templates by Schmidt (mid-June to early July) and the submission of all the other plates (mid-August at the latest). Bourgeois made a final attempt to bring the 'minimum dwelling' back to the forefront of the CIAM3 proceedings, proposing a set of parallel public-facing events with a more specific Belgian focus to be organized either at the tail end of the congress or immediately after its conclusion. This seemingly straightforward proposal was quickly accepted by the attending CIRPAC members, especially after Bourgeois guaranteed that this would be a side-event and would not overshadow CIAM3 as 'the congress in the absolute sense of the word'.[21] In hindsight, however, it introduced a further split in the programme of the Brussels congress that would result in the contentious organization of the parallel *Journées de l'Habitation Minimum* programme of talks and exhibition (see Chapter 7).

Even more bewilderingly, the discussion soon generated two further theme proposals. In different ways both were sponsored by Giedion himself. The first concerned the topic of horizontal sliding windows and formed part of his broader intention to feature in every future CIAM congress a mini-exhibition dedicated to a small technical detail. This new idea had appeared only recently in Giedion's private correspondence.[22] Given Le Corbusier's interest in the illumination of the dwelling and his intention to develop a specialist questionnaire on this topic for CIAM3, the proposal was received very positively by the Swiss architect, who in turn argued that innovation in sliding window technology ought to be discussed as a critical element of any type of dwelling, regardless of its size, intended use or resident. Bourgeois, on the other hand, was equally surprised and frustrated with the lack of prior consultation on this matter, since he and his Belgian national group were nominally the main organizers of CIAM3 in all its aspects. Once again CIRPAC gave the green light to this proposal without too much scrutiny or consideration of how it could be cogently integrated into the expanding web of CIAM3 discussion themes, questionnaires and exhibition events. Towards the end of the gathering Giedion observed how the original focus on the minimum dwelling had expanded into other types of habitation, perspectives, methodologies and scales of architectural analysis. Reiterating Gropius's proposal originally made at the first Paris meeting of February and resurrected three days earlier, Giedion added the theme of building height into the emerging thematic pastiche of CIAM3. This time Le Corbusier responded more favourably, connecting it to his own interest in the dwelling as a three-dimensional space ('cube'). His concluding intervention at the Paris meeting of 20 May was as determinative of the eventual programme of the Brussels congress as was his unorthodox introduction of the trope of 'minimum' in relation to the theme of CIAM2 at the preparatory meeting of February 1929. This time Le Corbusier proposed the theme of land subdivision as the conceptual pivot of the entire Brussels congress, with Schmidt, Gropius and himself devising three discrete but complementary questionnaires to expand the discussion from two- to three-dimensional construction, from the past and present to the future, and from realism to utopia.[23]

The communique issued by CIRPAC immediately after the two preparatory meetings in May 1930 captured eloquently how much had changed in the course of two otherwise chaotic gatherings in Le Corbusier's atelier in Paris.[24] The official overarching theme of CIAM3 was now stated as the rational land subdivision (*problème du lotissement rational du sol* in French; *rationelle Bebauungsweisen* in German). This shift was admittedly consistent with the direction of travel since the first preparatory meeting in February 1930, in an attempt to bridge the different perspectives of key CIAM members and mediate between their attempts to expand the more restrictive focus on the minimum dwelling. The latter was clearly becoming more and more like an unwanted bequest – and the absence of representatives from the Frankfurt team (May or Stam) from these meetings signalled more profound and consequential programmatic shifts within CIAM as a whole. What was particularly striking, however, was how the official meeting report contained no reference whatsoever to the 'minimum dwelling' and how much the discursive balance had swung towards the larger urban scale. In addition Le Corbusier's proposal to use questionnaires as a route to introducing further topics into the proceedings took the control of the congress agenda away from the hands of either the Zurich office or the Brussels organizers. Under the vague rubric of 'rational land subdivision' CIRPAC in effect sanctioned a multi-scalar and thematically de-centred congress, with the shape of the proceedings now largely depending on three very different questionnaires yet to be even drafted, let alone approved and distributed. Meanwhile the significant amount of time dedicated to discussing matters concerning the exhibition(s), the publications and the other parallel events at the two May preparatory sessions indicated that the core congress proceedings continued to be further upstaged by CIAM's associated public-facing events.

It took another preparatory meeting, four months later, to give final shape to the Brussels congress programme. The meeting, held in Frankfurt on 25 September 1930, was attended by a significantly wider, more diverse and more representative section of the CIAM membership than any similar gathering before or arguably afterwards.[25] Apart from Moser, Giedion and Bourgeois, there was a strong representation from Germany (Gropius, Häring, Stam, May) and Switzerland (Schmidt, Steiger), as well as representatives from the Netherlands (Gerrit Rietveld), Finland (Alvar Aalto), Poland (Syrkus), Hungary (Fred Forbát), the United States (Richard Neutra) and indeed the Soviet Union (Moisei Ginzburg). The expanded and nationally diverse attendance list attested to the diligent work of the Zurich secretariat in both co-opting new delegates and keeping the existing members as engaged as possible. There was no representation from France, however; even Le Corbusier, who had hosted and largely monopolized the preceding preparatory meetings, was absent from Frankfurt and, more alarmingly, going through yet another phase of detachment from CIAM after a spell of strong engagement in the first five months of the year. At the beginning of the meeting Giedion provided an overview of the congress programme and associated exhibition activities. 'Rational land management' now featured alongside 'low-, medium-, and high-rise construction' as major themes of the CIAM3 event, the latter having somehow transmogrified into the conceptual hub of the entire congress over the summer months. Tellingly there was hardly any mention of the 'minimum dwelling' in Giedion's overview, even when he referred to the discussion of the national reports on this very topic (the unfinished business of the questionnaires from CIAM2) scheduled for the final day of the Brussels congress.

The measured tone of Giedion's presentation belied the serious difficulties that the preparation effort for CIAM3 had encountered since the earlier meeting in Paris. In many respects the obstacles were similar to those that had bedevilled the preparation and conduct of the Frankfurt congress a year earlier: lack of centralized overview of the operation and of robust institutional structures; erratic behaviour of key CIAM members who were responsible for critical tasks such as the production of questionnaires or the organization of the exhibitions; unreliable and asymmetrically engaged national groups; lack of clarity regarding the definite shape of the congress proceedings and the nature of information/evidence requested. With multiple thematic strands running in parallel, each overly reliant on independent work carried out by a different CIAM figure, and an increasingly blurred distinction between congress and exhibition(s), CIAM3 ended up being far more at the mercy of competing visions and priorities than any of CIAM's early congresses. In the wake of the May meeting critical preparatory work had in effect been delegated to four separate hubs operating largely independent from each other and without a clear sense of coordination or direction. Bourgeois in Brussels turned his main attention to the parallel programme on the 'minimum dwelling' that he had only vaguely outlined at the Paris meeting, taking liberties without prior consultation that would dismay the Zurich central office and complicate further the task of coordination.[26] Gropius, who together with Giedion was the main proponent of the thematic shift from a two-dimensional focus on dwelling size and land management to a three-dimensional perspective hinging building form and height, was distracted over the spring and summer of 1930 by his key role in the Werkbund exhibition (Overy, 2004; Miller, 2017).[27] After initially playing a key role in determining the thematic profile of the congress, Le Corbusier became elusive and unpredictable over the spring and summer. The questionnaire that he had promised at the February and again at the May meetings arrived well into the summer and was distributed with considerable delay.[28] Furthermore, at various points over the summer and autumn he swung from inertia to short bursts of activity and back to detached silence, casting doubts as to whether he would even turn up in Brussels.[29] Schmidt continued to work effortlessly on his presentation scheme and associated questionnaire but was in the end defeated by the very ambition of his vision and the harsh test of limited time. By June it was clear that his original intention to include in the congress discussion and exhibition presentation a fourth dimension – the historical development of cities – could not be completed in time for the questionnaires to be distributed, collected and analysed ahead of the opening of CIAM3. In a last-ditch attempt to break the deadlock Stam was called in to assist Schmidt with finalizing a scaled-down but still usable version of the questionnaire for immediate circulation that also incorporated the bulk of Gropius's high-rise agenda.[30] Notwithstanding the misgivings of Gropius and other key CIAM members about Stam's disruptive behaviour and difficult character,[31] his renewed involvement in the preparations for CIAM3 came at the most critical moment to restore a semblance of focus and efficiency in the process

Just as things appeared to be getting back on track, however, May announced that he was about to end his five-year spell as chief architect of Frankfurt and embark on a new adventure in the Soviet Union from the coming autumn (Flierl, 2011; Bosma, 2014).[32] Until that point May's involvement in both CIAM matters and in the preparations for the Brussels congress had been very limited to begin with, even if he was nominally one of the key figures of the CIAM3 organizing committee. His experience and organizational nous, however, as well as his ability to mediate between opposing views and alleviate tensions – both within the organization and inside the troublesome Ring group in Germany – were critical assets for the early success and stability of CIAM. Therefore his forthcoming departure presaged trouble for CIAM's overall operation. To make matters worse, two other members at the helm of the preparation for the Brussels congress and exhibition – Stam and Schmidt – also announced their departure.[33] They were joined by other prominent members of the Frankfurt team (including Lihotzky) and by another

CIAM delegate, Forbat, who at the time was making his mark as designer and architect of various settlements in Berlin (Ingberman, 1994, 147–50; Jönsson, 2013).

The September 1930 preparatory meeting was the last CIRPAC event attended by May and the other 'brigade' members before their departure for the Soviet Union (Oorthuys and Möller, 1991, 14). In spite of Giedion's concerted efforts from the beginning to sidestep political discussions within the organization, it was evident even at the La Sarraz gathering that ideological divisions had a growing bearing on the debate about CIAM's fundamental programmatic priorities (Mumford, 2000, xii). As CIAM was preparing for its third congress, its leadership were pursuing a closer relationship with both the Soviet Union and (Fascist) Italy.[34] Preparations for a landmark (fourth) CIAM congress on urbanism to be held in Moscow in 1931 were already well-underway and became a priority immediately after the conclusion of the Brussels congress, when the growing presence of the Italian group within the organization raised the prospect of the following (fifth) congress to be held in Milan.[35] The official mantra that CIAM was a broad, inclusive and politically agnostic international forum based on shared professional and design principles alone could no longer compensate for the internal tensions that existing ideological fault lines generated. As membership continued to expand, these and other tensions – sometimes ideological, other times cultural and personal – became harder and harder to avoid, let alone reconcile. The increasingly strained equilibrium was always at the mercy of personal chemistry, dependent on who was in attendance and who was absent from any particular CIAM or especially CIRPAC gathering. The absence of Le Corbusier from the September meeting made it easier for the more brusque members to voice their criticism of the programmatic direction that CIAM3 had taken under his influence. When, for example, the discussion turned to the preparations for the planned mini-exhibition on sliding windows, Stam launched a stinging critique of the decision to turn such a 'luxury' item into one of the centrepieces of the congress. This, he argued, was at variance with the agreed emphasis on the social responsibility of the modern movement that had guided CIAM's activities since the La Sarraz declarations and had underwritten the choice of the 'minimum dwelling' as primary topic of the second and, in theory, third congress. For the more radical young socialist CIAM members the apparent decision to eschew the Existenzminimum in favour of niche technical topics indicated a much more profound and growing divergence between CIAM's executive group and the *Neue Sachlichkeit* members with outspoken Soviet sympathies.

Whether Stam's vocal criticism was also targeted personally at Le Corbusier and his growing influence on the shaping of CIAM's programmatic agenda is debatable. While it was Giedion who had made the original suggestion to include the sliding windows in the CIAM3 programme back in April, it was also well-known that Le Corbusier had already pioneered – and patented – the extensive use of the feature in many of his designs and executed projects in the second half of the 1920s (including his 'model' constructions for the Weissenhof estate in Stuttgart) (Prouvé and d'Ayot, 2006; Hölz, 2013, 23). At the 20 May meeting in Paris, it was Le Corbusier, not Giedion, who had stepped in to elucidate, expand and defend the proposal when questioned by Bourgeois. In the absence of potential vocal programmatic critics at that particular meeting, the Swiss architect had been able to stage-manage a spectacularly effective de facto acceptance of the new theme into the core of the CIAM3 planning activities. It appears, however, that things had moved on dramatically since then. The initial proposal for a parallel mini-exhibition on the horizontal windows as part of dwelling design had grown into a major event that not only moved well beyond the 'minimum dwelling' but also aligned with plans for a separate congress publication on the theme. News that Le Corbusier was still planning to send new exhibition material, typically at the eleventh hour, on the theme of 'fundamental elements of urbanism' caused a veritable backlash that went further than the sliding window issue and touched on other programmatic matters. Steiger, for example, voiced his disapproval at engaging with the urban scale as such a theme did not belong to the agreed CIAM3 agenda. This was a point that both he and his Swiss colleague Schmidt had already made in response to Le Corbusier's earlier efforts to introduce urbanism into the thematic mix of the Brussels congress. At the September meeting, however, they were joined by Häring whose hostility to the very use of the term and personal antipathy for Le Corbusier were equally well-known. Gropius, on the other hand, objected to the last-minute attempt to introduce a new 'special theme', in seemingly total disregard for all the previous preparatory work and hard-fought consensus.[36] Now it seemed that, in Le Corbusier's absence, all sorts of sedimented grudges, frustrations and antipathies were coming on the surface, as the impact of his growing influence on CIAM's direction was being increasingly felt and resented.

In a way it was ironic that a prime driver behind Le Corbusier's reorientation towards the broader frame of urbanism was his growing fascination with the experiments taking place in the Soviet Union in the late 1920s (Cohen, 1992; Moos, 2009, 171–2). At the May meeting that he hosted in his Parisian atelier he had praised effusively the Soviet officials and professionals for their revolutionary, yet entirely systematic, forensic and grounded in scientific insights approach to urban planning. On his part Giedion had worked hard to co-opt a Soviet delegation into the CIAM proceedings and encourage the swift formation of a national group representative of the Soviet constructivist architects. Fascination with the sweeping scale, ambition and programmatic ingenuity of the urban projects planned in the context of the first Soviet Five-Year Plan cut across ideological fissures inside the modern movement and added crucially to the momentum for a decisive switch to the urban scale of analysis in future congresses. Le Corbusier came to a similar conclusion with the socialist members of CIAM – namely, that the problems of housing in the interwar period could not be solved without first engaging the larger scale of urban planning; and that, in order to do so meaningfully, a profound transformation of the framework in which such problems were debated, understood and addressed was necessary. He was also convinced that the early Soviet experiments with new dwelling forms (e.g. collective and communal housing) and planning norms (e.g. new towns) sketched the most radical, indeed revolutionary path towards a 'new' architecture as the prime motor for a 'new' society. This is where the consensus ended, however, and the paths diverged sharply. Le Corbusier's aestheticised machiniste vision had clashed from a very early stage in the history of CIAM with the far more ideologically informed and socially engaged perspective of the committed socialists within the movement (McLeod,

1983; Somer, 2007, 20–4). For the Swiss architect the revolutionary impulse would come from the norms, forms and techniques of the 'new' architecture that he championed (see Chapter 4). The key missing ingredient was the formulation of a universal programme that extended across all architectural scales and reached its full expression in a novel modern doctrine of urbanism; but even this would come to nothing without actively seeking the sanction of political and economic centres of power – whether in Paris or Moscow or Rome or anywhere else. By contrast, CIAM's socialist constituency viewed this proposition as merely a 'palliative … but not a real cure' (Teige, 2002, 185). The latter group believed that only through subsuming the modern architectural vision to the logic of a social revolution, such as the one then underway in the Soviet Union, could the new architecture realize its transformative potential. To Le Corbusier's ideologically dubious and post-political vision of a technological leap into the future (Leach, 1999; Antliff, 2001), CIAM's socialist members juxtaposed an inverted order of priorities and action: planning and building could only meaningfully follow from – and then actively promote – the radical remaking of the political and social system (Tafuri, 1976, 100–4).

The conclusion reached at the Frankfurt preparatory meeting was that, although the formal shift to the urban scale did constitute a pivotal component of CIAM's programmatic future, this would have to wait until the following congresses. Since the decision to shelve Schmidt's ambitious analytical scheme on the historical development of urban forms, Giedion had repeatedly insisted that this would form an integral part of the programmatic scaffolding for CIAM's fourth congress.[37] Nevertheless, the meeting rubber-stamped the de facto demotion of the 'minimum dwelling' from the status of over-arching theme to a mere adjunct to the CIAM3 core proceedings on 'rational land subdivision'. In essence then the 'minimum dwelling', although still mentioned as one of the session topics on the official programme, had been largely eclipsed by the other two extended scales of the building form/height and land development, tucked into what was originally described as the 'administrative (final) day' of the congress and sharing the platform with other organizational issues such as the preparation for the following congress.[38]

## The Brussels congress

In his introductory speech at the opening of the main exhibition on 27 November Moser presented this shift in focus and scale as a logical and thoroughly planned evolutionary step.[39] Such an explanation misrepresented the haphazard genealogy of the third congress. In the first months of 1930 Giedion was privately despairing about the state of CIAM's internal affairs. Moser's impending departure was weighing heavily on the minds of Giedion and other leading CIAM leading figures throughout 1930. Giedion also feared that, in the vacuum left behind by Moser's resignation and the uncertainty regarding his successor, the 'secret war' raging between key members of the group (he mentioned explicitly Le Corbusier, Stam and May in this context) would tear CIAM apart.⁴⁰ The seeming inability of the members to 'agree even on fundamental issues such as a congress theme' was particularly distressing to him. At some point in January 1930 he confided to Gropius that, unless such agreement was made possible through a modicum of cooperation, he would rather see the whole venture terminated.⁴¹ He fought on against the odds, against a backdrop of intensifying programmatic disagreements, personality clashes and organizational problems, ensuring that Gropius remained involved, cajoling Le Corbusier, mediating between the fiercely antagonistic members of the German delegation, stirring every possible national group into action. But in early August he admitted defeat following news that May, Schmidt and Stam would no longer be able to carry out any preparatory work and might not even attend the proceedings.⁴² With Le Corbusier once again slipping into inert silence;⁴³ with growing uncertainty as to which of the national groups would even send delegates to Brussels; with delays in the dispatch of the questionnaires and the responses of the national groups;⁴⁴ with mounting difficulties in terms of collecting and organizing the material for the surfeit of exhibition activities in Brussels; and with growing complaints about Bourgeois's erratic handling of the CIAM3 organization,⁴⁵ Giedion decided to ask for a postponement of the event by six weeks (from early October to late November).⁴⁶ No matter how he had tried to play down the impact of Stam's and Schmidt's departure on the entire organization of CIAM3,⁴⁷ he was determined not to allow the operation to default to the already unreliable Brussels hub, especially since other key members such as Gropius had lost faith in, and patience with, Bourgeois.⁴⁸ For this reason Giedion asked Van Eesteren to step in and help with the final stages of the preparation.

In the end it took an extraordinary amount of work until the very opening day of the official congress to deal with the outstanding issues and fallouts from the tumultuous past few months.⁴⁹ There were numerous minor last-minute minor changes to the programme between in October and November that reflected some of the behind-the-scenes drama. In the final version the length of the congress was reduced by a day (the half-day originally planned for the 26th was removed from the official text and held instead as a special 'delegate session').⁵⁰ Speaker names and the order of the talks kept changing, with the Frankfurt-based Kaufmann-Böhm duo stepping in for May and with Neutra marking the first American presence in the organization's events. They joined Gropius and Le Corbusier, whose reengagement with the congress in September had caused another last-minute crisis as he too insisted on addressing the congress on the main theme of land management in an already packed first congress day. The organizers initially tried to accommodate him as the lead for the second congress day, asking him to provide a bridge between his own questionnaire and the windows exhibition. This suggestion, however, displeased Le Corbusier and raised once again the prospect of him failing to turn up in Brussels. In the end the importance of the Swiss architect's participation in CIAM3 convinced the organizers that his preferences had to be accommodated, offering him a keynote slot on the 27th and a thematic lead role for the 28th.⁵¹ Furthermore, after weeks of delays and organizational setbacks had cast a grave shadow on its very viability, the sliding windows exhibition was confirmed only ten days ahead of its official opening.⁵² It also received a fuller mention in the final version of the programme, in effect placing it on a near-equal footing with the main CIAM3 exhibition event on 'rational land development', with detailed introductions by Steiger (in German) and Barbe (in French).[53] Finally the 'administrative' designation of the closing day (29th) was abandoned in favour of a further full working session dedicated to the minimum dwelling – a welcome partial restitution for the otherwise striking demotion of the theme that was originally supposed to be the conceptual pivot of the entire Brussels congress.[54]

Chaotic preparation and thematic incoherence notwithstanding, CIAM3 produced a fascinatingly rich and sweeping panorama of ideas at arguably the most critical juncture in the history of the organization. The official proceedings kicked off on 27 November 1930 with a high-profile introductory event at the Brussels Palais de Beaux Arts and a visit to the exhibition on 'rational land development'. The actual congress business started in the afternoon, with a full programme of talks by Le Corbusier, Kaufmann-Böhm, Neutra and Gropius. In his address Le Corbusier wasted no time in shifting his frame of reference from individual building types to formulas for large-scale site development, as well as to the benefits of higher urban concentration and collective living. Noting a mismatch between the impressive technological development of the new *machiniste* era and the outdated current building and planning practices, he called for no less than a radical reorganization of existing cities. He argued that, first, entirely new forms and spatial arrangements of residential blocks and, second, rational concentration and distribution of functions would pave the way for a new conception of mixed private-collective urban living that satisfied the biological, sociological and emotional needs of the modern human far more effectively and efficiently than either peripheral settlements or non-urban alternatives. This could only be achieved productively through constructing significantly higher-rise buildings in or close to central zones and then setting the new building blocks on new vast natural sites for rest and recreation. Yet, for this radical plan to succeed and for any kind of modern urbanism to become operative, Le Corbusier claimed, a re-grouping of the land should be first promoted, erasing the traces of fragmentary property and replacing it with a rational model of collective land ownership.[55]

The talk prepared jointly by Herbert Böhm and Eugen Kaufmann was long, evidence-based and uncompromisingly technical. It succeeded in being the closest to the official topic of the session (low-, medium- and high-rise residential construction) while also retaining the theme of the minimum dwelling as its conceptual pivot. The reference to 'twelve-storey buildings' in the paper's title echoed Giedion's earlier efforts to introduce this specific dimension to the discussions in Brussels. The idea, strongly supported by Gropius,[56] was pursued at various stages in the winter and spring of 1930[57] and was abandoned over the summer. The two Frankfurt architects, however, stepped in to fill the gap, providing an impressively forensic examination of construction/maintenance costs and illumination/ventilation patterns for buildings types ranging from two to twelve floors, with examples drawn from a variety of realized projects in Frankfurt. Their approach contrasted sharply to the other keynotes, steering clear of the sweeping sociological assumptions that underpinned the talks of Le Corbusier or Gropius. Instead

Kaufmann and Böhm grounded their research on practical typological and distributive considerations concerning the correlation of cost, quality and quantity of affordable dwellings, this time however replacing individual dwelling size with building height as the main variable. Their research showed that, while one-floor constructions were the most expensive to construct and therefore unsuitable for the 'minimum dwelling' type, the cost benefits from buildings with six or more floors diminished rapidly with height, due to a number of extras required for this type of high-rise construction, such as elevators and complex central heating infrastructure. In addition, higher-rise constructions offered distinct disadvantages to particular population groups, such as families with children. In their opinion the proverbial sweet spot of the height-cost equation was the 4/5-floor building in rows and individual 'minimum' dwellings of 40–42 m$^2$ surface space, with higher-rise alternative types for single inhabitants and families without children also advisable but only in the peripheral areas of big cities.[58]

Gropius's address covered similar ground from a broader sociological perspective but reached very different conclusions. His starting premise was that the question of building height was not just a matter of cost or aesthetic preference but primarily of suitability for the sociological needs of the modern human being. In his view both high- and low-rise buildings offered distinct advantages in particular circumstances, unlike medium-height alternatives that constituted an unsatisfactory compromise that offered few of the individual benefits and most of the disadvantages of the other two types. Gropius defended the high-rise type against conventional criticisms about its hygienic and biological limitations, arguing that it was the most suitable solution for modern urban living. Unlike Le Corbusier, Gropius did not dismiss the low-rise residential solutions outright. For example, he claimed that houses with garden offered 'more quiet, more seclusion, more recreation facilities and living space in one's own garden, and the easier supervision of children'. He was adamant, however, that conventional criticisms of high-rise dwellings – poorly lit, ventilated, unhygienic, lacking in recreational space – had little to do with the multi-storey dwelling form itself. The cause of the problem, in his view, was that 'short-sighted legislation' had allowed the construction of higher-rise tenements and blocks 'to fall into the hands of unscrupulous speculators without adequate social safeguards'. The antidote was better design, increased site spacing between the high-rise buildings (from 1.5 to up to 3 times the height of the building), adequate provision of communal services and new building regulations that would set limits on the basis of density and not height.[59]

## The 'minimum dwelling' in CIAM3

The 'minimum dwelling' came at last into sharper focus on the morning session of the 29th November. This was the one chance to wind up the important unfinished business from CIAM2, taking advantage of the significant body of reports on the 'minimum dwelling' submitted by a significant number of national groups. At the September preparatory meeting Moser had pleaded with the national groups to provide high-quality empirical information for the congress reports and the exhibitions as soon as possible.[60] Clear guidelines for the preparation of the national reports had been issued relatively early in the CIAM3 planning cycle, with a stipulated three-part structure (overview of existing conditions concerning the 'minimum dwelling'; presentation of requirements for an ideal dwelling alternative; and description of the obstacles – financial, regulatory, cultural, etc. – that stood in the way of providing a solution to the problem of affordable, good-quality housing). This updated template, together with the other data provided through the questionnaires and the – by then rigorously standardized – exhibition materials, would enable the Brussels congress to approach the question in a more informed and constructive way with a view to expressing an official congress position on the 'minimum dwelling' that was lacking from the official outcomes of CIAM2.[61] The original guidelines appeared to place the review of present (sub-optimal) conditions and future (normative) directions on an equal footing, in an attempt to arbitrate between those CIAM members who favoured short-term pragmatism and those calling for a quasi-utopian reorientation of the discussion. In this respect it was the third part of the template – the obstacles/oppositions (*Widerstände/résistances actuelles*) – that emerged as the most significant component from a strategic point of view, as it charted the ways in which each national group considered its own subjective version of an alternative optimal future possible.

With the original deadline for the submission of the national group reports (30 June) slipping amidst the organizational chaos, only a handful had been submitted to the Zurich secretariat by the end of the summer. Predictably they varied in length, detail, areas of focus and findings. Some reports followed the suggested structure only tangentially, taking liberties with reordering, collating and stretching erratically different sections. In some cases, even entire sections – especially on the ideal conditions – were omitted or dispersed throughout the text in a way that made the process of extrapolating usable findings very difficult. At the September preparatory meeting Giedion singled out the Dutch national report for effusive praise, juxtaposing its clarity and measured tone to other, long-winded and lacking in precise focus, submissions. Indeed, the document submitted by the Dutch group was succinct but rigorously backed by statistical information about incomes, taxes, levels of rent, dwelling production across all sectors (private, state/municipal, cooperative) and financial instruments that supported the group's key findings about existing conditions and their proposals for future action. When it came to the discussion of ideal conditions, the Dutch report came out strongly in support of extending patterns of collective living, high(er)-rise building forms in urban areas, mechanization of production and technical innovation in all aspects of housing construction. Anticipating the shift to the urban scale that had already been signposted by Schmidt's proposals, the Dutch group also included recommendations concerning optimal hygienic requirements (especially the role of building orientation and window use for optimal illumination), good transport links, thoughtful planning of recreation areas and a more rational approach to zoning. It was, however, in the concrete ways in which key obstacles were outlined that the Dutch report excelled in programmatic terms. Historical legacies (predominance of the closed perimeter block), legal and administrative hindrances (outdated building legislation; lack of overall urban planning norms; the resistance of officials to the 'new' architecture) and financial limits (lack of financial instruments to ensure both production in scale and affordable prices; insufficient facilitation by state and municipalities) were shown to stand in the way of advancing particular normative propositions. Therefore, it was suggested, no credible and sustainable pathway to either the 'minimum dwelling' or rational site planning could be achieved without first revising the political, legal, financial and cultural context of modern architectural practice. All in all, the Dutch report managed an extraordinary feat – to tick all thematic boxes of CIAM3 (minimum dwelling, land development, building form/height, windows, hygiene, the transition to urban scale) in a mere six pages of objective, empirically backed, yet radically aspirational and constructive summary that was submitted on time.[62]

With the help of the extra time afforded by the six-week postponement of the congress and following a final plea issued at the Frankfurt preparatory meeting, a further eleven country reports arrived just on time to be summarized and included in the discussion that took place on the final day of CIAM3. Nearly all of them bemoaned the scarcity of high-quality yet truly affordable and available housing for the overwhelming majority of the working population and low-income families. This was the result of a combination of already familiar obstacles – poor and insufficient instruments of financial assistance; limited or inconsistent public involvement in housing construction as an alternative to private speculation; cultural mistrust of, if not outright hostility to, modern construction methods, materials and design forms shown by both public officials and the general population; outdated building regulations and land-development norms; and conservative heritage-preservation rules. While the overwhelming majority of the submissions avoided contentious political territory, a few national groups strayed from statistical and technical observations into overly ideological territory. The Danish report claimed that, since the capitalist system had no interest in the social idea of affordable dwelling for the masses, a sustainable solution to the housing question could be pursued only after radical social and political change. By contrast, the French text called for an end to the fragmentation of private property and a radical 'regrouping of land', making direct reference to earlier proposals for land reform advanced by the *Redressement Français*, a fringe pressure political group active in the interwar period and known for its hyper-technocratic corporatist ideas.[63] Le Corbusier's involvement with the Redressement in the late 1920s is well-documented, representing only one piece in the complex jigsaw of his ideologically incoherent and shady political links with radical third-way groups (Antliff, 2007, 119; Jarcy, 2015). What is also well-known is that the group's official publication had hosted Le Corbusier's radical proposal for a 'mobilisation of soil' – a concept that became part of CIAM's mainstream discourse from 1933 onwards but was also indirectly referenced in the French CIAM3 report. This was in effect a call for the French government to put an end to the vortex of land fragmentation by purchasing large plots of land and then integrating them into an overarching 'plan' commanded by a new kind of – technocratic, supra-political, not accountable to parliament – authority and entrusted to architects for rational development (Fishmann, 1982, 205–25; Mumford, 2000, 14–15; Hilpert, 2015, 203)).

Neither the French nor the Danish proposals were included in the congress summary of the country reports on the minimum dwelling, which restricted itself to technical recommendations.[64] Instead emphasis was placed on the – more anodyne – call for legal, financial and cultural change that would unlock the full transformative potential of the 'new' architecture for radical urban redevelopment in the near future. Since the official minutes from the CIAM3 discussion sessions ended up being unusable,[65] it is hard to reconstruct the actual details of the discussion on the minimum dwelling in Brussels. The delayed submission of the majority of the national reports meant that they had to be presented for the first time at the actual congress session, in a discussion that did not produce any final resolutions or official 'opinion' and left almost no trace (Somer, 2007, 34). This was a tellingly anticlimactic finale to the entire CIAM chapter on the 'minimum dwelling', from its meteoric rise to the heart of the organization's first working congress to its eventual eclipse by the other themes and scales that shaped the CIAM3 proceedings.

There was one further twist to the story, however. Shortly after the congress the CIAM secretariat asked the Czechoslovak delegate Karel Teige to provide an extensive critical overview of the updated national reports on the 'minimum dwelling'.[66] This contribution was only included in the official book publication for CIAM3 (Bourgeois et al., 1931). Teige was present in Brussels – his first and, as it turned out, sole appearance at a CIAM event).[67] He was the driving force behind the productive work and feedback of the recently formed Czechoslovak group to CIAM3, including the extensive analysis of social housing in Czechoslovakia that formed the basis of the group's contribution to the congress.[68] However, he ended up playing a more important role in the programme of the parallel Journées events than in the actual congress proceedings.[69] When it appeared, Teige's ex post facto summary resembled an alternative radical manifesto for the 'minimum dwelling' that never was. It contained a scathing critique of the idea that the 'minimum dwelling' was a problem of architectural design. Instead, he argued, 'the housing shortage is not just the result of the absolute increase of population in the cities ... [but] the product of insufficient supply [of smaller, more affordable dwellings]'. In his view, constructing sufficient good-quality and affordable homes could only be achieved through a radical transformation of the entire operation of the capitalist order and a parallel 'qualitative revolution' in patterns of living according to a wholesale collectivized template (Collins and Swenarton, 1987, 158). The gross mismatch between low wages and rising prices essentially created an affordability crisis; more gravely, it produced a 'subsistence level' class condemned to live in destitution. No matter how architects could reduce costs by refining the design or embracing standardization or even shifting functions from the private to the collective domain, Teige claimed, the problem could never be addressed without 'the overthrow of the existing constraints and crisis, material, social and cultural' (Teige, 1987; Specthenhauser and Weiss, 1999;

Kohlrausch, 2019, 95).[70] His critique erupted into a far more outspoken and polemical book-length publication on the 'minimum dwelling' that appeared in 1932 (Teige, 2002).

When it came to the question of building typologies according to height, the official congress verdict was similarly muted. The delegates acknowledged that low-rise models were uneconomical from the point of view of the 'minimum dwelling' but noted that there was limited evidence regarding the universal suitability of the high-rise alternative to reach definite conclusions as to whether it should become the standard norm for the 'minimum dwelling'.[71] This formulation was nothing more than an awkward and anodyne compromise. It barely disguised the lack of consensus among congress keynote speakers and delegates regarding the benefits and demerits of the high-rise housing typology. This was hardly surprising – after all, the IFHTP had attempted to settle the same issue at its 1928 and 1929 congresses but, in spite of the organization's default bias in favour of the single-family dwelling typology of the garden cities, failed to dismiss in a blanket manner the suitability of vertical construction in urban areas (see Chapter 3). Nevertheless, the extensive discussion on building form according to height in Brussels succeeded in one critical respect: by illustrating that the choice of building form was in itself subjected to wider forces, analyses and programmes of action, it confirmed CIAM's alignment with a broader scale perspective that subsumed 'minimum dwelling' and building typology, dwelling and site, under a more comprehensive vision of urban planning. As the new president Van Eesteren put it, 'only large-scale planning (*Großplannung*) brings change'.[72] This significant paradigmatic shift, conventionally associated with CIAM4, was actually rehearsed and legitimized, largely through trial and error, at the unsung Brussels congress.

In many respects then the 1930 Brussels congress could be read as a failure – of organization, of clear and well-defined focus, of community spirit and programmatic unity among the ranks of the group, of detailed outcomes. Its proceedings made clear that the fascination with the 'aesthetic of the scalar sublime' (Moravánzsky, 2017, 29) evinced in many presentations and deliberations at CIAM3 could no longer be contained even by the extended frame of 'rational land development' headlined in Brussels. The flexible ways in which the congress theme was interpreted by key CIAM figures such as Le Corbusier and Gropius sanctioned the organization's orientation towards the larger architectural scale (Johnson, 1994, 363–4). More importantly, however, it foreshadowed the push for magnitude as paradigm for architectural analysis/design – spatial amplitude, uninhibited verticalism and eventually a three-dimensional holism of spaces, forms and volumes. Magnitude was all about a defiant celebration of 'bigness' (Koolhaas and Mau, 1997, 509–16) – finding the widest possible architectural frame that resulted in the best strategy for planning, connecting and managing the various units and spaces inside it. Viewed from this perspective, CIAM3 was less an incremental scale step from CIAM2 (from the single dwelling to groupings of the grouping of dwelling in buildings and the planning of buildings as site); and even less an intermediate jump along a supposed path towards the urban scale that became the theme of CIAM4. Instead it resembled an initial stress test that explored, essentially as trial-and-error, how far the 'new' architecture could go in pursuit of programmatic 'bigness'. The scalar leap from Frankfurt to Brussels illustrated a deeper methodological tension – between the search for the elemental unit of design that could be then scaled up effectively as part of a modular approach; and the quest for the largest frame that could be managed as a single unit of architectural design and then be broken down into a series of smaller design segments. The insights gained cumulatively from the two congresses, together with a host of productive failures, cleared the path to what became eventually the official consecration of the 'big' urban scale as CIAM's favoured programmatic orientation.

# CHAPTER 7
# THE CIAM2 AND CIAM3 EXHIBITIONS

In so many respects the decision to hold CIAM's first working congress so soon after the founding of the organization was a risky decision. Organizational difficulties, uncertainty regarding membership and formation of national groups, as well as apparent programmatic disagreements and personal tensions among the participating architects meant that neither the theme of the first congress nor the way in which business was to be conducted at the congress were uncomplicated tasks. At some point in the spring and early summer of 1929 it was not even guaranteed that the event would take place, beset by tensions within the German group[1] as well as between German and French members regarding CIAM's remit and future shape.[2] Not surprisingly then the Frankfurt and Brussels congresses ended up being chaotic and frustrating. Nevertheless, following the conclusion of CIAM3 in late 1930, Giedion's mood had changed dramatically, divulging renewed optimism about the future prospects of the group.[3] What accounted for Giedion's dramatic shift to a more optimistic outlook within less than a year from his gloomy predictions for group's future had more to do with CIAM's rising international traction – evident in the diversity of individual/national membership, of the organization's steering group, CIRPAC, and of congress attendance, especially at the Brussels event – than with the congress proceedings themselves. The plan to hold the fourth congress in the Soviet Union, originally scheduled for 1931, provided a significant boost in self-confidence, especially since it opened up the prospect of a trans-national and -ideological convergence of modernist avant-gardes on a shared disruptive platform for architectural and planning action.

In addition, however, Giedion and the other members of CIRPAC had every reason to be satisfied with the publicity outputs generated from the two congresses in Frankfurt and Brussels. By the end of 1931 the young CIAM had managed to organize two influential and well-received exhibitions (one in Frankfurt on the Existenzminimum dwelling; the other in Brussels, dealing with the main theme of rational land subdivision) and to produce two book publications that gathered together each congress's keynotes and a curated selection of plans relating to each theme. In addition CIAM was involved in two further exhibition events, both in Brussels, dedicated to the minimum dwelling (*Journées de l'Habitation Minimum*) and to sliding windows used in housing design. Given all the significant practical difficulties involved in collecting and editing the reports, as well as in liaising with the publishers, Giedion could be excused for feeling considerable pride in seeing through all these communication events, critical for the international reputation of the new organization.

## The Minimum Dwelling

In hindsight the exhibitions and associated publications were the most consequential legacy of CIAM's first two working congresses. Both of them mutated into successful international travelling events, with a busy list of showings in a large variety of countries. CIAM's activities in this domain reached their peak with the – now legendary – exhibition associated with CIAM4 in 1933 and continued in relation to the 1937 congress in Paris (CIAM5) that interfaced with the equally mythologized world fair in the French capital (Mumford, 1992; Udovicki-Selb, 1997; Van Es et al, 2014; Udovicki-Selb, 2015). Yet it was the group's earlier, more experimental ventures aligned with Frankfurt and Brussels congresses that set the foundations for CIAM's reputation as a publicity-savvy hub of ideational aggregation that constructed the potent interwar narrative of the 'new' architecture. Giedion and the other leading members of CIRPAC were aware that CIAM, as a embryonic group and a late-comer in the communication sphere of interwar architecture, was competing not only with the architectural status quo but also with other relevant international organizations, some of which had an already established reputation and were as active in the international communication domain. The CIAM secretary understood that raising CIAM's profile depended both on its own outputs and on its ability to plug into existing communication structures and formats. He used the group's contacts to negotiate prominent CIAM presence in other important international exhibition events, such as the 1931 Berlin *Bauausstellung* and the 1933 Milan *Triennale*. The emphasis in these early years was on increasing the 'noise' of and about CIAM as far as possible and in this way to reach new audiences. In this context he worked together with other self-proclaimed publicists of the 'new' architecture beyond personal or ideological allegiances. His close relation with Pier Maria Bardi, the editor of the rationalist journal *Quadrante* and organizing nous of the substantial Italian engagement with CIAM4, underlines how willing he was to collaborate with like-minded propagandists of the 'new' architecture regardless of political affiliation (Rifkind, 2013; Kallis, 2018). The fact that Bardi had been the driving force of a campaign in 1930–31 to convince Mussolini that the 'new' architecture of rationalism ought to become the official art form of the (Fascist) state did not bother him even though he was already co-operating closely at the time with Soviet authorities and former CIAM members who were already working in the Soviet Union for the planned Moscow congress. Instead he relied on Bardi's own publicity activities to promote CIAM and its architectural programme, both within Italy and on the international field (e.g. Bardi travelled to south America in 1933 and used a series of lectures and exhibitions to also promote CIAM's activities). In this pursuit Giedion worked closely with other key figures of the group, such as Gropius and Le Corbusier, who shared his conviction that the most effective strategy for the success of the whole CIAM experiment was courting and eliciting political sanction, similar to Bardi's notion of modernist architecture as 'art of the state' (*arte di stato*).[4] In this supra-ideological campaign the importance of incessant publicity, eye-catching propaganda, international networking and a surfeit of all kinds of outputs shaped the strategy of CIAM during its crucial early years.

## The exhibition field in interwar Europe: Showcasing the 'minimum'

Of all the communication instruments that architects availed themselves of in the 1920s, exhibition events came to encapsulate the widest set of their aspirations and provide the most revealing insight into their utopian impulses. Exhibitions emerged as eminently productive 'contact zones' (Pratt, 1991; Schorch, 2013; Avermaete and Nuijsink, 2021) on three levels: first, as discursive events and staged interpretive contests over who was best placed to respond to contemporary social challenges and how best to promote solutions to pressing problems; second, between professional practitioners themselves; and third, between the agents of the 'new' architecture and the public. More than any other medium of self-expression and performance exhibitions provided architects and planners with the licence to express creatively their radical visions unencumbered by many practical constraints associated with practical work, to test and demonstrate the validity of their innovative hypotheses, and to provide proofs-of-concept for their non-mainstream design ideas. For architects identifying with the 'new' architecture these opportunities were particularly important because they offered a privileged public platform to rehearse and experience projections of the still abstract, 'not-yet' future that they propagated (see Chapter 3); and in the process to define a novel conception of living as a better alternative (or even successor) to the conventional 'bourgeois' ideas about taste, domesticity and dwelling. Therefore exhibitions functioned as authoritative sources of modernist discourse in which communication was both verbal and visual, concrete and ideational, expressed in both restrictive professional code and the universal medium of image and in some cases (e.g. exhibition of scaled models or real-size buildings) even physical experience (Forty, 2000, 13–14). The theme of the exhibition and the particular occasion that it was linked to provided unique opportunities, through and beyond exhibiting specimens, to talk about the horizons of the 'new' architecture (Blau, 1998, 365). It is thus not surprising that their importance as professional and popular milestones increased significantly from the turn of the twentieth century onwards.

Architecture- and design-themed exhibitions formed a particular subset of a much broader exhibitory culture. The medium of the exhibition per se had undergone dramatic changes since the nineteenth century. Modernity brought along mass audiences, mass publicity channels and new techniques of presentation as well as representation (Wesemael, 2001, 19–26). Exhibitions made the most of the new possibilities, mutating from their previous elitist or niche appeal to mass events and social trendsetters. Events geared to the domestic sphere (whether of decorative and functional object categories or homes as a whole) gradually expanded their frame of presentation in order to maximize their impact. Over time they shifted from showcasing in an isolated manner innovative items (initially individually crafted ones but from the turn of the century industrially produced varieties) to staging, projecting and promoting meticulously curated assemblages of components as total, all-encompassing and normative counter-arrangements for modern living (Ruhl, 2011, 303).[5] The prevailing discourse of progress aligned with ideas of national self-legitimization and pride, with civic and local identities, with the emergence of mass consumerism, and with increasing international mobility of ideas, people and trade (Williams, 1982, 58–106; Wesemael, 2001, 56; Filipova, 2015, 2). Beyond their obvious function of legitimizing the existing social order and popularizing the ideology of (national and/or human) progress, exhibitions became performative, participatory and experiential events that promoted a blend of informative, educational and anticipatory functions (Greenhalgh, 1988). The phenomenal success of earlier exhibition events in the nineteenth century – typically of either much broader character, such as world fairs, or specialized events, such as art exhibitions – generated a strong and steadily increasing supply-demand momentum to the exhibition culture. On the one hand, the popularity of exhibitions alerted potential actors (from state and public authorities to creative, professional and commercial organizations) to the opportunities offered by the medium in terms of enhancing publicity, attracting positive attention and, where appropriate, generating income. On the other hand, a seemingly exhibition-thirsty public turned up in ever-larger numbers for such events, eager to see important or new specimens and experience first-hand the buzz of the modern exhibition venue. As a result exhibitions grew in number, diversified in focus and character and attracted significantly more interest.

Architecture had played a key role in many landmark exhibition events of the nineteenth century, providing the backdrop to the main events and generating bespoke mega-structures that embodied the message of futural progress (e.g. Crystal Palace in 1851, Eiffel Tower in 1889 (Jones, 2011, 67–91)). As a primary exhibited specimen, however, architecture presented particular challenges from an exhibitory point of view. Practical questions of size, immobility and cost established a canon of architectural exhibition that initially involved either pictorial representations (technical drawings and impressionistic drawings) or scaled-down models. From the turn of the twentieth century, however, this category of exhibitions too was transformed, first, with the growth of interest in domestic architecture and design and, second, with new possibilities of showcasing specimens in real size, whether as interior or exterior or both (Colomina, 1999; Rohde, 2015).

Such was the profusion of architectural exhibitions in the years before and after the First World War and the diversity of their themes that it is impossible to mention them here. The dwelling became as much a key expression of the 'new' architecture as the hub of novel conceptions of living in the domestic and private sphere, of new model communities and cities, as well as of new societies. Dwelling became an integral part of a much wider range of design, artistic, architectural and planning conversations at the time (Cramer and Gutschow, 1984; Freestone and Amati, 2011). Even within the particular subset of architectural exhibitions where the house as an ensemble – container and sum of innovations – was the primary intended or de facto exhibit, the count of events taking place nationally and internationally in the interwar years was conspicuously high and the range of approaches almost as varied (Rohde, 2015). National events like the first major Bauhaus exhibition in 1923, the Stockholm exhibition in 1930 and the German Building Exhibition in 1931 exerted an influence that transcended their initially modest focus and audience. The German *Werkbund* organized a range of events that produced some of the most memorable vignettes and iconic structures of modern residential architecture in the interwar period – among them Cologne in 1914 ('New Architecture'), Berlin in 1924 ('Life without Ornaments'), Stuttgart in 1927 ('The Dwelling') and 1932 ('Living Necessities'), Breslau in 1929 ('Dwelling and Workplace'), as well as contributions to international design- and architecture-themes exhibition events. The homonymous Austrian, Swiss and Czechoslovak organizations that it inspired generated their own share of memorable architectural events, such as the exhibitions in Brno (1928), Vienna (1930, 1932), Basel (1930), Zurich (1931) and Prague (1931) (Figure 7.1). International recurring events like the periodical world fairs, the Triennale of Milan or

**Figure 7.1** Werkbund 'model' estates. In sequence: (1)–(2) WuWa in Breslau [*Die Form* 4/4(1929): 127]; (3)–(4) Vienna [*Die Form* 7(1931): 201–4]; (5)–(8) Weissenhof [5: Getty*, 6–8: author's]; (9)–(10) Neubühl in Zurich [9: Photo by Walter Mittelholzer, 10: author's photo]; (11)–(12) WoBa/Eglisee in Basel [11: Wohngenossenschaft Eglisee]; (13)–(16) Dammerstock in Karlsruhe [13–14: *Kunst und Künstler* 3 (1929): 129–30/15–16: author's photos].

the annual *Salon d'Automne* held in Paris, as well as special world events such as the 1925 International Exhibition of Modern Decorative and Industrial Arts held in Paris and the 1924 International Co-operative exhibition in Ghent (an extension of the regularly held international congress of the International Co-operative Alliance (Hilson, 2018, 64)) produced important moments that have since been treated as milestones in the emergence of modern architecture.

There was a fascinating ambivalence in all these staged projections of housing and living as it ought to be. Their premise was that the featured exhibits projected an aspiration not-yet fully achieved but within tantalizing reach; a proposition for a living 'optimum' with relatively modest means; a vision of the future presented in the present tense, branded not as a privilege of a small social elite but as an egalitarian idea now rendered attainable in the near future. The model settlements exhibited in the 1920s and 1930s were aspirational ideals in the sense that they summoned, abridged and performed a multitude of technical, organizational and design innovations as a 'new', radically different conception of living individually (as family units) and collectively (as settlements). Yet, even as they were inherently utopian, these model settlements expressed a pledge that modern architecture and design were on the cusp of capturing the new optimum as a realistic proposition, rehearsed in the microcosm of the exhibited model settlement and its individual model dwellings or staged as proof in an otherwise ephemeral setting. Their realizations were captured in numerous photographs and moving images that circulated across the world and then travelled – as two-dimensional plans, discursive formations and media representations – to other professional and public events. In this sense the model settlement transformed the abstract utopian projections of the 'new' architecture into inscribed facts – sources of inspiration, prototypes and guidelines, living proof that an alternative, better, even optimal future was within realistic reach as a universal ethical proposition (Latour, 1986).

When it came to the specific concern for affordable, in theory and intention at least, modern housing, these and other exhibition events became associated with a range of celebrity 'model' dwellings and houses realized as tangible fully formed prototypes in terms of both architectural design and domestic living. Some of these were ephemeral constructions while others were built with the intention to sell or rent afterwards. The Bauhaus-designed *Haus am Horn* in Weimar (built for the School's 1923 exhibition) was brandished as an experimental break-through in terms of its construction methods, external design and interior decoration and equipment (kitchen again being a primary focus of innovation) (Siebenbrodt, 2007; Seelow, 2018, 12–14). The experimental *casa minima*, designed by Osvaldo Borsani for the 1933 Triennale (Figure 7.2), offered a similar integration of concept, exterior and interior in a bespoke temporary structure erected solely for the purpose of the exhibition.[6] But it was the exhibition events featuring entire permanent 'model' settlements – configurations of different types of dwellings, typically designed by either teams of architects or individually by invited professionals, local or international – that provided the most varied and fascinating register of dwellings and houses in relation not only to their physical setting but also to one another. Some of the most influential dwelling and housing prototypes have emerged from within entire

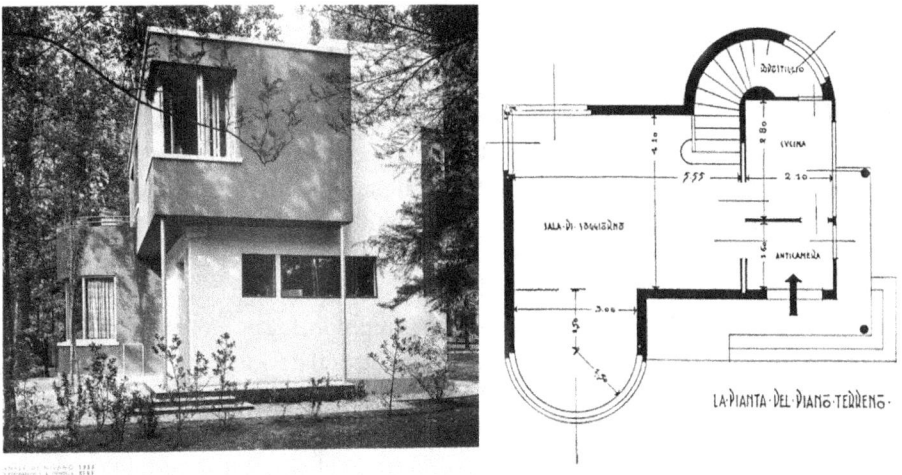

**Figure 7.2** 'Casa Minima', project by Alessandro Cairoli, G.B. Varisco and Osvaldo Borsani for the Mostra dell'abitazione, V Triennale, Milan 1933. Foto Crimella [Source: *Triennale Milano – Archivi*].

'model' settlements, such as those composing the Weissenhof estate in Stuttgart (1927) or the WuWa equivalent in Breslau (1929). There the featured innovations in architectural, spatial, technical and equipment design intersected with forward-thinking settlement planning ideas. The exhibitions of 'model' settlements marshalled different experimental dwelling typologies and spatial configurations in order to project optimal-yet-realisable alternative visions of living, within the domestic space as well as across a spectrum of scales from the private to the communal to the public.

No other exhibition-cum-model housing estate in the 1920s exemplified all these ambitions better than the fabled Weissenhof 'model' estate in Stuttgart. When the municipal authorities took the decision to work together with the Werkbund in designing and actually constructing an experimental modern housing complex in the outskirts of the city, as the highlight of the housing exhibition *Die Wohnung*, the city mayor Karl Lautenschlager emphasized the social utility of the experiment in terms of testing new hypotheses about high-quality yet affordable dwelling types as a solution to the city's post-First World War housing shortage. The policy document that gave the go-ahead for the construction of the estate emphasized avoiding extravagance and proposing instead new solutions that brought overall construction costs down without adversely affecting the quality of living or the innovative design that the dwelling units would provide to their future residents (Pommer et al., 1991, 22–3). The organizers of the exhibition appointed Ludwig Mies van der Rohe to oversee the project and allowed him considerable leeway in commissioning the architects and setting the design brief. Mies had intentionally opted for a project intended to produce a bold statement of programmatic purpose on behalf of the 'new' architecture.[7] The Stuttgart authorities afforded him a kind of near-total control over the project that was far from the case in other instances of exhibition events centred on a model settlement. His design and

## The Minimum Dwelling

logistical guidelines to the participating architects were deliberately elliptical – the prerequisites of flat roof and spatial innovation within the dwelling enclosure constituted the only prescriptive elements (Pommer, 1983). In the process the need to respond to the practical challenges of the housing crisis was overshadowed by his determination to produce a potent discursive statement of an unconditionally optimal transformation of living that involved the dwelling and its components but extended well beyond it (Stankard, 2002, 252). To achieve that he assembled an international team of well-known and rising avant-garde architects (among them many subsequent members of CIAM, like Gropius, Le Corbusier, Bourgeois, Frank and Stam) and mitigated cost prerequisites. Although not explicitly branded as an exercise in producing a 'model' solution to the specific problems of the minimum affordable dwelling, the Weissenhof estate set a new benchmark for exhibiting architecture as an ensemble of innovations across the entirety of scales from the individual object to the dwelling enclosure to its distribution in a community setting (Figure 7.3). Its success – in terms of visitor numbers, international publicity and as a commercial venture – spurred a rapid succession of similar initiatives organized by the Werkbund and other architectural organizations (Kirsch, 2013).

The Weissenhof experiment was predictably vulnerable to criticism from a variety of ideological and professional angles. Beyond attacks on the model estate for its perceived

**Figure 7.3** Examples of 'model' buildings constructed for the Weissenhof estate in Stuttgart: (1) Le Corbusier, (2) Behrens, (3) Scharoun, (4–5) Stam, (6) Oud, (7–8) Mies van der Rohe and (9) Frank [Source: Author's photos].

aesthetic monotony (a criticism that spurred opponents of the 'new' architecture to organize a counter-settlement that featured pitched roofs and more traditional building techniques (Voigt, 2012); Lampugnani, 1994), 'un-Germanness' or 'socialism' (Lane, 2013, 137; Rieben, 2019, 219), many critical views of the houses highlighted the estate's shortfalls as an egalitarian social experiment. The commercial functions of the exhibition – tied as it was to Werkbund's interest in marketing new products and selling aspirational living as consumer 'taste' – trumped the social dimension of the project. The exhibition of the dwellings with a curated selection of furniture items chosen because of their high quality and sales potential did very little to inform and educate the visitors about new ways to satisfy their needs with fewer well-designed domestic items. More importantly individual designers produced dwellings that ended up costing significantly more than any definition of 'affordable' could possibly justify (the two prototypes designed by Le Corbusier being the worst offenders in this respect), geared to more affluent middle-class potential buyers. Karel Teige's critical review of the Weissenhof estate came to a conclusion that underlined the deep ideological fractures within the modern movement in the interwar period: without a complete break with the present, the anticipatory potential of the 'new' architecture was forced in practice to accept too much of a compromise in its efforts to promote a radical, transformational programme 'for the new organisation of a new world' (Teige, 2002, 189–93).[8]

In contrast to the freedom of creative expression and relative financial largesse that characterized the Weissenhof exhibition, many subsequent exhibition events dedicated to the 'minimum' affordable dwelling deliberately put the consideration of 'minimum' cost at the heart of the design brief. The model settlement in the Garbatella garden suburb of Rome constructed as a side-event of the 1929 IFHTP congress (see Chapter 3 and Figure 3.3) was based on clear guidelines in terms of both (low) maximum cost and ease of execution (to be completed within four months) (Kallis, 2020a, 604). The projects commissioned for the Swiss Werkbund exhibitions in Basel (Eglisee) and Zurich (Neubühl) also followed strict guidelines of cost and standards that imposed a significantly higher number of design prerequisites on the architects than in the case of Weissenhof (Rieben, 2019). The Werkbund model settlement constructed in Vienna between 1930 and 1932 marked a departure from the big blocks of the 1920s because funding was now only made available on the basis of proposing single-family detached dwellings. The 1929 exhibition in Breslau was conceived as an exploration of innovative techniques and typologies that addressed the particular local challenges of producing affordable dwellings that were small yet adhering to elevated modern standards of comfort and hygiene, easy to construct, suited to the particular local natural and social conditions, and economical enough to enable mass deployment but also humane, individual and respectful of local traditions (Ascher Barnstone, 2016, 58; Syring and Kirschenmann, 2004, 12–14) (Figure 7.1). The international character of the designer team put together in Stuttgart also proved an exception, with most interwar model housing/settlement exhibitions involving overwhelmingly local architects.

The advantage of designing and presenting dwellings as part of a unified, planned and ambitiously scaled ensemble lay in transforming individual dwelling solutions into complete, multi-scalar and multi-faceted discursive statements of what modern affordable dwelling ought to be and how it could be achieved in sufficient scale to address the social question. When the city of Karlsruhe decided to hold a competition for a large model housing estate in 1926, its authorities chose to experiment with a range of new solutions beyond the menu of existing reduced-size options (Kleinwohnung) brought together organically in a single settlement project. The 'new' architecture's promise of better and more housing that was cheaper to produce and affordable to rent or buy afterwards convinced Karlsruhe's municipal leadership to turn the planned Dammerstock estate into a laboratory of testing new scenarios for individual, family and community living. The competition served numerous objectives. The city was seeking an efficient and effective formula in order to address the immediate challenge of affordable housing shortage that it, like most cities in the interwar years, faced at the time. In addition, however, the competition brief invited submissions that deliberately researched new typologies and methods of construction in order to ascertain the most efficient use of space and resources. Utilitarian dwelling (*Gebrauchswohnung*), the theme of the scheme and an associated exhibition that was organized in 1929, highlighted how the discourse of the 'minimum' had by that time become fully absorbed into the utopian pursuit of solving the housing question as a whole. Like in the case of Stuttgart and Breslau later, Karlsruhe opted for a settlement as a unified conception that offered not just a practical accommodation of the new housing typologies but a model of living across the entire range of private and public domains.

The ensuing Dammerstock settlement was conceived as a microcosm of both a new kind of dwelling and of a new conception of living in the city – a usable settlement on its own and a hub of scenarios for future anthropological and social transformation. The exhibition-settlement combo was presented in the language of concrete utopia: Herman Schneider, the head of the municipal building office, prefaced the exhibition catalogue by claiming that it was no longer a utopian belief to expect modern architecture to work out a way to produce 'as perfect as possible' dwellings that could be made available to, and become affordable by, most, if not all German families. The competition was won by Gropius, who designed the overall plan for a 750-dwelling settlement and produced twenty-three prototypes, in apartment blocks of varying heights and row houses, that catered for a range of family sizes and room configurations. Having overall responsibility for the entire site allowed Gropius to innovate across all scales and configure systems of integration between the individual dwelling ration (which he calculated for each dwelling prototype, ranging from a minimum of 10 $m^2$ to 20 $m^2$ with the typical value around 12–14 $m^2$); the family enclosure (from 49 $m^2$ upwards); and the communal areas within each building and across the entire settlement (Gössel et al., 2001, 159). The message was clear: the solution to the problem did not exhaust itself in the functional and technical reconceptualization of the dwelling itself but involved its re-integration into a radically new conception of living within the community. The combination of micro-communities assembled in high-rise residential blocks and rigorous spatial organization of life at the level of the entire settlement could revolutionize the function of the dwelling itself, maximizing the social impact of design and construction innovation.

## The CIAM2 and CIAM3 Exhibitions

Even as fierce a critic of 'model' dwelling as Teige recognized that the experimental housing estates of the 1920s and 1930s represented a critical 'transitory' stage along the path of utopian transformation (Teige, 2002, 367). His teleological belief in the panacea of revolution and collective living aside, he was perceptive enough to recognize that the models mapped new horizons of expectation and set new standards of 'optimum' living that would supplant bourgeois notions of domesticity. They also represented an assemblage of – heterogeneous and often contradictory – signs that exceeded the object of design or the realized product (Hays, 1995, 121). Even if Teige argued that 'the most far-reaching solution to the housing problem is still in paper and cannot as yet be realised', he acknowledged that built models and prototypes had a cumulative transformational effect in cultural terms. Rather than approaching the problem of the minimum affordable dwelling as a savage reduction of conventional bourgeois mental images of life, the 'new' architecture had proposed alternative conceptions of living based on the rigorous calculation of 'real' human needs and modern functions that incorporated the dwelling into the frame of a different, more equal society. This, in the end, ought to be the yardstick for judging the 'minimum' dwelling as a utopian proposition – how the design of the private and semi-private space could achieve a new 'optimum' by generating conditions for a better life both within *and* outside the dwelling, one in tandem with the other. For Teige model dwellings and estates represented meaningful 'hypothetical architecture', not-yet realizable as a universal proposition, not-yet clearly defined as toolkit but important nonetheless as a series of discursive events that articulated utopia as a radical possibility within reach (Teige, 2000, 299–301). In this context model experiments offered a space where alternative radical ideas could flourish and a public stage for local and/or young, lesser-known architects to project imagination – and speak through their own small chunks of concrete utopia.

### The minimum dwelling on show: Exhibiting CIAM2

One of the earliest references to the importance of deliberately aligning the formation of CIAM with an exhibition came from its president Karl Moser. Although he was forced to cancel his participation to the La Sarraz founding meeting at the very last moment, he wrote to Giedion with a list of suggestions for the immediate steps in the wake of the June 1928 gathering. In his letter he stressed the importance of taking swift action to plan the next congress and start thinking of a 'sufficiently complete exhibition featuring new constructions from architects and engineers … that could afterwards be shown in different countries'.[9] The matter was apparently not discussed at La Sarraz, eclipsed by the animated discussions on the six points of the wide-ranging programme and on agreed versions of the programmatic declarations in French and German (Mumford, 2000, 16–27). Yet the need to maintain the momentum of the fledgling organization not only in professional but also in communication terms was at the heart of Giedion's and Moser's strategy before and just after the founding meeting.

## The Minimum Dwelling

It was in the margins of the crucial February 1929 Basel preparatory meeting (see Chapter 5) that the topic of the exhibition was raised by Le Corbusier. Once a modicum of consensus on the theme of the small-size apartment had been tentatively achieved, he proposed a more specific exhibition event aligned to the congress's theme and featuring relevant ideas and work carried out in different participating countries. In contrast to Stam's preference for a show exclusively focused on the work carried out in Frankfurt at the time, May, Bourgeois and Moser endorsed the proposal for a broader exhibition event as a way of reaching out to the public and performing an essential propaganda function of highlighting the advances in habitation made possible by the 'new' architecture since the First World War.[10] As the entire La Sarraz gathering in 1928 and the first two days of the forthcoming Frankfurt congress were conducted behind closed doors to ensure an honest exchange of professional views, the inauguration of the exhibition would coincide with the open-door congress sessions of the third day and thus provide ample opportunities for an outward-facing publicity campaign. The Frankfurt organizers – essentially May, Stam and the local *Oktobergruppe* of radical architects – began the preparations for the congress and the exhibition, battling against a tight timetable and a pile of missed deadlines. A set of guidelines for the exhibition materials were formulated at the the same time as the instructions for the congress questionnaires, ensuring as much uniformity of presentation as possible for floor and site plans, sections and facades.[11]

The organizer of the Frankfurt event Ernst May had promised the full backing of the city authorities to the congress and the associated exhibition; yet it was only in August that he approached them with a concrete proposal regarding the publicity side of the events. In his pitch to the municipal authorities for political and above all financial support, he emphasized how the event's focus on the 'minimum dwelling' aligned with the city's ambitious programme of affordable housing in the previous five years and how it represented a recognition of Frankfurt's trailblazing record in this field. He went to great lengths to emphasize how the exhibition would be of 'significant interest to the public and especially the working citizens' and asked for a generous subsidy of 15,000 marks to cover the communication side of the event.[12] 1929, however, was not 1925 in terms of financial largesse. Against a backdrop of economic insecurity and budget cuts, the city authorities eventually agreed to a lower package of financial assistance up to 10,000 marks and placed limits on how the funds ought to be spent in relation to the public activities.[13]

Revised guidelines and timetable for the exhibition were issued to the national groups in August, this time with an almost desperately urgent tone.[14] CIAM's national groups were asked to send materials under four categories (one-room apartments for single people, boarding houses, elderly hostels; dwellings for childless couples; and apartments for small and large families), organized according to the number of sleeping rooms on a range from one to six. At the final preparatory meeting that took place in Karlsruhe in late September it was also agreed to run a busy schedule of guest events featuring targeted political, administrative and industrial figures, with a view to promoting the work of the featured architects (Barr, 2011, 30–1). This was of crucial importance, as the CIAM leadership had always placed emphasis on using the organization's activities to elicit political sanction for their vision of architecture and planning. In the months

## The CIAM2 and CIAM3 Exhibitions

leading up to the congress Giedion used every opportunity to invite further participants and to coax more exhibition plans from silent national groups.[15] By that time he admitted privately that, if the Frankfurt event could not be what he had originally intended, he still hoped that it would be successful in both professional and propaganda terms – hence the importance of the success of the exhibition.[16]

On 26 October, the third day of the congress, the city inaugurated the exhibition in the *Werkbundhaus* (Figure 7.4). The panegyrical tone of the occasion eclipsed the organizational and financial trials and tribulations that had preceded it. As it happened, the municipal authorities eventually were convinced to make a big publicity investment in the occasion, preparing two parallel exhibitions (one to the recently deceased Frankfurt architect Adolf Meyer; the other to the artist Käthe Kollwitz) to accompany the main CIAM show.[17] The exhibition itself proved popular, notwithstanding the fact that it shied away from more popular presentation formats such as building models and plans or recreated interiors typical of other housing exhibitions in the 1920s. Instead it consisted of a number of panels in more or less standardized graphical and textual format, each featuring a single floor plan, often accompanied by section and ground views, and identified simply by reference to the city in which the exhibited solution derived from.[18] The selection of featured examples was by all standards an eccentric one. As expected, Frankfurt itself provided the largest number of panels in an attempt to showcase the

**Figure 7.4** Interior view of the CIAM2 exhibition in Frankfurt [Source: *DNF* 3/11(1929): 213–5].

169

range, diversity and quality of the affordable housing projects executed throughout May's peripheral Trabanten settlements. Together with examples from a host of other cities, Germany supplied more than a third of the total number of panels. Breslau, the city where May had spent the first half of the 1920s as head of the *Schlesische Heimstätte* (see Chapter 2), was also given prominent place, though instead of examples from the WuWa Breslau exhibition the featured projects came from the settlements of Klein-Tschansch (Księże Małe) and Zimpel (Sępolno) (Kononowicz, 1996). Already formed national groups with active representatives, like in Poland, Belgium, Switzerland or The Netherlands, fared better in comparison to those national delegations mired in internal organizations problems, like France, Czechoslovakia or Italy, or those that had not yet been formed, as was the case in the Scandinavian countries, Britain or the Soviet Union. The absence of Le Corbusier from the congress and the ongoing problems surrounding the formation of a French group meant that France was conspicuously under-represented at the exhibition. Some other national groups managed to dispatch a decent sample of work – among them Hungary and Spain; Italy, on the other hand, was the source of only two, highly unrepresentative projects. Personal antipathies got in the way too: particular architects with portfolios that were otherwise relevant to the exhibition's theme were absent.[19] Lastly the selection reflected a conscious bias in favour of works that qualified as 'new' architecture, leading to the exclusion of a number of other housing projects that followed alternative programmes – the kinds of which were typically represented in the IFHTP congresses of the time. The main outlier of the Frankfurt exhibition was Vienna. The city where the idea of the mass-produced, good-quality and truly affordable dwelling was pioneered in the interwar period was represented by five projects, the majority of which, however, were attributable to architects who had later joined May's team in Frankfurt (e.g. Franz Schuster, Anton Brenner).

Most of the featured examples concerned projects already or about to be built. The portfolio of Frankfurt focused mostly on examples from the more recent projects of Praunheim II and III, Hellerhof and Westhausen, as well as the projected garden city of Goldstein (the largest settlement designed by May that was meant to begin construction in 1929 but was postponed due to financial difficulties and was eventually replaced by an emergency settlement after May and most of his team had departed for the Soviet Union) (Figure 7.5). Preference for realised projects was grounded in pragmatism on part of the congress organizers, who wanted to showcase the transformative effects of the 'new' architecture as lived experiences and not as mere wishful thinking. However this did not preclude 'paper' architecture from being included into the exhibition lineup, whether out of relevance to the theme or in order to keep a modicum of cross-national balance. The majority of the Spanish contributions (Salvador; Vallejo; Zarranz and Madariaga) were related to a 1929 national competition about 'minimum dwellings'.[20] Entries by André Lurçat and Le Corbusier derived from their experimental work on the so-called 'Maison Loucheur' that they proposed as a dwelling typology for the ambitious building programme of affordable dwellings launched by the French government in 1928 (Benton, 1984). Along a similar vein, one of the Frankfurt entries concerned Kaufmann's submission to the competition for the 'experimental' estate of Haselhorst-Spandau in

**Figure 7.5** Examples of Frankfurt dwelling plans exhibited at the CIAM2 exhibition [Source: CIAM. *Die Wohnung Für Das Existenzmiminum*. Edited by CIAM, Englert & Schlosser, 1930].

Berlin, for which the architect received second place behind Gropius's project.[21] One of Bourgeois' submissions related to a 1927 project that combined the traditional spatial scheme of a peripheral garden city with duplex apartments arranged in multi-floor elongated blocks (Ledent, 2019, 202). Gerrit Rietveld presented an experimental study on his idea for a fully prefabricated and transportable 'core house' that he designed for the city of Utrecht (Kuipers, 2013, 91–5).[22] Stuttgart was represented at the exhibition not through any of its more celebrated Weissenhof model dwellings but by studies of experimental dwellings devised by the brothers Heinz and Bodo Rasch. Examples from the Soviet Stroikom studies of collective housing complexes conducted in the late 1920s (see Chapter 4) were also shown in a special section of the exhibition dedicated to hotel-apartments. A further interesting example came from Klein's studies of optimal dwelling space utilization that he had conducted for the RFG – a rare point of thematic intersection with the 1928 IFHTP Paris congress, where Klein's study had also been exhibited (see Chapter 3). 'Model' housing projects were also selectively co-opted in the exhibition programme. While the Weissenhof estate in Stuttgart and the WuWa one in Breslau were absent, the Swiss Werkbund's WoBa Eglisee estate in Basel (projects by Artaria and Schmidt (Rieben, 2019)), the preliminary project of the Artaria-Schmidt partnership for the low-cost housing scheme of Bäumlihofstrasse in the same city and the Dammerstock Siedlung in Karlsruhe (multiple designs by the scheme's architects Gropius and Otto Häsler)[23] were included in the exhibition programme.

But the event also provided a unique opportunity to less well-known residential experiments to gain prominence. The impressively active Polish group, headed by Szymon and Helena Syrkus and featuring their collaborators in the avant-garde journal *Praesens*, compiled a striking portfolio of both executed 'model' projects and experimental schemes from Warsaw (Żoliborz estate) and Łodz (submitted to the competition for a model settlement in the Polesie Konstantynowskie district) (Czaplinska-Archer, 1981; Wenderski, 2018; Kohlrausch, 2019, 94–5, 105–14; Matysek-Imielińska, 2020, 19–60).[24] The Hungarian portfolio featured typologies by a group of young rationalists who were inspired by the work of Gropius and Le Corbusier in an attempt to challenge the neo-baroque academic revival in Hungary during the 1920s. They clustered around the modernist journal *Tér és Forma* and produced an innovative register of plans for affordable, small-size dwellings that put Gropius's idea of the 'dwelling ration' into practical and thoughtful use (Ritoók and Sebestyén, 2018). At Frankfurt György Rácz presented his own reflection on the 'living cell' with an eight-bed apartment study divided into 9 m² cells for two (with single beds) and featuring a complex hierarchy of semi-private spaces (basins shared between two cells; large living room; single toilet facilities) and a modular design that allowed the living room to expand by removing the cell partitions and provide the family with a more usable and pleasant space for relaxation. In his second contribution to the exhibition Rácz produced variations on the one-room apartment, again following the 9 m² cell module but also scaling the type to a two-bed variant while keeping overall surface area to a minimum (14.7 m² and 29.5 m² for one and two people, respectively). In addition the Hungarian leading delegate Farkas Molnár submitted another study for a two-storey dwelling with eight beds and small but separate kitchen, following a similar reduced-size cell analogy for the sleeping areas.[25]

In morphological and typological terms the curated selection of dwellings exhibited at Frankfurt was similarly eclectic. The original structure that was stipulated in the preparatory guidelines – six categories based on the number of bedrooms – was in the end simplified by reducing the number of sections to three (dwellings in one-, two- and multi-family houses). In an attempt to reconcile underlying programmatic differences between proponents of urban concentration versus adherents to the model of decentralization, the exhibition featured examples from garden cities (e.g. Floréal and Logis in Brussels; Goldstein in Frankfurt; Sępolno in Breslau), a large number of peripheral settlements, as well as apartments integrated into the existing urban fabric or intended for this use. 'Cell'-like solutions were represented in the first section (in addition to the special annex devoted to hotel solutions), while examples of apartments in larger multi-family blocks covered a wide range of programmatic solutions, from the low- and medium- to high-rise and from row-houses to detached large multi-storey apartment blocks. Except for the Soviet Stroikom special case that reflected an affirmative endorsement of socialized living or for the other 'special' cases where communal areas were justified by the hotel-like function of the project, all other featured examples followed the conventional assumption that a dwelling was a privatized space for its residents. Only one of the Viennese examples (Schuster) made explicit reference to communal washing facilities within the broader block. Racz's smallest design, on the other hand, reflected a collective design hypothesis but was presented and captioned in a more subtle way by referencing 'new conceptions in the modes and aims of living'.

A similarly wide range of organizational and distributive solutions can be observed across the examples presented at the exhibition. With the exception of the few case studies included as indications of poor design practice, the organizers assumed an agnostic position vis-a-vis different typological solutions that they offered to the questions of centralization-versus-decentralization or low-versus-high rise. Many examples of multi-family dwellings featured more conventional internal staircases but about a third of the case studies opted for the gallery access model, with loggias and balconies observed frequently. When it came to kitchen design, functional models that tended towards either reduced-size separate rooms or even smaller kitchen niches were the norm, with associated sizes ranging from the relatively large room of Gropius's and Breuer's example from the Torten estate in Dessau (11.7 m$^2$) to the minute niches of many Frankfurt and Viennese submissions (as small as 2 m$^2$). All featured dwellings offered at least a toilet (though the Torten example was unique in placing it outside) but a significant number also comprised either shower or a full bathroom suite. Flexibility and adaptability were evident in cases where the architects either explicitly provided floor plan variations (e.g. designs by Racz and Bourgeois; or Franz Roeckle's dwellings for the Dammerstock estate) or suggested alternative configurations facilitated by movable furniture (e.g. Lihotzky's Frankfurt example and Rietveld), flexible partitions (e.g. Johann Wilhelm Lehr's example from Goldstein) or altogether different spatial distributions of adjacent apartments within the same building (e.g. Schuster's Frankfurt design).

As expected, overall dwelling size was also given a central place in the graphic illustrations of the plans. When planning for the event and formulating guidelines for the national groups, the CIAM organizers had underlined the link between the exhibition's theme (good-quality but above all economically produced and affordable dwellings for the economically weaker classes) and dwelling size reduction. More specific guidance underlined the need for efficient design solutions that were typically in the region of 40 m$^2$ and ought not to exceed 70 m$^2$ for the largest families.[26] The exhibited specimens provided an even wider gamut of solutions in terms of size reduction. In the first (one-family) section of the exhibition, the dwellings ranged from 14.7 m$^2$ (Rácz's 'cells' in Budapest) to the comparatively generous apartments designed by members of the Spanish delegation (both Madrid examples by Vallejo and Zarranz-Madariaga exceeded 70 m$^2$). In-between these two extremes architects provided different scenarios of habitation (bed numbers varied from 2 to 8 m$^2$, with overall floor areas between 30 m$^2$ and 69.4 m$^2$). The individual 'dwelling ration' – in most cases *c.* 11 m$^2$ – was at its lowest in Rietveld's Utrecht study (around 6.5 m$^2$, largely because of the multi-use living area and the small size of two of the bedrooms in the upper floor) and in all of Rácz's examples (courtesy of the architect's strict modular approach that used the redefined 'cell' as the strict scale for every variation), peaking at more than 15 m$^2$ in Schuster's spacious example. In spite of its relatively smaller number of examples, the two-family section offered a similarly wide range of sizes – from 25 m$^2$ (Salvador's 'minimal' apartment) to 52.7 m$^2$ (one of Le Corbusier's plans for the Maison Loucheur). A very interesting example was provided by Otto Häsler from his settlements in Celle (Italienische Garten, Georgsgarten and finally Galgenberg): in its standard form, it was a 33 m$^2$ apartment for two but it could easily be scaled up to an eight-bed version by progressively adding small cell-like single-bed cubicles to the plan (Antz et al., 2018, 7–11). The variety of typological solutions was significantly wider in the last exhibition category (dwellings in multi-family houses). Floor areas ranged from 23 m$^2$ (Bernhard Hermkes' special solution for single-room apartments in his working women's blocks in Frankfurt) to Klein's spacious large-family dwellings that could exceed 90 m$^2$, with most examples falling between 40 m$^2$ and 60 m$^2$. This section was dominated by the various Frankfurt examples but also included some outliers, such as Rietveld's study of an apartment block featuring an elevator and an even more bewildering entry from the social housing portfolio of Milan's Institute of Social Housing (ICP) – a traditional apartment block from the Regina Elena quarter (1925–28) (Agustoni, 2007, 39) (Figure 7.6).

In contrast to the frustration felt by key CIAM figures about the conduct of the congress, the internal appraisal of the exhibition was more positive. The event was well-received and fulfilled the publicity expectations of both the CIAM leadership and the Frankfurt hosts. Hannes Meyer, who was present at La Sarraz but did not attend the subsequent congresses, praised the show for its 'exceptional' presentation and contribution to knowledge on the minimum dwelling.[27] Bourgeois was clearly inspired by CIAM's

**Figure 7.6** Dwelling plans from the CIAM2 exhibition [Source: CIAM. *Die Wohnung Für Das Existenzmiminum*. Edited by CIAM, Englert & Schlosser, 1930].

theoretical approach to housing to the point that he embarked upon designing (together with Louis Herman de Koninck) a 'model' Existenzminimum-dwelling settlement in the context of the 1930 world fair in Liège (Tribouillet quarter).[28] It was the afterlife of the exhibition, however, that proved its – and the congress' – most productive legacy. After Frankfurt Giedion arranged for the exhibition to become an international mobile event showcasing and popularising CIAM's work. The US delegate Richard Neutra proposed to take over the organization of a congress in the near future and host the travelling exhibition.[29] This promising idea remained on paper but it whetted the appetite of the CIAM leadership for promoting the exhibition as an ongoing event with international significance. The eventual agreed itinerary featured first Basel (December) and Zurich (January–February 1930), then Warsaw (March), Stuttgart, Munich, Madgenburg and Hamburg, before the exhibition could find its way to Brussels in October 1930 in order to coincide with CIAM's third congress.[30] In its numerous local iterations the itinerant exhibition exceeded the expectations of the CIAM leadership in terms of publicity, social appeal and professional interest. The two events in Switzerland took the form of more conventional museum exhibitions that largely replicated the original Frankfurt show, albeit accompanied by new detailed catalogues (curated by Hans Schmidt) and a more pronounced focus on Swiss examples.[31] The real contribution of the events in Basel and Zurich (Figure 7.7) lay in the quality of the opportunities that they offered to reflect further on and refine the core theme of the 'dwelling for the Existenzminimum'. Schmidt refracted the Frankfurt discussions and the exhibition examples through his own programmatic emphasis on the architect's 'social' responsibility and pushed further two key messages. The first was that technical and design innovation had disrupted the conventional correspondence between dwelling size and quality of life, arguing that what the pre-First World War apartment could do with 50 m$^2$ the 'new' dwelling could satisfy or even exceed through half the size. The second message from Schmidt's framing of the Swiss iteration of the exhibition was that no real change in the dwelling conditions for the working classes was conceivable without a root-and-branch reform of the legal and political framework of urban planning. Meanwhile the Polish version of the exhibition in Warsaw (*Mieszkanie Najmniejsze*, 1–21 March 1930) provided a unique opportunity to the local CIAM group around the journal Praesens and the Warsaw Housing Cooperative to engage in and showcase further experiments in thoughtful, socially responsible dwelling size reduction and design innovation (Figure 7.7). In addition to exhibiting the material of the travelling Frankfurt show alongside photographs and ideas/plans produced by local architects, the event was aligned with particular aspects of the domestic social housing discourse and the programmatic priorities of the architectural avant-garde groups in Poland, leading to further 'ideas' competitions and events that resulted in a range of new 'model' dwellings in the new housing estates under construction in the outskirts of Warsaw (e.g. the Żoliborz estate) (Crowley, 1992, 87–9; Matysek-Imielińska, 2020, 62–5).

What happened in Frankfurt informed and in some cases influenced directly architectural discourse and exhibition activities well beyond the list of CIAM2 attendees and their contacts. Both the Ring and the Werkbund aligned their subsequent exhibition

## The CIAM2 and CIAM3 Exhibitions

**Figure 7.7** Instances of the CIAM2 travelling exhibition – Zurich (January–February 1930) and Warsaw (March 1930) [Source: (1) Archives of the Zurich University of the Arts, GBA-1930-D01-400 / (2) *Narodowe Archiwum Cyfrowe*, 1-U-8482].

and 'ideas' competition initiatives with the discourse of the 'minimum dwelling', albeit in ways that also referenced the typological lineage of the Kleinwohnung in Germany (Becker, 1991). The 1930 Werkbund Paris exhibition co-organized by Gropius and Breuer reflected on the same themes that were at the heart of CIAM's early congresses (size of dwelling, height and density of buildings, minimalism in design, social responsibility to design affordable dwellings) and Gropius stayed in close contact with Giedion in order to strengthen the programmatic alignment between the two groups, repeatedly asking for exhibition materials and publicity support (Rössler, 2014, 70–84). In Sweden the 1930 Stockholm exhibition offered a unique stage for CIAM members Markelius and Uno Åhrén, as well as other modern architects like Gunnar Asplund, to align the minimalist functional design philosophy with indigenous historical building traditions and social questions concerning affordable housing and efficient urban planning (Menin et al., 2003, 54–8; Marklund and Stadius, 2010, 617–9; Monterumisi, 2017, 81, 88). Aalto organized the special 'minimum dwelling' (*Pienasuntonäyttely*) section of the 1930 Arts and Crafts exhibition organized in Helsinki.[32] He also produced an influential programmatic statement of his understanding of the 'housing problem' in an article published in 1930 that resonated with ideas and nomenclature derived from CIAM's contemporary discourse of the biological, sociological and technical requirements of the modern dwelling.[33] In all these exhibition events the unabashed programmatic partisanship of the organizers offered the kind of prescriptive clarity that the Frankfurt congress had shunned because of the disagreements among its members and the emphasis on promoting the widest possible transnational collaboration. Schmidt, for example, was candid about the technical and design requirements of the optimal 'minimum dwelling': with a 14–16 m$^2$ living area, a reduced-size yet functionally designed kitchen (ideally as a niche), and flexible, multi-use spaces for different parts of the day, the typical size that he had in mind was *c.* 40 m$^2$ for a typical family dwelling. Aalto, on the other hand, followed similar design and social assumptions but stipulated a more generous size norm that extended up to *c.* 60 m$^2$ for the same typical family (Kim, 2005, 358–9).

The second communicative device in CIAM's strategy – the publication of a volume featuring a combination of congress contributions and exhibition materials – proved a much more contentious and problematic affair. In the closing statement of his address to the Frankfurt congress Giedion had described this initiative as the 'main emphasis' of CIAM's efforts following the Frankfurt event.[34] Both May and Gropius agreed, stressing how the official publication would build on and extend the itinerant exhibition's international publicity effects.[35] The publication's significance as legacy for both the congress and the exhibition was clear in Giedion's thinking immediately after the conclusion of CIAM2.[36] In addition, however, it was expected that the volume would help recoup some of the costs involved in the exhibition itself that the city of Frankfurt's financial contribution could not cover fully.[37] The main problem was that the publication necessitated its own preparatory work plan (editing of talks, reproduction of plans) that was onerous time-wise and costly. Given the early CIAM's challenging budgetary situation, the work was awkwardly divided between Frankfurt, where the publisher was based, and Zurich, with Giedion in theory assuming responsibility for the editorial work. The initial plan was to abridge the keynote talks in order to shift the publication's emphasis to the exhibition itself and keep production costs at bay[38] but both Le Corbusier and Gropius objected to this and in the end the keynotes were reproduced verbatim.[39] Meanwhile the Frankfurt organizers used their proximity to the publisher to shape the publication, taking liberties with the editing of the texts and reserving particular parts of the congress proceedings for the municipal magazine *Das Neue Frankfurt*. This angered Gropius who in a stream of letters in November-December 1929 and again throughout March 1930 remonstrated with Giedion against the Frankfurt organizer's behaviour, accusing them of exploiting the congress publication as a propaganda medium for the promotion of their own work and programmatic ideas about housing and planning. Gropius even threatened that he would have to forego his participation at the following congress or withdraw from CIAM altogether.[40] The issue of the publication came up repeatedly in the various planning meetings in the winter and spring of 1930, dividing the delegates and frustrating efforts to turn the volume into the kind of major publishing event that Giedion and others had originally in mind. In the end problems with the way in which the Frankfurt organizers had negotiated the contract with the publisher and a series of unforeseen onerous financial implications resulted in a significantly diminished publication without translated contributions but at least with a detailed cross-section of the originally exhibited dwelling plans (Henderson, 2013, 436–40).[41]

## Exhibiting CIAM3

The following congress in Brussels turned out to be in fact an umbrella event for four mini-congresses. The incongruent profusion of themes (minimum dwelling, land subdivision, high-versus-low rise building, sliding windows) (see Chapter 6) produced a similar surfeit of potential exhibition events that added to the organizational chaos and complicated CIAM's communication strategy. Bourgeois was expected to coordinate the various exhibition activities collapsed into CIAM3 while also aligning them with the visiting legacy CIAM2 show. In theory there would be one umbrella exhibition event coinciding with the congress, encompassing and unifying the itinerant Frankfurt exhibition, new plans on land subdivision and urban planning drafted by the national groups for CIAM3, possibly a specific show on dwelling interiors from the work carried out in Frankfurt, and a further event that would present a curated list of innovative work carried out under the programmatic banner of the 'new' architecture, ideally accompanied by photographic material. At the February preparatory meeting the planned exhibition event was described as 'the most important manifestation of modern architecture realized until today'.[42] Things, however, started becoming more complicated during the spring, as both Giedion and Bourgeois started taking liberties with the thematic coverage and the publicity side of the congress. In April Giedion approached Le Corbusier with an idea to introduce a 'construction detail' event that could be exhibited in the context of every congress, suggesting to him the theme of the sliding windows for CIAM3.[43] The idea was taken up enthusiastically by Le Corbusier and formally proposed as part of the official congress and exhibition programme at the May preparatory meeting in Paris. Although initially Bourgeois protested at the suggestion of the separate exhibition event on the sliding windows, he then proceeded to announce his own departure from the originally agreed exhibition agenda: a special 'conference' dealing with the problems of affordable housing in Belgium with the expected participation of CIAM members, originally planned to begin immediately after the closing of the CIAM3 congress and its main exhibition event, with the added benefit that it would stimulate further interest in the contribution of the 'new' architecture in this domain.[44] There were few details about this new event provided by Bourgeois at that stage and, given the brief and generally positive discussion that followed the announcement, it would be safe to assume that the attendees sanctioned the proposal. At any rate most of the proceedings in Paris appeared to be reassuringly focused on the preparation of the main exhibition on rational land subdivision that was expected to show 'how the problem of the Existenzminimum dwelling can be addressed through [urban] planning and change of regulations'. A team consisting of Bourgeois, Henveaux, Stam and Verwilghen would lead preparations for the main exhibition, working together with May, Giedion and the Frankfurt authorities to deal with the logistics of bringing the CIAM2 exhibition material to Brussels.[45]

In the period between the May preparatory meeting and August, however, co-ordination once again broke down. Throughout July communications to the delegates appeared to assume that the main exhibition event at Brussels would be the one dedicated to the rational land subdivision; everything else – the visiting Frankfurt exhibition and Bourgeois' event – were treated as little more than supplementary occasions.[46] Giedion kept asking for updates on the progress of the preparations from Brussels, uncertain as to whether there would be a parallel event on the city of Frankfurt as had been proposed in February. Meanwhile Stam seemed intent on monopolizing the organization of CIAM3's main exhibition, directing every detail from Frankfurt.[47] As for Bourgeois he kept quiet about the advance planning for his event, limiting himself to reassuring letters to Giedion and Moser about the progress of the preparation for CIAM3.[48] When he did send more details about his special 'conference' (by that time having graduated to a mammoth *Journées de l'Habitation Minimum* event), the scale of the departure from what had been originally agreed became evident and alarmed Moser and Giedion. The distressing revelation that Bourgeois had used his privileged position as organizer of CIAM3 to insert what was essentially a parallel congress and an alternative exhibition event to the programme came only days after news that key CIAM members were about to depart for the Soviet Union and could no longer be actively involved in the group's activities.[49] The original programme of lectures and activities of the Journées that Bourgeois shared with the Zurich office featured a series of lectures by CIAM members, still including May and Stam as key speakers. The main concern, as Giedion confessed to Moser, was that the Journées would overshadow the congress itself, making the exhibition on the rational land subdivision appear like a secondary adjunct to the programme of Bourgeois's event.[50] On his part Moser expressed his unease with the prospect of an organizational breakdown that could affect the quality of the main exhibition, since Stam and to an extent May were directly involved in the preparations.[51]

The compound crisis caused by the departure of key CIAM figures for the Soviet Union and Bourgeois's announcement about the shape of his Journées prompted the decision to postpone the congress by seven weeks to late November.[52] In spite of the extra time, however, the situation got worse. When the revised programme for the Journées was circulated, it became clear that Bourgeois had arranged for his event to precede the opening of CIAM3, with its total duration now stretching to six full days. The publicized programme for the event was by all means impressive. Lectures by Giedion, Gropius, Le Corbusier, Van Eesteren, Syrkus and the Italian delegate Alberto Sartoris complemented a bespoke exhibition event. The exhibition itself featured no less than seven sections, apparently absorbing both the CIAM3 and CIAM2 exhibitions, the Belgium-focused show, the showcase of Frankfurt's social housing programme, and two further technical events on kitchen and bathroom design. To make matters worse, the draft programme for the event made no mention of CIAM or the third congress, featuring instead an independent organizing committee with a number of prominent Belgian public figures and Bourgeois as secretary but no other CIAM member.[53] The final straw came only two weeks before the opening date of the congress. Bourgeois wrote to Giedion that all exhibition events would be inaugurated in tandem on 22 November inside the rooms of the Palais des Beaux Arts of Brussels. However this meant that, having allocated the largest rooms to the Journées and to the exhibition on the city of Frankfurt, the only remaining space available for the congress was too small to accommodate comfortably all the delegates. Giedion was once again aghast. Although he was eager to avoid a head-on collision with Bourgeois so close to the official opening of the already delayed congress and seemed respectful of the amount of effort that Bourgeois had invested into his own conference-exhibition, he was also determined to ensure that CIAM3 and its exhibition would be treated as the main event. At that stage he called upon first the Dutch member Cornelis Van Eesteren, who had remained largely aloof from the preparations of the Brussels congress and became involved only after replacing Stam as congress delegate (Somer, 2007, 34–7),[54] and then his Swiss colleague Steiger to intervene in order to reproportion the various events in favour of the CIAM3 exhibition.[55] On his part Bourgeois did his best to reassure CIAM that his decision to proceed with the Journées was dictated by financial considerations, claiming that the proceeds from the exhibition and the financial support of the Belgian authorities went a long way towards relieving the budget pressures from the organization of CIAM3.

In the end both the Journées and the main CIAM3 exhibition lived up to their publicity expectations. Stam's impressive work in producing a standardized schema for the visual presentation of the material on land subdivision set the foundations for a more streamlined exhibition event than the preceding one in Frankfurt.[56] In the original guidelines for the exhibition plans circulated in late March 1930, when Schmidt was in charge of the operation, the anticipated presentation scheme was both over-complicated (no less than eleven fields of information were required for each project, relating both to the individual dwelling, to the building, the site and the city as a whole) and incomplete in its precise graphical format.[57] In the face of persisting delays in assembling the exhibition material and developing a new visual presentation scheme for the material Stam took over the operation and simplified the process by reducing the number of information fields and adopting the visual scheme used in Frankfurt a year earlier.[58] In a symbolic shift of focus, the featured plans were re-categorized according to each featured building's height (low-, medium-, high-rise or mixed) rather than by the size of the dwelling itself as was the case in CIAM2.⁵⁹ Each example was accompanied by information about its location and site coverage; circulation, density, orientation and distance between buildings; social composition of the residents; and land prices. A separate table displayed data about dwelling typology, number of beds per dwelling, total number of storeys and floor plans. In contrast to the CIAM2 exhibition most already executed projects were identified by their precise location and date of execution, as well as photographic illustrations; but there was also a significant number of examples of experimental projects, usually accompanied by sketches. Inevitably there were gaps in the information provided, primarily because the material supplied by the national groups was often incomplete.⁶⁰ The overall result, however, was a significantly more informative and engaging presentation that allowed for easier comparisons across all exhibited case studies.

There were continuities and overlaps between the featured projects at the CIAM2 and CIAM3 exhibitions. Familiar names from Frankfurt (Hellerhof and Westhausen), Karlsruhe (Dammerstock), Berlin (Hasselorst), Brussels (*Cité Moderne*) and Paris (Le Corbusier's variations of his sweeping urban planning schemes) made a reappearance in the Brussels exhibition, albeit now presented and analysed as sites rather than individual dwellings. However shifts in CIAM membership patterns between 1929 and 1930 and the attendance of new national delegations at Brussels supplied a wealth of new specimens from locations and projects that had not featured a year earlier. The presence of Teige from Czechoslovakia and Aalto from Finland provided the impetus for a more extensive and thought-provoking representation of architectural work from their two countries. Even the United States was now included in the list (Radburn) on occasion of Richard Neutra's participation in the Brussels proceedings with one of the keynote addresses on high-rise residential development. Conversely the acrimonious withdrawal of Josef Frank from the organization (see Chaptre 5) removed the only source of information from Austria. Ongoing problems inside the Italian group meant that once again Italy was grossly underrepresented, with only two examples from Milan that were mostly used as 'primitive' or suboptimal examples of site management. The German, Dutch, Swiss and Belgian cases continued to be the best-represented – a reflection of the productive work carried out by the respective national groups. Recent projects, such as the Neubühl estate in Zurich, Schorenmatten in Basel or Buiksloot and Transvaalburt in north Amsterdam, appeared alongside earlier examples (e.g. the garden settlements of Floreal-Le Logis and Kapelleveld in Brussels; the estates of Kiefhoek in Rotterdam, Im Vogelsand in Basel; Gagfah in Frankfurt; and Hardturmstrasse in Zurich). Once again there was an interesting mix of executed projects, ideas developed for particular sites and more abstract experimental design solutions that tested a universal typological proposition, as stipulated in the various guidelines issued by CIAM regarding the exhibition's content. (Figures 7.8-7.9).

Interestingly only a smaller subset of the featured projects were explicitly labelled as 'Existenzminimum' with the majority of the dwellings described as suitable for workers. There was also a number of exclusively middle-class and mixed settlements, as well as examples that explicitly referenced the degree of shift towards communal living or

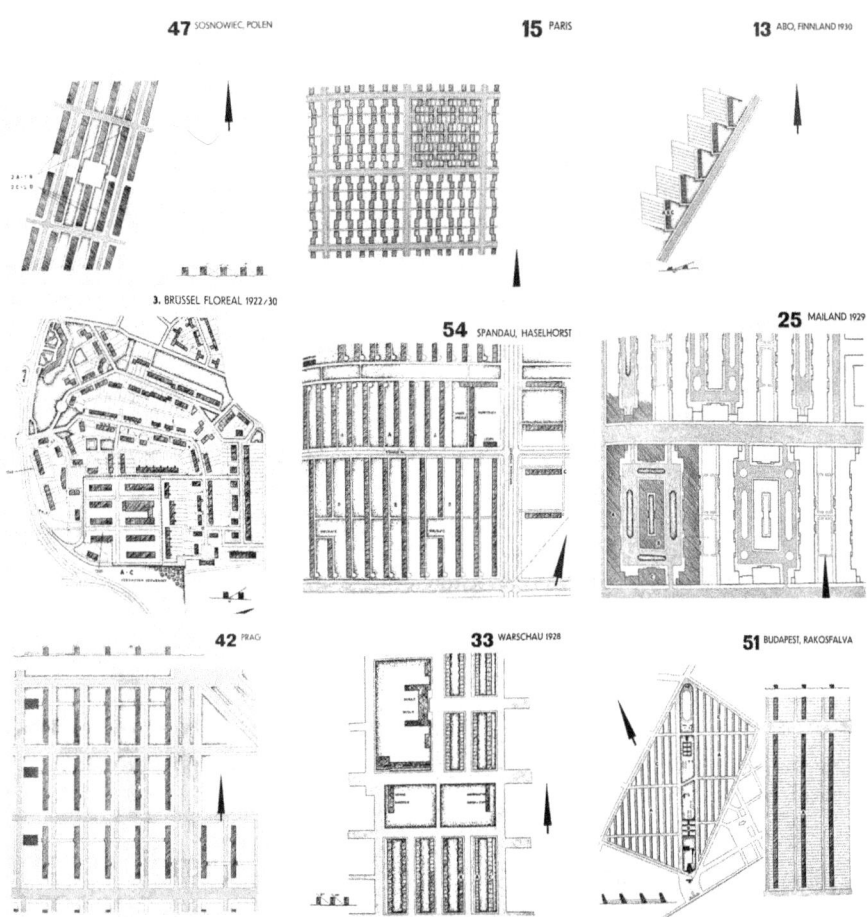

**Figure 7.8** Settlement plans featured in the CIAM3 exhibition [Source: Bourgeois, Victor, et al. *Rationelle Bebauungsweisen: Ergebnisse des 3. Internationalen Kongresses für Neues Bauen*. Stuttgart: J. Hoffman, 1931].

collective living. The mixed perspective on dwelling, building and settlement meant that the CIAM3 exhibition was a programmatically richer affair than its Frankfurt predecessor, integrating to a reasonable extent a range of interests in typological variation, biological requirements and sociological parameters of modern habitation. Yet it was clear from both the exhibition's structure and the mode of visual presentation that the focus of the CIAM3 exhibition had shifted decisively away from the individual dwelling – the cornerstone of the Frankfurt event – and towards ever-larger scales of reference. The featured projects provided little information about their internal organization beyond overall size/bed count and whatever further insights could be inferred from the – downsized and fragmentary – floor plans of individual dwellings that supplemented the settlement information. Instead most of the information highlighted

**Figure 7.9** Examples of estates featured at the CIAM3 exhibition: (first row) Kiefhoek (Rotterdam); (second row) Kapelleveld (Brussels); (third row) Cité Moderne (Brussels) [Source: Author's photos].

how individual residential building types interfaced with each other in the space of the settlements and formed together distinct urban microorganisms. Significantly neither dwelling size nor individual 'dwelling ration' were presented as primary qualitative indicators: the majority of featured examples assumed a personal ration of $c.$ 9–11 m$^2$ regardless of their social classification. In this sense the main Brussels exhibition shed little new light on the 'minimum dwelling' discussion that was carried on from Frankfurt and took up the final day of the CIAM3 congress proceedings; but it did promote the minimum (in size and design) as an egalitarian indicator of better-quality living.

The programmatic tensions that had nearly derailed the preparations for the Brussels congress were only partly and often awkwardly reconciled in the exhibition lineup. As a result the featured projects covered variations in settlement type (garden city, peripheral settlement, urban development), building height (anything from one to fourteen storeys), class and social agenda of the residents (with affordability receding as a major consideration behind the selection of projects) and typology (anything from single-family houses to multi-storey apartments blocks to 'living cells' in socialized settlements or boarding houses). Paradoxically this larger diversity made direct comparisons between the featured projects more difficult, as the data provided for some categories of dwellings derived from different assumptions about the reference unit. This problem was evident in the third section of the exhibition dedicated to high-rise developments – a fully-fledged theme of the CIAM3 congress. Examples of collective living supplied by the Czechoslovak and Polish groups in particular provided data about their size and bed count that often bypassed the single dwelling or 'cell' and were based instead on the sum of these spaces in a single building or even across the whole settlement project. Some of the projects exhibited in Brussels (e.g. the Erismannhof settlement designed by Karl Kündig und Heinrich Oetiker or examples from the Dammerstock estate in Karlsruhe) intentionally sought to mix working- and middle-class dwellings to promote actively the formation of multi-class local communities. By contrast more radical designs from Poland and appeared to reject the idea that spatial proximity between socially heterogeneous families would facilitate social mixing and advance a broader agenda of egalitarianism. The example of the Rakowiec working-class estate in Warsaw underlined instead how the need to elevate the quality of life of those with low incomes was best served through prioritizing affordability and sufficient supply of good-quality dwellings for those who needed them at the expense of lofty ideas about social interaction that could otherwise be regarded as de facto accepting the forces of socio-economic inequality inherent in capitalist societies (Matysek-Imielińska, 2020, 282–4). The Czechoslovak submissions in particular (Josef Havlíček and Karel Honzík's plans for a collective quarter in Vršovice based on the collective – Koldom – housing typology (Zarecor, 2011, 21; Seelow, 2017, 4); and Jan Gillar's and Josef Špalek's designs for fully socialized housing complexes in the Ruzyn district of Prague) experimental translations of contemporary Soviet ideas about a new form of collective living living, postulating a root-and-branch reconceptualization of the entire housing and planning culture through a project of revolutionary socio-economic transformation (Teige, 2002, 3, 251, 308, 341–3).

At the official opening of the Brussels congress and of the main exhibition on 27 November 1930 the outgoing president Moser together with Bourgeois and Van Eesteren did their best to drum up enthusiasm for the occasion and to paper over the multiple cracks of the preceding months. There was effusive praise for the Journées, not just for the quality of the exhibition materials but also for the theoretical contributions that they hosted and the discussions that they fostered in the particular Belgian context. In a deliberate show of unity the opening talks presented the Journées as evidence that the work of CIAM could be supremely useful as a guide for effective reformist action by national and local political authorities. Thus the speakers' main concern was to re-unify the preceding Journées with CIAM3 and its exhibitions into a single narrative of 'new' architecture that was now presented as being on the verge of making a significant impact on both political and social processes.[61] There was also considerable public and professional interest in all CIAM exhibitions, including the last-minute show curated by Le Corbusier on the sliding windows. The intention of the CIAM leadership was for the main collection on rational land subdivision to become the new version of the organization's itinerant exhibition, replacing and partly absorbing the Frankfurt one on the 'minimum dwelling' that had fulfilled its publicity brief through a full programme of international iterations throughout 1929–30. It soon became clear, however, that a similar – though less extensive – programme of international events would also need to be planned for the sliding windows show that Le Corbusier was only too keen to promote.

The post-congress fate of all the exhibitions hosted under CIAM3 depended on the ability of the organizing team in Brussels to prepare the exhibits for international dispatch – something that was complicated by Bourgeois's short illness and communication hiatus soon after the conclusion of the CIAM3 proceedings. By mid-December Giedion expressed serious concerns about the fate of both exhibitions, calling on Van Eesteren to intervene and speed things up. The initial plan was for the main exhibition to travel from Brussels to Germany and then to Switzerland in January but the initial optimism soon evaporated in the face of Bourgeois's inaction.[62] As the opening date of the exhibition in Zurich was fixed for 15 February 1931, it became clear that there was no time for the show to be shown in another location before reaching Switzerland.[63] The Zurich event turned out to be an important one, with the main CIAM exhibition complemented by a parallel show organized by Gropius and dedicated to his pet issue of high-rise construction. Gropius, Le Corbusier and Van Eesteren were all present for the official opening.[64] Beyond that point the plan was for the exhibition to travel to Germany in order to be shown as part of the important Berlin international building exhibition (*Internationale Ausstellung für Städtebau und Wohnungswesen*) in June 1931 before travelling further to Amsterdam, Basel, Milan, Madrid and Barcelona. CIAM's participation in the Berlin event had been identified as a critical component of the group's publicity strategy as far back as the early autumn of 1930, when initial contacts were made to host a special congress as part of the exhibition programme and arrange for an official CIAM visit to the exhibition premises.[65] Additional ideas continued to be discussed in 1931 and 1932 featuring shows in Finland and Sweden, Greece, again Switzerland and Italy, and even Soviet Union, as part of the planned but repeatedly postponed fourth congress.[66]

The situation regarding the publication(s), on the other hand, appeared more promising at the beginning but soon encountered different complications. The painful saga of the CIAM2 volume had convinced Giedion that he needed to wrest control of the operation from either the Brussels or the Frankfurt offices and transfer significant responsibility to the more dependable Van Eesteren in his new capacity as CIAM president.[67] Bourgeois was understandably upset about this change, perceiving it as yet another attempt to isolate him from the leadership of the group, coming shortly after the decision to bypass him in favour of Van Eesteren for the position of CIAM president. Van Eesteren handled the ensuing fallout with Bourgeois carefully and a new crisis was averted; but the sudden change in the management of the publication added an extra element of administrative complexity to the process, with exhibition materials held in Brussels and then travelling in Switzerland being managed from Amsterdam and involving a Frankfurt-based publisher.[68] Initial contacts with the same Frankfurt publishers behind the CIAM2 publication (Englert & Schlosser) about a trilingual publication based on the congress (with abridged keynotes this time) and its main exhibition plans on rational land subdivision were promising. At the February 1931 meeting of the committee charged with the preparation of the Moscow congress that took place in Basel in order to coincide with the opening of the CIAM3 exhibition at the local *Museum für Gestaltung*, Giedion explained optimistically that the all-important terminus for the publication was the Berlin exhibition in June.[69]

Once again, however, the complexities involved in arranging for a large number of material to get reproduced and printed for publication in the midst of an exhibition cycle criss-crossing national borders proved much harder to manage than Giedion had initially anticipated. The intention to have a second publication dedicated to the sliding windows exhibition come out at the same time as the main CIAM3 volume complicated matters further, adding to the workload and slowing down the entire production process.[70] As a result, delays in preparing the visual aspects and collating the textual contributions meant that the main volume was pushed back until the autumn, missing the originally intended deadline of the Bauausstellung in Berlin in June.[71] Similar unforeseen complexities involved in the process of editing and standardizing the material slowed down the production cycle of the second publication on the sliding windows.[72] The bankruptcy of the Frankfurt publisher in charge of the project meant that a new publishing company (Julius Hoffmann in Stuttgart) had to take over the publication and distribution of the volume (as well as the continuing production of the previous book based on CIAM2), causing further delays and cost to the already overstretched CIAM budget.[73]

The main exhibition volume eventually came out in early November 1931, featuring summaries of the keynotes, Teige's reflection on the CIAM2 reports on the Existenzminimum, the key findings of the national group reports in a mixture of German and French, the congress' final declarations on the theme of high-versus-low rise construction, as well as a selection of the exhibited plans presented in full detail and annotated in three languages with the addition of English translations (Bourgeois et al., 1931). In addition to the main congress-exhibition publications, however, Giedion pursued a number of further avenues for publication in order to maximize the propaganda effect of the group's recent activities. On Gropius's advice he produced a series of shorter publications throughout 1931 showcasing the activities and projects of members and especially national groups through the widely read German architectural journal *Bauwelt*.[74] Essays on the 'new' architecture in Germany, Finland, the Netherlands, Switzerland, Sweden, Italy and Spain appeared in 1931–2 as part of CIAM's strategy of maximizing the use of diverse publication outlets for enhancing the group's international reputation and allowing national groups to be more actively engaged in the publicity effort.[75]

The itinerary of the CIAM3 main exhibition was disrupted by inevitable delays and last-minute changes but the international exposure that it offered was significant, eclipsing the previous exhibition on the minimum dwelling. The primary focus remained on the preparation of CIAM's participation in Berlin – both an exhibition and an extraordinary mini-congress event. By virtue of his proximity and links to the organizers Gropius took over the preparations for the CIAM representation at the Berlin event, trying repeatedly to inject urgency into the operation of collecting, preparing and dispatching the exhibition material to Berlin.[76] The slow pace of CIAM's internal processes frustrated him: deadlines were repeatedly missed and preparations were affected by the typical communication breakdowns between Zurich, Brussels, Amsterdam and Frankfurt.[77] The sliding windows collection proved the hardest to manage because of transport difficulties, customs charges and the withdrawal of a number of construction firms that had sent models to Brussels.[78] The main CIAM3 exhibition, however, made it to Berlin.[79] Alongside the primary Bauausstellung, Mies van der Rohe curated a real-size model exhibition on contemporary dwelling designs (*Die Wohnung unserer Zeit*), in which Le Corbusier also exhibited a version based on his *Ville Radieuse* (Gameren, 2013; Hilpert, 2015, 72–3). As a counter-gesture to the mainstream housing exhibitions in Berlin, another exhibition was organized by the Collective for Socialist Building, in which alternative dwelling models derived from ongoing experiments in the Soviet Union were displayed in deliberate juxtaposition to the 'bourgeois' model apartments shown by the Bauausstellung.[80] Inside the ranks of CIAM Gropius used his de facto driving position in all matters regarding the Berlin extraordinary congress and exhibition to bring the theme of high-rise construction to the heart of CIAM's proceedings. Le Corbusier kept pressing for the jump to the urban scale of reference, aligning his already expressed programmatic preference with the preparation of the fourth congress (and its planned associated exhibition on the 'functional city'), at that point still expected to take place in the Soviet Union. On his part Giedion was eager to marshall the entire publicity apparatus from CIAM2 and 3 in order to present the full gamut of the group's work at the future Moscow congress.[81]

After Berlin the CIAM3 exhibition travelled back to Switzerland for an extended show in Basel in the autumn of 1931. The plan was for the show to continue its route to Amsterdam before arriving in Barcelona to coincide with the already fixed date of the delegate meeting in the spring of 1932. Within Spain the exhibition also travelled to Madrid but not to San Sebastian as originally planned,[82] before making its way to Amsterdam in May. The other major planned engagement involved Milan in the autumn but it was hoped that the exhibition could make further detours, most likely in the Scandinavian countries following interest from Sweden and Finland.[83] The plan fell through, however, and the exhibition had to remain 'in no man's land' over the summer of 1932 before returning once again to Zurich in order to be dispatched to the premises of the Milanese syndicate of architects in September.[84] The longer the wait for the fourth congress was getting as a result of a series of postponements demanded by the Soviet authorities the more the CIAM3 travelling exhibition was getting a new lease of life. After the successful CIRPAC side-event at the 1933 Triennale (*Saletta di CIAM*) the exhibition was meant to make brief stops at Rotterdam and even Athens but in the end it was routed to Geneva to be ready for the long-planned journey to the Soviet Union that never happened.[85]

*****

The ways in which Giedion promoted the exhibitions and publications emanating from CIAM's first two working congresses reflected his conviction that, in their immediacy, materiality and multivalence, they represented and bespoke the transformative horizons of the 'new' architecture more effectively than anything the congress proceedings could ever produce. In addition, unlike the drama of congress discussions largely behind closed doors, the publicity events were essential outward-facing devices that distilled programmes, enacted alternative future scenarios and left behind a lasting trace that could easily become generative of more discussion and propaganda. Although the publicity aspects of CIAM congresses appear to have emerged as little more than an afterthought in the buildup to the La Sarraz gathering in 1928, supplementing the 'real' business of networking and professional discourse, they ended up being the most enduring and impactful legacies of CIAM2 and CIAM3. They were inserted into an already burgeoning inter- and trans-national field of interaction among professionals professing a commitment to the 'new' architecture. Together with the congresses, the architectural competitions and the kaleidoscope of published work in various formats and outlets, they constituted CIAM's 'communicative dimension' (Goldhagen, 2005, 162–3), where normative ideas about architecture were inscribed and shared as enduring material representations through text, image, plan or model. From this point of view, CIAM4 represented a regression: beyond the makeshift exhibition in Athens with its limited travelling trajectory in the years following the congress, the fabled publication never came out as a complete record of the discursive and exhibited content of the Athens congress (Mumford, 2000, 91). This was not because of lack of will or change of publicity strategy on CIAM's part: at the Amsterdam (1935) and La Sarraz (1936) gatherings, the link between the outward-facing publicity events and the group's all-important propaganda potential that could influence political decision-making was repeatedly emphasized.[86] In response to the growing financial difficulties involved in the production of the CIAM4 publication, Van Eesteren had proposed an alternative staggered approach: prioritizing a 'popular' book on the congress and exhibition to appear before the following 1937 congress in Paris that, after sufficient promotion from national groups, could finance a second, 'professional' publication on CIAM4.[87] Nothing came out of these deliberations, as the planning for CIAM5 soon monopolized the group's focus and energy. Therefore, in the absence of clear and agreed programmatic resolutions from the first three congresses, and in the light of an increasingly adverse international situation for the 'new' architecture in the 1930s, the role that the legacy CIAM2/3 exhibitions and publications were called to fulfil became even more significant.

# CONCLUSIONS

'A hoax: magic that didn't work': This was Rem Koolhaas's final, typically apodictic verdict on the modernist alchemy of trying to do more and better with less, 'transform(ing) quantity into quality through abstraction and repetition'. In so many respects, the metaphor can be used to describe the trajectory of CIAM's brief encounter with the question of mass affordable dwelling in 1928–30. Reyner Banham's critique of modernism certainly featured a scathing attack on this very alchemical proposition 'of the maximum of comfort. … with the minimum of drudgery' (Banham, 1969, 121). Damned for either betting on a mythologized fallacy of *machiniste* rationalism (Curl, 2018, 54) or for promising a revolution divorced from fundamental or meaningful social change (Ioannidou, 2006, 73–7), CIAM's short-lived affair with the (Existenz)minimum remains contentious and polarizing. The one, supposedly definitive congress on the 'dwelling for the Existenzminimum' (CIAM2) concluded amidst a frustrating sense of non-finito that prompted the organizers to extend the discussion to the next meeting (CIAM3), only to see it eclipsed by a series of other themes that dealt with larger architectural frames. With no official congress resolutions and no programmatic guidelines extrapolated from the congress deliberations or hundreds of pages of contributions from the distinguished keynote speakers, the discussion on the modernist 'minimum dwelling' appeared almost as intractable and elusive in 1930 as it had appeared to the CIAM members in 1928. Surely the organizational weaknesses of a fledgling international organization, the chaotic congress preparation and the heterogeneity of CIAM's membership did affect the fruitfulness of the discussions that unfolded during and in the margins of the two congresses. Yet, at the end of the Brussels congress, there appeared to be no route back to any discussion of the dwelling scale of design; instead the jump to the urban scale and the focus on the theme of the 'functional city' were identified by the CIAM steering group as the next phases in CIAM's work. Just like the disappearance of the nomenclature of the Existenzminimum so soon after its unlikely peak in 1929–30, the dwelling – let alone the 'minimum' dwelling as the foundation of the 'new' architecture and living faded away on CIAM's programmatic and discursive compass.

Was this swift transition to the urban scale anything other than an unspoken admission of defeat and an earnest realization that the ambitious pursuit of a dwelling alchemy had brought the organization to a programmatic cul de sac? In an early draft prepared for the inauguration of the special exhibition *Journées de l'habitation minimum* that ran in parallel to CIAM3 in Brussels, CIAM's outgoing president Karl Moser argued that the organization's discussions on the 'minimum dwelling' had finally gained international traction by 'penetrating public opinion' and becoming adopted by governments as state policy. Given all the turmoil and resentment that the cavalier organization of this special event by the Belgian organizers of CIAM3 had caused in the buildup to the congress, this kind of ex post facto effusive praise should be taken with reticence. Nevertheless, in a subsequently crossed-out section of the draft, Moser also acknowledged that 'the discussion [about the minimum dwelling] has often gone beyond the frame of this problem to reach that of urban planning'.[1]

The de facto relegation of the discussion on the 'minimum dwelling' in Brussels was reflective of an organizational shift of focus that had already been well underway in the months ahead of the Brussels congress and took hold as preparations for the eagerly anticipated Moscow congress on the 'functional city' gathered pace. It would be fair to note that such a shift was the product of contingencies rather than of design or, even less, consensus. Yet the narrative of an organic and orderly scale transition from the dwelling design to settlement planning to urbanism took hold in CIAM's discourse in the months following the Brussels congress. That this was more than ex post facto agitprop is evident by the fact that it was reproduced by key figures of the organization such as the incoming president Van Eesteren and the key member of the very active Swiss group Rudolf Steiger in closed-door meetings in the first half of 1931.[2] Long before CIAM constructed a partisan genealogy that promoted the Athens Charter as a revolution foretold at the first meeting of La Sarraz in 1928 and forged purposefully at the two subsequent congresses, the organization had embraced an intriguingly similar perspective internally through a process of reflection and strategic/programmatic readjustment. The key difference between these two readings lies in different assessments of intentionality behind the shift: while subsequent narratives depicted CIAM4 as climax of an alleged evolutionary continuum from the first to the fourth congresses, Moser's comment for the opening of the Brussels exhibition in November 1930 bespoke a far more improvised, trial-and-error attitude that was significantly more in line with the inclusive and experimental nature of the early CIAM.

If the yardstick of CIAM's engagement with the 'minimum dwelling' in 1929–30 was the definition of a particular universal housing typological panacea that could generate better-quality and more affordable dwelling at a cost that would enable its mass deployment by public authorities to fully cover increasing demand, then the Frankfurt and Brussels congresses patently failed. No matter how pivotal the dwelling was acknowledged to be as a hub of radical social transformation, architectural agency alone could not alchemise a revolution. While planning for the extraordinary congress that took place in the margins of the Berlin *Bauausstellung* in June 1931, the profound programmatic clash between intellectual and empirical approaches that had bitterly divided CIAM members in Frankfurt and Brussels[3] once again came to the fore (Mumford, 2000, 59–61). In his – eventually book-length – published reflection on the 'minimum dwelling' Karel Teige argued that there could be no shortcut to the utopian condition of better and more affordable housing for all, no modernist architectural alchemy that could bypass the prerequisite of political and social revolution. The 'minimum dwelling' in the singular, as a universal design panacea, simply could not and did not exist. The 1929 and 1930 congresses charted a bewildering plethora of possible practicable pathways to a better future but were far more effective in identifying the obstacles to their realization, as indeed was the subject of one of the questionnaires distributed to members ahead of CIAM3 and discussed in Brussels. Put simply, the housing question was not the problem to be solved but a facet, however significant, of a wider and more complex equation that defied universality, eluded consensus and in the end far exceeded architecture itself.

Nevertheless, in the aftermath of the Brussels congress, the mood within CIAM's ranks was noticeably ebullient, in sharp contrast to the downbeat tone that had followed CIAM2. This had of course a lot to do with the anticipation of the Moscow congress on the 'functional city' that absorbed the bulk of CIAM's energies immediately after the conclusion of CIAM3. Yet the planned shift to the urban scale in preparation of CIAM4 seemed to validate the longer-term ambitions of the organization to make its mark in the exciting field of urbanism that was evident since its early gatherings in La Sarraz (1928) and the first preparatory meeting for the Frankfurt congress that took place in Basel (February 1929). If earlier calls to embrace the urban scale as reference for CIAM's deliberations had been brushed aside in favour of the minimum dwelling, the blind alleys that skewed and frustrated the road from La Sarraz to Frankfurt and then to Brussels seemed to refocus attention to the importance of the urban planning scale as the optimal basis for addressing a range of architectural questions, dwelling included. In this crucial respect CIAM's apparent failure to tackle conclusively the question of the minimum dwelling in 1929–30 foregrounded the interconnectedness of architectural scales and subsumed the housing question into an expanded modular system of analysis that joined the room and its components to the dwelling to the building to the block to the settlement and eventually to the city plan. The trial-and-error experimental approach had already fed into the planning of the Brussels congress, where the initial focus on the dwelling was in the end eclipsed by the broader questions of building height and land use.[4] Once the taboo of debating exclusively the original single-dwelling scale had been de facto breached, the path to the extension towards urban planning lay open.

The other main reason as to why the organizational mood post-CIAM3 was notably more effervescent had to do with the unanticipated extent of CIAM's success in the communicative side of the operation. It is no coincidence that the fate of the congress exhibitions and the publications on the minimum dwelling received so much attention at the first meeting after CIAM3 and in the discussions that took place at the 1931 Berlin extraordinary congress. Giedion made it very clear that extending international collaboration via more and more inclusive congress work was a key target for the group's future, alongside planning for an exciting congress in Moscow.[5] In spite of the logistical nightmare and the organizational hiccups, the congress publicity and outreach events exceeded the expectations of the CIAM steering group. Much more than the congress proceedings they captured, curated effectively, synthesized and disseminated CIAM's vision for the 'new' architecture as an intellectually rich yet practical and realizable vision. If Sarah Goldhagen has accurately read the output of the interwar modernist avant-gardes as primarily discursive acts, then the exhibitions and the publications from the two congresses nurtured, advanced and diffused the debate. In this respect, the apparent lack of congress resolutions on the minimum dwelling was a setback but one that was compensated for by the richness of the ideas, voices and works that the early CIAM had brought together and collated into successful communication events. This, rather than any supposedly canonical document qua Athens Charter, was the most valuable and enduring legacy of the Frankfurt and Brussels congresses.

In the end the early CIAM proved unable to bridge its ideological, programmatic and methodological dichotomies. CIAM2 and CIAM3 were as much about 'practical' utopia as about radical transformative action in response to social emergency; as much about visionary futures as about tangible change in the present tense; as much about sociological analysis as about statistical empirical research; as much about partisan propagation as about inclusion. This inner tension may have been frustrating at the time of preparing and hosting international congresses. It may have exasperated those members who were looking for a definitive political and/or programmatic commitment that would bind CIAM and transform it into a potent canonizing force in modern architecture. These voices, already present in 1928–30, continued to press the group for definitive ideological, sociological or programmatic commitments even in the wake of the Brussels meeting and ahead of the Moscow planned super-event. Yet, in hindsight, the unresolved conflict of views and prescriptions was a blessing in disguise. If CIAM's early dwelling congresses were deemed by the organizers to have fallen short of expectations at the time, this was a failure of the most productive variety, based on a fierce mobility of ideas and people, on engagement and on creative friction. It was this intellectual and discursive friction that transformed CIAM2/3 – and all the drama that unfolded in preparation and in ex post facto appraisal of the two congresses – from seeming dead ends into catalysts for new experimental pathways.

Judged against the yardstick of an intellectual 'contact zone' CIAM's early congress milestones, as well as whatever transpired in the intervening time, were extraordinarily prolific and gratifying. By definition the contact zone is primarily a special domain – intellectual and physical, ideational and interpersonal – forged through co-presence and exchange. Such a contact zone is formed by a shared commitment to address a common challenge, plugging into and at the same time generating networks of participants and relationships. The production of ideas is thus judged by the accident of co-present, interacting multiplicities that come into contact, conflict, exchange and negotiation, undergoing in the process multiple, largely unpredictable adaptations and translations (Avermaete and Nuijsink, 2021, 334). In a contact zone the primary focus shifts from the actual outcomes to the dynamics of interaction and friction. In this sense, it is not canonization but its opposite – spectral heterogeneity and contention – that becomes the litmus of success. According to this standard, the choice of the 'minimum dwelling', precisely in its expansive ambivalence, as the common challenge that the network came together in order to deliberate, proved eminently successful as a magnet of diverse people and ideas. This is evidenced in the intellectual rigour of the participants' contributions to the congresses and in the vigorous discussions that they generated – before, at and in the wake of the meetings. But it was in the exhibitions and the associated publications that the full potential of the contact zone was realized. In fact, much more than the records of the congress textual contributions, discussions or resolutions, these mobile curated events and artefacts, proved to be the most lasting legacy of the organization's engagement with the minimum dwelling. The exhibition shows mutated into successful international travelling events, with a busy list of showings in a large variety of countries. Moser's original suggestion, ahead of the La Sarraz founding meeting, to align each congress with outward-facing communication events such as general and thematic exhibitions of the 'new' architecture that could then travel internationally and enhance the reputation of the group, set the tone of CIAM's subsequent heavy investment in the communication potential of such events. The exhibitions that accompanied the Frankfurt and Brussels congresses set the foundations for CIAM's reputation as a communication-savvy, inclusive laboratory of ideas and programmes that reshaped the emerging interwar narrative of the 'new' architecture. In parallel the official publications captured and inscribed the kaleidoscope of views expressed by the network participants, glossing over programmatic disagreements and the apparent lack of concrete resolutions from the two congresses.

For a duet of congresses supposedly dedicated to the minimum dwelling (singular) and inserted into the genealogy of 'small'-in-size habitation (the original German nomenclature used at the preparatory meetings for the Frankfurt congress explicitly named the Kleinwohnung as the focus of the proceedings), discussion of dwelling size was unsurprisingly pervasive yet surprisingly uncontroversial. If CIAM's encounter with mass housing plugged itself into, and benefitted from, intellectual groundwork on the 'minimum' that predated it by many decades and on affordable dwelling typologies that stretched back to the nineteenth century, the way in which it arrived at the investigation of rational design in terms of sizing and scaling ended up being transformational. There may have been diverse 'minimum' understandings and strategies in either the congress keynotes or the featured exemplars submitted to the exhibitions, pointing to a wide spectrum of 'dwelling rations' and optimal dwelling configurations; yet such a divergence of verdicts was welcomed as part of the congress's exploratory and practicable approach to dwelling design. The areas of often bitter disagreement concerned not size per se – and not the individual dwelling decontextualized – but the distribution of dwellings across other scales, from the building to the settlement to the urban form. Building height proved a sensitive issue, as did the dilemma of urban concentration versus peripheral settlements and suburbanization or adaptation of garden-city typologies. The de facto key theme of CIAM3 – rational land use/subdivision – did shift the focus beyond the minimum dwelling but also served as a far more flexible and all-encompassing conceptual platform for a frank exchange of different views held by CIAM's members. Even in the critical field of the exhibitions the CIAM3 event subsumed all that had divided the delegates at Frankfurt and Brussels under a modular perspective that spanned architectural scales while crucially acknowledging their interconnectedness. The apparent exasperating impasse concerning the minimum (i.e. high quality, rationally designed and affordable) dwelling refocused attention to dwellings as planned modular ensemble in context. By the end of the Brussels congress it seemed that the key to an optimal size-quality-cost-affordability calculus did lie in rational design – just not of the single dwelling but of dwellings in the plural form, as practical, scalable and realizable units generative of an optimal new way of living for all.

# Conclusions

Nevertheless, the novel intellectual grounding of the 'minimum dwelling' in the 1920s and 1930s made a critical contribution to the formation of a new architectural consciousness that from the very beginning extended well beyond the individual dwelling and encompassed the entire urban frame. Though short-lived and soon to be eclipsed, CIAM's discussion of the Existenzminimum transformed the moral complexion of mass low-cost, reduced-size and 'minimal' dwelling. If CIAM's encounter with housing plugged itself into, and benefitted from, intellectual groundwork on the 'minimum' that predated it by many decades and on affordable dwelling typologies that stretched back to the nineteenth century, the way in which it arrived at the investigation of rational design in terms of sizing and scaling was transformational. It achieved this primarily by giving a 'social' meaning to the problem, as part of the pursuit of an elusive golden ratio of utopian aspiration and realism grounded on a flexible equilibrium of quality, cost and affordability that could ensure universal deployment in the present tense. Unlike the IFHTP, which approached the challenge as a 'problem' to be mitigated in the margins of architectural practice, for CIAM the problem of the 'minimum dwelling' was both a vexing challenge and the ultimate aspiration. The frame was universal and egalitarian: CIAM's 'minimum dwelling' was conceived as an ethical proposition – a community asset, judged less on the quality of each single unit that it provided and more on its capacity for promoting better-quality housing for as many as possible – and ideally for all members of a community. In its wake, the size-reduction rationale of the Kleinwohnung, the design language of 'less is more', as well as the debates on centralization versus peripheral settlement or low-versus-high rise were proposed as complementary, flexible variables subsumed under an overriding ethical project of providing good-quality housing to everyone. CIAM sought, however in the end unsuccessfully, to give architects the overarching social agency to become the arch-alchemists and soon-to-be builders of a perfect society.

Inadvertently then CIAM's frustrating adventures with the minimum dwelling in 1928–30 exchanged one alchemy for another. In seeking to define the symbolic limes of the incipient group (Latour, 2005, 33), the scale singularity of housing was swapped gradually, through trial-and-error and reflection, for the modular expansiveness of rational design across diverse scales. Housing did not lose its critical place as the intimate hub of 'new living' but was inserted into a significantly more complex scheme of all-encompassing architectural agency. The emerging focus on urbanism became CIAM's de facto new limes but the utopian streak that had animated the pursuit of a new minimum as rational, austere and optimal, visionary and practical, ethical and pragmatic, canon of the 'new' architecture lost none of its earlier salience. The quest for a *practical* utopia that balanced creatively intellectual ambition and realistic execution not only survived the apparent programmatic impasse in Frankfurt and Brussels but grew in scope and ambition in subsequent years. If anything, the focus of the CIAM3 exhibition on mostly realized featured projects but alongside a curated selection of aspirational 'paper' architecture straddled the divide between an unfolding architecture-as-revolution and the taste of a not-yet utopian direction.

# NOTES

## Chapter 1

1. 'Improved Dwellings for Artisans and Labourers', *The Week*, 12.2.1876, 170–2.
2. 'Inauguration of Peabody Buildings', *The Architect*, 5.8.1871, 70.
3. *Amtliche Berichte über die Verhandlungen der Charlottenburger Stadtverordneten, Versammlung in den öffentlichen Sitzungen*, Session 8.5.1912, 208.

## Chapter 2

1. Labussière, J.A. (1913), *Premier Concours pour la Construction d'Habitations à Bon Marché de la Ville de Paris*. Paris: Ville de Paris.
2. May, E., 'Notheime', *SH* 2 (1920), 1010.
3. May, E., 'Siedlungspläne', *SH* 1 (1920), 7 (Part I); and *SH* 3 (1920), 5–11 (Part III).
4. May, E., 'Wolkenkratzer zur indirekten Abhilfe über Wohnungsnot', *SH* 5 (1920), 19–21.
5. May, E., 'Kleinwohnungstypen', *SH* 1 (1920), 14–17.
6. May, E., 'Aussichten für die Bauwirtscaft im Jahre 1920', *SH* 1 (1920), 13–14.
7. May, E., 'Wohnungsfürsorge', *SH* 5 (1924), 406–12; emphasis added.
8. May, E., 'Wie weit kann die Wohnfläche des Kleinhauses eingeschränkt werden?', *SH* 2 (1921), 38–43.
9. May, E., 'Die Grundtypen der Schlesischen Heimstätte mit Finanzierungstabelle', *SH* 5 (1924), 71–8 and 99–117.
10. May, E., 'Das Mittelstandshaus mit Einbaumöbeln der Schlesischen Heimstätte auf der betriebswirtschaftlichen und Bauausstellung in Breslau', *SH* 5 (1924), 143–9.
11. Krug, T. 'Die Bautätigkeit von Schlesischen Landgesellschaft in Kleinsiedlungssachen im Jahre 1919', *SH* 1 (1920), 11.
12. Mueller, S., 'Die Wohnungsbautätigkeit in Oberschlesien', *SH* 5 (1924), 312–15.
13. Kämper and Wildermuth, 'Die Finanzierung der Arbeiter- und Mittelstandswohnungen in Deutschland', IFHTP (1929), II, 61–71.
14. IfS, Personalakten 65.099: Description of advertised post of Stadtrat, 17.1.1925.
15. IfS, Personalakten 65.099: Ernst May's application, 9.2.1925.
16. May, E., 'Wohnungspolitik der Stadt Frankfurt am Main', *DNF*, 1/5 (1927), 93–104.
17. Goettel, J., 'Vorschlag für eine billigste Wohnung', *DNF* 2/6 (1928), 111.
18. Hagen, W., 'Biologische und soziale Voraussetzungen der Kleinstwohnung', *DNF* 3 (1929), 222–4.

19. May, E., 'Fünf Jahre Wohnungsbautätigkeit in Frankfurt am Main', *DNF* 2/3 (1930), 20–51.
20. May, E., 'Kleinstwohnungen', *Zentralblatt der Bauverwaltung*, 49/19 (8.5.1929), 297.

## Chapter 3

1. IFHTP (1924), Vol. 1: Papers, 11.
2. Hein, E., 'Die Bodenpolitik der Gemeinde Wien', IFHTP (1926), 1–19.
3. Musil, F., 'Wohn- und Verkehrsverhältnisse in ihrer gegenseitigen Abhängigkeit', IFHTP (1926), Vol. 1, 151–5.
4. Muesmann, A., 'Kleinhaus und Großhaus und ihre Bedeutung für den Stadtorganismus', IFHTP (1926), Vol. 1: Papers, 205–27.
5. IFHTP (1926), Vol. 3: Reports, 170–83.
6. Musil, F., 'Die Volkswohnungen dear Gemeinde Wien', *Das Neue Wien*, III (1927), 49–112.
7. Hein, 'Die Bodenpolitik', 9.
8. Musil, F., 'Wohn- und Verkehrsverhältnisse', 153–4.
9. IFHTP (1926), Vol. III, 52–4, 63–4.
10. IFHTP (1926), Vol. III, 91–3; cf. Elgood, Frank M, 'Houses or Tenements in England. A Comparison with Special Relation to their Situation', IFHTP (1926), Vol. I, 166–73.
11. IFHTP (1926), Vol. III, 69–70 and 140–1.
12. IFHTP (1926), Vol. III, 124–5.
13. Keppler, A., 'L'Habitation des Très Pauvres aux Pays-Bas', and Lopez Valencia, Federico, 'Housing of the Very Poor in Spain', IFHTP (1928), Vol. 1: Papers: 39–46 one 57–61, respectively).
14. Mitchell, M. E., 'Housing of the Very Poor in England', IFHTP (1928), Vol. II: Programme and General Reports, 16–19.
15. IFHTP (1928), Vol. III: Report, 59.
16. For example, Sellier, H., 'L'Habitation des Tres Pauvres', IFHTP (1928), Vol. II, 14.
17. IFHTP (1928), Vol. III, 93–4.
18. Gorla, G., L'Habitation des Très Pauvres en Italie, IFHTP (1928), Vol. I, 49–56.
19. Sellier, H., 'L'Habitation des Tres Pauvres', IFHTP (1928), Vol. II, 14–15.
20. Schmidt, R., 'House Building Costs', IFHTP (1928), Vol. II, 40–3; and Vol. I, 78–206 for the full range of session papers.
21. Final Assembly, 5 July 1928, Reports on Discussions during the Congress, IFHTP (1928), Vol. III, 194–6.
22. 'La prima Mostra Nazionale dell'Abitazioni e dei Piani Regolatori', *Capitolium* 10 (1929), 489–97.
23. IFHTP (1929), Vol. II: 24–33.
24. IFHTP (1929), Vol. II: 38.
25. 'Planning Apartment Housing Schemes in Large Towns', Session of 14 September 1929, IFHTP (1929), Vol. II: 64.
26. IFHTP (1929), Vol. I, 215–25.

## Notes

27. IFHTP (1929), Vol. I, 164–8 and 205–11.
28. IFHTP (1929), Vol. I, 197–20.
29. IFHTP (1929), Vol. II, 80.
30. IFHTP (1929), Vol. I, 284.
31. IFHTP (1929), Vol. II, 77–8.
32. Contribution of Victor Bachinsky (Moscow) to the session on 'Density', IFHTP (1929), Vol. III, 181–2.
33. For example, when the splinter IVW was planning a joint housing conference with the IHC in Berlin for 1931, it extended an invitation to CIAM to be represented in the proceedings, stressing that the IVW's interests in the mass affordable urban dwelling intersected with CIAM's discussion of the 'minimum dwelling' in Frankfurt and Brussels. See CIAM/Giedion/Museen & Behörden/30: Kampffmeyer to Giedion 19.12.1930. On his part CIAM's secretary Sigfried Giedion actively pursued closer ties with a wide range of both national and international housing organizations – among them, the RFG, the IVW, and the ILO, though not directly the IFHTP (even if it should be stressed that Kampffmeyer held membership in both the Federation and the IVW post-1929). See CIAM/Giedion/Museen & Behörden/29.

## Chapter 4

1. Stam, 'Das Maß. Das richtige Maß. Das "Minimum" Maß', *DNF* 3, no. 2 (1929), 29–30.
2. Wichert, F., 'Zeitwende+Kunstwende', *DNF* 1, no. 1 (1926), 15–24.
3. Gropius, W., 'Das Wohnhaus dear Neuzeit', *Innerdekoration* 37(1926), 310.
4. Doesburg, T. v., 'Stuttgart Weißenhof 1927, Die Wohnung', *Het Bouwbedrijf* 4, no. 24 (1927), 556–9; translated in (Doesburg, 1990, 164–7).
5. Le Corbusier, 'Wie wohnt man in meiner Stuttgarten Häusern', *DNF* 2, no. 1 (1928), 13–15.
6. Breuer, M., 'Die Werkbundausstellung in Paris 1930', *Zentralblatt der Bauverwaltung* 50/27 (1930), 477–81.
7. Meyer, H., 'Die Neue Welt', *Das Werk* 13, no. 7 (1926), 205–24, in DAM, 164-201-001; translated in (Schnaidt, 1965, 91–5).
8. Meyer, H., 'Die Siedlung Freidorf: erbaut durch Hannes Meyer, Basel', *Das Werk* 12 (1925): 40–51.
9. DAM 164-201-011/012: Hannes Meyer, 'The architect in the class struggle' (1932).
10. Ginzburg, M., 'Communal House A1', *Sovremmennaia Arkhitektura (Contemporary Architecture)*, no. 4–5 (1927): 130–43 (in Russian).
11. Ginzburg, M., 'Constructivism as a Method of Laboratory and Teaching Work', *Sovremennaja Arhitektura* (Contemporary Architecture), 6 (1927), 160–6 (in Russian); translated and reprinted in (Ginzburg et al., 2017, 603–4).
12. Teige, K., 'Contemporary International Architecture', *ReD* 2 (1928–29), 269–73.
13. Gropius, W., 'Der grosse Baukasten', *DNF* 1/2 (1926–27), 25–30; Walter Gropius, 'Das Wohnhaus der Neuzeit', *Innerdekoration* 37 (1926), 310; Gropius, Walter, 'Wie bauen wir billigere, bessere, schönere Wohnungen', *Die Form* 9 (1927), 275–7.

14. Klein, A., 'Grundrissbildung und Wohnungsgestaltung', *Wasmuths Monatshefte für Baukunst und Städtebau*, 12/2 (1928), 74–8.
15. Klein, A., 'Beiträge zur Wohnungsfrage als praktische Wissenschaft', *Zeitschrift für Bauwesen*, 10 (1930), 239–52, here 249.
16. See, for example, his public attack on some of the designs presented at the Weissenhof exhibition in Klein, A., 'Versuch eines Graphischen Verfahrens zur Bewertung von Kleinwohnungsgrundrissen', *Wasmuths Monatshefte für Baukunst und Städtebau*, 11 (1927), 296–8.
17. Klein, A., 'Wirtschaftliche Grundrissbildung und Raumgestaltung', *Städtebau* 15 (1931), 539–41.
18. Klein, A., 'Rationelle Gestaltung von Kleinwohnungs-Grundrissen', *Das Wohnen* 3/2 (1928), 23–6.
19. Klein, A., 'Einundzwanzig eingerichtete Kleinwohnungen auf der Ausstellung "Heim und Technik" München 1928', *Baumeister*, 7 (1928), 201–43, here 209.

## Chapter 5

1. EEST/4.212: Giedion to Le Corbusier, 25.5.1928.
2. EEST4.212: Giedion to Lissitzky, 21.5.1928.
3. EEST4.210: Giedion to Van Eesteren, 20.6.1928; CIAM/K/1928/Giedion: Giedion to Oud, 22.6.1928.
4. EEST/4.210: Giedion to Van Eesteren, 21.5.1928.
5. CIAM/K/1928/Giedion: Giedion to Le Corbusier, 21.6.1928.
6. EEST4.210: Giedion to Van Eesteren, 5.7.1928.
7. CIAM/K/1928/Giedion: Giedion to Van Eesteren, 5.7.1928, especially in the German version of the document (Mumford, 2000, 24–7).
8. CIAM/K/1928 S: Schmidt to Giedion, 6.3.1928.
9. CIAM/K/1929 G: Giedion to Gropius, 16.5.1929.
10. CIAM/K/1929 G: Gropius to Giedion, 7.1.1929.
11. CIAM/K/1928/Giedion: Giedion to Häring, 10 and 24.7.1928.
12. CIAM/K/1928/Giedion: Giedion to Gropius, 25.7.1928.
13. EEST/4.214: Giedion to Van Eesteren, 12.7.1928.
14. EEST/4.2: Protocol of the La Sarraz Meeting, Closing Session; CIAM/K/1928/Giedion: Giedion to Bourgeois.
15. CIAM/K/1928/Giedion: Giedion to Gropius, 22.12.1928.
16. CIAM/2-1-14F.
17. 'Der internationale Verband für Wohnungswesen', *Das Wohnen*, 4 (1929), 7–8.
18. EEST/4.215: Gropius to Giedion, 10.5.1929.
19. CIAM/K/1929 G: Gropius to Schmidt, 13.6.1929.
20. CIAM/K/1929/Giedion: Giedion to May, 21.6.1929.
21. CIAM/K/1929 G: Gropius to Giedion, 20.5.1929.

## Notes

22. CIAM/K/1929/Giedion: Giedion to Gropius, 2.4.1929.
23. CIAM/K/1929/Giedion: Giedion to Bourgeois, 15.2.1929.
24. CIAM/2-1-15F/D: Extract from the Basel meeting's protocol; and 2-1-16: press report on the Basel meeting.
25. CIAM/K/1929 S: Syrkus to Giedion, 20.3.1929.
26. CIAM/K/1929 M: Moser to Giedion, 28.2.1929; EEST4.214: Wagner to Giedion, 19.4.1929.
27. CIAM/K/1929/Giedion: Giedion to Gropius, 16.5.1929.
28. CIAM/K/1929/Giedion: Giedion to Breuer, 14.5.1929.
29. CIAM/K/1929/Giedion: Giedion to May, 21.6.1929; CIAM/K/1929 M: May to Giedion, 11.7.1929.
30. CIAM/K/1929 G: Gropius to Giedion, 10.5.1929.
31. EEST/4.214: Giedion to May 16.5.1929; EEST4.215: Gropius to Giedion, 25.5.1929.
32. CIAM/2-1-21: Agenda of the Karlsruhe meeting.
33. EEST/4.214: Giedion to Gropius, 10.9.1929.
34. CIAM/K/1929 G: Gropius to Giedion, 10.10.1929; EEST/4.214: Giedion to Van Eesteren, 5.10.1929.
35. CIAM/2-1-22D/F: Guidelines for the Frankfurt Congress.
36. CIAM/K/1929/Giedion: Giedion to Gropius, 26.2.1929 and 2.4.1929; Giedion to Bourgeois, 2.4.1929 / Giedion to Le Corbusier, 2.4.1929.
37. CIAM/K/1929 S: Syrkus to Giedion, 3.4 and 10.7.1929.
38. CIAM/K/1929/Giedion: Giedion to Schmidt 6.7.1929.
39. CIAM/K/1929/Giedion: Giedion to Bourgeois, 12.9.1929.
40. CIAM/2-2-33D and 2-2-35F.
41. CIAM/K/1929 S: Stam to Giedion, 3.6.1929.
42. CIAM/K/1929 M: Moser to Giedion, 5.7.1929.
43. EEST/4.214: Giedion to Gropius, 22.6.1929; Giedion to May, 21.6.1929.
44. CIAM/K/1929 S: Stam to Moser, 14.8.1929.
45. CIAM/K/1929 M: Moser to Giedion, 17.6.1929.
46. CIAM/K/1929/Giedion: Giedion to May, 16.5.1929.
47. CIAM/K/1929/Giedion: Giedion to Le Corbusier, 27.7.1929.
48. CIAM/K/1929/Giedion: Giedion to Le Corbusier, 21.8.1929.
49. CIAM/K/1929/Giedion: Giedion to Krejcar, 30.7.1929.
50. CIAM/K/1929/Giedion: Giedion to Teige, 4.10.1929; CIAM/K/1929 T: Teige to Giedion, 14.10.1929.
51. CIAM/K/1929/Giedion: Giedion to Ginzburg, 13.9.1929; and Giedion to Lissitzky.
52. CIAM/K/1929 T: Taut to Giedion, 2.9.1929.
53. EEST/4.215: Sellier to Giedion, 23.10.1929.
54. CIAM/2-2-62D: Agenda for the 'expert' part of the congress.
55. EEST/4.215: Gropius to Giedion, 10.5.1929.
56. cf. CIAM/2-4-1: Referrat von Giedion.

# Notes

57. CIAM/2-3-1, 1-2: Protocol of the 24.10.1929 Session; Giedion, 1930, 38–42.
58. CIAM/2-2-21D: Guidelines for the exhibition 'the Dwelling for the Existenzminimum'; and 2-2-51D: Announcement for the Frankfurt Congress, no date.
59. Giedion, S., 'Bauen in der Schweiz', *DNF*, 3/6 (1929), 105–21.
60. CIAM/2-2-64D.
61. CIAM/K/1929/Giedion: Giedion to May, 21.6.1929.
62. CIAM/K/1929/Giedion: Giedion to Bourgeois, 21.8.1929 and Giedion to Sellier, 17.10.1929.
63. CIAM/K/1929 S: Schmidt to Giedion, 20.4.1929.
64. CIAM/2-3-1: Protocol of the CIAM2 session on 24.10.1929, 5.
65. CIAM/K/1929 M: Meyer to Giedion, 11.1929; and Moser to Krejcar, 7.2.1929.
66. CIAM/2-2-64D.
67. CIAM/2-4-1: Summary of Bourgeois's keynote – 'Das Programm der Kleinstwohnung'.
68. CIAM/2-3-1: Protocol of session of 24.10.1929, 3-4.
69. CIAM/2-3-1, 13-15: Protocol of the 25.10.1929 session.
70. CIAM/2-3-1, 1-7: Summary of the Proceedings of 24-25.10.1929.
71. CIAM2-4-31F/D: Summary and discussion points based on Questionnaire No. 2.
72. CIAM2-4-32DA: Draft theses of the 2nd congress in Frankfurt, 1929.
73. CIAM/2-3-1: Protocol for the meeting on 25.10.1929, 15–16.
74. CIAM/K/1929 M: May to Giedion, 30.10.1929.
75. CIAM/K/1929 F: Frank to Giedion, 5.11.1929.
76. CIAM/K/1929/Giedion: Giedion to Gropius, 29.11.1929.
77. CIAM/K/1929/Giedion: Giedion to Gropius, 7.12.1929.
78. Bier, J., 'Der zweite Internationale Kongress für Neues Bauen', *Die Form* 4/22 (1929), 617–9.
79. Bauhaus IV/1929, 18; J Gantner, Report on Frankfurt Congress, *DNF* 11/1929; Journal de la Construction, 15.3.1930; all in CIAM/2-6-1.
80. May, E., 'Die Wohnung für Das Existenzminimum', *DNF* 3/11 (1929), 209–12.

## Chapter 6

1. CIAM/K/1929/Giedion: Giedion to Neutra, 30.10.1929; CIAM/3-1-14, 22-4; 'Dritte internationaler Kongreß für Neues Bauen,' *Stein Holz Eisen*, 4 (1930), 4.
2. CIAM/K/1929 M: May to Giedion, 29.11.1929.
3. For example, CIAM/K/1929/Giedion: Giedion to Ginzburg, 31.10.1929.
4. CIAM/K/1930/Giedion: Giedion to Moser, 7.1.1930.
5. CIAM/K/1930 G: Gropius to Giedion, 14.1 and 1.2.1930.
6. CIAM/K/1930 M: Moser to Giedion, 20.1.1930.
7. CIAM/K/1930/Giedion: Giedion to Gropius, 27.1.1930.
8. CIAM3-1-11F: Extensive summary of the 3 February 1930 meeting.

## Notes

9. CIAM/3-1-13F/D: Press communique regarding the 2 February 1930 CIRPAC meeting in Paris.
10. EEST4.7: Report on the meeting of the CIRPAC Swiss Group, 13.8.1929.
11. CIAM/K/1930 G: Gropius to Giedion, 1.2.1930.
12. E.g. CIAM/K/1930 K: Keay to Giedion, 3.2.1930.
13. CIAM/3-1-11F, 34; CIAM/K/1930/Giedion: Giedion to Gropius, 5.2.1930.
14. CIAM/3-1-11F, 22–4.
15. CIAM/3-1-11F, 26–7.
16. CIAM/3-1-11F: February preparatory meeting, 26–9, 42–3.
17. CIAM/3-1-12F/D: Communique on the Paris preparatory meeting, 5.2.1930.
18. CIAM/K/1930/Giedion: Giedion to Le Corbusier, 14.3.1930.
19. CIAM3-1-15: Swiss Group's study of Swiss cities, 30.4.1930.
20. CIAM3-1-22F: Minutes of the 20 May 1930 Paris meeting.
21. CIAM3-1-22F, 3.
22. CIAM/K/1930/Giedion: Giedion to Le Corbusier, 8.4.1930.
23. CIAM3-1-22F, 13–14.
24. CIAM3-1-25F: Report of the preparatory committee for the Brussels congress of 1930.
25. CIAM3-1-35: Minutes of the Frankfurt preparatory meeting, 25.9.1930.
26. EEST4.219: Giedion to Moser, 8.8.1930.
27. CIAM/K/1930 G: Gropius to Giedion, 16.6.1930.
28. EEST4.16: Circular to the congress delegates, 18.7.1930.
29. CIAM/K/1930/Giedion: Giedion to Le Corbusier, 8.4, 25.4, and 3.10.1930.
30. CIAM/K/1930/Giedion: Giedion to Gropius, 10.7.1930.
31. CIAM/K/1930 G: Gropius to Giedion, 1.2.1930.
32. EEST/4.219: May to Moser, 25.7.1930.
33. EEST/4.219: Giedion to Stem, 1.8.1930; EEST4.218: Giedion to Bourgeois, 8.8.1930.
34. See Moser's relevant comments in CIAM3-1-22F: Protocol of the 20 May 1930 meeting, 10.
35. CIAM/K/Giedion 1931: Giedion to Bottoni, 22.7.1931.
36. CIAM3-1-35, 8–10.
37. CIAM/K/1930/Giedion: Giedion to Gropius, 10.7.1930.
38. CIAM3-2-61 and 63F/D: versions of the official CIAM3 programme.
39. CIAM/3-4-21D: Introductory talk by Moser, 26.11.1930; cf. a similar argument in Bourgeois et al., 1931, 5-6.
40. CIAM/K/1930/Giedion: Giedion to Moser, 29.1.1930; and Giedion to May, 29.1.1930.
41. CIAM/K/1930/Giedion: Giedion to Gropius, 27.1.1930.
42. CIAM/K/1930 M: May to Giedion, 31.7.1930.
43. CIAM/K/1930/Giedion: Giedion to Le Corbusier, 3.10.1930.
44. CIAM/K/1930 L: Giedion to Le Corbusier, 7.11.1930.
45. See, for example, Gropius's increasing frustration with the lack of response from Brussels in CIAM/K/1930 G: Gropius to Giedion, 11.9 and 11.10.1930.

# Notes

46. EEST4.218: Giedion to Bourgeois, 6.8.1930; EST 4.15: Letter to CIAM3 delegates, 25.8.1930.
47. CIAM/K/1930/Giedion: Giedion to Gropius, 11.8.1930.
48. CIAM/K/1930 G: Gropius to Giedion, 15.11.1930.
49. CIAM/K/1930 E: Van Eesteren to Giedion, 16.11.1930.
50. CIAM/3-4-21D/F.
51. CIAM/K/1930 B: Bourgeois to Giedion, 30.10.1930; CIAM/K/1930/Giedion, Giedion to Le Corbusier, 3.10, 5.11, and 7.11.1930.
52. CIAM/K/1930/Giedion: Giedion to Gropius, 17.11.1930.
53. CIAM/3-4-28F: Summary of the report on horizontal sliding windows, 28.11.1930.
54. CIAM3-2-61DA: Draft of the CIAM3 programme.
55. Le Corbusier, 'Le parcellement du sol des villes,' in (Bourgeois et al., 1931, 48–57); Summary of talk by Le Corbusier: CIAM/3-4-1; Le Corbusier, 'Rapport sur le parcellement du sol des villes et les immeubles destinés à l'habitation', *Tekhné* 4/7(1931), 141–7.
56. EEST4.218: Gropius to Giedion, 11.4.1930.
57. CIAM/K/1930/Giedion: Giedion to Gropius, 27.1.1930 / Giedion to Keay, 29.1.1930 / Giedion to Robertson, 10.3.1930; and CIAM/K/1930 K: Keay to Giedion, 2.2.1930.
58. CIAM/3-4-11D: Böhm and Kaufmann, 'Untersuchung der Gesamtbaukosten zwei- bis zwölf-geschossiger Bauweisen'.
59. CIAM3-4-12F: Gropius, 'Maison basse, maison moyenne ou maison haute' – and CIAM3-4-23D/F for executive summary.
60. CIAM3-1-35, 13.
61. EEST4.16: Communique concerning the national reports, 3.1930.
62. CIAM3-4-41D: Dutch group's report on the question of the Existenzminimum; cf. EEST4.17: Minutes of the meeting of the Dutch group, 2.7.1930.
63. Both documents in CIAM/Kongress Brüssel 1930/ Landesberichte; and in EEST4.17 and 4.18.
64. CIAM3/Kongress Brüssel 1930/Landesberichte: Summary of national reports on the minimum dwelling; reproduced in Bourgeois et al., 1931, 71-3.
65. EEST4.218: Giedion to Teige, 31.1.1931.
66. EEST4.27: Minutes of the preparatory meeting for the fourth congress, 15.2.1931.
67. CIAM/K/1930 T: Teige to Giedion, 21.2 and 17.5.1930.
68. CIAM3-4-42D.
69. EEST4.20: Programme of the Journées de l'Habitation Minimum; CIAM/K/1930 T: Teige to Giedion, 17.11.1930.
70. Teige, K., 'Die Wohnungsfrage der Schichten des Existenzminimums', in Bourgeois et al., 1931, 64-70.
71. CIAM/3-4-4: 'Opinion du congrès au sujet de la question des maison basses, moyennes ou hautes'.
72. Van Eesteren, C., 'Rationelle Bebauungsweisen'. In *Ausstellung Walter Gropius – Rationelle Bebauungsweisen, Kunstgewerbemuseum der Stadt Zürich (Wanderausstellung der III. Internationalen Kongresses des Neuen Bauen, 14.2-15.3.1931*, in CIAM/3-7-21D, 19–24.

# Notes

## Chapter 7

1. Bardi, P. M., *Rapporto sull'architettura (per Mussolini)* (Rome: Critica Fascista, 1931).
2. CIAM/K/1929/Giedion: Giedion to May, 30.4.1929.
3. CIAM/K/1929/Giedion: Giedion to Gropius, 6.5.1929 (two letters), 16.5.1929, and 22.6.1929.
4. CIAM/K/Giedion 1931: Giedion to Aalto, 13.1.31.
5. Doesburg, T. v., 'Stuttgart-Weissenhof 1927: Die Wohnung', *Het Bouwbedrijf*, 4/24 (1927), 556–9.
6. 'L'arte nella casa', *Domus*, Fascicolo dedicato alla Triennale di Milano, 9/65 (1933), 1–30.
7. Deutsche Werkbund, *Bau und Wohnung* (Catalogue of the Weissenhof exhibition) (Stuttgart: Akad. Verlag, 1927), 7.
8. Teige, K., 'Mezinárodní soudobá architektura', *ReD*, 2/9 (1928–29), 269–73, translated as 'Contemporary International Architecture' (1928) in (Benton et al., 1975, 200–2).
9. CIAM/K 1928: Moser to Giedion, 25.6.1929.
10. CIAM/2: Protocol of the Basel preparatory meeting, 2.2.1929, 15.
11. CIAM/2.2.1-2.2.2: Vorbereitung des Zweiten Internationalen Kongresses für Neues Bauen and Richtlinie für die Ausstellung: Frankfurt 1929.
12. IfS Magistratsakten S2.634: May to Magistrates, 21.8.1929; Nosbisch to Magistrates, 15.8.1929.
13. IfS Magistratsakten S2.634: Finance Department to May, 16.8.1929; Protokoll-Auszug Nr. 1613, 23.9.1929.
14. CIAM/2.2.21F: Letter to the groups, 8.1929; CIAM/2.2.22D: Announcement regarding the Exhibition.
15. CIAM/K/1929/Giedion: Giedion to Figini, 18.10.1929.
16. CIAM/K/1929/Giedion: Giedion to Gropius, 6.7.1929/ 27.7.1929/ 10.9.1929.
17. EEST/4.215: Opening Address at the Inauguration of the Exhibition, 26.10.1929.
18. Kaufmann, E., 'Die internationale Ausstellung "Die Wohnung für das Existenzminimum"', *DNF*, 3/11 (1929), 213–7.
19. As an example, the name of Cologne-based Wilhelm Riphahn was suggested by Giedion directly to May as relevant to the exhibition in spite of the architect's more traditional architectural formation but was not followed up (EEST/4.214: Giedion to May, 19.8.1929).
20. 'Concurso della vivienda minima', *Arquitectura*, 8 (1929), 286–99; Amós Salvador, 'Sobre il problema della vivienda minima', ibid., 300.
21. 'Forschungssiedlung Spandau-Haselhorst', *Bauschrift für Bauwesen*, 79/4 (1929), 79–110, here 90–3.
22. 'Kleine Woningen te Utrecht. Architekt Rietveld', *i10*, 17/18 (1928), 91–3.
23. Martin, K., 'Sonderheft Dammerstocksiedlung', *Kunst und Handwerk*, 79/12 (1929), 373–92; Behne, Adolf, 'Dammerstock', *Die Form*, 6 (1929), 163–6.
24. Cf. CIAM/K/1929 S: Syrkus to Giedion, 20.3.1929.
25. Farkas, M., 'A masodik nemzetkösi kongresszus az új építésért', *Tér és Forma*, 3 (1930), 10–14.

# Notes

26. CIAM/K/1929/Giedion: Giedion to Teige, 4.10.1929.
27. CIAM/K/1929 M: Meyer to Giedion, 12.11.1929.
28. CIAM/K/1929 B: Bourgeois to Giedion, 4.4.1929.
29. EEST/4.9: Meeting of delegates in Frankfurt, 26.10.1929; CIAM/K/1929 M: Moser to Giedion, 6.11.1929.
30. 'Internationale Ausstellung "Die Wohnung für das Existenzminimum"', *DNF*, 3/11 (1929), 226 and 4/1 (1930), 71.
31. CIAM/2-7-2: Exhibition catalogue from the Basel and Zurich shows – *Die Wohnung für das Existenzminimum, Basel Gewerbemuseum, 8–29 December 1929*; *Ausstellung: Die Wohnung für das Existenzminimum, 8 Januar–15 Februar 1930, Wegleitungen des Kunstgewerbemuseums der Stadt Zürich*, No. 91.
32. EEST/4.215: Aalto to Moser, no date.
33. Aalto, 'Asuntomme probleemina', *Domus*, 8–10 (1930), 176–89, translated in Aalto, 1998, 76–84.
34. EEST/4.11: 'Die internationale Kongresse für neues Bauen', draft of Giedion's keynote.
35. CIAM/K/1929 M: May to Giedion, 6.11.1929.
36. CIAM/K/1929/Giedion: Giedion to Neutra, 30.10.1929.
37. EEST/4.9: Meeting of delegates in Frankfurt, 23.10.1929.
38. CIAM/K/1929 M: Moser to Giedion, 27.12.1929.
39. EEST/4.214: Gropius to Giedion, 26.2.1930.
40. CIAM/K/1929 M: Gropius to Giedion, 27.11.1929; CIAM/K/1930 G: Gropius to Giedion, 11.3.1930 and four letters dated 21.3.1930.
41. EEST/4.14: Protocols of the preparatory meeting for CIAM/3 in Paris, 17.5 and 20.5.1930.
42. CIAM/3-1-11F: Report on the meeting of 3.2.1930 in Paris; cf. the provisional list of exhibition themes for CIAM3 published in *DNF*, 4-2/3 (1930): 71.
43. CIAM/K/1930/Giedion: Giedion to Le Corbusier, 8.4.1930.
44. EEST/4.14: Meeting of the preparatory committee for CIAM3 in Paris, 20.5.1930.
45. EEST/4.14: Meeting of the preparatory committee for CIAM3 in Paris, 17.5.1930.
46. EEST/4.16 Circular to the delegates, 18.7.1930.
47. CIAM/K/1930 B: Giedion to Bourgeois, 7.7.1930 and 17.7.1930.
48. CIAM/K/1930 B: Bourgeois to Giedion, 12.7.1930.
49. EEST/4.219: May to Moser, 25.7.1930.
50. EEST/4.219: Giedion to Moser, 8.8.1930.
51. EEST/4.219: Moser to Stam, 1.8.1930; CIAM/K/1930 B: Giedion to Bourgeois, 7.7.1930.
52. CIAM/K/1930 B: Bourgeois to Giedion, 8.8.1930.
53. EEST/4.20: Draft Programme for the Journées de l'Habitation Minimum.
54. EEST/4.217: Giedion to Van Eesteren, 24.10.1930.
55. EEST/4.17: Giedion to Van Eesteren, 13.11.1930.
56. CIAM/K/1930 B: Bourgeois to Giedion, 11.7.1930; Giedion to Gropius, 10.7.1930.
57. EEST/4.16: Guidance on the country reports and the exhibition for CIAM3, March 1930.

## Notes

58. EEST/4.218: Giedion to Stam, 8.8.1930; Giedion to May, 8.8.1930; cf. EEST/4.16: Guidance on the preparation of the exhibition material, 8.7.1930; CIAM/K/1930 S: Schmidt to Giedion, 31.6[sic].1930; and Giedion to Bourgeois, 7.7.1930.
59. EEST/4.16: Guidance and clarifications on the CIAM3 exhibition by Bourgeois and Van Eesteren, 7.11.1930.
60. EEST/4.23: Draft list of specimens for the CIAM3 exhibition, 24.5.1930.
61. EEST/4.20: Draft and final version of the opening speeches at CIAM3, 27.11.1930.
62. EEST/4.217: Giedion to Van Eesteren, 19.11.1930.
63. EEST/4.217: Giedion to Van Eesteren, 30.12.1930.
64. CIAM/K/1931/Giedion: Giedion to Aalto, 13.1.1931.
65. CIAM/Giedion/Museen & Behörden/30: Letter from Deutsche Bauausstellung Berlin to CIAM, 14.10.1930.
66. CIAM/42-04-1-2: Protocol of the Extraordinary Meeting of CIAM, Berlin 4-5.6.1931, Protocol of 5.6.1931 session; CIAM/42-04-1-6: Points for the Moscow preparatory meeting for CIAM4, no date; CIAM/K/1932 P: Giedion to Papadaki, 20.9.1932.
67. CIAM/K/1930 G: Gropius to Giedion, 6.12.1930.
68. CIAM/K/1931 B: Bourgeois to Giedion, 18.5.1931 and 10.9.1931.
69. CIAM/42-04-1-12D, Minutes of the 15.2.1931 meeting of the preparation committee for CIAM4.
70. CIAM/42-04-1-12D: Preparatory Meeting for the 4th CIAM/Congress, 15.2.1931; 42-04-1-2: Giedion's report on the publication at the 5.6.1931 meeting of the Berlin extraordinary CIAM/congress.
71. CIAM/K/1931/Giedion: Giedion to Schmidt, 16.4.1931.
72. EEST/4.28: Minutes of the Berlin congress session of 5.6.1931, 11.
73. CIAM/42-04-1-41D: Circular to delegates, 25.2.1932.
74. CIAM/K/1931 G: 24.1.1931, 6.2.1931; Giedion K 1931: Giedion to Pollini, 22.7.1931; CIAM/K/1931 B: Bourgeois to Giedion, 10.9.1931; CIAM/K/1931 T: Teige to Giedion, 14.5.1931.
75. EEST/4.31: Circular to delegates, 19.11.1931; CIAM/K/1931/Giedion: Giedion to Schmidt, 16.4.1931; CIAM/42-04-1-4-3F: Report from the CIRPAC meeting in Barcelona, 29-31.3.1932, 4.
76. CIAM/K/1931 G: Gropius to Giedion, 14.1.1931; CIAM/42-04-1-12F: Report on the preparatory meeting for CIAM4 in Zurich, 15.2.1931, 2.
77. CIAM/K/1931 G: Gropius to Giedion, 31.3.1931.
78. CIAM/3-7-21D: exhibition booklet for Gropius's Zurich exhibition 1931, 15; CIAM/K/1931 B: Bourgeois to Giedion, 4.5.1931; CIAM/K/1931 B: Van Eesteren to Giedion, 8.1.1931.
79. EEST/4.28: Minutes of the Berlin congress session of 5.6.1931, 8–9.
80. CIAM/42-04-1-2: Programme of the exhibition Proletarische Bauausstellung.
81. CIAM/K/1931/Giedion: Giedion to Schmidt, 16.6.1931.
82. CIAM/K/1932/Giedion: Giedion to Sert, 22.2.1932.
83. CIAM/K/1932/Giedion: Giedion to Van Eesteren, 9.6.1932.
84. CIAM/K/1932/Giedion: Giedion to Van Eesteren, 27.8.1932; Giedion to Pollini, 6 and 14.9.1932.

85. CIAM/K/1933/Giedion: Giedion to Papadaki, 27.8 and 19.9.1932; CIAM/K/Giedion 1933: Giedion to Pollini and Bottoni, 13 and 16.2.1933.
86. CIAM/5-1-39: Proposals for the reorganisation and intensification of national groups.
87. CIAM/5-1-71: Meeting of La Sarraz, 9–12.9.1936, 4–9.

## Conclusions

1. HNI EEST 4.20 (CIAM3), Moser's draft speech, 27.11.1930.
2. EEST 4–29: Minutes of the second plenary session of the Berlin extraordinary congress (6.6.1931), 15.
3. CIAM, 3-1-11: Minutes from the meeting of the organising committee of the 3. Congress, Paris 3.2.1930, 27.
4. EEST 4.29: Minutes of the second plenary session of the Berlin extraordinary congress (6.6.1931), 13–14.
5. CIAM4/42-04-1-2-3: Circulaire à Messieurs les Délégués, 13.5.1931.

# BIBLIOGRAPHY

### Archives

CIAM: CIAM Archive / Giedion Archive at the Institute for the History and Theory of Architecture *(Institut für Geschichte und Theorie der Architektur, GTA)*, ETH, Zurich, Switzerland.
DAM: German Museum of Architecture *(Deutsches Architekturmuseum, DAM)*, Frankfurt, Germany.
EEST: Archive of Van Eesteren in The New Institute *(Het Nieuwe Instituut, HNI)*, Rotterdam, The Netherlands.
IFHTP: Garden City Collection, Letchworth Garden City Heritage Foundation, Letchworth, UK.
IfS: Archive of the Institute of City History *(Institut für Stadtgeschichte, IfS)*.
Triennale: Historical Archive of the *Triennale di Milano*, Milan, Italy.

### Journals

*Baumeister*
*Bauwelt*
*Capitolium*
*Das Neue Frankfurt*
*Das Werk*
*Das Wohnen*
*Die Form*
*Domus*
*Het Bouwbedrijf*
*Innerdekoration*
*ReD*
*Schlesisches Heim*
*Sovremmennaia Arkhitektura*
*Städtebau*
*Tekhné*
*The Architect*
*The Week*
*Wasmuths Monatshefte für Baukunst und Städtebau*
*Zeitschrift für Bauwesen*
*Zentralblatt der Bauverwaltung*

### Publications

*Architecture Today* (2001), 'Editorial', 114–18: 1–9.
Adam, T. (2007), 'Housing Charities and the Provision of Social Housing in Germany and the United States of America, Great Britain, and Canada in the Nineteenth Century', in B. Harris

# Bibliography

& P. Bridgen (eds), *Charity and Mutual Aid in Europe and North America Since 1800*, 158–88, London and New York: Routledge.

Adam, T. (2009), *Buying Respectability: Philanthropy and Urban Society in Transnational Perspective, 1840s to 1930s*, Bloomington and Indianapolis IN: Indiana University Press.

Adler, G. (2004), 'Tessenow in Hellerau: The Materialisation of Space', PhD in the History of Architecture, Kent Institute of Art and Design, University of Kent.

Agustoni, A. (2007), 'Percezioni, Iterazioni, Identità. La Dimensione Spaziale della Vita Sociale', in A. Agustoni, P. Giuntarelli & R. Veraldi (eds), *Sociologia dello Spazio, dell'Ambiente E Del Territorio*, 26–42, Milan: FrancoAngeli.

Albert, M. & N. Chomsky (2017), *Practical Utopia: Strategies for a Desirable Society*, Oakland CA: PM Press.

Albrecht, H. (1891), *Die Wohnungsnot in den Großstädten un die Mittel zu ihrer Abhülfe*, Munich: R Oldenbourg.

Alfani, G. & R. Frigeni (2016), 'Inequality (un)perceived: The emergence of a discourse on economic inequality from the Middle Ages to the Age of Revolution', *The Journal of European Economic History*, 45 (1): 21–66.

Allan, G. (2013), *A Hundred Years at the Global Spearhead: A Century of IFHP 1913-2013*, Copenhagen: International Federation for Housing & Planning.

Anderson, S. (2003), 'Deutscher Werkbund – The 1914 Debate: Hermann Muthesius versus Henry van de Velde', in B. Farmer & H. Louw (eds), *Companion to Contemporary Architectural Thought*, 462–7, London and New York: Routledge.

Andrusz, G.D. (1984), *Housing and Urban Development in the USSR*, Basingstoke: Palgrave.

Antliff, M. (1997), 'La cité française: Georges Valois, Le Corbusier, and fascist theories of urbanism', in M. Affron & M. Antliff (eds), *Fascist Visions: Art and Ideology in France and Italy*, 134–70, Princeton NJ: Princeton University Press.

Antliff, M. (2001), 'The Artist as Producteur: Le Faisceau, Le Corbusier, and Fascist Theories of Urbanism', in H.D. Christensen, Y. Hjort, Ø. Hjort & N.M. Jensen (eds), *Rethinking Art Between the Wars*, 13–46, Copenhagen: Museum of Tusculanum Press and University of Copenhagen.

Antliff, M. (2007), *Avant-Garde Fascism: The Mobilization of Myth, Art, and Culture in France, 1909-1939*, Durham and London: Duke University Press.

Antz, C., C. Gries, U. Maasberg & R. Prinz, eds (2018), *Neues Bauen Neues Leben*, Munich and Berlin: Deutscher Kunstverlag.

APUR (Atelier Parisien d'urbanisme) (2017), *Les Habitations à Bon Marché de la ceinture de Paris: étude historique*, Paris: APUR.

Arnold, K.-P. (1993), *Vom Sofakissen zum Städtebau: Die Geschichte der Deutschen Werkstätten und der Gartenstadt Hellerau*, Dresden and Basel: Verlag der Kunst.

Ascher Barnstone, D. (2016), *Beyond the Bauhaus: Cultural Modernity in Breslau, 1918-33*, Ann Arbor MI: University of Michigan Press.

Aureli, P.V. (2014), 'The Dom-ino Problem: Questioning the Architecture of Domestic Space', *Log* (30): 153–68.

Aureli, P.V. (2017), *The Room of One's Own*, Milan: Black Square.

Avermaete, T. & C. Nuijsink (2021), 'Architectural Contact Zones: Another Way to Write Global Histories of the Post-War Period?', *Architectural Theory Review*, 25 (3): 350–361.

Aymonino, C. (1971), *L'Abitazione Razionale: Atti Dei Congressi C.I.A.M. 1929-1930*, Venice: Marsilio.

Baf, S. (1997), *Trieste 1900-1999: Cent'Anni di Storia*, Trieste: Publisport.

Banham, R. (1969), *The Architecture of the Well-Tempered Environment*, Chicago: University of Chicago Press.

Barnstone, D.A. (2017), *The Break with the Past: Avant-Garde Architecture in Germany, 1910-1925*, London and New York: Routledge.

## Bibliography

Barr, H. (2011), 'Frankfurt 1929: der Kongress tagt. Eine Rekonstruktion des CIAM II', *Neues Wohnen 1929/2009. Frankfurt und der 2. Congrès International d'Architecture Moderne; Beiträge des internationalen Symposiums in Frankfurt am Main 22. - 24. 10.2009*, Berlin: Jovis.
Bauer, C.K. (2020), *Modern Housing*, Minneapolis: University of Minnesota Press.
Baxter, J.E. & A.H. Bullen (2011), '"The World's Most Perfect Town" Reconsidered: Negotiating Class, Labour and Heritage in the Pullman Community of Chicago', in L. Smith, P. Shackel & G. Campbell (eds), *Heritage, Labour and the Working Classes*, 258–74, London and New York: Routledge.
Bay, C. (1977), 'Human Needs and Political Education', in R. Fitzgerald (ed), *Human Needs and Politics*, 1–26, Rushcutters Bay NSW, Oxford, and New York: Pergamon Press.
Bayliss, D. (2001), 'Revisiting the Cottage Council Estates: England, 1919–39', *Planning Perspectives*, 16 (2): 169–200.
Becker, H. (1991), 'Wettbewerbe und Wohnungsbau - Weichenstellungen für mehr Planungs- und Wohnkultur', in K. Novy & F. Zwoch (eds), *Nachdenken Über Städtebau*, 89–104, Braunschweig and Wiesbaden: Vieweg.
Becker, H. & S. Knott (1992), *Geschichte der Architektur- und Städtebauwettbewerbe*, Stuttgart, Berlin, and Cologne: Kohlhammer.
Benton, T. (1984), 'Le Corbusier and the Loi Loucheur', *AA Files* (7): 54–60.
Benton, T., C. Benton & D. Sharp, eds (1975), *Architecture and Design, 1890–1939: An International Anthology of Original Articles*, New York: Whitney Library of Design.
Berge, A.E.F.L. (1992), *Mission and Method*, Cambridge and New York: Cambridge University Press.
Berghaus, G., ed. (2000), *International Futurism in Arts and Literature*, Berlin and New York: De Gruyter.
Bernardi, J. (1995), 'Le Corbusier's Curutchet House: The Pleasures of Memory', *83rd ACSA Annual Meeting - History/Theory/Criticism*, 83rd ACSA Annual Meeting Proceedings, 101–5.
Berndt, C. (2004), 'The "Hobrecht Plan" (1862) and Berlin's urban structure', *Urban History*, 31 (3): 400–19.
Bertani, E. (2014), 'Nel risolvere il problema delle abitazioni: il contributo di Giuseppe Gorla al dibattito urbanistico internazionale', in R. Riboldazzi, G. Ernesti & M. Grønning (eds), *Atelier 2 L'Urbanistica Moderna Italiana nel Contesto Internazionale. Atti della XVII Conferenza Nazionale SIU. L'urbanistica Italiana nel Mondo, Milano 15–16 Maggio 2014*, 156–62, Milan: Planum.
Bevilacqua, M. G. (2011), 'Alexander Klein and the Existenzminimum: A "Scientific" Approach to Design Techniques', *Nexus Network Journal*, 13 (2): 297–313.
Biles, R. (2010), *From Tenements to the Taylor Homes*, University Park PA: Pennsylvania State Press.
Billiani, F. & L. Pennacchietti (2019), *Architecture and the Novel Under the Italian Fascist Regime*, Basingstoke: Palgrave.
Blake, P. (1960), *The Master Builders*, New York: Alfred A Knopf.
Blau, E. (1998), 'Reviewing Architectural Exhibitions', *Journal of the Society of Architectural Historians*, 57 (3): 256–366.
Blau, E. (1999), *The Architecture of Red Vienna, 1919–1934*, Cambridge MA and London: MIT Press.
Blau, E. (2006) 'Isotype and Architecture in Red Vienna: The Modern Projects of Otto Neurath and Josef Frank', *Austrian Studies*, 14, Culture and Politics in Red Vienna: 227–59.
Bloch, E. (1995), *The Principle of Hope*, Cambridge MA: MIT Press.
Bollnow, O.F. (1961), 'Lived-space', *Philosophy Today*, 5 (1): 31–9.
Booth, C. (1902), *Labour and Life of the People in London*, London: Macmillan.

Bosch Abarca, J. (2017), 'Theodor Goecke. La vivienda pequeña en el debate urbano alemán de final del S.XIX', *VLC arquitectura*, 4 (2): 87.

Bosma, K. (2014), 'New Socialist Cities: Foreign Architects in the USSR 1920-1940', *Planning Perspectives*, 29 (3): 301-29.

Boughton, J. (2018), *Municipal Dreams: The Rise and Fall of Council Housing*, London: Verso books.

Bourgeois, V., S. Giedion & C. Van Eesteren (1931), *Rationelle Bebauungsweisen: Ergebnisse Des 3. Internationalen Kongresses Für Neues Bauen*, Stuttgart: J. Hoffman.

Brott, S. (2013), 'Architecture et révolution: Le Corbusier and the fascist revolution', *Thresholds*, 41: 146-57.

Brott, S. (2016), 'The Ghost in the City Industrial Complex: Le Corbusier and the Fascist Theory of Urbanisme', *Journal of Architecture and Urbanism*, 40 (2): 131-42.

Brott, S. (2017), 'The Le Corbusier Scandal, or, was Le Corbusier a Fascist', *Fascism*, 6 (2): 196-227.

Brysch, S. (2019), 'Reinterpreting Existenzminimum in Contemporary Affordable Housing Solutions', *Urban Planning*, 4 (3): 326-45.

Buchanan, I. & C. Irr (2006), *On Jameson: From Postmodernism to Globalization*, Albany NY: SUNY Press.

Buchli, V. (1998), 'Moisei Ginzburg's Narkomfin Communal House in Moscow: Contesting the social and material world', *Journal of the Society of Architectural Historians*, 57 (2): 160-81.

Buchli, V. (1999), *An Archaeology of Socialism: The Narkomfin Communal House, Moscow*, Oxford and New York: Berg Publishers.

Buchli, V. (2017), 'The Social Condenser: Again, Again and Again—The Case for the Narkomfin Communal House, Moscow', *The Journal of Architecture*, 22 (3): 387-402.

Buder, S. (1990), *Visionaries and Planners: The Garden City Movement and the Modern Community*, Oxford and New York: Oxford University Press.

Bullock, N. (1988), 'First the Kitchen: Then the Facade', *Journal of Design History*, 1 (3-4): 177-92.

Campbell, J. (2015), *The German Werkbund: The Politics of Reform in the Applied Arts*, Princeton NJ: Princeton University Press.

Carmony, D.F. & J.M. Elliott (1980), 'New Harmony, Indiana: Robert Owen's Seedbed for Utopia', *The Indiana Magazine of History*, 161-261.

Carriou, C. (2005), 'La spatialisation des Habitations à Bon Marché', *Communication aux journées*.

Celedon, A. (2013), '"And the Wicked Will Be Ashes under the Soles of the Feet of the Good"', *Materia Arquitectura*, 8: 74-7.

Champy, F. (2009), 'L'engagement des professionnels comme conséquence de tensions consubstantielles à leur pratique: l'architecture moderne entre les deux guerres', *Sociétés Contemporaines*, 73 (1): 97-119.

Chermayeff, S. & C. Alexander (1963), *Community and Privacy: Toward a New Architecture of Humanism*, Garden City, NJ: Anchor Books, Doubleday.

Ciucci, G. (1999), 'The Invention of the Modern Movement', in K.M. Hays (ed), *Oppositions Reader: Selected Essays 1973-1984*, 552-75, Princeton NJ: Princeton Architectural Press.

Clark, K. (1995), *Petersburg, Crucible of Cultural Revolution*, Cambridge MA: Harvard University Press.

Clingan, C.E. (2000), 'More Construction, More Crisis: The Housing Problem of Weimar Germany', *Journal of Urban History*, 26 (5): 630-44.

Co-op (2012), *Profiles of a Movement: Co-operative Housing around the World*, CECODHAS Housing Europe and ICA Housing.

Cohen, J.-L. (1987), *Le Corbusier Et La Mystique del'URSS: Théories Et Projets Pour Moscou, 1928-1936*, Brussels and Liege: Mardaga.

## Bibliography

Cohen, J.-L. & E. Jeanneret (2014), 'The Dom-ino Intrigue', *Log* (30): 122–37.
Cohen, J.L., (1992), *Le Corbusier and the Mystique of the USSR: Theories and Projects for Moscow, 1928-1936*, Princeton NJ: Princeton University Press.
Collins, C.C. & M. Swenarton (1987), 'CIAM, Teige and the Housing Problem in the 1920s', *Habitat International*, 11 (3): 153–9.
Colomina, B. (1999), 'Das Wohnhaus als Schaustück', in R. Ferguson (ed), *Am Ende Des Jahrhunderts: 100 Jahre Gebaute Visionen*, 126–65, Ostfildern-Ruit: Cantz Verlag.
Conrads, U., ed. (1971), *Programs and Manifestoes on 20th-Century Architecture*, Cambridge MA: MIT Press.
Cooke, C. (1995), *Russian Avant-Garde: Theories of Art, Architecture and the City*, London: Academy Editions.
Cooke, C. (2005), 'Cities of Socialism: Technology and Ideology in the Soviet Union in the 1920s', in T. Deckker (ed), *Modern City Revisited*, 26–55, London and New York: Taylor & Francis.
Cooper, C. (2005), 'Places, "Folk Devils" and Social Policy', in P. Somerville & N. Sprigings (eds), *Housing and Social Policy: Contemporary Themes and Critical Perspectives*, 69–102, London and New York: Routledge.
Corbusier, L. (1924), *Vers une Architecture*, Paris: G. Crès.
Cortjaens, W. (2011), '"The German Way of Making Better Cities": German Reconstruction Plans for Belgium during the First World War', in N. Bullock & L. Verpoest (eds), *Living With History, 1914-1964: Rebuilding Europe after the First and Second World Wars and the Role of Heritage Preservation*, 44–59, Leuven: Leuven University Press.
Cramer, J. & N. Gutschow (1984), *Bauausstellungen: Eine Architekturgeschichte Des 20. Jahrhunderts*, Stuttgart: Kohlhammer.
Crawford, C.E. (2014), 'The Innovative Potential of Scarcity in SA's Comradely Competition for Communal Housing, 1927', *archiDOCT*, 1 (2): 32–53.
Crowley, D. (1992), *National Style and Nation-State*, Manchester: Manchester University Press.
Curl, J. S. (2018), *Making Dystopia*, Oxford and New York: Oxford University Press.
Curtis, W.J.R. (1986), *Le Corbusier - Ideas and Forms*, London: Phaidon Press.
Curtis, W.J.R. (1996), *Modern Architecture since 1900*, London: Phaidon London.
Czaplinska-Archer, T. (1981), 'Polish Architecture and the Contribution of Helena and Szymon Syrkus', *Architectural Association Quarterly*, 13 (1): 37–44.
D'Amuri, M. (2013), *La Casa per Tutti nell'Italia Giolittiana. Provvedimenti e Iniziative per la Municipalizzazione dell'Edilizia Popolare*, Milan: Ledizioni.
Daniel, J.O. & T. Moylan, eds (1997), *Not Yet: Reconsidering Ernst Bloch*, London and New York: Verso.
Davidovici, I. (2017), 'Tafuri on hous-"ing": Housing History as City-making Praxis', *Joelho: Revista de Cultura Arquitectonica* (8): 36–51.
Dearstyne, H. (1986), *Inside the Bauhaus*, London: London Architectural Press.
De Carlo, G. (1970), 'Il pubblico dell'architettura', *Parametro*, 3 (4): 4–12.
DeHaan, H.D. (2013), *Stalinist City Planning*, Toronto, Buffalo, and London: University of Toronto Press.
Djalali, A. (2015), 'The Architect as Producer: Hannes Meyer and the Proletarianisation of the Western Architect', *Footprint*, 17: 27–46.
Doesburg, T.V. (1990), *On European Architecture: Complete Essays From Het Bouwbedrijf 1924-1931*, Basel: Birkhauser.
Dogliani, P. (2002), 'European Municipalism in the First Half of the Twentieth Century: The Socialist Network', *Contemporary European History*, 11 (4): 573–96.
Domhardt, K.S. (2012), 'The Garden City Idea in the CIAM Discourse on Urbanism: A Path to Comprehensive Planning', *Planning Perspectives*, 27 (2): 173–97.
Doxiadis, C.A. (1972), 'The Formation of the Human Room', *Ekistics*, 33 (196): 218–29.

Dreier, P. (1997), 'Philanthropy and the Housing Crisis: The Dilemmas of Private Charity and Public Policy', *Housing Policy Debate*, 8 (1): 235-93.

Dumont, M.J. (1991), *Le Logement Social à Paris 1850-1930: Les Habitations à Bon Marché*, Liege: Mardaga.

Eesteren, C.V. (1997), *The Idea of the Functional City*, Rotterdam: Nai Uitgevers Pub.

Eisenman, P. (2014), 'Aspects of Modernism: Maison Dom-ino and the Self-Referential Sign', *Log* (30): 139-51.

Eisenschmidt, A. (2019), *The Good Metropolis: From Urban Formlessness to Metropolitan Architecture*, Basel: Birkhäuser.

Ekici, D. (2018), 'In Praise of Poverty: The Middle-class Dwelling and Asceticism in Early Twentieth-century Germany', *The Journal of Architecture*, 23 (4): 563-79.

Elsaesser, T. (2006), 'The Camera in Kitchen. Grete Schütte-Lihotzky and Domestic Modernity', in C. Finna (ed), *Practicing Modernity: Female Creativity in the Weimar Republic*, 27-49, Würzburg: Königshausen & Neumann.

Evans, S. (2014), *Sowjetisch Wohnen: Literatur- und Kultur-geschichte der Kommunalka*, Bielefeld: transcript.

Falser, M. (2015), 'Picturesque modernities in Eurasian contact zones: negotiating architectural regionalisms in universal and colonial exhibitions (Paris 1931 and 1937)', in EAHN (ed), *Entangled Histories, Multiple Geographies. Papers from the International Scientific Thematic Conference EAHN 2015 Belgrade/Serbia*, 221-7, Belgrade: EAHN and University of Belgrade.

Fehl, G. (1988), 'Der Kleinwohnungsbau, die Grundlage des Stadtebaus? Von "offenen Kleinwohnungen" in Berlin und vom verfolgten Reformprojekt der "abgeschlossenen Kleinwohnung"', in G. Fehl & J. Rodriguez-Lores (eds), *Die Kleinwohnungsfrage: Zu den Ursprüngen des Sozialen Wohnungsbaus in Europa*, 95-134, Hamburg: Hans Christian Verlag.

Fehl, G. (1990), 'Fordismus und Städtebau um 1930- "Auflösung" oder "Auflockerung" der Großstadt', *Wissenschaftliche Zeitschrift / Hochschule für Architektur und Bauwesen Weimar*, Vol. 36.1990, (1-3): 61-66.

Fijalkow, Y. (2006), 'Taudis, habitat insalubre, logement indigne: évolution et enjeux des stratégies de désignation. 19ème-20ème siècle', in Depaule, J._C. (dir.), *Les Mots de la stigmatisation urbaine*, 20_40, Paris: Éditions UNESCO.

Filipova, M. (2015), *Cultures of International Exhibitions 1840-1940: Great Exhibitions in the Margins*, Farnham and Burlington VT: Ashgate.

Fishmann, R. (1982), *Urban Utopias in the Twentieth Century: Ebenezer Howard, Frank Lloyd Wright and Le Corbusier*, Cambridge MA: MIT Press.

Flierl, B., ed. (1965), *Hans Schmidt: Beiträge Zur Architektur, 1924-1964*, Berlin: Verlag für Bauwesen.

Flierl, T. (2011), '"Perhaps the greatest task an architect ever faced" - Ernst May in the Soviet Union (1930-1933)', in C. Quiring, W. Voigt, P. Schmal & E. Herrel (eds), *Ernst May: 1886-1970*, 157-96, Munich, London and New York: Prestel.

Ford, C. (2018), 'The Paris Housing Crisis and a Social Revolution in Domestic Architecture on the Eve of the First World War', *Journal of Modern History*, 90: 580-620.

Forty, A. (2000), *Words and Buildings: A Vocabulary of Modern Architecture*, New York: Thames & Hudson.

Frasch, T. & T. Wyke (2015), 'Housing the Workers: Re-visiting Employer Villages in Mid-19th-Century Europe', in J.O. Czierpka, Kathrin Thorade, Nora (ed), *Regions, Industries, and Heritage*, 173-97, London: Palgrave.

Freestone, R. & M. Amati (2011), 'Exhibitions and Town Planning Culture: An Australian Perspective', *A/Z*, 8: 25-39.

Freestone, R. & M. Amati, eds (2014), *Exhibitions and the Development of Modern Planning Culture*, London and New York: Routledge.

# Bibliography

Gameren, D.V. (2013), 'Die Wohnung unserer Zeit Berlin', *DASH Delft Architectural Studies on Housing*, 09: Housing exhibitions, 92–101.

Gartman, D. (2009), *From Autos to Architecture*, New York: Princeton Architectural Press.

Gaskell, S.M. (1986), *Model Housing: From the Great Exhibition to the Festival of Britain*, London and New York: Mansell.

Gaspari, O. (1997), 'Alle origine del movimento comunale europeo: dall'Union Internationale des Villes al Consiglio dei Comuni d'Europa 1913-1953', *Memoria e* Ricerca, 10: 147–63.

Gatrell, P. & L. Zhvanko, eds (2019), *Europe on the Move: Refugees in the Era of the Great War*, Manchester: Manchester University Press.

Geddes, P. (1949), *Cities in Evolution*, London: Williams & Norgate.

Geertse, M. (2015), 'Cross-Border Country Planning Dialogue in Interwar Europe', *SAGE Open*, 5 (3): 1–12.

Geerse, M. (2016), 'The International Garden City Campaign: Transnational Negotiations on Town Planning Methods 1913-1926', *Journal of Urban History*, 42 (4): 733–52.

Geertse, M.A. (2012), 'Defining the Universal City. The International Federation for Housing and Town Planning and Transnational Planning Dialogue 1913-1945', Architecture, Vrije Universiteit Amsterdam, Amsterdam.

Giedion, S. (1930), 'Die internationalen Kongresse für Neues Bauen', in CIAM (ed), *Die Wohnung für das Existenzmiminum*, 5–9, Frankfurt: Englert & Schlosser.

Giedion, S. (2019), *Befreites Wohnen*, Zurich and Leipzig: Lars Müller Verlag.

Ginzburg, M., I. Leonidov & N.S. Kuzmin (2017), 'New Translations from Contemporary Architecture', *The Journal of Architecture*, 22 (3): 584–628.

Glendinning, M. (2013), *The Conservation Movement: A History of Architectural Preservation: Antiquity to Modernity*, London and New York: Routledge.

Glendinning, M. (2021), *Mass Housing*, London and New York: Bloomsbury Visual Arts.

Gold, J.R. (1998), 'Creating the Charter of Athens: CIAM and the Functional City, 1933–43', *Town Planning Review*, 69 (3): 225–47.

Gold, J.R. (2007), *The Practice of Modernism: Modern Architects and Urban Transformation, 1954-1972*, London and New York: Routledge.

Gold, J.R. (2013), *The Experience of Modernism*, London and New York: Taylor & Francis.

Goldhagen, S.W. (2005), 'Something to Talk about: Modernism, Discourse, Style', *Journal of the Society of Architectural Historians*, 64 (2): 144–67.

Gössel, P., G. Leuthäuser (2001), *Architecture in the Twentieth Century*, Cologne, London, Madrid, New York, Paris, Tokyo: Taschen.

Gould, E. & R. Lovell (1895), *The Housing of the Working People*, Washington DC: U.S. Government Printing Office.

Greenhalgh, P. (1988), *Ephemeral Vistas: The Expositions Universelles, Great Exhibitions and World's Fairs, 1851-1939*, Manchester: Manchester University Press.

Gregh, E. (1979), 'The Domino Idea', *Oppositions*, 15 (16): 61–82.

Griffin, R. (2007), *Modernism and Fascism: The Sense of a Beginning Under Mussolini and Hitler*, Basingstoke: Palgrave.

Gropius, W. (1930), 'Die soziologischen Grundlagen der Minimalwohnung für die stadtische Industriebevölkerung', in CIAM (ed), *Die Wohnung Für Das Existenzmiminum*, 17–27, Frankfurt: Englert & Schlosser.

Gropius, W. (1995), 'Réponses au questionnaire Ja! Stimmen des Arbeitsrates für Kunst', in J. Aron (ed), *Anthologie du Bauhaus*, 51–4, Brussels: Éditions Didier Devillez.

Gruber, H. (1991), *Red Vienna: Experiment in Working-Class Culture, 1919-1934*, New York and Oxford: Oxford University Press.

Grulois, G. (2011), 'La construction épistémologique de l'urbanisme en Belgique', *Belgeo* (1–2): 5–16.

# Bibliography

Gustiaux, R. (2015), 'La loi Loucheur de 1928. Contexte, filiation et diversité des positionnements politiques autour du logement social dans les années 1920', *Pour Mémoire*, 15: 162–77.

Hagen, J. & R.C. Ostergren (2020), *Building Nazi Germany: Place, Space, Architecture, and Ideology*, Lanham, Boulder CO, New York and London: Rowman & Littlefield Publishers.

Hake, S. (2008), *Topographies of Class*, Ann Arbor MI: University of Michigan Press.

Harris, R. (1999), 'Slipping through the Cracks: The Origins of Aided Self-help Housing, 1918–53', *Housing Studies*, 14 (3): 281–309.

Harris, T.M. (2012), 'The German Garden City Movement: Architecture, Politics and Urban Transformation, 1902–1931', PhD Dissertation Graduate School of Arts and Sciences, Columbia University.

Harrison, J. (2017), 'The Origin, Development and Decline of Back-to-back Houses in Leeds, 1787–1937', *Industrial Archaeology Review*, 39 (2): 101–16.

Häußermann, H. & W. Siebel (2021), Soziologie des Wohnens. Eine Einführung in Wandel und Ausdifferenzierung des Wohnens, in S. Schipper & L. Vollmer (eds), *Wohnungsforschung: Ein Reader*, 263–302, Bielefeld: transcript Verlag.

Hautmann, H. & R. Hautmann (1980), *Die Gemeindebauten des Roten Wien 1919–1934*, Vienna: Schönbrunn.

Hays, K.M. (1995), *Modernism and the Posthumanist Subject: The Architecture of Hannes Meyer and Ludwig Hilberseimer*, Cambridge MA: MIT Press.

Hays, K.M. ed. (1999), *Oppositions Reader: Selected Essays 1973–1984*, New York: Princeton Architectural Press.

Hays, R.A. (1995b), *The Federal Government and Urban Housing*, Albany: SUNY Press.

Heidegger, M. (2006), 'Building Dwelling Thinking', in J. Morra & M. Smith (eds), *Spaces of Visual Culture*, 66–76, London: Routledge.

Henderson, S.R. (2002), 'Ernst May and the Campaign to Resettle the Countryside: Rural Housing in Silesia, 1919–1925', *Journal of the Society of Architectural Historians*, 61 (2): 188–211.

Henderson, S.R. (2010), 'Römerstadt: The Modern Garden City', *Planning Perspectives*, 25 (3): 323–46.

Henderson, S.R. (2013), *Building Culture: Ernst May and the New Frankfurt Am Main Initiative, 1926–1931*, New York: Peter Lang.

Hernández, J.M. & C. Nuijsink (2020), 'Introduction / Architecture as Exchange: Framing the Architecture Competition as Contact Zone', *Footprint*, 26: 1–5.

Heynen, H. (1999), *Architecture and Modernity: A Critique*, Cambridge MA and London: MIT press.

Hilberseimer, L. (1927), *Grossstadtarchitektur*, Stuttgart: Hoffmann.

Hill, J. (2003), *Actions of Architecture: Architects and Creative Users*, London and New York: Routledge.

Hilpert, T. (2015), *Century of Modernity: Architektur und Städtebau: Essays und Texte*, Wiesbaden: Springer-Verlag.

Hilson, M. (2018), *The International Co-Operative Alliance and the Consumer Co-Operative Movement in Northern Europe, c. 1860–1939*, Oxford and New York: Oxford University Press.

Hochhaeusl, S. (2013), 'From Vienna to Frankfurt Inside Core-House Type 7: A History of Scarcity through the Modern Kitchen', *Architectural Histories*, 1 (1): 1–19.

Holcombe, A.N. (1910), 'The British Minimum Wages Act of 1909', *The Quarterly Journal of Economics*, 24 (3): 574–7.

Holmes, C. (2006), *A New Vision for Housing*, London and New York: Routledge.

Holtfrerich, C.-L. (2011), *Die Deutsche Inflation 1914–1923: Ursachen und Folgen in Internationaler Perspektive*, Berlin and New York: Walter de Gruyter.

## Bibliography

Hölz, C. (2013), 'L'architecte créateur d'espace intérieur: le classique moderne', in C. Schittich (ed), *Intérieurs: Espace, Lumière, Matériaux*, 16–29, Basel: Birkhäuser.

Horne, J.R. (2002), *A Social Laboratory for Modern France: The Musée Social and the Rise of the Welfare State*, Durham NC and London: Duke University Press.

Hsu, C.-C. & C.-M. Shih (2006), 'A Typological Housing Design: The Case Study of Quartier Fruges in Pessac by Le Corbusier', *Journal of Asian Architecture and Building Engineering*, 5 (1): 75–82.

Huber, B. (1993), *Die Stadt des Neuen Bauens: Projekte und Theorien von Hans Schmidt*, Wiesbaden: Springer.

Hyman, P. (2002), 'Fair/Living/Family/Minimum/Social Wages: Historical and Recent New Zealand debates', *Labour, Employment and Work in New Zealand*, 107–15.

ICA (1908), *7th Congress, Cremona. Report of the Seventh International Co-Operative Congress (Cremona, September 1907)*, London: ICA.

ICAM (1913), *L'Istituto Comunale per Abitazioni Minime a Trieste nel Decennio 1902–1912*, Trieste: Tipografia della Società dei Tipografi.

IFTCPGC (International Federation for Town and Country Planning and Garden Cities) (1924), *International Town Planning Conference Amsterdam 1924*, 2 vols (I: Papers, II: Reports), London, IFTCPGC.

IFHTP (1926): *International Housing and Town Planning Congress, Vienna 1926*, 3 vols (I: Papers, II: Papers, III: Reports), London: IFHTP.

IFHTP (1928): *International Housing and Town Planning Congress, Paris 1928*, 3 vols (I: Papers, II: Programme and General Reports, III: Reports), London: IFHTP.

IFHTP (1929): *International Housing and Town Planning Congress, Roma 1929*, 2 vols (I: Papers, II: Programme and General Reports), London: IFHTP.

Ingberman, S. (1994), *Abc: International Constructivist Architecture, 1922–1939*, Cambridge MA: MIT Press.

Ioannidou, E. (2006), 'The (Existenz-)Minimum Dwelling', PhD Dissertation, Bartlett School of Architecture, University College London.

Jackson, N. (2016), *The Modern Steel House*, London and New York: Taylor & Francis.

Jäger-Klein, C. (2005), *Österreichische Architektur des 19. und 20. Jahrhunderts*, Vienna and Graz: Neuer Wissenschaftlicher Verlag.

Jahn, H.A. (2014), *Das Wunder des Roten Wien*, Vienna: Phoibos Verlag.

Jameson, F. (1985), 'Architecture and the Critique of Ideology', in J. Ockman (ed), *Architecture, Criticism, Ideology*, Princeton NJ: Princeton Architectural Press.

Jarcy, X.D. (2015), *Le Corbusier, Un Fascisme Français*, Paris: Albin Michel.

Jeanneret, L.C.P.O.C.E. (1987), *Towards a New Architecture*, London: London Butterworth-Architecture.

Jerram, L. (2007), *Germany's Other Modernity: Munich and the Building of Metropolis, 1895–1930*, Manchester: Manchester University Press.

Jerram, L.W. (2011), *Streetlife: The Untold History of Europe's Twentieth Century*, Oxford: Oxford University Press.

Johnson, P.A. (1994), *The Theory of Architecture: Concepts Themes & Practices*, New York: Wiley.

Jones, G.S. (2014), *Outcast London: A Study in the Relationship between Classes in Victorian Society*, London: Verso.

Jones, P. (2011), *The Sociology of Architecture: Constructing Identities*, Liverpool: Liverpool University Press.

Jones, P.B. (1999), *Hugo Häring: The Organic versus the Geometric*, Stuttgart and London: Axel Menges.

Jönsson, R. (2013), 'Fred Forbat and the History of Functionalism', *Nordic Journal of Architectural Research*, 16 (4): 79–85.

Kafkoula, K. (2013), 'On Garden-city Lines: Looking into Social Housing Estates of Interwar Europe', *Planning Perspectives*, 28 (2): 171–98.

Kähler, G. (1985), *Wohnung und Stadt: Hamburg, Frankfurt, Wien*, Wiesbaden: Springer.
Kallis, A. (2017), 'Rome's Singular Path to Modernism: Innocenzo Sabbatini and the "Rooted" Architecture of the Istituto Case Popolari (ICP), 1925–1930', *Papers of the British School at Rome*, 85: 269–301.
Kallis, A. (2018), 'Futures Made Present: Architecture, Monument, and the Battle for the "Third Way" in Fascist Italy', *Fascism*, 7 (1): 45–79.
Kallis, A. (2020a), '"Minimum Dwelling" All'italiana: From the Case Popolari to the 1929 "Model Houses" of Garbatella', *Journal of Urban History*, 46 (3): 603–21.
Kallis, A. (2020b), 'From "Minimum Dwelling" to "Functional City": Reappraising Scale Transitions in the Early History of CIAM (1928–33)', *Planning Perspectives*, 36 (1): 125–45.
Karch, B. (2018), *Nation and Loyalty in a German-Polish Borderland: Upper Silesia, 1848–1960*, Cambridge: Cambridge University Press.
Kermode, F. (2000), *The Sense of an Ending: Studies in the Theory of Fiction with a New Epilogue*, Oxford and New York: Oxford University Press.
Kim, H.-S. (2005), 'A Study on Alvar Aalto and His Experimentation in Villa Mairea', PhD Dissertation, School of Architecture, University of Sheffield, Sheffield.
Kindt, O., ed. (1982), *Heinrich Tessenow: Geschriebenes Gedanken Eines Baumeisters*, Braunschweig/Wiesbaden: Friedr. Vieweg & Sohn.
Kirk, T. (2005), *The Architecture of Modern Italy. Volume 2: Visions of Utopia 1900 – Present*, New York: Princeton Architectural Press.
Kirsch, K. (2013), *The Weissenhofsiedlung, Stuttgart: Experimental Housing Built for the Deutscher Werkbund, Stuttgart, 1927*, Stuttgart: Edition Axel Menges.
Koch, D. (2016), 'On Avoidance: Reflections on Processes of Socio-spatial Structuring', *cea*, 4 (2): 67–78.
Kohlrausch, M. (2019), *Brokers of Modernity: East Central Europe and the Rise of Modernist Architects, 1910–1950*, Leuven: Leuven University Press.
Kononowicz, W. (1996), 'La cité-jardin Sepolno à Wroclaw (1919–1935)', in Girard, P. and B. Fayolle Lussac (eds), Patrimoine (ed), *Cités, Cités-Jardins: Une Histoire Européenne. Actes du Colloque de Toulouse, 18–19 Novembre 1993*, 171–89, Pessac: Maison des Sciences de l'Homme d'Aquitaine.
Koolhaas, R. (1995), 'Whatever Happened to Urbanism?', *Design Quarterly*, 164.
Koolhaas, R. & B. Mau (1997), *S, M, L, XL*, New York: Monacelli Press.
Kopp, A. (1970), *Town and Revolution Soviet Architecture and City Planning 1917–1935*, London: Thames and H.
Korbi, M. & A. Migotto (2019), 'Between Rationalization and Political Project: The Existenzminimum from Klein and Teige to Today', *Urban Planning*, 4 (3): 299–314.
Koselleck, R. & M.W. Richter (2006), 'Crisis', *Journal of the History of Ideas*, 67 (2): 357–400.
Kress, C. (2011), *Adolf Sommerfeld/Andrew Sommerfield: Bauen Für Berlin 1910–1970*, Berlin: Lukas.
Krieger, N. & A.-E. Birn (1998), 'A Vision of Social Justice as the Foundation of Public Health: Commemorating 150 Years of the Spirit of 1848', *American Journal of Public Health*, 88 (11): 1603–6.
Kuchenbuch, D. (2016), 'In Search of the "Human Scale": Delimiting the Social in German and Swedish Urban Planning in the 1930s and 1940s', *Journal of Urban History*, 42 (6): 1044–64.
Kuczynski, R.R. (1921), *Das Existenzminimum und Verwandte Fragen*, Berlin: HR Engelmann.
Kühl, U. (2001), *Der Munizipalsozialismus in Europa /Le Socialisme Municipal en Europe*, Munich: Oldenbourg.
Kuipers, M. (2013), 'Rietveld and Nieuwe Zakelijkheid in Architecture', in R. Grüttemeier, K. Beekman & B. Rebel (eds), *Neue Sachlichkeit and Avant-Garde*, 81–111, Amsterdam: Rodopi.

# Bibliography

Ladd, B. (1990), *Urban Planning and Civic Order in Germany, 1860–1914*, Cambridge MA and London: Harvard University Press.
Lallement, M. (2012), 'An Experiment Inspired by Fourier: JB Godin's Familistère in Guise', *Journal of Historical Sociology*, 25 (1): 31–49.
Lambrichs, A. (2000), 'Les cités-jardins en Belgique', *Ciudades: Revista del Instituto Universitario de Urbanística de la Universidad de Valladolid* (6): 57–74.
Lane, B.M. (1986), 'Architects in Power: Politics and Ideology in the Work of Ernst May and Albert Speer', *The Journal of Interdisciplinary History*, 17 (1): 283–310.
Lane, B.M. (2006), *Housing and Dwelling: Perspectives on Modern Domestic Architecture*, London and New York: Routledge.
Lane, B.M. (2013), *Architektur und Politik in Deutschland 1918–1945*, Braunschweig and Wiesbaden: Friedr. Vierweg & Sohn.
Larsen, S.U., ed. (2001), *Fascism outside Europe: The European Impulse against Domestic Conditions in the Diffusion of Global Fascism*, Boulder Co: Social Science Monographs.
Latour, B. (1986), 'Visualization and Cognition: Drawing Things Together', in H. Kuklick (ed), *Knowledge and Society: Studies in the Sociology of Culture Past and Present*, 1–40, London: Jai Press.
Latour, B. (2005), *Reassembling the Social*, Oxford and New York: Oxford University Press.
Leach, N. (1999), 'Architecture or Revolution?', in N. Leach (ed), *Architecture and Revolution: Contemporary Perspectives on Central and Eastern Europe*, 112–23, London and New York: Routledge.
Leatherbarrow, D. (2017), 'Le Corbusier: A Modern Monk', in A. Rabaça (ed), *Le Corbusier: History and Tradition*, 90–114, Coimbra: Coimbra University Press.
Le Corbusier & P. Jeanneret (1946), *Œuvre Complète de 1910–1929*, Paris: Éditions d'architecture.
Ledent, G. (2019), 'From Ideal Proposals to Serial Developments: Victor Bourgeois's Schemes in the Light of Post-War Developments in Brussels', *Urban Planning*, 4 (3): 196.
Lenger, F. (2012), *European Cities in the Modern Era, 1850–1914*, Leiden: Brill.
Levitas, R. (1990), 'Educated Hope: Ernst Bloch on Abstract and Concrete Utopia', *Utopian Studies*, 1 (2): 13–26.
Levitas, R. (2010), *The Concept of Utopia*, Oxford: Peter Lang.
Lévy, A. (1988), 'Le Corbusier et la question de l'innovation architecturale et urbaine', *Les Annales de la Recherche Urbaine*, 37 (1): 55–67.
Lewin, D. (1913), 'Theorie Existenzminimums. Inaugural-Dissertation zur Erlangung der Doktorwürde eingereicht der philosophischen Fakultät der Ruprecht-Karls-Universität zu Heidelberg', Faculty of Philosophy, Ruprecht-Karls-Universität zu Heidelberg, Heidelberg.
Lewis, M. (1922), *The Story of Utopias*, New York: Boni and Liveright.
Lieberman, B. (1998), *From Recovery to Catastrophe: Municipal Stabilization and Political Crisis*, New York and Oxford: Berghahn Books.
Llewellyn-Smith, H. (1929), 'The New Survey of London Life and Labour', *Journal of the Royal Statistical Society*, 92 (4): 530–58.
Long, C. (2016), 'Josef Frank, CIAM and the Assault on the Unified Ideal', *OASE*, 97: 53–60.
Lorbek, M. (2018), 'Idealizations of the Kleinhaus: On the Typology of the Small Single-Family House in Germany, 1920s–1960s', *Architectural Histories*, 6 (1): 1–17.
Luckin, B. (2006), 'Revisiting the idea of degeneration in urban Britain, 1830–1900', *Urban History*, 33 (2): 234–52.
Lueder, C. (2017), 'Evaluator, Choreographer, Ideologue, Catalyst: The Disparate Reception Histories of Alexander Klein's Graphical Method', *Journal of the Society of Architectural Historians*, 76 (1): 82–106.
MacCarthy, F. (2019), *Gropius: The Man Who Built the Bauhaus*, Cambridge MA: Belknap Press of Harvard University Press.

# Bibliography

Maderthaner, W. (2017), 'Das kommunale Experiment des Roten Wien – die „Veralltäglichung "der Utopie?', in A. Amberger & T. Möbius, *Auf Utopias Spuren: Utopie und Utopieforschung. Festschrift für Richard Saage zum 75. Geburtstag*, 207–27, Wiesbaden: Springer Fachmedien Wiesbaden.

Mallgrave, H.F. (2009), *Modern Architectural Theory*, Cambridge: Cambridge University Press.

Maltby, J. & J. Rutterford (2016), 'Investing in charities in the nineteenth century: the financialization of philanthropy', *Accounting History*, 21 (2–3): 263–80.

Maltz, D. (2006), *British Aestheticism and the Urban Working Classes, 1870–1900: Beauty for the People*, Basingstoke: Palgrave.

Mannheim, K. (2013), *Ideology and Utopia*, London and New York: Routledge.

Marklund, C. & P. Stadius (2010), 'Acceptance and Conformity: Merging Modernity with Nationalism in the Stockholm Exhibition in 1930', *Culture Unbound: Journal of Current Cultural Research*, 2 (5): 609–34.

Marzot, N. (2002), 'The Study of Urban Form in Italy', *Urban Morphology*, 6 (2): 59–74.

Matysek-Imielińska, M. (2020), *Warsaw Housing Cooperative*, Cham: Springer.

McEwan, C. (2018), 'Ludwig Hilberseimer and Metropolisarchitecture: The Analogue, the Blasé Attitude, the Multitude', *Arts*, 7 (92): 1–15.

McLeod, M. (1983), '"Architecture or Revolution": Taylorism, Technocracy, and Social Change', *Art Journal*, 43 (2): 132–47.

Medina, C.D. & J. Monclús, eds (2018), *Urban Visions: From Planning Culture to Landscape Urbanism*, Cham, Switzerland: Springer.

Meganck, L., L. Van Santvoort & J. de Meyer (2013), *Regionalism and Modernity: Architecture in Western Europe, 1914–1940*, Leuven: Leuven University Press.

Menin, S., F. Samuel & M.A. Samuel (2003), *Nature and Space*, London and New York: Routledge.

Messana, P. (2011), *Soviet Communal Living: An Oral History of the Kommunalka*, Basingstoke: Palgrave.

Mies van der Rohe, L. (1971), 'Industrialised building', in U. Conrads (ed), *Programs and Manifestoes on 20th-Century Architecture*, 81–2, Cambridge MA: MIT Press.

Milan, A. (2019), 'Wilhelm Riphahn in Cologne (1913–1963): Urban Policies and Social Housing between Innovation and Conservation', *Urban Planning*, 4 (3): 134–53.

Milyutin, N.A. (1975), *Sotsgorod: The Problem of Building Socialist Cities*, Cambridge MA and London: MIT Press.

Miller, W. (2017), 'Points of View: Herbert Bayer's Exhibition Catalogue for the 1930 Section Allemande', *Architectural Histories*, 5 (1): 1–22.

Millins, D., A. Murie & P. Leather (2006), *Housing Policy in the UK*, Basingstoke: Palgrave.

Misa, T.J. (2008), 'Appropriating the International Style: Modernism in East and West', in M. Hård & T.J. Misa (eds), *Urban Machinery: Inside Modern European Cities*, 71–97, Cambridge MA: MIT Press.

Monterumisi, C. (2017), 'Towards the "People's Home": First Housing Districts in Stockholm', *Joelho: Revista de Cultura Arquitectonica* (8): 80–95.

Moos, S.V. (2009), *Le Corbusier: Elements of a Synthesis*, Rotterdam: 010 Publishers.

Moravánzsky, Á. (2017), 'Blow-Up: The Powers of Scale', *Journal of Architectural Culture*, 80: 22–35.

Movilla Vega, D. (2020), 'Housing and Revolution: From the Dom-Kommuna to the Transitional Type of Experimental *Vivienda y Revolución. El Concurso entre Camaradas de la OSA, la Sección de Tipificación del Stroykom y la Casa Experimental de Transición Narkomfin (1926-1930)*', PhD DIssertation, Escuela Técnica Superior de Arquitectura, Universidad Politécnica de Madrid.

Mumford, E. (1992), 'CIAM Urbanism after the Athens Charter', *Planning Perspectives*, 7 (4): 391–417.

## Bibliography

Mumford, E. (2019), 'CIAM and Its Outcomes', *UP*, 4 (3): 291–8.
Mumford, E.P. (2000), *The CIAM Discourse on Urbanism, 1928-1960*, Cambridge MA: MIT Press.
Muthesius, H. (1918), *Kleinhaus und Kleinsiedlung*, Munich: Bruckmann.
Nerdinger, W. (2013), 'Rationalisierung zum Existenzminimum - Neues Bauen und die Ästhetisierung ökonomischer und politischer Maßgaben', in A. Hellinger, B. Waldkirch, E. Buchner & H. Batt (eds), *Die Politik in der Kunst und die Kunst in der Politik*, 87–108, Wiesbaden: Springer Fachmedien.
Noonan, J. (2006), *Democratic Society and Human Needs*, Montreal: McGill-Queen's University Press.
Oberlander, H.P. & E.M. Newbrun (2011), *Houser*, Vancouver: UBC Press.
Oorthuys, G. & W. Möller (1991), *Mart Stam 1899-1986*, Milan: Editrice CIPIA.
Ottillinger, E.B. (2009), 'Die andere Moderne. Wiener Wohnungseinrichtungen der Zwischenkriegszeit, in E.B. Ottillinger (ed), *Wohnen Zwischen den Kriegen: Wiener Möbel 1914-1941*, 15–63, Vienna: Böhlau Verlag.
Overy, P. (2004), 'Visions of the Future and the Immediate Past: The Werkbund Exhibition, Paris 1930', *Journal of Design History*, 17 (4): 337–57.
Panerai, P., J. Castex, J.-C. Depaule & I. Samuels (2004), *Urban Forms: The Death and Life of the Urban Block*, Oxford, Woburn MA: Architectural Press.
Passanti, F. (1987), 'The Skyscrapers of the Ville Contemporaine', *Assemblage* 4: 53–65.
Paterson, G.R. (1917), 'Wage-Payment Legislation in the United States', *Bulletin of the US Bureau of Labor Statistics*, No. 229, Washington DC: Government Printing Office.
Payre, R. & P.-Y. Saunier (2000), 'Municipalités de tous pays, unissez vous! L'Union Internationale des Villes ou l'Internationale municipale (1913-1940)', *Amministrare*, 30 (1–2): 217–39.
Perelman, M. (2015), *Le Corbusier: Une Froide Vision du Monde*, Paris: Editions Michalon.
Peters, H.A. (1933), *Die Wohnungswirtschaft Hamburgs vor nach dem Kriege*, Hamburg: Hamburger Verlag für Grundeigentum und Wohnungswesen.
Petz, U.V. (1990), 'Margarethenhöhe Essen: Garden City, Workers' Colony or Satellite Town', *Planning History*, 12 (2): 3–9.
Pick, D. (1993), *Faces of Degeneration: A European Disorder, c. 1848-1918*, Cambridge NY and Melbourne: Cambridge University Press.
Picon, A. (2014), 'Dom-ino: Archetype and Fiction', *Log*, 30: 169–75.
Pittman, T.S. & K.R. Zeigler (2007), 'Basic Human Needs', in A.W. Kruglanski & E.T. Higgins (eds), *Social Psychology: Handbook of Basic Principles*, 473–89, New York and London: Guilford Press.
Poerschke, U. (2014), *Architectural Theory of Modernism: Relating Functions and Forms*, London and New York: Routledge.
Pommer, R. (1983), 'The Flat Roof: A Modernist Controversy in Germany', *Art Journal*, 43 (2): 158–69.
Pommer, R., C.F. Otto & K.P. Harrington (1991), *Weissenhof 1927 and the Modern Movement in Architecture*, Chicago: University of Chicago Press.
Pont, M.L. (2014), 'International Municipalism between the Wars: Local Government as Modernizing Agents', in N.J. Doyle & L. Sebesta (eds), *Regional Integration and Modernity: Cross-Atlantic Perspectives*, 21–42, Lanham MD, Boulder CO, New York and London: Lexington Books.
Pooley, C.G. (1992), 'Housing Strategies in Europe, 1880-1930: Toward a Comparative Perspective', in C.G. Pooley (ed), *Housing Strategies in Europe, 1880-1930*, 325–48, Leicester, London and New York: Leicestere University Press.
Popp, R. (2018), *Fritz Schumacher und der Dulsberg*, Munich and; Hamburg: Dölling und Galitz Verlag.

# Bibliography

Porotto, A. (2016), 'Utopia and Vision: Learning from Vienna and Frankfurt', *Joelho: Revista de Cultura Arquitectonica* (7): 84–103.

Porotto, A. (2017a), 'Pietre che parlano. Gli Höfe della Vienna socialista', *Esempi di Architettura*, 4: 53–66.

Porotto, A. (2017b), 'Kleinwohnung vs Existenzminimum: Social Housing Types from Inter-war Years', Athens: ATINER Conference Paper Series.

Porotto, A. (2019), 'A Wealth of Typological Solutions from the Twenties: Vienna and Frankfurt', *La Casa: Espacios Domesticos, Modes de Habitar, Granada 23-25 January 2019*, 842–55.

Porotto, A. (2019b), *L'intelligence des formes. Le projet de logements collectifs à Vienne et Francfort*, Geneva: Métis Presses.

Pott, P. (2009), *Moskauer Kommunalwohnungen 1917 bis 1997: Materielle Kultur, Erfahrung, Erinnerung*, Zurich: Pano Verlag.

Power, A. (1993), *Hovels to Highrise: State Housing in Europe Since 1850*, London and New York: Routledge.

Pratt, M.L. (1991), 'Arts of the Contact Zone', *Profession*, 33–40.

Prouvé, J. & C.D. d'Ayot (2006), *Jean Prouvé: The Poetics of the Technical Object*, Weil am Rhein: Vitra Design.

Pruden, S. (2018), '"Absolutely Palpable Utopias": The Expressionist Ideas behind Bruno Taut's GEHAG Housing Estates', *Mount Royal Undergraduate Humanities Review (MRUHR)*, 5: 10–17.

Rendell, J. (2017), *The Architecture of Psychoanalysis: Spaces of Transition*, London and New York: I B Tauris.

Riboldazzi, R. (2009), *Un'Altra Modernità: L'Ifhtp E La Cultura Urbanistica Tra Le Due Guerre 1923-1939*, Rome: Gangemi Editore.

Riboldazzi, R. (2013), 'Historical Heritage, Landscape and Modernity: Aspects of the Italian Contribution to the IFHTP Congresses between the Two Wars', *Planning Perspectives*, 28: 399–419.

Riboldazzi, R. (2013b), 'The IFHTP Congresses between the Wars: A Source for Studies on Modern Town Planning', *Town Planning Review*, 84: 159–70.

Rieben, R. (2019), 'Contested Architecture: The "Woba" Residential Colony in Basel, 1930', *Urban Planning*, 4 (3): 212–22.

Rifkind, D. (2012), '"Everything in the State, Nothing against the State, Nothing outside the State": Corporativist Urbanism and Rationalist Architecture in Fascist Italy', *Planning Perspectives*, 27 (1): 51–80.

Rifkind, D. (2013), 'Pietro Maria Bardi, Quadrante and the Architecture of Fascist Italy', *Modernidade Latina*.

Ritoók, P. & Á.A. Sebestyén (2018), 'Communicating "space and form": The history and impact of the journal Tér és Forma as the Hungarian pipeline of Modernism, *Docomomo Journal*, 59: 18–25.

Roberts, D.D. (2006), *The Totalitarian Experiment in Twentieth-Century Europe: Understanding the Poverty of Great Politics*, New York: Routledge.

Robertson, M. (2018), *The Last Utopians: Four Late Nineteenth-Century Visionaries and Their Legacy*, Princeton NJ: Princeton University Press.

Rodgers, D.T. (1998), *Atlantic Crossings*, Cambridge MA and London: Harvard University Press.

Rodogno, D., B. Struck & J. Vogel (2015), 'Introduction', in D. Rodogno, B. Struck & J. Vogel (eds), *Shaping the Transnational Sphere: Experts, Networks and Issues from the 1840s to the 1930s*, 1–20, New York and Oxford: Berghahn.

Rohde, T. (2015), 'Die Bau-Ausstellung zu Beginn des 20. Jahrhunderts oder "Die Schwierigkeit zu wohnen"', PhD Dissertation, Bauhaus-Universität Weimar, Weimar.

Rössler, P. (2014), *The Bauhaus and Public Relations*, London and New York: Routledge.

## Bibliography

Rousset, I. (2020), 'The Industrious, the Laboring, and the Sunken: Berlin's Mietskaserne and the Housing Question', *Journal of Urban History*, 47 (6): 1275–1300.
Rowe, P.G. (1995), *Modernity and Housing*, Cambridge, Mass: MIT Press.
Rowntree, B.S. (1901), *Poverty: A Study of Town Life*, London: Macmillan.
Rudolph, N.C. (2015), *At Home in Postwar France: Modern Mass Housing and the Right to Comfort*, New York and Oxford: Berghahn Books.
Ruhl, C. (2011), 'Architekturausstellungen – Von der Präsentation zum autonomen Raum der Architektur', in W. Sonne (ed), *Die Medien Der Architektur*, 302–30, Berlin and Munich: Deutscher Kunstverlag.
Rutar, S. (2006), 'Wohnen in Trieste um der Jahrhundertwende', in A. Janatková & H. Kozińska-Witt (eds), *Wohnen in der Grossstadt, 1900–1939: Wohnsituation und Modernisierung im Europäischen Vergleich*, 55–76, Stuttgart: Franz Steiner Verlag.
Sadler, S. (2004), 'An Avant-Garde Academy', in A. Ballantyne (ed), *Architectures*, 33–56, Oxford: Blackwell.
Saldern, A.V. (1991), '"Statt Kathedralen die Wohnmaschine". Paradoxien der Rationalisierung im Kontext der Moderne', in F. Bajohr, W. Johe & U. Lohalm (eds), *Zivilisation und Barbarei: Die Widersprüchlichen Potentiale der Moderne: Detlev Peukert Zum Gedenken*, 168–92, Hamburg: Christians.
Saunier, P.-Y. (2004), 'Circulations, connexions et espaces transnationaux', *Genèses*, 57 (4): 110–26.
Saunier, P.-Y. (2007), 'The ILO as Organizer: Shaping the Transnational Housing Scene in the 1920s'.
Saunier, P.-Y. (2008), 'Les régimes circulatoires du domaine social 1800–1940: Projets et ingénierie de la convergence et de la différence', *Genèses*, 71 (2): 14–21.
Saunier, P.-Y. (2010), 'Borderline Work: ILO Explorations onto the Housing Scene until 1940', in J. Van Daele, M.R. García, G. Van Goethem & M. van der Linden (eds), *ILO Histories. Essays on the International Labour Organization and Its Impact on the World during the Twentieth Century*, 197–220, Bern: Peter Lang.
Savorra, M. (2015), 'La casa razionale', in F. Irace (ed), *Storie di Interni. L'Architettura dello Spazio Domestico Moderno*, 47–77, Rome: Carocci.
Scheffler, K. (1913), *Die Architektur der Grosstadt*, Berlin: Cassirer.
Schlögel, K. (1998), 'Kommunalka-oder Kommunismus als Lebensform: Zu einer historischen Topographie der Sowjetunion', *Historische Anthropologie*, 6 (3): 329–46.
Schmid, S. (2019), *A History of Collective Living: Forms of Shared Living*, Basel: Birkhäuser.
Schnaidt, C., ed. (1965), *Hannes Meyer: Buildings, Projects and Writings*, Teufen: Niggli.
Schnoor, C. & C. Kromrei (2013), 'Immeuble-villas between Le Corbusier and Albert Gessner', 807–19.
Schorch, P. (2013), 'Contact Zones, Third Spaces, and the Act of Interpretation', *Museum & Society* 11 (1): 68–81.
Schubert, D. (2021), 'Fritz Schumacher – Neglected German town planner and urban reformer in Hamburg and Cologne', *Planning Perspectives*, 36 (1): 1–19.
Schuldenfrei, R. (2018), *Luxury and Modernism: Architecture and the Object in Germany 1900–1933*, Princeton NJ and Oxford: Princeton University Press.
Schumacher, F. (1919), *Die Kleinwohnung. Studien zur Wohnungsfrage*, Leipzig: Quelle & Meyer.
Schumacher, F. (1932), *Das Werden einer Wohnstadt: Bilder vom Neuen Hamburg*, Hamburg: Georg Westermann.
Schuster, F. (1927), *Eine Eingerichtete Kleinstwohnung*, Frankfurt: Englert und Schlosser.
Schuster, F. (1929), *Ein Möbelbuch: Ein Beitrag zum Problem des Zeitgemässen Möbels*, Frankfurt: Englert und Schlosser.
Schütte-Lihotzky, M. (2019), *Warum Ich Architektin Wurde*, Vienna: Residenz Verlag.

Schwartz, F.J. (1996), *The Werkbund: Design Theory and Mass Culture before the First World War*, New Haven CT: Yale University Press.

Scott, A.M. (2012), *Experiences of Poverty in Late Medieval and Early Modern England and France*, Farnham; Burlington VT: Ashgate.

Seelow, A. (2017), 'Function and Form: Shifts in Modernist Architects' Design Thinking', *Arts*, 6 (4): 1.

Seelow, A. (2018), 'The Construction Kit and the Assembly Line – Walter Gropius' Concepts for Rationalizing Architecture', *Arts*, 7 (4): 1–29.

Seelow, A.M. (2016), 'From the Continent to the North – German Influence on Modern Architecture in Sweden', *Konsthistorisk tidskrift/Journal of Art History*, 85 (1): 44–62.

Sert, J.L. (1942), *Can Our Cities Survive? An Abc of Urban Problems, Their Analysis, Their Solutions*, Cambridge MA: Harvard University Press.

Shapiro, A.-L. (1985), *Housing the Poor of Paris, 1850–1902*, Madison WI and London: University of Wisconsin Press.

Shvidkovskiĭ, D.O. (2007), *Russian Architecture and the West*, New Haven CT and London: Yale University Press.

Siebenbrodt, M. (2007), 'Das Haus am Horn in Weimar–Bauhausstätte und Weltkulturerbe: Bau, Nutzung und Denkmalpflege', in M. Petzet & J. Ziesemer (eds), *Heritage at Risk: Patrimoine En Péril. ICOMOS World Report 2006/2007 on Monuments and Sites in Danger, Heritage at Risk*, 112–8, Altenburg: E. Reinhold Verlag.

Sieder, R. (1985), 'Housing Policy, Social Welfare, and Family Life in "Red Vienna", 1919–34', *Oral History*, 13 (2): 35–48.

Silverman, D.P. (1970), 'A Pledge Unredeemed: The Housing Crisis in Weimar Germany', *Central European History*, 3 (1–2): 112–39.

Simmel, G. (1903), 'Die großstädte und das geistesleben', in T. Petermann (ed), *Die Großstadt: Vorträge und Aufsätze zur Städteausstellung*, 187–206, Dresden: Zahn & Jaensch.

Simmons, D. (2015), *Vital Minimum: Need, Science, and Politics in Modern France*, Chicago: University of Chicago Press.

Sloterdijk, P. & D. Fabricius (2007), 'Cell Block, Egospheres, Self-Container', *Log* (10): 89–108.

Smets, M. (1977), *L'Avènement de la Cité-Jardin en Belgique: Histoire de l'Habitat Social en Belgique de 1830 à 1930*, Brussels and Liège: P. Mardaga.

Snowden, F.M. (2002), *Naples in the Time of Cholera, 1884–1911*, Cambridge: Cambridge University Press.

Somer, K. (2007), *The Functional City: The CIAM and Cornelis Van Eesteren, 1928–1960*, Rotterdam and The Hague: NAi Publishers & EFL Foundation.

Sonne, W. (2009), 'Dwelling in the metropolis: Reformed urban blocks 1890–1940 as a model for the sustainable compact city', Progress in Planning, 72 (2): 53–149,

Specthenhauser, K. & D. Weiss (1999), 'Karel Teige and the CIAM: The History of a Troubled Relationship', in E. Dluhosch & R. Švácha (eds), *Karel Teige, 1900–1951: L'Enfant Terrible of the Czech Modernist Avant-Garde*, 217–55, Cambridge MA: MIT Press.

Stabile, D.R. (2009), *The Living Wage: Lessons from the History of Economic Thought*, Cheltenham: Edward Elgar.

Stankard, M. (2002), 'Re-Covering Mies van der Rohe's Weissenhof: The Ultimate Surface', *Journal of Architectural Education (1984–)*, 55 (4): 247–56.

Stavrides, S. (2016). *Common Space*, London: Zed Books.

Steadman, P. (2014), *Building Types and Built Forms*, Kibworth Beauchamp: Matador.

Steinmann, M., ed. (1979), *CIAM: Dokumente 1928–1939*, Basel and Stuttgart: Birkhäuser.

Stieber, N. (1998), *Housing Design and Society in Amsterdam: Reconfiguring Urban Order and Identity, 1900–1920*, Chicago IL and London: University of Chicago Press.

Stoppioni, B. (2007), 'Hugo Haring and "Der Ring". Origins of an Alternative to the Lecorbusian Moderno', *Critica d'Arte*, 69: 131–55.

## Bibliography

Stromberg, T. (1992), 'Sweden', in C.G. Pooley (ed.), *Housing Strategies in Europe, 1880–1930*, 11–39, Leicester, London and New York: Leicestere University Press.

Stübben, J. (1907), *Der Städtebau: Handbuch der Architektur*, 2nd ed. Books.Google.Com. Stuttgart: A. Kröner.

Syring, E. & J.C. Kirschenmann (2004), *Hans Scharoun, 1893–1972: Outsider of Modernism*, Cologne: Taschen.

Tafuri, M. (1969), 'Per una critica dell'ideologia architettonica', *Contropiano*, 2 (1): 31–79.

Tafuri, M. (1976), *Architecture and Utopia: Design and Capitalist Development*, Cambridge MA and London: MIT Press.

Tarn, J.N. (1973), *Five Per Cent Philanthropy: An Account of Housing in Urban Areas between 1840 and 1914*, Cambridge: Cambridge University Press.

Teige, K. (1987), 'The Housing Problem of the Subsistence Level Population: Summary of the National Reports at the International Congress for New Building (CIAM), 1930', *Habitat International*, 11 (3): 147–151.

Teige, K. (2000), *Modern Architecture in Czechoslovakia and Other Writings*, Los Angeles: Getty Research Institute.

Teige, K. (2002), *The Minimum Dwelling*, Cambridge MA, London: MIT Press.

Tessenow, H. (1916), *Hausbau Philanthropy: An Dergleichen*, Berlin: B. Cassirer.

Tessenow, H. (1982), *Heinrich Tessenow: Geschriebenes Gedanken Eines Baumeisters*, Otto Kindt (ed.), Otto Kindt. Braunschweig/Wiesbaden: Friedr. Vieweg & Sohn.

Thompson, P. (2012), 'What Is Concrete about Ernst Bloch's "Concrete Utopia"?', in M.H. Jacobsen & K. Tester (eds), *Utopia: Social Theory and the Future*, 33–46, Farnham and Burlington VT: Ashgate Publishing, Ltd.

Tomita, H. & M. Ishii (2014), 'The Influence of Hannes Meyer and the Bauhaus Brigade on 1930s Soviet Architecture', *Journal of Asian Architecture and Building Engineering*, 13 (1): 49–56.

Torp, C. (2011), *Konsum und Politik in der Weimarer Republik*, Göttingen: Vandenhoeck & Ruprecht.

Udovicki-Selb, D. (1997), 'Le Corbusier and the Paris Exhibition of 1937: The Temps Nouveaux Pavilion', *Journal of the Society of Architectural Historians*, 56 (1): 42–63.

Udovicki-Selb, D. (2015), 'Reinventing Paris', *Journal of the Society of Architectural Historians*, 74 (2): 179–200.

Uhlig, G., N. Kohler & L. Schneider (1994), *Fenster: Architektur und Technologie im Dialog*, Braunschweig and Wiesbaden: Friedr. Vieweg & Sohn.

Urbanik, J. (2014), 'Notheime – Ergonomically Designed Crisis Houses of the Building Cooperative "Schlesische Heimstätte"', in C. Stephanidis & M. Antona (eds), *Universal Access in Human-Computer Interaction: Design for All and Accessibility Practice: 8th International Conference, Uahci 2014, Held as Part of HCI International 2014, Heraklion, Crete, Greece, June 22–27, 2014, Proceedings*, 303–13, Cham, Heidelberg, New York, Dordrecht and London: Springer.

Van Es, E., G. Harbusch, B. Maurer, M. Pérez, S.K. & D. Weiss, eds (2014), *Atlas of the Functional City: CIAM 4 and Comparative Urban Analysis*, Bussum: Thoth Publishers.

Van Loo, Anne (1996), 'La cité-jardin, laboratoire du mouvement moderne en Belgique', in Girard, P. and B. Fayolle Lussac (eds), *Cités, Cités-Jardins: Une Histoire Européenne. Actes du Colloque de Toulouse, 18–19 Novembre 1993*, 33–51, Pessac: Maison des Sciences de l'Homme d'Aquitaine.

Villani, L. (2012), *Le Borgate del Fascismo*, Milan: Ledizioni.

Voigt, W. (2012), 'Modern in Intention? Paul Schmitthenner Revisited', *DASH Delft Architectural Studies on Housing*, 6: 16–33.

Von Saldern, A. (2009), '"Neues Wohnen": Housing and Reform', in A. McElligott (ed), *Weimar Germany*, 207–33, Oxford: Oxford University Press.

Vujosevic, T. (2013), 'Living Efficiently: The Aesthetic of the Russian One-Room Habitat in the 1920s', *Society of Architectural Historians, Australia and New Zealand (SAHANZ) Annual Conference 2013*, 739–48.
Wagner, M. (1925), *Amerikanische Bauwirtschaft*, Berlin: Vorwärts.
Wagner, P. (2016), *Stadtplanung für die Welt?*, Göttingen: Vandenhoeck & Ruprecht.
Wenderski, M. (2018), *Cultural Mobility in the Interwar Avant-Garde Art Network: Poland, Belgium and the Netherlands*, London and New York: Routledge.
Wesemael, P.V. (2001), *Architecture of Instruction and Delight*, Rotterdam: 010 Publishers.
Williams, R.H. (1982), *Dream Worlds: Mass Consumption in Late Nineteenth Century France*, Berkeley, Los Angeles, Oxford: University of California Press.
Willimott, A. (2017), '"How Do You Live?": Experiments in Revolutionary Living after 1917', *The Journal of Architecture*, 22 (3): 437–57.
Wisselgren, P. (2017), *The Social Scientific Gaze: The Social Question and the Rise of Academic Social Science in Sweden*, London and New York: Routledge.
Wolfe, R. (2011), 'The Graveyard of Utopia'. Online publication, available at https://thecharnelhouse.org/2011/11/22/the-graveyard-of-utopia-soviet-urbanism-and-the-fate-of-the-international-avant-garde/
Wurster, C.B. (1934), *Modern Housing*, Boston and New York: Houghton Mifflin Company.
Young, J. (2011), 'Heidegger's Heimat', *International Journal of Philosophical Studies*, 19 (2): 285–93.
Zarecor, K.E. (2011), *Manufacturing a Socialist Modernity: Housing in Czechoslovakia, 1945–1960*, Pittsburgh PA: University of Pittsburgh Press.

# INDEX

Aalto, Alvar 74, 126, 144, 178, 182
Amsterdam 61, 62, 67, 73, 108, 182, 186, 188, 189
Architecture
   and agency 6, 7, 79, 81, 83, 89, 131, 191, 195
   and bigness 35, 36, 155–156
   and revolution 6, 8, 28, 70, 77, 79, 80, 81–85, 86, 89, 90, 101, 106, 141, 148, 154, 167, 190, 191, 195
   and social responsibility 3, 6, 36, 50, 77, 101, 109, 110, 114, 130–131, 133, 146, 176–177, 195
   and utopia 2, 4, 6, 7, 8, 9, 11, 19, 20, 28, 50, 58, 76, 77, 78, 79, 80, 83, 84, 89, 90, 91, 99, 100, 101, 105, 133, 139, 141, 152, 159, 162, 166, 167, 191, 195
   [See also *Utopia*]
   modular 5, 9, 28, 30, 48, 51, 55, 81, 93, 100, 103, 120, 131, 137–138, 156, 172, 174, 192, 194–195
   multi-scalar 4, 7, 9, 50, 55, 144
Artaria, Paul 109, 117, 172
Asplund, Gunnar 178
Athens Charter (1933) 106, 111, 191, 193

Bad Dürrenberg (Germany) 102, 103
Bardi, Pier Maria 158
Barshch, Mikhail 93
Bauer, Catherine 23, 37
Bauhaus 88, 99, 108, 127, 160, 162
Behrens, Peter 127, 164
Belgium 21, 60, 61, 74, 138, 170, 180, 181
Berlage, Hans 74, 108
Berlin 19, 22, 25, 31, 32, 33, 35, 36, 52, 66, 67, 74, 76, 79, 87, 102, 116, 146, 158, 161, 172, 182, 186, 187, 188, 191, 192
Bernoulli, Hans 74
Bloch, Ernest 78
Böhm, Herbert 149, 150, 151
Booth, Charles 13, 15, 16, 17
Borsani, Osvaldo 162, 163
Bourgeois, Victor 3, 60, 74, 108, 109, 112, 117, 119, 121–122, 123, 124, 125–126, 128, 136, 138, 140, 142–146, 149, 154, 164, 168, 172, 173, 179–181, 183, 185, 186, 187
Brenner, Anton 54, 170

Breslau (Wrocław) 37, 38, 39, 41, 42, 43, 49, 50, 51, 108, 161, 163, 165, 166, 170, 172
   post-First World War housing programme 37–43
   [See also *Exhibitions*]
Breuer, Marcel 85, 99, 112, 114, 173, 177
Britain 14, 18, 19, 20, 22, 23, 24, 59, 60, 62, 109, 170

Calza Bini, Alberto 70, 71
Celle (Germany) 174
Chadwick, Edwin 14
CIAM
   and historiography 12, 106–107, 116
   and ideological/programmatic tensions 127–131, 133, 134, 139, 146, 147, 158, 193
   and IFHTP 3, 74–75, 127, 133, 137–138, 155, 170, 172, 195
   and publicity 10, 48, 112, 120, 130, 157, 158, 159, 160, 164, 168, 169, 174, 176, 178, 179, 181, 185, 186, 187, 188, 189, 192, 194
   early CIAM 3–5, 107–109, 123–124, 134–135, 145, 193
   [See also *CIAM Congresses; CIRPAC*]
CIAM Congresses
   CIAM1 (1928) 2, 75, 106–112, 116, 118, 119, 122, 126, 129, 131, 146, 167, 168, 174, 189, 191, 192, 194
   and early discussions on and housing 109–112
   CIAM2 (1929) 1, 3, 10, 97, 98, 106, 107, 112–133, 134, 135, 136, 137, 139, 140, 141, 143, 144, 151, 152, 155, 157, 167–179, 180, 181, 182, 186, 187, 188, 189, 190, 192, 193, 194
   [See also *Exhibitions/CIAM2 exhibition*]
   aftermath of 128–133
   as publicity event 129
   linguistic confusion 122–128
   preparation 112–119
   publication 178–179
   CIAM3 (1930) 1, 2, 3, 10, 106, 107, 108, 111, 116, 134–156, 157, 158, 179–188, 189, 190, 191, 192, 193, 194, 195
   [See also *Exhibitions/CIAM3 exhibition*]

# Index

and high-rise 137–138, 143, 151
and land subdivision 134, 135, 137, 140, 141, 143–144, 148, 157, 179–181, 185, 186, 194
*Journées de l'Habitation Minimum* (1930) 142, 154, 157, 180–181, 185, 190
preparation 135–148
publication 186–189
CIAM4 (1933) 2, 106, 111, 117, 126, 134, 155, 158, 188, 189, 191, 192, 193
Athens Charter 106, 111, 191, 193
planning for the Moscow Congress (cancelled) 2, 90, 95, 142, 146, 148, 158, 187, 188, 191, 192, 193
[*See also* **Exhibitions**]
CIRPAC (*Comité International pour la Résolution des Problèmes de l'Architecture Contemporaine*) 112, 115, 118, 123, 135, 136, 137, 138, 142, 143, 144, 146, 157, 158, 188
Cité Moderne (Brussels) 60, 182, 184
City
and countryside 6, 20, 36, 133, 173, 194–195
and overcrowding 11, 14, 15, 17, 26, 31, 37
and poverty 7, 12, 13, 14, 15, 16, 17, 20, 31, 60, 67, 68, 69
nineteenth-century city 15, 17, 23
Communism 96, 97
Czechoslovakia 109, 118, 154, 170, 182

Denmark 73, 139, 153, 154
Dessau (Germany) 66, 101, 173
*Dom-kommuna* (Soviet Union) 91, 94–98
Doxiadis, Apostolos 30
Dulsberg (Hamburg) 44, 45
Dwelling [*see* **Housing**]
Dwelling ration 3, 86, 97–101, 121, 166, 172, 174, 184, 194
[*See also* **Housing**]

Eggericx, Jean-Jules 60
Eiffel Tower 160
Exhibitions 10, 59, 65, 69, 71, 80, 81, 144, 152, 157, 158, 159, 160, 161, 163, 165, 169, 176, 181, 182, 185, 186, 188, 189, 192, 193, 194
as contact zones 3, 8, 9, 10, 58, 74, 81, 159, 193
CIAM2 exhibition 167–179
CIAM3 exhibitions 179–188
German Building Exhibition (*Bauausstellung*, Berlin, 1931) 158, 160, 187–188, 191
Great Exhibition (London, 1851) 19, 160

International Co-operative exhibition (Ghent, 1924) 162
International Exhibition of Modern Decorative and Industrial Arts (*Exposition Internationale des Arts Décoratifs et Industriels Modernes*, Paris, 1925) 82, 162
and modern architecture 159–167
*Salon d'Automne* (Paris, 1922) 82, 162
*Salon des Artistes Décorateurs* (Paris, 1930) 99
Stockholm Exhibition (1930) 160, 178
*Triennale* (Milan, 1933) 158, 161, 162, 163, 188
Weissenhof exhibition (*Die Wohnung*) (Stuttgart, 1927) 82, 84, 85, 146, 161, 163, 164, 165, 172
Werkbund housing exhibitions 36, 145, 160–161
WoBa (Basel, 1930) 161, 172
WuWa (Breslau, 1929) 161, 163, 170, 172
*Existenzminimum* 1, 2, 3, 4, 5, 6, 8, 9, 10, 24–27, 121, 122, 123, 124, 125, 129, 131, 132, 133, 137, 146, 157, 176, 180, 182, 187, 190, 195
decline 131–133, 155–156, 190–191
linguistic confusion 122–128, 137
[*See also* **Kuczynski**; **Minimum**]

Fascism 48, 71, 86, 109, 146, 158
First World War 2, 6, 8, 9, 24–26, 28, 29, 35, 36–38, 43, 44, 46, 47, 48, 57, 59–62, 64, 65, 70, 75, 76–78, 81, 82, 105, 120, 160, 163, 168, 176
as rupture 76–78
Fourier, Charles 19
France 14, 19, 20, 23, 32, 34, 35, 60, 70, 84, 121, 124, 144, 170
*Habitations à Bon Marché* (HBM) 32, 34, 70, 73, 119
*Habitations à Loyer Modéré* 32
Loucheur Law 70, 121, 124
Frank, Josef 73, 112, 126, 129, 130, 164, 182
Frankfurt 1, 2, 3, 4, 10, 35, 37, 38, 40, 41, 46, 49–58, 73, 74, 75, 78, 86, 97, 98, 106, 107, 108, 112, 113, 114, 115, 116, 117, 118, 119, 120, 122, 123, 124, 125, 127, 128, 129, 130, 131, 132, 134, 135, 136, 137, 138, 139, 140, 143, 144, 145, 148, 149, 150, 153, 156, 157, 158, 168, 169, 170, 171, 172, 173, 174, 176, 178, 179, 180, 181, 182, 183, 184, 185, 186, 187, 188, 191, 192, 193, 194, 195
'New Frankfurt' programme 49–58, 79, 179
Freidorf (Basel) 88

227

# Index

Garbatella (Rome) 71, 72, 165
Geneva 108, 140, 188
Germany 8, 21, 22, 23, 32, 35, 36, 38, 43, 46, 50, 60, 64, 66, 69, 101, 102, 112, 144, 145, 170, 177, 186, 187
Giedion, Sigfried 2, 3, 97, 98, 106, 108, 109, 110, 112, 113, 116, 117, 118, 119, 120, 121, 122, 123, 124, 125, 127, 129, 130, 131, 132, 134, 136, 137, 138, 139, 140, 141, 142, 143, 144, 145, 146, 147, 148, 149, 150, 152, 157, 158, 167, 169, 176, 178, 179, 180, 181, 186, 187, 188, 192
    and dwelling ration 98
    and liberated living 3, 123, 131
    as CIAM's driving force 109, 149
Ginzburg, Moisei 9, 86, 90, 95, 96, 97, 108, 119, 144
Goldstein (Frankfurt) 170, 173
Gorla, Giuseppe 68
Göttel, Jacobus 52
Gropius, Walter 3, 9, 75, 76, 79, 84, 86, 97, 99, 100, 101, 104, 108, 109, 111, 114, 116, 117, 119, 121, 122, 124, 125, 126, 127, 128, 129, 130, 136, 137, 138, 140, 141, 142, 143, 144, 145, 147, 149, 150, 151, 155, 158, 164, 166, 172, 173, 177, 178, 179, 181, 186, 187, 188
    and dwelling ration 98–101
    and high-rise 127, 137–138, 141–142, 145, 151, 166, 186

*Habitations à Bon Marché* (affordable dwellings, France, HBM) 32, 34, 35, 70, 119, 124
Hagen, Wilhelm 32, 52, 127
Hamburg 35, 43, 44, 45, 46, 55, 176
    Housing programme 44–46
Häring, Hugo 108, 112, 114, 115, 118, 125, 127, 140, 144, 147
    [*See also* **Ring**]
Häsler, Otto 172, 174
Hein, Ernst 63
Hellerau (Germany) 35, 54
Hellerhof (Frankfurt) 170, 182
Hilberseimer, Ludwig 51, 85, 127
Hill, Octavia 17, 22, 71, 103
Housing
    affordable 1, 2, 4, 5, 6, 8, 9, 21, 25, 26, 27–29, 32, 33, 34, 37, 38, 42, 43, 44, 46, 47, 48, 50, 52, 55, 57, 60, 62, 63, 67, 68, 69, 70, 75, 84, 85, 86, 98, 99, 101, 104, 107, 114, 120, 121, 122, 124, 126, 128, 130, 131, 142, 151, 152, 153, 154, 162, 163, 164, 165, 166, 167, 168, 170, 172, 174, 178, 180, 190, 191, 194, 195

and cell 9, 51, 77, 85–89, 90, 91, 93, 94, 96, 97, 98, 104, 105, 120, 122, 137, 172, 173, 174, 185
and co-operative movement 22
and dwelling ration 95, 97–101
and family unit 88, 90, 95, 97–100, 103, 105, 121–122, 126–128, 162, 166
and Fordism 79, 101
and frictionless living 69, 103–104
and gender roles 24, 40, 41, 54, 100, 103, 121, 126
and laissez-faire economics 12, 13, 18, 20, 22, 27, 37
and philanthropy 8, 18–20, 21–23, 27, 89
and size reduction 40, 48, 83
and small size 30–36, 50, 124
and social responsibility of the architect 3, 6, 36, 50, 77, 101, 109, 110, 114, 130–131, 133, 146, 176–177, 195
and Taylorisation 88
and taxation 21, 24, 26–27, 44, 47, 68, 69
and 'very poor' 67–69
as human need 14–18
as living machine 83, 101
as universal right 5, 50, 80, 89, 90, 98, 133, 162, 165, 184, 195
calculus 27–29
collective 7, 9, 18, 46, 57, 70, 77, 78, 88, 89, 90, 91, 93, 94, 95, 96, 97, 98, 99, 103, 108, 110, 122, 124, 127, 128, 147, 150, 152, 154, 167, 172, 173, 183, 185
communal 9, 19, 28, 46, 52, 63, 65, 73, 77, 91, 95, 96, 97, 98, 99, 100, 137, 147, 151, 163, 166, 173, 182
high-rise 52, 73–75, 109, 127, 137–138, 141–142, 144, 125, 150–151, 155, 166, 173, 181, 182, 185, 186, 188
informal settlements ('slums') 17, 20, 23, 28, 34, 73, 75
kitchen 24, 32, 35, 36, 39, 40, 41, 46, 49, 52, 54, 64, 91, 93, 96, 121, 126, 162, 173, 178, 181
legislation 20–21, 23, 34, 43, 70
    Loucheur law (France, 1928) 70, 121, 124
    Luzzatti Law (Italy, 1903) 21
    UK Planning Acts 21, 60
minimum dwelling 1, 124, 125
model housing
    *casa minima* (1933) 162–163
    *Haus am Horn* (1923) 162
    Narkomfin (1928–32) 95–96
model settlements
    Dammerstock (Karlsruhe, 1928–29) 161, 166, 172, 173, 182, 185
    Eglisee (Basel, 1930) 161, 165, 172

# Index

Garbatella (Rome, 1929) 71–72, 165
Haselhorst-Spandau (Berlin, 1930–35) 170
Neubühl (Zurich, 1930–32) 161, 165, 182
Tribouilet (Liège, 1930) 176
Weissenhof (Stuttgart, 1927) 82, 84, 85, 146, 161, 163, 164, 165, 172
reform of 15–23
social dimension of 12, 100, 113, 114, 123, 165
supply–demand 27–28
Housing typologies
Bassena-type (Vienna) 36
Becque housing typology 34, 70
Citrohan 51, 81, 82, 84, 85
Co-op Zimmer 86–89
Dom-Ino 51, 81, 82
*dom-kommuna* 91–97
dwelling cell (*Wohnzelle*) 85
*Hof* 49, 57, 64, 65, 187
*Kommunalka* (communal apartments, Soviet Union) 97
Loucheur (Maison) 84, 170, 174
row-housing 45, 50
small-size apartment 1, 6, 8, 32, 35, 36, 38, 40, 41, 43, 45, 51, 52, 54, 55, 56, 63, 64, 65, 66, 86, 104, 115, 116, 120, 123, 124, 125, 126, 133, 166, 177, 194, 195
Stroikom housing types (Soviet Union) 91–96, 172, 173
[*See also* **Kleinwohnung**; **Kleinstwohnung**]
Zola housing typology 34, 35, 70
Howard, Ebenezer 74
Hungary 112, 144, 170, 172

IFHTP (International Federation of Housing and Town Planning) 2, 3, 9, 47, 51, 59–75, 102, 107, 114, 127, 133, 137, 138, 155, 165, 170, 172, 195
[*See also* **International Garden Cities and Town Planning Association (IGCTPA)**]
Congresses
Paris (1928) 67–71
Rome (1929) 71–74
influence on CIAM 74–75
Vienna (1926) 61–66
Im Vogelsand (Basel) 182
International Co-operative Alliance 162
International Federation for Housing (*Internationaler Verband für Wohnungswesen*, IVW) 60, 62, 74, 114
International Garden Cities and Town Planning Association (IGCTPA) 59, 61, 62. [*see also* **IFHTP**]

International Housing Congress (IHC) 59, 61
International Union of Local Authorities (*Union Internationale des Villes*, UIV) 59, 61, 74, 107
Italy 21, 32, 70, 71, 72, 85, 108, 109, 112, 146, 158, 170, 182, 186, 187
Institute of Social Housing (ICP) 68, 70, 71, 174

Jeanneret, Pierre 79, 81, 82, 85, 117, 119, 123

Kampffmeyer, Hans 127
Kapelleveld (Belgium) 60, 182, 184
Karlsruhe 112, 117, 161, 166, 168, 172, 182, 185
Kaufmann, Eugen 51, 149, 150, 151, 170
Kitchen
Frankfurt kitchen 54
living kitchen 39
Viennese kitchen 48
Klein, Alexander 1, 9, 36, 46, 55, 69, 70, 101–104, 115, 125, 170, 172, 174
and frictionless living 69, 103–104
*Kleinstwohnung* (smallest-size apartment) 1, 43–46, 52, 54, 55, 56, 115, 125
Kleinwohnung (small-size apartment) 6, 8, 32–46, 51, 63, 64, 65, 66, 86, 104, 115, 116, 120, 123, 124, 125, 126, 133, 166, 177, 194, 195
Kollwitz, Käthe 169
Koolhaas, Rem 7, 155, 190
Krejcar, Jaromír 118
Kuczynski, Robert Réné 24–26

La Sarraz (CIAM meeting, 1928) [*see* **CIAM Congresses/CIAM 1**]
Land (reform of) 113, 114, 116, 137, 153
Le Corbusier, (Charles-Édouard Jeanneret) 3, 9, 51, 75, 79, 81, 82, 83, 84, 85, 86, 90, 101, 108, 109, 110, 111, 112, 113, 114, 117, 118, 121, 122, 123, 124, 126, 130, 136, 137, 138, 139, 140, 141, 142, 143, 144, 145, 146, 147, 148, 149, 150, 151, 153, 155, 158, 164, 165, 168, 170, 172, 174, 178, 179, 181, 182, 185, 186, 188
and architecture as revolution 79, 81–85, 121
and cell 85–86
and fascism 148, 153
and housing as 'machine for living' 83, 101, 147
and urban concentration 122, 141–142
and urban scale 110–111, 122, 126, 136–137, 147, 150, 155
fascination with the Soviet Union 147–148
*Plan Voisin* 85, 141
Towards a New Architecture (book) 81, 83

229

# Index

Ville Contemporaine 141
Ville Radieuse 188
Weissenhof estate designs 164–165
Le Logis-Floréal (Belgium) 60
League of Nations
   competition for the Headquarters of (1927) 61, 108
Letchworth Garden City (UK) 66
Lewin, David 15, 24, 26
Liberalism 11, 12, 13, 18, 24, 26, 88
Lihotzky, Margarete 48, 49, 51, 54, 65, 173
   kitchen innovation 49, 64–65
Lissitzky, El 108, 119
Liverpool 23, 73
Łodz (Poland) 172
London 13, 15, 17, 19, 22, 23, 37, 74
   housing conditions in East London 15, 16
Loos, Adolf 55, 108
Loucheur, Louis 60, 70, 121, 124
Lurçat, André 127, 170

Maslow, Abraham 15
   [See also **Needs**]
May, Ernst 3, 37, 38, 39, 40, 41, 43, 49, 50, 51, 52, 55, 57, 60, 73, 74, 79, 86, 108, 109, 112, 113, 114, 115, 116, 118, 119, 120, 122, 123, 124, 125, 126, 127, 129, 131, 132, 133, 135, 136, 138, 140, 141, 142, 143, 144, 145, 146, 147, 148, 149, 168, 170, 178, 179, 180, 188
   and *Existenzminimum* 122–123, 125, 132–133
   departure for the Soviet Union 145–146
   in Breslau 37–43
   in Frankfurt 49–56
Mendelsohn, Erich 108
Mercadal, Fernando García 108
Meyer, Hannes 9, 51, 86, 87, 88, 89, 90, 108, 109, 118, 127, 139, 169, 174
   and Co-op Zimmer 86, 87, 88
Mies van der Rohe, Ludwig 79, 84, 108, 163, 164, 188
*Mietskaserne* 31, 36, 38
Milan 43, 68, 73, 146, 158, 161, 163, 174, 182, 186, 188
Milinis, Ignatii 95
Milyutin, Nikolai Alexandrovic 9, 86, 96
Minimum 13, 14, 20, 25, 32, 45, 48, 97, 101, 102, 117, 123, 128, 162
   and large scale in architecture 194–195
   and minimalism 1, 3, 78, 82, 83, 90, 96, 177
   as deficit 8, 15, 35, 83
   as optimal 1, 5, 6, 9, 10, 11, 29, 40, 41, 55, 59, 61, 63, 65, 66, 72, 78, 82, 90, 91, 93, 95, 98, 99, 101, 102, 103, 121, 131, 137, 140, 152, 162, 163, 164, 172, 178, 192, 194, 195

   [See also ***Existenzminimum***]
Mobilities 19, 41, 99, 103, 158, 160, 162, 193
   and CIAM exhibitions 176, 186–188, 189, 194
Model housing [see **Housing**]
Modernism 5, 7, 9, 78, 80, 81, 98, 105, 106, 190
   and minimum 78–81
   and new architecture 76, 88, 90, 110, 116, 148
   as alchemy 7, 28, 43, 45, 48, 77, 103, 190, 191, 195
   as discursive act 3, 8, 9, 57, 61, 62, 75, 77, 80, 81, 104, 105, 107, 111, 116, 131, 137, 143, 159, 162, 164, 166, 167, 189, 190, 192, 193
Modernity 11, 127, 159–160
Moholy-Nagy, Lászl 99
Molnár, Farkas 172
Moser, Karl 112, 115, 118, 125, 135, 136, 140, 142, 144, 148, 151, 167, 168, 180, 185, 190, 191, 194
Munich 35, 176
Musil, Franz 63, 65
Muthesius, Hermann 35, 36, 39

Narkomfin (Moscow) 95–96
Needs (human) 12–15
Netherlands 21, 74, 144, 170, 187
Neutra, Richard 144, 149, 150, 176, 182

*Oktobergruppe* 118, 168
Organisation of Contemporary Architects
   (*Organizatsiya Sovremmennaia Arkhitektura*, OSA) 90, 91, 92, 95, 96
Oud, Jacobus 108, 164

Pessac (France) 82, 85
Poland 37, 38, 108, 113, 144, 170, 176, 185
Practical utopia [see **Utopia**]
Praunheim (Frankfurt) 170

Rácz, György 172, 174
Rakowiec (Warsaw) 185
Research Society for Economic Efficiency
   in Building and Housing
   (*Reichsforschungsgesellschaft für Wirtschaftlichkeit im Bau-und Wohnungswesen*, RFG) 69, 114, 172
Revolution
   and rupture 4, 6, 11, 76, 77, 78, 79, 83, 101
   Bolshevik Revolution (1917) 24, 26, 77
   search for a blank canvas 82
   [See also **Architecture**]
Rietveld, Gerrit 144, 172, 173, 174
*Ring* 108, 112, 118, 130, 140, 145, 176
Rome 71, 72, 74, 138, 148, 165
Rotterdam 73, 182, 184, 188
Rowntree, Seebohm 13, 17

# Index

Sabsovich, Leonid 90, 95
Sartoris, Alberto 108, 112, 181
Scharoun, Hans 60, 164
Schmidt, Hans 3, 85, 86, 97, 99, 109, 110, 112, 113, 114, 115, 117, 119, 122, 123, 124, 125, 126, 127, 128, 129, 131, 135, 139, 140, 141, 142, 143, 144, 145, 147, 148, 149, 152, 172, 176, 178, 181
    and cell 85
    and building regulations 122–123, 126, 142
    and dwelling ration 98–99
    and social mission of architecture 176
Schorenmatten (Basel) 182
Schumacher, Fritz 35–36, 43–45, 55
Schuster, Franz 54–56, 63, 118, 125, 170, 173, 174
Sellier, Henri 60, 68, 119, 124
Socialism 7, 14, 88, 89, 90, 97, 101, 102, 109, 139, 146, 147, 148
Soviet Union 37, 48, 70, 79, 88, 89, 90, 91, 96, 97, 118, 135, 142, 144, 145, 146, 147, 148, 157, 158, 170, 180, 186, 188
    and new life (*novyi byt*) 90, 91, 96
    architecture in 81–85
    Bolshevik Revolution (1917) 24, 26, 77
    Five-Year Plan (1928) 89, 147
Spain 108, 113, 170, 187, 188
Stam, Mart 51, 86, 108, 109, 112, 118, 127, 128, 135, 136, 138, 139, 141, 143, 144, 145, 146, 148, 149, 164, 168, 180, 181
Steiger, Rudolf 140, 141, 142, 144, 147, 150, 181, 191
Stroikom (Building Committee of the Russian Republic (*Stroitel'nyi komitet*) 91, 93, 94, 96, 172, 173
Sweden 178, 186, 187, 188
Switzerland 74, 108, 112, 144, 170, 176, 186, 187, 188
Syrkus, Helena 3, 172
Syrkus, Szymon 3, 108, 113, 116, 144, 172, 181

Taut, Bruno 76, 119
Teige, Karel 5, 9, 86, 97–98, 109, 118, 131, 135, 148, 154, 155, 165, 167, 182, 185, 187, 191
    and critique of western modernism 97, 155, 165, 167, 191
    and Minimum Dwelling (book, 1932) 5, 155
    and report on minimum dwelling at CIAM3 154–155

Tessenow, Heinrich 35, 54
Törten estate (Dessau) 173
*Trabanten (satellites)* 50, 52, 141, 170
Trieste 21

Unwin, Raymond 37, 51, 60, 66, 68, 71, 74
Urbanism 110
    CIAM's shift to the urban scale 136–142
    high-density versus decentralization 6, 43, 44, 49, 50, 65, 66, 74, 89, 133, 150, 173, 184, 194, 195
Utopia 3, 4, 7, 8, 69, 76, 78, 81, 89, 91, 95, 97, 100, 139, 141, 143, 166, 167, 193, 195
    [*See also* **Architecture**]
    not-yet defined 78, 80–81, 105, 159, 162, 167, 195
    practical utopia 4–7, 69, 195
Utrecht 172, 174

Vallejo, Luís 113, 170, 174
Van Eesteren, Cornelis 108, 109, 149, 155, 181, 185, 186, 189, 191
*Verein für Socialpolitik* (Association for Social Policy, VfS) 22, 35
*Verein zur Verbesserung kleiner Wohnungen* (Association for the Improvement of Small Dwellings) 32–33
Verwilghen, Raphael 60, 74, 138, 139, 140, 180
Vienna 37, 46–49, 54, 57, 61, 62, 63, 64, 65, 67, 69, 71, 137, 161, 165, 170
    and *Hof* (court) 49, 57, 64, 65, 187
    and Kleinwohnung 46
    and *Volkswohnungen* (people's palaces) 65
    Red Vienna housing programme 46–49, 54
Vinck, Emile 60, 68
Vladimirov, Vladimir 93

Wagner, Martin 51, 62, 66, 79, 116, 119
Warsaw 172, 176, 177, 185
Warsaw Housing Cooperative 176
Weimar Republic 43, 44, 46, 50, 123, 162
    and housing as constitutional right 43
Welwyn Garden City (UK) 66
Werkbund 35, 36, 51, 64, 100, 145, 160, 161, 163, 164, 165, 172, 176, 177
    housing exhibitions of 36, 145, 165
Westhausen (Frankfurt) 55, 170, 182

York 13, 17

www.ingramcontent.com/pod-product-compliance
Lightning Source LLC
Chambersburg PA
CBHW071831300426
44116CB00009B/1506